MW00462269

Exploring

THE GOSPEL
OF MARK

THE JOHN PHILLIPS COMMENTARY SERIES

Exploring
THE GOSPEL
OF MARK

An Expository Commentary

JOHN PHILLIPS

kregel
PUBLICATIONS

Grand Rapids, MI 49501

Exploring the Gospel of Mark: An Expository Commentary

© 2004 by John Phillips

Published in 2004 by Kregel Publications, a division of Kregel, Inc., P.O. Box 2607, Grand Rapids, MI 49501.

Library of Congress Cataloging-in-Publication Data
Phillips, John.
    Exploring the Gospel of Mark: an expository commentary / by John Phillips.
        p.   cm.
Includes bibliographical references.
    1. Bible N.T. Mark—Commentaries. I. Title.
BS2585.53 .P48 2004
226.3'07—dc22   2003022209

ISBN 0-8254-3381-9

Printed in the United States of America

04 05 06 07 08 / 5 4 3 2 1

Summary Outline

Introduction

John Mark was the son of a well-to-do Jerusalem woman whose home was one of the meeting places of the early church (Acts 12:12, 25). Mark undoubtedly knew all of the church's early leaders. Not only were his parents Jews but he also was a relative of Barnabas (Col. 4:10), one of the leaders of the early Jewish church. Peter calls Mark his "son" (1 Pet. 5:13), either because he led him to the Lord or because he was one of his disciples.

Mark accompanied Paul and Barnabas on their first missionary journey as far as Perga, where he left them and returned to Jerusalem. He seems to have become disillusioned about missionary work and alarmed at the turn of events. When the team reached the mainland from the island of Cyprus, Mark saw quite clearly that Saul, who was now calling himself Paul, had completely eclipsed Uncle Barnabas. Moreover, Paul was proposing an itinerary that would take the missionary team through the Cilician Gates, over the Taurus Mountains, and into Galatia. Mark was alarmed at the dangers that any such enterprise entailed. Brigands, wild beasts, and difficult terrain lay ahead. Mark quit (Acts 12:25; 13:5, 13). He had come along on this missionary venture to be the "minister" (servant) of Saul and Barnabas, to run their errands and do the chores. But enough was enough! He went back home.

Later, when Paul consulted Barnabas about a second missionary journey, Barnabas agreed to the idea. However, he wanted to take Mark along again. Doubtless he argued that his young nephew was sorry, that he had learned his lesson, and that he deserved a second chance, but Paul refused to consider any such thing. He and Barnabas had such a sharp disagreement over the matter that, in the end, they decided to go their separate ways. Paul headed off on his second missionary enterprise, and Barnabas took Mark with him back to Cyprus, where he was known and where he had once owned property (Acts 15:36–39).

Not that Paul wrote Mark off completely. We are told, for instance, that Mark was with him at the time of his first imprisonment in Rome (Col. 4:10; Philem. 24). Later, he was at Babylon from which city he joined Peter in sending greetings to Christians in various places (1 Peter 5:13). At the time of Paul's second and final imprisonment at Rome, Mark seems to have been with Timothy at Ephesus. Paul wrote to Timothy from his prison and urged him to come to him as soon as possible. He was to bring Paul's cloak and his books—and also Mark. "He is profitable to me for the ministry," Paul said (2 Tim. 4:11). Mark had failed once as a servant, but now he had earned a reputation as a servant.

Somewhere in the interval, between Paul's castigation of Mark and his commendation of Mark, someone possibly handed Paul a manuscript and said, "Here, Paul, read this."

We can picture Paul reading that manuscript with ever growing interest. We can hear him say, "That is very good indeed! A true gospel of Christ! Who wrote it? Peter?"

"No!" he would be told, "John Mark wrote it."

"Well!" Paul would say, "Barnabas was right about Mark after all."

One ancient tradition says that Peter sent Mark to Egypt, where he founded the church at Alexandria and that he became the bishop of that church. He seems eventually to have suffered martyrdom in that famous city.

That Mark's gospel should portray Jesus as God's perfect *Servant* is fitting. Mark's key verse states, "The Son of man came not to be ministered unto, but to minister, and to give his life a ransom for many" (Mark 10:45). This text divides his gospel into two parts. First, we see the Lord Jesus giving His life in *service* (chaps. 1–10), then we see Him giving His life in *sacrifice* (chaps. 11–16).

It is widely accepted that Mark's gospel reflects the teaching of Peter. The church father Papias (A.D. 60–150), affirmed as much. Papias is said to have obtained this information not much later than A.D. 100 and that he obtained it from one who was a contemporary of the apostles. Papias calls Mark "Peter's interpreter," presumably because Peter preached and taught in his native Aramaic and Mark translated his words into Greek.[1]

The internal evidence of Mark's gospel suggests that it was written for primarily the Romans, just as Matthew's gospel was written for the Jews, Luke's for the

---

1.Graham Scroggie, *A Guide to the Gospels* (London: Pickering and Inglis, 1948), 134.

Greeks, and John's for the church. Mark's gospel has comparatively few Old Testament quotations. It explains Jewish customs, ignores the Mosaic Law, indicates when the Passover lamb was killed, and so on. All of these facts point to a Gentile audience. Scholars tell us that Mark's Greek is rough-and-ready but admirably suited to the slaves and freedmen who formed some of the earlier Christian congregations at Rome.

Mark's gospel likely was written about A.D. 50, which would make it one of the earliest of the New Testament writings. It is an expansion of Peter's sermon at Caesarea (Acts 10:34–43). Mark begins with the ministry of John the Baptist and ends with the ascension of the Lord Jesus. Graham Scroggie suggests that Mark was one of the half-dozen men who accompanied Peter to the house of Cornelius on the historic occasion when the door of the church was opened to the Gentiles (Acts 10–11).

Mark begins his gospel at the point when Peter joined himself to the Lord. He seems to have been particularly interested in the Lord's Galilean ministry, especially in His activities at Capernaum, where Peter lived. So the hand that penned this gospel was the hand of Mark; the voice that speaks is the voice of Peter.[2] Of the 678 verses that comprise Mark's gospel, 285, in whole or in part, contain the actual words of Christ. Also, a very large part of Mark's gospel is incorporated into Matthew's and Luke's gospels.

Graham Scroggie depicts Mark's gospel as a "day" of service:

> Introduction (1:1–13). The Day Before
> (a) Acclamation (1:14–45). Dawn
> (b) Opposition (2:1–3:6). Morning
> (c) Separation (3:7–6:6). Forenoon
> (d) Consummation (6:7–8:26). Midday
> (c) Instruction (8:27–10:52). Afternoon
> (b) Condemnation (11:1–13:37). Evening
> (a) Crucifixion (14:1–15:47). Night
> Conclusion (16:1–20). The Day After[3]

In expounding this gospel, I have given a detailed, analytical, alliterated outline and a running verse-by-verse commentary on the biblical text. Come then, and explore the gospel according to Mark.

---

2. Ibid., 179.
3. Ibid., 223.

PART 1

The Servant Gives His Life in Service

Mark 1:1–10:52

Section 1: The Servant's Work (1:1–3:35)

  A. The Servant's work begun (1:1–45)

    1. The mystery (1:1–2)

      a. A beginning (1:1)

        (1) The essential humanity of the Servant (1:1a–b)

          (a) Who He was: Jesus (1:1a)

          (b) What He was: Christ (1:1b)

        (2) The essential deity of the Servant (1:1c)

      b. A book (1:2)

        (1) The Old Testament prophets (1:2a)

        (2) The Old Testament promise (1:2b)

    2. The messenger (1:3–4)

      a. The person (1:3)

        (1) A description (1:3a)

        (2) A dwelling (1:3b)

        (3) A demand (1:3c)

      b. The proclamation (1:4)

        (1) Its visual dimension (1:4a)

        (2) Its verbal dimension (1:4b–c)

          (a) Repentance (1:4b)

          (b) Remission (1:4c)

    3. The multitude (1:5–8)

      a. John's success (1:5)

        (1) They came (1:5a)

        (2) They confessed (1:5b–c)

          (a) Symbolically (1:5b)

          (b) Specifically (1:5c)

      b. John's simplicity (1:6)

        (1) His dress: appearances crucified (1:6a)

        (2) His diet: appetite crucified (1:6b)

      c. John's subject (1:7–8)

        (1) The promise of the coming of the Son of God (1:7)

          (a) His superior might (1:7a)

          (b) His superior majesty (1:7b)

        (2) The promise of the coming of the Spirit of God (1:8)

          (a) The symbolic baptism of John (1:8a)

(b) The supernatural baptism of Jesus (1:8b)
4. The Master (1:9–13)
   a. The visit (1:9)
      (1) The place from whence the Savior came (1:9a)
      (2) The purpose for which the Savior came (1:9b)
   b. The vision (1:10)
      (1) The place from whence the Spirit came (1:10a)
      (2) The purpose for which the Spirit came (1:10b)
   c. The voice (1:11)
      (1) The place from whence the Father spoke (1:11a)
      (2) The purpose for which the Father spoke (1:11b)
   d. The victory (1:12–13)
      (1) A portentously different experience (1:12)
      (2) A particularly dreary experience (1:13a)
      (3) A perfectly diabolical experience (1:13b)
      (4) A potentially dangerous experience (1:13c)
      (5) A periodically delightful experience (1:13d)
5. The move (1:14–15)
   a. The time (1:14–15a)
      (1) Human time (1:14)
         (a) Prison for the messenger (1:14a)
         (b) Proclamation by the Master (1:14b–c)
            i. Where He preached (1:14b)
            ii. What He preached (1:14c)
      (2) Heaven's time (1:15a)
   b. The truth (1:15b–e)
      (1) Prophetic truth (1:15b)
      (2) Predominant truth (1:15c–d)
         (a) Convicting people (1:15c)
         (b) Converting people (1:15d)
      (3) Practical truth (1:15e)
6. The men (1:16–20)
   a. Two men working with their nets (1:16–18)
      (1) Their diligence (1:16)
      (2) Their obedience (1:17–18)
         (a) The challenge (1:17)
         (b) The choice (1:18)

    b. Two men working on their nets (1:19–20)
      (1) Their diligence (1:19)
      (2) Their obedience (1:20)
        (a) A new Lord to be followed (1:20a)
        (b) An old loyalty to be forsaken (1:20b)
7. The miracles (1:21–45)
  a. In the house (1:21–34)
    (1) In His Father's house (1:21–28)
      (a) The instruction (1:21)
        i. The site (1:21a)
        ii. The Sabbath (1:21b)
        iii. The synagogue (1:21c)
      (b) The interest (1:22)
        i. Their astonishment (1:22a)
        ii. His authority (1:22b)
      (c) The interruption (1:23–28)
        i. The demoniac cries out (1:23–25a)
          a. We hear the demons speak (1:23–24)
            1. What they discerned (1:23–24)
            2. What they dreaded (1:24b)
            3. What they declared (1:24c)
          b. We have the demons silenced (1:25a)
        ii. The demons cast out (1:25b–28)
          a. The command (1:25b)
          b. The compliance (1:26)
          c. The comments (1:27–28)
            1. His fame discussed by the crowd (1:27)
              (i) They were astonished at what He taught
              (ii) They were astonished at what He wrought
            2. His fame discussed in the country (1:28)
    (2) In His friends' house (1:29–34)
      (a) The private healing (1:29–31)
        i. The place (1:29a)
        ii. The people (1:29b)
        iii. The problem (1:30–31)
          a. Immediate help (1:31–31a)

b. Immediate health (1:31b)

(b) The public healings (1:32–34)

   i. The scene (1:32a)

   ii. The sick (1:32b–33)

      a. The cases (1:32b)

      b. The crowds (1:33)

   iii. The Savior (1:34)

      a. The diseased cured (1:34a)

      b. The demoniacs cleansed (1:34b–c)

         1. The demons expelled instantly (1:34b)

         2. The demons expelled imperially (1:34c)

b. On the highway (1:35–45)

(1) The Lord (1:35–37)

  (a) A quiet time sought (1:35)

     i. The Lord's plan (1:35a)

     ii. The Lord's purpose (1:35b)

  (b) A quiet time spoiled (1:36–37)

     i. The unnecessary interruption (1:36)

     ii. The unnecessary information (1:37)

(2) The land (1:38–39)

  (a) The towns (1:38)

  (b) The tour (1:39a)

  (c) The Teacher (1:39b–c)

     i. Visiting their synagogues (1:39b)

     ii. Vindicating His sermons (1:39c)

(3) The leper (1:40–45)

  (a) His coming (1:40)

     i. His great daring (1:40a)

     ii. His great desire (1:40b)

  (b) His cleansing (1:41–43)

     i. The compassion of Jesus (1:41)

        a. His heart involved (1:41a)

        b. His hand involved (1:41b)

     ii. The command of Jesus (1:41c–42)

        a. The word declared (1:41c)

        b. The work done (1:42)

  (c) His commission (1:43–45)

     i. How it was delivered (1:43–44)

   a. What was refused to this man (1:43–44a)
   b. What was required of this man (1:44b–c)
    1. The provisions of the law (1:44b)
    2. The priests of the law (1:44c)
  ii. How it was disregarded (1:45)
   a. The people He contacted (1:45a)
   b. The problems He caused (1:45b)

It has been estimated that Matthew incorporated 96 percent of the gospel of Mark, five-sixths of its actual wording, into his gospel. That is not to say that Matthew, who was both an apostle and an eyewitness of the ministry of Christ, simply took Mark's gospel and embedded it into his own. But he does seem to have used it extensively when putting together his own gospel. This possibility is quite understandable if Mark was reflecting Peter's preaching.

The difference between the two gospels is more a matter of method than of material. Mark is direct, brief—to the point of being blunt—and full of unique touches that help bring the Lord to life for us. He shows us Jesus as a Man of action, a worker and a servant. He includes little discourse and much action. By contrast, Matthew was methodical, Luke was an artist in both language and style, and John was a theologian. Mark's gospel is forceful and down to earth. It is conversational, abrupt, graphic, and pragmatic; it abounds with references to everyday things. It tells us about the Lord's looks, gestures, and emotions, including His anger and displeasure. Mark was fond of details. His key words are *immediately* and *straightway*.

—⁊⁊⁊—

Section 1: The Servant's Work (1:1–3:35)
 A. The Servant's work begun (1:1–45)
  1. The mystery (1:1–2)

This is such a busy little gospel! From the very first chapter, we are caught up in a whirl of activity:

> *The beginning of the gospel of Jesus Christ, the Son of God; As it is written in the prophets, Behold, I send my messenger before thy face, which shall prepare thy way before thee. (1:1–2)*

Mark tells us how it all began. Indeed, his gospel is frequently concerned with the beginnings of things.[1] Each of the four evangelists begins at a different point in the gospel story. Matthew begins with the ancestry and birth of the long-awaited Jewish Messiah. Luke begins with the birth of John the Baptist. John goes back before the beginning of time to the Lord's preincarnate existence as the Word. Mark's beginning is at a point later than all of the other gospels—with the actual ministry of John the Baptist.

The word that Mark uses for "gospel" is *euangelion.* It was used in the Roman world (which so attracted Mark) to announce that a new emperor had ascended the throne. That was supposed to be "good news." The Holy Spirit appropriates the word. A long-announced Savior had come, and that indeed was good news because this Savior would be both a Sovereign and a Servant.

Mark gives this long-awaited Messiah His proper title—"Jesus Christ, the Son of God." The Jews needed some good news badly because God had not spoken to them for four hundred years, and terrible years they had been. It had all come down to the fact that, in Jerusalem, an Edomite monster of a man named Herod the Great sat on the throne of Israel. The Promised Land itself had dwindled in size and importance to a small and despised province in a vast and alien empire. Moreover, the land was ruled from Caesarea on the coast, a wholly Roman city. A pagan Roman governor (Pontius Pilate) presided over the local interests of a Gentile emperor (Augustus) in far-off Rome, and the emperor was demanding that divine honors be bestowed on him. It was all bad news for the Jewish people. Moreover, it was a mystery to them. Were they not the chosen people? Was not Palestine the Promised Land? Why had God been so silent for so long? Was there to be no end to their sufferings and humiliation?

But good news came at last! John the Baptist was its herald. John himself had been the subject of an ancient prophecy (Mal. 3:1; Isa. 40:3), and his coming marked a new beginning. The Messenger had come! The Messiah was on His way! God had invaded the planet, and things could never be the same again. The Messenger's task was to prepare the way for the coming King.

2. The messenger (1:3–4)

The voice of one crying in the wilderness, Prepare ye the way of the Lord, make his paths straight. John did baptize in the

---

1. See Mark 1:1, 45; 4:1; 5:17, 20; 6:2, 7, 34, 55; 8:11, 31–32; 10:28, 32, 41, 47; 11:15; 12:1; 13:5; 14:19, 33, 65, 69, 71; 15:8, 18.

wilderness, and preach the baptism of repentance for the remis-
sion of sins. (1:3–4)

Mark begins with *the person* (1:3). John the Baptist was born to be a priest. Early in life, however, and doubtless spurred on by the wondrous circumstances of his birth, John decided that what Israel needed was not another priest after the order of Aaron but another prophet after the order of Elijah.

The Hebrews had fallen on bad times quite apart from Roman oppression. Dead formalism characterized their religion. The roots of this formalism, which had been sprouting in Malachi's day, now ran deep. Rabbinical tradition had largely replaced the Bible. John the Baptist knew all about the hypocrisy of the Pharisees, the skepticism of the Sadducees, the materialism and opportunism of the Herodians, and the fanaticism of the Zealots. The faith of the fathers, applauded in Hebrews 11, had now become "the Jews' religion" (Gal. 1:13).

Someone needed to cut a path through the tangled undergrowth of the deadening, man-made tradition. The Messiah was coming! It was high time that someone spoke out. So John became what Mark calls "the voice of one crying in the wilderness." John did not seek the big cities, and he did not stalk the streets of Jerusalem. Rather, he sought solitary, lonely places that were off the beaten track down by the riverside. He did not go to the people. He made the people come to him, and come they did until vast crowds thronged into the wilds to hear him preach.

Today we would send crusade teams to supervise various aspects of the ministry. We would create a vast organization to mobilize helpers, handle funds, make arrangements, and follow up converts. But John the Baptist needed no massed choirs, instrumentalists, song leaders, or soloists. A hired arena was not for him. He had no need to cover the countryside with posters and swamp the postal system with brochures. He needed no budgets and no appeal for funds. Nor did he need to arrange for special transportation to bring in the crowds. He just raised his voice in the wilderness, and the crowds came!

Next, Mark tells of *the proclamation* (1:3). "Prepare!" he said. As John used the word, it had all of the force of a peremptory military command.

"Make his paths straight!" The highways of John's native land were winding, twisting affairs. The traveler would be forced to climb a long, steep hill, then his path would wind through a valley, then it would bend around some obstacle, and later it would follow the path of a river. The Romans, for whom Mark wrote, scoffed at such archaic trails. They built magnificent roads throughout their empire. Their great "interstates" ran dead straight, scorning all obstacles. Did a river or gorge stand in the way? Their engineers bridged it. Was a mountain astride the path? The Romans moved it or cut a road right through it. The emperor's business demanded haste. The straighter the road, the swifter his couriers could ride or his legions march. The Roman interstate system comprised fifty thousand miles of first-class military highways and two hundred thousand miles of secondary highways. Romans would have appreciated this part of John's message—"Make his paths straight."

"Make his paths straight!" cried John. It was a clarion call to his own countrymen to clean up their lives and clear away all moral and religious obstacles that might hinder the coming King.

John's preaching, however, had a visual as well as a verbal dimension: baptism was a symbol of repentance. The Mosaic Law mandated sundry "washings," but those were quite different from baptism.[2] Some scholars think that, by New Testament times, the Jews had adopted baptism as an initiatory rite for Jewish proselytes, but John's baptism had nothing to do with that. Nor is it to be confused with Christian baptism (Acts 19:1–7).

John's baptism focussed on repentance. John did not want proselytes; he wanted penitents. His baptism could not wash away sin, but his preaching could produce conviction of sin. Those who repented under John's preaching simply, and in a most public way, signified their *repentance* by being immersed in the Jordan. Cleansing would have to await the ministry of the Messiah.

3. The multitude (1:5–8)

And there went out unto him all the land of Judaea, and they of Jerusalem, and were all baptized of him in the river of Jordan, confessing their sins. And John was clothed with camel's hair, and with a girdle of a skin about his loins; and he did eat locusts and wild honey; (1:5–6)

First, we have *John's success* (1:5). The people came! His base of operations was at one of the fords of the Jordan River, and his preaching seems to have coincided with a sabbatical year, a time when people would be free from their agricultural labors and able to undertake a pilgrimage to the Jordan to hear this revolutionary preacher. In any case, the people came. Both the more sophisticated Judeans and

---

2. In the Old Testament, baptism was embedded in the types—Noah, for instance (1 Peter 3:2–21), and Moses (1 Cor. 10:1–2).

the even more cultured and polished people of Jerusalem came. The common people came, and many of them were convicted of their sin and took their stand in the Jordan, confessing their sin and joining the ever growing ranks of those who were watching for the coming Messiah.

John's lifestyle gave his sermons a cutting edge; he practiced what he preached. The simplicity of his dress and diet made an immediate impact on those who came to hear him. They saw a man clothed in camel's hair and wearing a leather girdle. He seems to have deliberately chosen attire that would remind people of the great Old Testament prophet Elijah (2 Kings 1:7–8; Mal. 4:5). The people would note both his dress and his diet. John did not need to be wined and dined. He lived like an ascetic, content to eat the unpalatable locust, along with some wild honey for sauce.

But John's subject—Christ—was calculated to stir the most sluggish soul! He preached the coming of Christ and produced a spiritual awakening the like of which had not been seen for centuries. Admittedly, a flurry of patriotic fervor and religious zeal had occurred at the time of the Maccabees, but it had been four hundred years since the nation had last really heard from God. Malachi's closing Parthian shot (4:4) suggests that Malachi himself did not see or anticipate any response to his own preaching. Well! Let the people wait for Elijah to come back!

So now John, clothed like Elijah, raised his voice. A new day had come! The fiery, desert prophet who had suddenly surfaced must have been discussed from one end of the land to the other. "Have you been to hear him yet?" "Did you know that my mother-in-law was baptized last month?" It augured well for the coming of Christ because, although the ruling religious establishment dismissed John as a crackpot, they feared him. So did Herod. As for the common people, they believed, heart and soul, that John was a prophet of the living God.

We note, also, *John's simplicity* (1:6). John behaved the way a prophet, in the popular mind, was supposed to behave. Those who came to hear him had no desire to wear a hair shirt and eat dried locusts, but that John did so appealed to them. That was how prophets were supposed to dress, how prophets were supposed to eat, and how prophets were supposed to preach.

Then came John's subject (1:7–8)—first, the promise of the coming of *the Son of God:*

> *And preached, saying, There cometh one mightier than I after me, the latchet of whose shoes I am not worthy to stoop down and unloose. (1:7)*

John preached about the coming of the Son of God. John himself was mighty, and the people trembled before his fiery eloquence. Even powerful, wicked Herod Antipas was afraid of him. The Pharisees and the Sadducees cringed when he denounced them as "a generation of vipers," but they dared not touch him. John was mighty, but when compared with the One who was coming, he was nothing. He was mighty, but the coming One was *Almighty.* Between John and Jesus a great gulf was fixed, not a gulf of degree but of kind. John was a mere man; Jesus was a Man but much more than man. John was a voice; Jesus was the Word. John called for repentance; Jesus demanded rebirth. John was a messenger; Jesus was the Messiah. John's mother and the mother of Jesus are believed to have been sisters, but one could not speak of John's father in the same breath with the Father of the Lord Jesus Christ.

No wonder John declared that he was not fit to stoop down and untie the sandals of the coming One! Ten thousand times ten thousand angels gladly would have given up the rule of a thousand galaxies to do that, but they were no more worthy than John.

There was another promise—the coming of *the Spirit of God:*

> *I indeed have baptized you with water: but he shall baptize you with the Holy Ghost. (1:8)*

"Mightier than I," said John, "I indeed have baptized you with water: but he shall baptize you with the Holy Ghost." John's mission, to bring people to repentance, had been successful with the common people. All kinds of people had come—businessmen and farmers, housewives and soldiers, mothers and fathers, young and old, rich and poor, Judeans and Galileans—people from all segments of society. He pointed them to Christ. John baptized them with water, but that was as far as he could go.

"He shall baptize you with the Holy Ghost!" he said. That was it! There was all the difference in the world between John's symbolic baptism with water and Jesus' supernatural baptism with the Spirit. John showed people their natural hearts; Jesus gave people new hearts. John brought people to the Jordan, to the river of death; Jesus brought people to the river of life.

On one occasion, David Livingstone, the intrepid pioneer missionary to Africa, brought some natives with him from the deep interior to the coast. There the land suddenly ended. One of the astonished Africans said, "We followed the white father through forests and across plains, up mountains and into deep valleys. The land went on and on. Then, all of a sudden, it came to an end. 'There is no more of me,' it said." John said much the same. "I have brought you to the water. There is no more of me, no more that I can do. Here is the end of John. Now you need Jesus. 'He must increase, but I must decrease'" (John 3:30).

4. The Master (1:9–13)

First, we have *the visit:*

> *And it came to pass in those days, that Jesus came from Nazareth of Galilee, and was baptized of John in Jordan. (1:9)*

"In those days!" That is an arresting statement. Never in the history of this planet have there been days like those days.

We think, for instance, of the early days when Adam walked the glades and glens of the Garden, the monarch of all that he surveyed. All that he knew in those pristine days were health, happiness, and holiness. But he had not yet been tempted. From the darkness of space, the sleepless eye of a being watched tirelessly and with ceaseless malice for the moment when this man would fall.

Then, too, there were the days when Noah sailed the stormy sea, triumphant over tempest blast and awesome waves. But it was a sad triumph, after all, because all about him the world was being torn apart under the wrath of a holy God.

There was the day when Abraham packed his bags, loaded his camels, and headed for the Promised Land. Every place on which he pressed his foot, from the Euphrates to the Nile, was to be his. But he nearly lost it all in Egypt, nearly lost it all with Hagar, and nearly lost it all to a Philistine king because Abraham, as great as he was, had feet of clay.

There were the days when Moses humbled Egypt to the dust and freed Israel, bringing two or three million people out of the house of bondage and bound for Canaan. But Moses had his "mixed multitude" with which to contend, and the whole glorious expedition nearly collapsed at Kadesh Barnea. And again he faced problems when pagan Balaam expounded his subtle doctrine to Balak, the king of Moab: "If you cannot conquer them, my lord, then corrupt them."

There were "those days" when David, crowned with glory and honor, ascended to the throne to found a deathless dynasty. But that was before he met Bathsheba and before he had to write his tear-drenched penitential psalms.

In all of "those days" since Adam, we look in vain for a perfect Man, one who was able to stare back into that sleepless eye and dare fallen Lucifer himself to come and do battle with Him. So it was that "those days" of which Mark speaks arrived. In "those days," John the Baptist preached repentance and the imminent appearing of the long-awaited Christ. In "those days," "the fulness of the time" came, and God "sent forth his Son, made of a woman, made under the law" (Gal. 4:4). He grew up in obscurity until the day of His showing to Israel. Then the voice of John, which stirred the whole land, stirred His soul too.

He "came," Mark says, "from Nazareth of Galilee." Contempt was widespread in Judea for both Galilee and Nazareth, especially in rabbinical circles. Galileans were easily picked out by their dialect, grammatical errors, and mispronunciation of words. The Roman emperor, Julian the Apostate, derided Christ as "the *Galilean* God" and challenged Him to defend Himself against the might of Rome. In the end, Julian died fighting the Christians of the empire. As he lay dying of his wounds, he caught up a handful of his blood and threw it toward heaven, crying, "Thou hast conquered, O thou *Galilean.*" The wonder of it all is that Jesus was not ashamed to be known as a *Galilean.* Indeed, many of His mightiest miracles, and much of His most tremendous teaching, was done in Galilee.

As for Nazareth, it is not once mentioned either in the Old Testament or by the Jewish historian Josephus. Yet, it lies only ten miles from Megiddo. It was hidden in a basin formed by surrounding hills, and the Jews despised it because of its irreligion and lack of morals. Jesus did not shrink from the title "Jesus of Nazareth," although its population was of a mongrel character, its dialect was rough and provincial, and its people were seditious and despised. In time, the Christians themselves were called "Nazarenes." It was a term of contempt, which stamped them, in the popular mind, as followers of an equally despised Jesus. In His own day, the Lord's association with Nazareth branded Him, in the mind of His enemies, as a false Messiah. The Bible said that Bethlehem, not Nazareth, was to be the Messiah's city.

"Those days" that Jesus spent in Nazareth are wrapped in almost total silence. His half brothers, James and Jude, who came to be of note in the church, and His cousins, James and John, who from the first, were prominent among the apostles, are all silent about "those days." They cover His public ministry, a scant three and a half years, only lightly. The four Gospels focus on the closing events of Christ's life. Indeed, the four Gospels themselves are little more than mere memos.

Those hidden days, in Nazareth, doubtless will be unfolded for us in eternity. John tells of those days that "the world itself could not contain the books that should be written" about them (John 21:25). When we learn the full story of "those days," we shall cry with the queen of Sheba, "The half was never told us!" (2 Chron. 9:6).

In *those days* "Jesus came . . . and was baptized of John in Jordan." He came from a despised town and a despised province to a despised river. "Are not Abana and Pharpar, rivers of Damascus, better than all the waters of Israel?" sneered leprous Naaman when Elisha told him that he must bathe in the Jordan if he wished to be healed (2 Kings 5:10–12).

The *purpose* for which Christ came was almost as extraordinary as the *place* from whence He had come. He came "to be baptized of John in Jordan." John's baptism was one of repentance. Did Jesus need to repent? No, indeed! John, himself, was horrified at the thought. Before him stood "the Holy One of God." John, good and godly man that he was, was overcome by a sense of his own sinfulness in the presence of this One. Rather Jesus should baptize him than that he should baptize Jesus. But Christ firmly overruled all of his objections. Jesus stepped into Jordan's waters, hurrying on their way to burial in the Dead Sea, and John plunged Him beneath the waves. Thus, He identified Himself publicly with the ruined race that He had come to save. His baptism in the Jordan was a vivid picture of His coming baptism in the river of death at Calvary.

We have, next, *the vision:*

And straightway coming up out of the water, he saw the heavens opened, and the Spirit like a dove descending upon him: (1:10)

Then came the vision and the voice. The heavens opened! The Spirit appeared! Up Christ came from that watery grave! Down the Spirit came from above to rest on Him. From then on, the Lord Jesus, who had always been filled with the Spirit, was now also anointed with the Spirit.

An opened heaven! Heaven would open again and again from that point. Heaven and earth, after all, are never that far apart—nor, for that matter, are earth and hell.

Something about it all is symbolic—Jesus "coming up" and the Spirit "coming down." Pentecost was only fifty days from Passover and the Feast of Firstfruits. Jesus "came up out" of the waters of death, leaving in His wake a conquered tomb and an empty grave. Up! Up! Until earth was left behind and an opened heaven received Him to His seat at the right hand of the Majesty on high. Then the Spirit came down to stay, and a new day was born—the day of the dove!

Wrath, vengeance, judgment, and righteous retribution were all now postponed, and grace was given its centuries of empire on the earth. Instead of the severity of God, we experience the grace of God. The Lord goes up; the Spirit comes down. The Spirit is still here—reproving, regenerating, and restraining—and here He will remain until Jesus comes again.

Now comes *the voice:*

> *And there came a voice from heaven, saying, Thou art my beloved Son, in whom I am well pleased. (1:11)*

The beloved Son was there! The Spirit of God was there! The Father Himself was there! Three persons, one God. Each member of the Godhead is actively involved in bringing salvation to a lost world.

The Father's accolade set the seal of divine approval on the silent years from the Lord's birth to His baptism. The Father had observed Him in that Nazareth home—as a babe, as a boy, as a brother, and as a businessman. He had observed Him in the home, at school, on the playground, at the well, in the village, and in the shop. He had observed Him in the secret place. He had been the unseen Listener to every conversation; the unseen Guest at every meal; the unseen Witness to every act; and the unseen Recorder of every secret thought, imagination, and desire. Here is His verdict on those hidden thirty years: "This is my beloved Son, in whom I am well pleased!"

So the public approval of the Father was voiced at Jordan's bank as this glorious Person stood there with the water still pouring from His clothes.

And now, to work! But first, a final test. The divine visit, the divine vision, and the divine voice are now to be followed by a divine victory.

Humanly speaking, while the extraordinary manifestation of the Godhead was fresh in everybody's mind, this would have been a strategic moment to march on the capital. Why waste such marvelous publicity? For the simple reason that this was not a publicity stunt. God scorns cheap publicity. So, no sooner was Jesus publicly and miraculously declared to be God's beloved Son than He disappeared.

We note, also, *the victory:*

> *And immediately the Spirit driveth him into the wilderness. (1:12)*

The word here for "driveth" is *ekballō,* a very strong word indeed. It means literally "to cast out," or "to throw out from within." It is used of the Lord's expulsion of demons (Mark 1:34, 39). The first thing that the anointing Spirit of God did was drive the Lord Jesus into the desert, where He was held in the grip of intense mental concentration. He was now to engage the Devil himself in single combat.

The economy of words in Mark's account of the temptation is startling. It is all over and done with in one verse! Matthew gives us the fullest account; Luke's account is fairly brief. John does not mention it at all because John was concerned with the deity of Christ, and the Lord, as God, could not be tempted (James 1:13).

> *And he was there in the wilderness forty days, tempted of Satan;*
> *and was with the wild beasts; and the angels ministered unto*
> *him. (1:13)*

"He was there," says Mark, underlining the *Person* and the *place!* The two are put in stark contrast. "*He* was there." He, the Creator of the universe, the One who planted that garden eastward in Eden, the One who is the Author of all beauty and life. "He was *there*"—in that waste, howling wilderness; in that frightful desert, surrounded by scenes of desolation and death. It was the home of the scorpion and the serpent. It was a place where the fierce sun did nothing but bake and blast and burn. One word from Him and that desert would have blossomed as the rose. But no such word came. He was to meet the Devil on his own ground, the Evil One who was the author of all such scenes. Thorns, thistles, and thirsty soil are *his* fingerprints on this planet, not God's.

Although Mark does not detail the temptation itself, he does add an interesting touch of his own. During that forty-day sojourn in the wilderness, Jesus was "with the wild beasts." He was *with* them. They were not wild to Him. They came to be companions to Him, to render their homage unto Him, not as their Creator but to the last Adam, their sovereign Lord. They were tame to Him and were His courtiers and comrades in the days of His solitude.

And Satan was there. Mark implies that the temptation was continuous. He uses a present tense participle, speaking of continuous action during the forty-day period. Matthew records the intense climax, Mark the daily battle. The word for "tempted" means "to put to the test."

But, if He was there with the wild beasts and the Evil One, He was also with the angels. Mark's contrast is arresting: "with the wild beasts; and the angels. . . ." The verb is in the imperfect tense, pointing to continuous action. Throughout the whole period, marked by increasing bodily weakness and by intensifying satanic pressure, the angels stood by to minister to His spiritual needs.

5. The move (1:14–15)

Note *the time* (1:14):

> *Now after that John was put in prison, Jesus came into Galilee, preaching the gospel of the kingdom of God.*

Note, also, *the truth* (1:15):

> *And saying, The time is fulfilled, and the kingdom of God is at hand: repent ye, and believe the gospel.*

Between verses 13 and 14 we must make room for the passing of a whole year. During this period, the Lord performed His first signs and miracles and gave some of His earliest teaching. He traveled, too, between Galilee and Judea. The miracles were performed mostly in Galilee, and the teaching was given primarily in Judea. This period has been called "the year of obscurity," and we would know little or nothing about it if not for the gospel of John.

Mark commences his record of the Lord's ministry at the point where John the Baptist was imprisoned by Herod, and Jesus left Judea, returned to Galilee, and began a more public and intensive crusade.

John was put into prison. That was his reward for becoming a veritable Elijah to awaken the nation's conscience. According to Josephus, John the Baptist was committed to the strong fortress of Machaerus. It marked the extreme point south in Peraea. It was the boundary fortress in the southeast (toward Arabia), so its safety was of the greatest importance. The Romans did everything possible to make the place, which was strong by nature, completely impregnable.

Herod the Great built a town along the shoulder of the hill and surrounded it with walls fortified by towers. The castle stood even higher. It, too, was surrounded by walls and flanked by towers 160 cubits high. Inside was a magnificent palace. Cisterns, storehouses, and arsenals had been provided in case of a prolonged siege. The highest point of the fort was on the west, where it looked sheer down into a valley. On the north and the south, the fort was equally cut off by valleys, which could not be filled up for siege purposes. On the east was a valley one hundred cubits deep, but it terminated in a mountain opposite Machaerus, which was evidently the one weak point.

In the west, at the end of this long fortress and looking southward is a square fort. The highest and strongest part of the defenses is the eastern citadel on a steep slope 150 yards up. This small keep is exactly one hundred yards in diameter. Still standing are the remains of a well of great depth and a deep cemented cistern with the vaulting of the roof. More terrible are two dungeons, one of them deep, deep down—the terrible prison where Herod kept John. Edersheim says, "As we look down into its hot darkness, we shudder in realising that this terrible keep had for nigh ten months been the prison of that son of the free 'wilderness,' the bold herald of the coming kingdom, the humble, earnest, self-denying John the Baptist."[3]

And now we picture the deep dungeon in the citadel on the one side, and, on the other, down that slope, the luxurious palace of Herod. There he sat with his adulterous, murderous wife while the shouts of wild revelry and drunken merriment rose around!

What must John have thought? What had happened to the kingdom that he had come to announce was near at hand? Where was the Christ? What was He doing? Was He eating and drinking with publicans and sinners the whole time while he, John the Baptist, was suffering for Him?[4]

John had declared concerning the Lord Jesus, "He must increase, but I must decrease" (John 3:30). He had not reckoned, however, on imprisonment and death.

Meanwhile, Satan was foiled. True, "John was put in prison," but "Jesus came into Galilee, preaching!" It was a bad setback for Satan. He had suffered a resounding defeat in the desert. Now the Son of the living God was abroad in the land, doing exactly what the Old Testament prophet had foretold, preaching in Galilee (Matt. 4:13–16; Isa. 9:1–2).

Galilee was cosmopolitan. It was a region where Roman, Greek, and Jew mixed and intermingled because the population of Galilee was as much Gentile as it was Jewish. Tiberias was a good example. Herod Antipas built and named it in honor of the emperor Tiberius (A.D. 14–57). No strict Jew would go there, however, because it was built on top of a cemetery. Foreign customs were much in evidence there, and it was the capital of Galilee in Jesus' day. Jesus, Mark reminds

---

3. Alfred Edersheim, *The Life and Times of Jesus the Messiah* (Grand Rapids: Eerdman's, 1959), 1:658–66.
4. Ibid.

us, went to Galilee. Whereas John had sought out the wilderness, Jesus sought out the great thoroughfares. John expected the people to come to him; Jesus went to the people.

Jesus' message was much the same as John's: "The time is fulfilled, and the kingdom of God is at hand: repent ye, and believe the gospel."

"Believe!" That was the message. Repentance? Yes! But also redemption, reconciliation, and regeneration. Within a decade, a whole new vocabulary would be needed to describe the wondrous truths that now were about to be revealed.

The Lord's message contained a *prophetic* element: "The time is fulfilled." The world had been waiting some four thousand years to hear someone say that! Throughout the Old Testament, from Genesis 3 to Malachi 4, the Messiah had been portrayed as the coming One. Now He had come! Prophecy had been fulfilled, was even then being fulfilled, and would continue to be fulfilled. The time had come! The hour had arrived!

The Lord's message also contained a *predominant* element: "The kingdom of God is at hand." The prophets had painted pictures of that kingdom in bright, bold shades and tints. The promised King would smite all of Israel's foes. He would reign as David had reigned, putting down all of His foes. He would reign as Solomon had reigned, in prosperity and peace. The deserts would garb themselves with the splendor of Eden. The lion would lie down with the lamb and eat straw like an ox. Harvests would be so bountiful that the plowman would overtake the reaper. Crime and disease would be banished, and death itself would be put under severe restraint. A man would be but a youth at a hundred, and men would learn war no more. All nations would undertake annual pilgrimages to Jerusalem to pay their tribute to the King of Kings. The Hebrew people would reign with Christ as His ambassadors, governors, and administrators. Bold colors indeed!

But somber browns, drab grays, and overpowering blacks were also dabbed on the prophetic canvas. The prophets spoke of a Messiah who would be "despised and rejected of men; a man of sorrows, and acquainted with grief" (Isa. 53:3). They spoke of His hands and feet being pierced. They told of deep, chilly waters rolling over His soul and of His voice crying out because He was forsaken of God.

"The kingdom of God is at hand." The Lord was well aware that the way to the crown was by way of the cross. The Jews, however, refused to recognize this fact, and even His disciples shied away from it. But Jesus saw it all.

Therefore, His preaching included a *practical* note: "Repent ye, and believe the gospel." The spiritual must transcend the physical. There must be "repentance toward God, and faith toward our Lord Jesus Christ" (Acts 20:21). The Lord reinforced the message of John, who was now silenced and shut up in prison. The people must turn from their sin. They must believe on the Lord Jesus Christ. Repentance signifies a change of direction; faith toward the Lord Jesus signifies a change of devotion.

6. The men (1:16–20)
  a. Two men working with their nets (1:16–18)

Now as he walked by the sea of Galilee, he saw Simon and Andrew his brother casting a net into the sea: for they were fishers. And Jesus said unto them, Come ye after me, and I will make you to become fishers of men. And straightway they forsook their nets, and followed him. (1:16–18)

Doubtless, the Lord had walked beside that little lake a hundred times in the years of His growing up. After all, Nazareth was only twenty miles from Capernaum, on the lake, where He had relatives. Indeed, the Palestine of Jesus' day was only about 140 miles long and about 23 miles wide in the north and 80 miles wide in the south. Jesus probably knew every nook and cranny of the shore. So the Lord walked the shoreline of the lake, as He had done many times before. Only this time He walked with a special purpose in mind.

The Sea of Galilee itself is about sixty miles from Jerusalem. It is from 80 to 160 feet deep. It lies 680 feet below the level of the Mediterranean. Nine cities, including Tiberias, bordered it, each having a population of some fifteen thousand or more. Half of the Lord's recorded miracles were performed in the immediate vicinity of the Sea of Galilee.

It is a very little lake in terms of size, but it is a veritable "sea" in terms of significance. It is a mere dot on the geography of our planet, but it is a vast ocean in the thinking and hymnology of the church. It is important because of what happened there. It dominates the Gospels, just as the Gospels themselves have dominated the thinking of mankind for two thousand years. It was near the Sea of Galilee that Jesus gave us the Sermon on the Mount and many of His parables. There His name first leaped to fame. There, too, He found most of His closest followers and friends, as Mark reminds us.

For example, that is where He called "Simon and Andrew his brother." Simon! He became one of Mark's heroes. Doubtless, Mark received his information about this momentous meeting from Simon himself. But Mark, as usual, was in a hurry, and he leaves out many details that the other Evangelists supply. Even so, Mark cannot wait to tell us about Jesus' meeting with Peter. "He saw Simon." Mark says as an afterthought, "and Andrew his brother." In fact, Andrew came to Christ before Peter; indeed, Andrew first brought Peter to Jesus. Mark ignores all of that. It had already taken place sometime earlier. Mark is in a hurry to tell us about Peter and Jesus. In any case, he is not recording Peter's conversion but his call.

"He saw Simon!" Everyone saw Simon Peter or, at least, heard him! Simon was always the center of a crowd. He was always where the action was. At sports, Simon had to bat first. At play, Simon had to be the groom if they were playing weddings, and the rabbi if they were playing funerals—or better still, the corpse! Especially if the game included a resurrection!

"He saw Simon." But He saw more than that. He saw "Peter." As Michelangelo saw David in a block of marble, so Jesus saw an apostle in a rugged fisherman. He saw Simon casting his net, but at the same time He saw three thousand souls being saved by a single sermon that Peter would deliver on a coming Pentecost. He saw Peter, and He saw Gentiles being added to the church. He saw Peter, and He saw a man carrying a cross to Execution Hill, faithful unto death, even the death of the cross. He saw Peter, and He saw a name being written down in glory, engraved with an iron pen and lead into the rock forever, cut into the foundation stones of the celestial city. He saw Andrew's name, too, because in his own quiet, retiring way, Andrew was as big a man as his blustering brother Peter. Each time we meet Andrew in the Gospels, he is bringing someone to Jesus. The Lord saw that.

We tend to overlook the quiet man. But not Jesus! He has as much room for Andrew as for his big brother. Andrew had been the first of the two to come to Jesus. He soon came back with his brother in tow. He was just as diligent casting his net that day as Peter was. It pleased the Lord to see these brothers, so different in type and temperament, working together, busy and in harmony.

"Occupy till I come," is the Lord's word to us all (Luke 19:13). The Lord did not call idle people to be His disciples; He called busy people. It pleased Him to see these men getting on with the tasks that they knew how to do best during the period of waiting for Him to come with His imperative call.

"Come ye after me, and I will make you to become fishers of men." Barely a dozen words! That was all it took.

Much about this Messiah of whom John the Baptist had preached must have seemed mysterious to Simon and Andrew. He had performed no miracle as yet.

John had reluctantly baptized Him, and the awesome voice had rung out from heaven. But then the Master had disappeared into the depths of the desert. Doubtless, the two brothers had wondered about His disappearance. Now, here He was, strolling along the lakeside toward them.

By this time, Simon and Andrew probably had compared notes with their partners, James and John, who had met Christ sometime ago, just as they had. They must have thought that this was a low-key, haphazard way to go about claiming the throne of David.

Then, too, was the fact that they had probably known Jesus of Nazareth on the human level for years! The mother of James and John was Salome, who seems to have been a sister of the Virgin Mary. If so, then James and John were His cousins. Surely stories about the strange circumstances that had surrounded the birth of Jesus must have been current, at least in the family circle. His reputation for absolute goodness was well known. But, if He was the Messiah, why did He wait so long to proclaim it? And why was He content to live in Nazareth, of all places?

But all doubts were now banished. Jesus had come. His call rang out, and Simon and Andrew responded at once—as did James and John a little while later when they, too, were called. The voice that rang out was full of authority. "Come ye after me!" Jesus said. Peter, a born leader, was invited to become a follower. "I will make you to become fishers of men," Jesus added. They did not hesitate for a moment. One moment they were fishermen; the next minute they were followers.

b. Two men working on their nets (1:19–20)

> And when he had gone a little farther thence, he saw James the
> son of Zebedee, and John his brother, who also were in the ship
> mending their nets. And straightway he called them: and they left
> their father Zebedee in the ship with the hired servants, and went
> after him. (1:19–20)

Peter and Andrew followed Him a little way along the lake and came to where James and John were just as busy as they had been. They were engaged in a different task, but they were equally as diligent.

Zebedee seems to have been a man of means because he was able to hire helpers and possibly had contacts of importance in Jerusalem. If his wife, Salome, was indeed Mary's sister, as seems likely, then she, too, was of royal descent. So were James and John, who, along with Peter, soon formed an inner circle among the disciples.

Little did these men know where following Jesus would eventually take them! Peter's path would take him to Jerusalem, Joppa, Antioch, and over the seas and far away. Tradition says that he went to Rome. By all accounts he went to Babylon. John's path would take him to distant Ephesus and, at last, to Patmos, a place of which he probably had never heard in those early Galilean days. Little did these fishermen know that day that they would be numbered among the most famous people of all time or that they would write books that would be as much a part of the Bible as the familiar writings of Moses and Malachi.

James and John! What another study in contrasts! James became the first apostolic martyr, John the last apostolic messenger. James would show us how to die for Christ, John how to live for Christ. The Lord Jesus nicknamed the pair the "sons of thunder." To John Jesus committed the care of His mother as He hung upon the cross of Calvary. As for the parents of these apostles, they represent all mothers and fathers who generously give their sons and daughters to Jesus, even though they are their pride and joy, partners in their daily affairs, and the anticipated support of their old age.

When they were called, one pair of brothers was *casting* their net; they represent the evangelist. They saw immediate results for their labors. The other pair was *mending* their nets; they represent the pastor-teacher. Their work was more tedious and not so spectacularly rewarding. The church needs both types of leaders. Jesus called Peter and Andrew first, then James and John. Similarly, the work of the evangelist comes first, followed by the patient toil of those who keep the affairs of the local church in good repair.

With both calls the response was immediate. With both calls Mark uses his favorite word *straightway*, or *immediately*, to describe it. Mark's gospel emphasizes the servant character of both Christ and the Christian. Instant, prompt, and cheerful obedience is the mark of the servant.

The Lord's first four disciples were fishermen! That seems odd by human standards. He was going to found a kingdom and build a church. Surely He should have gone to the capital for His men. Surely He should have combed the rabbinical schools for scholars and gone to the Sanhedrin for men skilled in government and law. Surely, if He was to take on the might of Rome, He would need men of military genius, not mere Galilean fishermen. His ways, however, are not our ways. He was not looking for potential soldiers but pastors and teachers. So He went to ordinary people. He would take on Rome in due course, not by battle and policy and intrigue but by faith and hope and love. The blood of the martyrs would be the seed of the church. The bulk of

Christians in the Roman world were to be drawn from the ranks of slaves and freedmen. They would be encouraged to know that when Jesus chose His disciples, He chose workingmen.

So Jesus called, and Mark notes that "they left their father Zebedee in the ship with the hired servants, and went after him." Zebedee still had competent help to carry on the business, but he must have sorely missed his boys.

We know very little about Peter and Andrew. They were partners with James and John so, doubtless, they were fairly well off. We do know that Peter was married and that he had a house in Capernaum. Apparently, too, the Lord made Peter's home His base of operations when He began His public ministry.

> 7. The miracles (1:21–45)
>   a. In the house (1:21–34)
>   (1) In His Father's house (1:21–28)
>   (a) The instruction (1:21)

And they went into Capernaum; and straightway on the sabbath day he entered into the synagogue, and taught. (1:21)

Mark wastes no time in getting down to business. He devotes less than two dozen verses to getting all of the preliminaries out of the way to show the Romans and the rest of the world God's perfect Servant at work. He began with a miracle—in startling contrast to John the Baptist, who performed no miracles (John 10:41).

The Sabbath found Jesus in His place in the local synagogue in Capernaum. The ruler of the synagogue did not hesitate; he turned the pulpit over to Jesus. We are not told what Jesus taught that day, but we can be sure that the Lord had everyone's attention. We know the style and substance of the Lord's preaching from other portions of the Gospels. He would teach about the kingdom that was now being offered to Israel. He would emphasize the need for regeneration as the way into that kingdom and for holy living as proof of citizenship in it. The message would be lavishly illustrated from everyday objects and events, and it would be thoroughly documented by many an Old Testament reference or allusion.

The impact was immediate. "They were astonished at his doctrine" (1:22). Moreover, absolute assurance and authority was in His teaching, and it gripped their hearts. Until now, they had fed on the dry husks of rabbinical teaching. They had grown accustomed to the rabbis' oral traditions, many of which were contrary to the Word of God. Jesus cut aside all of this tangled undergrowth and let the people see for themselves the tall trees of Old Testament biblical truth.

Some of the Lord's best teaching was done in and around Capernaum; some of His mighty miracles were performed there too. The people of Capernaum did not react *indignantly* to the Lord's teaching, as did the people of Nazareth (Luke 4:16–30), but, in the end, they were just as bad. They reacted *indifferently*. Familiarity bred contempt in them as it had in the hearts of the people of His hometown of Nazareth, and, in the end, He handed Capernaum over to judgment (Matt. 11:23–24). However, for the moment, He was "a nine-day wonder." The people of Capernaum contrasted His preaching with that of the local and visiting rabbis whom they had heard so often and who had confused them and complicated their lives with endless rituals, rules, and regulations.

(b). The interest (1:22)

> *And they were astonished at his doctrine: for he taught them as one that had authority, and not as the scribes. (1:22)*

The scribes were the intelligentsia of the nation and, after the nation's return from Babylon, the most important men in the kingdom. Originally, they had been raised up to guard the Scriptures from corruption and to copy them for circulation. They were diligent in this task, counting every letter on every page and counting everything else that could be counted to protect copies from scribal errors.

They also constituted themselves guardians of the so-called "oral law." According to rabbinical theory, God gave to Moses the *written* Word and the *oral* word. The written Law was the Old Testament Scripture; the "oral law" was what the rabbis preserved in their teaching and traditions. It had a kind of life all its own. It kept on growing and expanding. This ever growing body of beliefs included a record of rabbinical decisions on questions of ritual *(Halacoth)*, a legal code arising from those decisions *(Mishna)*, a collection of Hebrew sacred legends *(Gemara)*, commentaries on the Old Testament *(Midrashim)*, and reasonings on this ever expanding body of traditional teaching *(Hagada)*. As a mystical offshoot of all of these was the *Kabbala*, which specialized in highly imaginative and allegorical speculations of a mystical and semimagical nature. For many centuries, this mass mixture of truth and error of tradition was preserved solely in the vast memories of the rabbis and the scribes because it was forbidden to be written down. It later made up the *Talmud,* which virtually replaced the Scriptures themselves among the Jews.[5]

The Lord cut right through this tangled mass of religious red tape, took the people back to the Bible, spoke in everyday terms, and drew His illustrations from everywhere. He spoke to heart and mind, conscience and will. And He spoke with authority, the Holy Spirit bearing witness to the truth of His Word. Even His enemies declared, "Never man spake like this man" (John 7:46). The people in the Capernaum synagogue were among the first to hear Him.

We can be sure that He did not begin by denouncing what He called "the traditions of the elders," although He did that later in no uncertain terms. For now, He ignored it. "A certain man," He would say, "had two sons." Or, "the kingdom of heaven is like a mustard seed." Or, "Blessed is the man who." It was all so simple, so sound, and so stirring.

(c) The interruption (1:23–28)

And there was in their synagogue a man with an unclean spirit;
and he cried out, (1:23)

Along with messages such as they had never heard before came miracles such as they had never seen before. The Devil was in the synagogue that Sabbath, waiting for an opportunity to disrupt the service. We do not know how often this demoniac had been to the synagogue before; quite likely he was a regular attendee. The Devil had little to fear from the usual synagogue service. Certainly the man with the unclean spirit had never heard there anything that had disturbed him before. But this new kind of preaching was something else. The teaching of the scribes had never touched the awful depths of depravity that reigned in this man's tormented soul, but the preaching of Jesus did. It provoked a sudden and electrifying response. We can well imagine the thrill of fear and shock that ran through the congregation when the voice of the demoniac rang out.

Saying, Let us alone; what have we to do with thee, thou Jesus of
Nazareth? art thou come to destroy us? I know thee who thou art,
the Holy One of God. (1:24)

---

5. See John Phillips, *Exploring the World of the Jew* (Neptune, N.J.: Loizeaux Brothers, 1993).

Note the switch of personal pronouns between the plural and the singular. Confusion of personalities is common enough in cases of demon possession. The demon who inhabited this man was terrified by the person of the Lord Jesus and by the awesome holiness that clothed Him. The demon could not stand that. He knew exactly who Jesus was, this Man from Nazareth. He was the Holy One of God. The holiness of Jesus burned into the demon's consciousness like a red-hot iron.

The demons puzzle us. They are evil spirits in the grip of wickedness beyond the ordinary human kind. Moreover, they have a craving to possess bodies, and they seize human bodies when they can. They would prefer the bodies of swine to no bodies at all. They seem to be under the authority of Satan, and he uses them to hold men captive. However, they are not of the same order as fallen angels. Angels can assume bodily form (Gen. 18:1–33) and have no need to steal human bodies. One suggestion is that demons are the disembodied spirits of a pre-Adamic race of beings of whom now no trace or record remains. We know little or nothing, from the biblical standpoint, of what transpired on our planet before the coming of man. We do know that the world was ruined (Gen. 1:2) and that it was not created that way (Isa. 45:18). Possibly our planet and its solar system was part of the hegemony of Lucifer before his fall, and maybe the state of chaos described in the opening verses of Genesis was part of that fall.

In any case, the demon inhabiting this wretched man in the synagogue recognized Jesus instantly and confessed Him at once. The demon used the plural in addressing the Lord: "Let us alone; what have *we* to do with thee? " Either the man was possessed by more than one evil spirit, or the demon was speaking for evil spirits in general. The demon demanded that he be left alone, that the Lord not interfere with him. At the same time, it recognized that between Him and them a great gulf was fixed. The demon(s) knew, also, that Jesus possessed all of the power of the Godhead.

Demons are the only ones in the New Testament to address the Christ of God as "Jesus." He said to His disciples, "Ye call me Master and Lord: and ye say well; for so I am" (John 13:13). It was a form of insolence and bravado and an involuntary display of their dreadful wickedness that demons dared to address Him so. He invariably silenced them and ejected them and made them the prisoners of His will.

It was His holiness, however, that burned like fire in the soul of the poor man's tormenting demon. It was like lightning, which both burns and sheds dazzling light. His holiness, before which even the shining seraphs shrink (Isa. 6:2), exposed the abysmal vileness and wickedness of this foul spirit. He shrank from it, called out against it, and writhed beneath its glare.

> *And Jesus rebuked him, saying, Hold thy peace, and come out of*
> *him. And when the unclean spirit had torn him, and cried with*
> *a loud voice, he came out of him. (1:25–26)*

Jesus silenced the demon at once. "Hold thy peace, and come out of him." The demon's insolence was rebuked, and his vile tongue, which for once told the truth, was tied. Jesus wanted no testimonials from such a source. Moreover, this tenancy of this poor man's body was terminated.

Throughout the Gospels, the Lord's ministry was contested by Satan and unprecedented demon activity. The hosts of hell seem to have been mobilized to oppose the Son of God. His response was simply to cast out every demon that crossed His path. Thus, He exposed the terrible dangers that imperil mankind and revealed His own absolute lordship over all of the situations and conditions of life. He had already defeated Satan personally in the wilderness. Now He sowed havoc in his realm. Moreover, He is the same yesterday, today, and forever.

Even when face-to-face with the Son of God, this foul spirit made his exodus from his victim as painful and as public as possible. He had to have one last jab and one last word. But come out he did, and the poor man was set free. Mark does not dwell on the outcome, but it must have been like the dawn of a new day. The blind man whom Jesus healed, testified, "Once I was blind, but now I can see." This formerly possessed man could have said, "Once I was bound, but now I am free!" Once again he had control of his body and mind.

> *And they were all amazed, insomuch that they questioned among*
> *themselves, saying, What thing is this? what new doctrine is this?*
> *for with authority commandeth he even the unclean spirits, and*
> *they do obey him. (1:27)*

As for the people in the synagogue that Sabbath, they were astounded. "What new doctrine is this?" they asked. They had never seen any of their preachers do anything to compare with what Christ had just done, but it was no "new doctrine" at all. It was timeless truth, stripped of all traditionalism and error, truth backed by a life in touch, moment by moment, with heaven. The demons recognized that fact, even if the people didn't.

Doubtless, too, that is what the world today is waiting to see in the church—evidence of Christ in our midst. The world is tired of our legalism, ritualism, rationalism, and hypocrisy. It is tired of our sterile teaching, psychological preaching, worn-out cliches, "charismatic" extremism, phony ecumenism, and dead sermons. It is waiting to see doctrine wedded to Holy Spirit power. Then, as when the demons were cast out, the careless, Christ-rejecting world will be all eyes and ears.

> *And immediately his fame spread abroad throughout all the region round about Galilee. (1:28)*

The entire northern part of the country was alerted to the fact that a prophet was abroad in the land. Matthew tells us that an ancient prophecy was fulfilled because God always works in accordance with His own Word: "The land of Zabulon, and the land of Nephthalim, by the way of the sea, beyond Jordan, Galilee of the Gentiles; The people which sat in darkness saw great light; and to them which sat in the region and shadow of death light is sprung up" (Matt. 4:15–16; cf. Isa. 9:1–2).

This part of the country was a no-man's-land, a buffer zone, between the world of Jerusalem, Judea, and Jewry to the south and the world of the Gentiles to the north. As we have seen, it contained a mixture of Jews and Gentiles. It was almost as much despised by the Hebraist Jews of the south as by the Gentile world itself. It was "Galilee of the Gentiles" indeed (Matt. 4:15). Yet, it was there that the Lord displayed just who He was—"a root out of a dry ground" (Isa. 53:2).

(2) In His friends' house (1:29–34)

First, we have *the private healing* (1:29–31):

> *And forthwith, when they were come out of the synagogue, they entered into the house of Simon and Andrew, with James and John. (1:29)*

The Lord, having performed a notable miracle in His Father's house, now performed a miracle in His friend's house. After the Sabbath synagogue service, Jesus and His disciples headed for Peter's place for a meal and a rest. Doubtless,

Peter's wife had gone on ahead to get things ready and to minister to her sick mother. The way Mark describes it, it was not far to Peter's house. Mark no doubt came to know the house very well when he became Peter's translator. It seems, too, that Peter's house had become the Lord's home away from home.

What kind of a house was it? Likely enough it was made of stone. It was big enough to accommodate Peter, his wife, his mother-in-law, possibly his brother Andrew, and a guest. In all probability, it had the usual stairs leading up one of the outside walls to the flat roof, a favorite place for the family and friends to congregate when the day's work was done. Very likely, it offered a great view of the lake and the surrounding hills—as well as the neighbors' yards and the narrow streets and the nearby synagogue, not to mention the waterfront with its boats drawn up onshore or launching out across the lake.

H. V. Morton describes a typical Palestinian home thus:

> One of the houses which I visited might have remained unchanged since the time of Christ. The man was attending to the animals, two donkeys and a foal, which were tied up to the rock in the cave. In the room above the woman was sifting some small grain, like millet, through a sieve. From time to time she talked to her husband as he busied himself in the room beneath.
>
> The living-room was, like most rooms in the East, bare of furniture. In a corner of it were the matting beds rolled up and tucked away out of sight.
>
> The thought came to me that the nearest approach to the kind of building in which Christ was born is probably a Connemara cabin. I remember once going to a wake in a little white cabin rather like these Bethlehem houses, except that it was all on one floor. The living-room was separated from the animals' quarters by a pole and a curtain of sacking. The noise of beasts stamping came clearly to us as we sat round the turf fire. I remember thinking at the time that perhaps the Nativity took place in the same humble surroundings.[6]

Probably Peter's house was not that much different. We can be sure that Jesus was much loved in that home. In urging hospitality on the saints, the Holy Spirit

---

6. H. V. Morton, *In the Steps of the Master* (London: Rich and Cowan, 1934), 126.

says, "Be not forgetful to entertain strangers: for thereby some have entertained angels unawares" (Heb. 13:2). Peter and his family entertained the One whom angels worship.

> *But Simon's wife's mother lay sick of a fever, and anon they tell him of her. (1:30)*

Perhaps they told Him about Peter's sick relative on the way home. Maybe they blurted it out: "Peter's mother-in-law is sick. She has a fever." Doubtless they told Him, hoping that He would heal her. After all, what was a mere fever to a Man who could heal a demoniac? Surely He could take care of a mere fever!

From this incident we learn that Peter, at least, among the ranks of the apostles, was a married man with domestic responsibilities. He had a wife to support; perhaps he supported her mother too. We tend to think of the Lord's disciples as being young and unattached, footloose and fancy-free. However, in Peter's case at least, that was not so.

We can be quite sure that the Lord was considerate of Peter's situation. The four Evangelists record several fairly long preaching tours of Jesus. But as far as we know, most of the time He either stayed close to His home in Capernaum or came back to it often. (The bulk of all of the gospel narratives is taken up with just one week in the Lord's life.) Peter's home, then, seems to have been adopted by the Lord as His home once He moved to Capernaum to stay.

So, on that Saturday morning, after that extraordinary Sabbath service, they all headed for Peter's house. And they told Him something that He already knew— Peter's wife's mother was sick.

Peter's wife! What was she like? How old was she? How long had she and Peter been married? What was her name? Was she a local girl? Who were her parents? Did they have any children? What were her interests? Evidently, she was a good daughter to her mother and hospitable to Peter's friends. We see only her shadow here. On the one side of her are Peter and Andrew. On the other side is her mother. In between is the Lord. We'll get to know her better someday, when we get to heaven and the books are opened and she comes in for her reward. Then the Lord's home will be her home! Glory!

> *And he came and took her by the hand, and lifted her up; and immediately the fever left her, and she ministered unto them. (1:31)*

As soon as He arrived at Peter's house, the Lord made His way to where the sick woman lay. He took her hand and lifted her up. And at once the fever fled! Of course it did! The fact that disease vanished at His touch is no more incredible than that demons fled at His Word. What *would* have been incredible is if these things had *not* happened. He was the Creator of the universe, in control of all of the factors of time, space, and matter, and now manifest in the flesh. Omniscient knowledge and omnipotent power were His. It would have been strange indeed if He had sat down to His meal but left the suffering woman to toss upon her bed and Peter's wife to run to and fro, distracted by her mother's cries.

One touch from Him, however, and the older woman was up and about, back into the kitchen, appearing with bowls of food for the guests. "She ministered unto them!" It is the natural response of a heart that has known the transforming touch of the Christ of God.

Next, we have *the public healings* (1:32–34):

> *And at even, when the sun did set, they brought unto him all that*
> *were diseased, and them that were possessed with devils. And all*
> *the city was gathered together at the door. (1:32–33)*

They probably spent that afternoon in rest, but the Sabbath ended at sundown, and that was why the people had been waiting. Word had run through the neighborhood, and Peter's house was besieged. "All the city," says Mark, "was gathered together at the door." They stood, in one vast, diverse group in front of Peter's house, eager for miracles. And still they came, as varied as the moods of the sea, with one thing in common: they knew their need—no one had to convince them of that—and that is halfway to a cure. They had heard of Jesus, found out where He was, and had come. They surrounded Peter's house. They overflowed into the street. They looked eagerly for the Savior. It was a foretaste of Pentecost. Peter was not adequate for the situation, of course, but Jesus was.

Everyone in town came! The ruler of the synagogue and the local rabbi, fishermen and their wives and children, the local tax collector and the shopkeepers. The skeptics came. The curious came. The rich and the poor, the bond and the free, and the young and the old. One and all they came. Those at the back called to those at the front. Those at the front surged against the door.

> *And he healed many that were sick of divers diseases, and cast out*
> *many devils; and suffered not the devils to speak, because they*
> *knew him. (1:34)*

Each case presented itself before Him, cases that fill our medical textbooks. People with ailments that had no name, or that had a name but had no cure, were brought to Him. However, the Great Physician, the One who never lost a case or charged a fee, had come. Enough miracles were performed that night to fill a book, enough miracles to satisfy even the most hardened skeptic. Never in history had the world seen the like of what happened that day at Peter's front door.

As for the demons, He silenced them even as He expelled them. To this day, no demon can confess that Jesus Christ is come in the flesh (1 John 4:1–3). "They knew him!" Indeed they did, but we are not told how. Certainly His blazing holiness exposed their abysmal wickedness, and His unquestioned authority exposed their stolen strength. Perhaps they recognized His voice from some previous encounter in another age. In any case, they knew Him to be the Son of God. Men might have been strangely blinded as to who it really was who was in their midst, but the demons had no doubts at all.

b. On the highway (1:35–45)
(1) The Lord (1:35–37)

> *And in the morning, rising up a great while before day, he went*
> *out, and departed into a solitary place, and there prayed. (1:35)*

It was still dark when He left the house the next morning. The day before had been a long day, stretching on into the evening hours. It had been an awesome day. Years later, Peter could still remember it as though it were but yesterday. He told his young disciple, Mark, about it, and Mark tells us about it.

Evidently, He went to bed that night, and in that He was like us. He had a body of flesh and blood that called for rest. So He went to bed. But He was up again a few hours later. Silently, He put on His robe and sandals and just as silently He slipped out of the house. He also was like us in that He needed to get alone with His Father in heaven. His outer Man having been renewed by a few hours of sleep, His inner Man had to be renewed too. And He needed guidance for the day, which was even then tingeing the eastern sky with the first rosy signs of the dawn.

About what did He and the Father talk? We have several of the Lord's model prayers to enlighten us. The "Lord's Prayer," the *paternoster* as it is called, is evidently a skeleton outline of the Lord's own approach to prayer. The High Priestly Prayer, recorded by John (chap. 17), gives us a better idea of the substance of His prayers.

To concentrate in prayer, He needed solitude and silence. He could find none in Peter's crowded house. Before long, Peter's mother-in-law would be up and about, lighting the fire and starting the breakfast. Peter would be calling for Andrew to come on down to the beach to see the night's catch. It was all as it should be. The Lord slipped away before the events of another day could come crowding in. He needed to be alone with God.

> *And Simon and they that were with him followed after him. And when they had found him, they said unto him, All men seek for thee. (1:36–37)*

Although they had been with Him for such a short time, they had a good idea where their missing Master would be. Moreover, they had already become so attached to Him that they could not imagine a day without Him.

"All me seek for thee!" they said when they found Him. That augured well, they thought. Such a popular Messiah could soon build a following, then an army. The disciples had rosy visions of the movement's catching fire, spreading swiftly through Galilee and the adjacent districts, spreading to the south, taking Judea by storm—all helped forward by mighty miracles. Once the Jerusalem establishment joined the movement, it would not be long before the Diaspora would be enlisted in the cause. All it would take would be just one Jerusalem Passover, when tens of thousands of Jews from all over the world would be in the capital. Just let them see the new Messiah in action, hear His stirring call, and see His stunning miracles! The disciples could envision the whole thing! Last night's miracles had opened their eyes. What could Rome do against a Jewish army that was protected by miracles and supported by an enthusiastic population at home and an energetic Jewish fifth column in every country, state, and city abroad? The disciples could see the whole thing! And to think that it all started in Peter's house! "All men seek for Thee," they said.

(2) The land (1:38–39)

> *And he said unto them, Let us go into the next towns, that I may preach there also: for therefore came I forth. (1:38)*

"There are other places," He said, not a bit moved by their news. As yet, they still didn't have even the faintest understanding of His method, His message, or His mission. As for His miracles, on which they placed so much reliance, the Lord did not even mention them. He placed no particular value on them. A following that was based on miracles would need increasingly more miracles, and such a following would soon fade away when the miracles were withdrawn.

He had come to preach. He wanted followers who were grounded on God's Word. But it could not be the debased and diluted Word as taught by the rabbis; it had to be God's Word as He Himself knew, understood, interpreted, and practiced it. The disciples did not yet understand that fact, and they would not really understand it until after Pentecost.

> *And he preached in their synagogues throughout all Galilee, and cast out devils. (1:39)*

The Lord toured the cities and villages of Galilee, preaching in the synagogues that dotted the countryside and that, in those early days, provided Him with such a ready base of operations. Although the rabbis had cluttered divine truth with their man-made traditions, at least they still read the Bible in the synagogues. So in synagogue after synagogue, the Bible was opened and read—and He preached.

Paul did the same when his turn came. Roman roads provided the means of access, a common Greek language provided the means of communication, and Jewish synagogues provided the congregations. No wonder Paul wrote that Jesus came in "the fulness of the time" (Gal. 4:4).

Jesus was welcome everywhere. Everyone wanted to see a miracle, and Jesus performed many of them, especially casting out evil spirits, which seemed to have descended like locusts on the land. Casting out demons was one of the Lord's ways of waging war on Satan's kingdom on earth.

(3) The leper (1:40–45)

We note *his coming:*

> *And there came a leper to him, beseeching him, and kneeling down to him, and saying unto him, If thou wilt, thou canst make me clean. (1:40)*

And He cleansed lepers. As far as we know, only three lepers were cleansed throughout the entire Old Testament period—Moses, Miriam, and Naaman.[7] But Jesus cleansed them as a matter of course.

Leprosy! The very word filled people with horror. The Jews regarded it as "the stroke of God." The leper carried about in his body corruption, contamination, and death. Society ostracized and rigidly segregated him lest he contaminate others of the community. If anyone wandered into his vicinity, he had to cover his mouth and cry, "Unclean! Unclean!" to warn the other person away. He was excommunicated from the religious life, functions, and feasts of the nation. His only companions were other lepers in the same pitiable condition as himself. He could not work because who would want the goods and services of a leper? He could not come and go as he pleased. He endured a living death, because his disease spread and was incurable. Often, it began in a small way. He lost the feeling in his fingers, in his feet, and in his limbs. Before long, he presented a dreadful spectacle with rotted stumps where once had been healthy limbs. He had no hope. He was cut off from his family, from his former friends, and from the fellowship of the people of God. All he could look forward to was death. No wonder leprosy is often viewed as a type and picture of sin.

This man was a leper, but he was one who had made a wise decision; he would come to Christ. He would defy the interdict under which he lived. He would dare the thunderous edicts and penalties of the law; he would come to Christ.

Acting on that decision took a great deal of courage. For one thing, crowds always surrounded Jesus, and who could predict the actions of a crowd? The man might well have been stoned long before he reached the Christ. So what? He was dying anyway. He had nothing to lose and everything to gain. Possibly his fellow lepers tried to dissuade him because none of them accompanied him. No matter! He would come. And so it was that he commenced his lonely journey to Jesus. And behold! A path opened up before him. The disciples, "bold" enough to chase away the mothers and children who sought to come to Christ, were not so forward in chasing away this leper. On the contrary, we can be sure that when they saw him coming, heard his leper's cry, and saw the crowds parting before him, they kept their distance. They would want to keep well enough away from a leper!

This man did not approach Christ with the modern proud "Name it! Claim it!" attitude. He had too great an appreciation of his terrible condition to come,

---

7. And possibly David.

like Naaman, demanding salvation. On the contrary, he came beseeching, "If thou wilt, thou canst make me clean." That was flawless faith.

We note, also, *his cleansing* (1:41–43):

> *And Jesus, moved with compassion, put forth his hand, and touched him, and saith unto him, I will; be thou clean. (1:41)*

In all probability, some people there were moved with criticism: "Of all the nerve! A man like that! Coming to Christ indeed! He should be ashamed of himself! He ought to be stoned. He's a public menace." But Jesus was moved with compassion. He was able to identify Himself with the unhappy man whose life had been so ruined and ravaged by this "stroke of God." He would touch him, transform him, and, thereafter, forever identify him with Himself.

The whole scene is a microcosm of the plan of salvation. It was the Lord's infinite compassion and wondrous saving power that made "so great salvation" possible. He *touched* this wretched man. That was love in action. Not since he became known as a leper had anyone deliberately touched him.

There was something else too. Jesus "saith unto him, I will; be thou clean." That was "the word of his power" (Heb. 1:3). Who else but God could speak worlds into being, command light to shine, or order the distribution of land or sea (Gen. 1)? Who else but God could command a leper to be clean? This was

> . . . the same Almighty word
> Chaos and darkness heard,
> And took their flight . . .

in the early dawn of time. Only now "the Word was made flesh," and Deity was robed in Humanity. "I will!" Jesus said, "Be clean." Just like that!

> *And as soon as he had spoken, immediately the leprosy departed from him, and he was cleansed. (1:42)*

Throughout his gospel, Mark seems to have been impressed by the swiftness with which the Lord's commands were obeyed. He spoke! It was done! There was no long and painful surgery; no protracted convalescence; no extended course of treatment; no stretched-out regime of therapy, exercise, and diet; and no medicine to be taken four times a day for months on end. There was instant cleansing for the leper, instant cure for the diseased, instant life for the dead, instant sight for the blind, and instant expulsion of demons. And there was instant cancellation of sin.

That is the difference between religion and regeneration. Religion has an agenda. It calls for meritorious good works, for fasts and flagellation, for rites and rituals, for penance and pilgrimages, for sacrifices and self-denials, for priests and payments. But religion never yet cleansed a leper or gave a guilty conscience peace.

Such is religion. All religions are born of human ingenuity, philosophy, and wisdom, and all religions are the same—salvation must be earned, purchased by good work. By contrast, regeneration (what John and Peter call "the new birth") is instantaneous, miraculous, and eternal. "As soon as he had spoken," says Mark, "immediately the leprosy departed from him, and he was cleansed."

We note, also, *his commission* (1:43–45), and *how it was delivered* (1:43–44):

And he straitly charged him, and forthwith sent him away; (1:43)

Having cleansed the leper, Jesus sent him away. The modern so-called "faith healer" would have kept him around as a useful advertisement. He could be put on the platform to give his testimony. He would draw the crowds. That, however, was the very thing that Jesus wanted to avoid. The Jerusalem crowds, which would shout, "Hosanna!" one day, would just as readily shout, "Crucify!" the next day. So Jesus gave this cleansed leper his orders and sent him away. That was as much for the man's own good as for any other reason.

Nowadays we make heroes out of notable celebrities who get saved. We lionize them, put them on the platform and on national television, get them to give their testimonies, tout them all over the country, put them on talk shows, and praise them and applaud them. What they really need is quiet and seclusion, a small-group fellowship, and time to grow in grace and increase in the knowledge of God. "Lay hands suddenly on no man" is a sound biblical principle (1 Tim. 5:22). So Jesus sent the man away. That must have astonished the disciples—perhaps by now, though, they were getting used to the Lord's unorthodox methods.

And saith unto him, See thou say nothing to any man: but go thy way, shew thyself to the priest, and offer for thy cleansing those things which Moses commanded, for a testimony unto them. (1:44)

The Lord not only sent the man home but also told him not to talk about his healing. One thing he must do, however; he must present himself to the priest that he might be legally certified clean by the representative of the Mosaic Law. Also, the priest himself needed to know that this unusual Messiah was a healer indeed!

The instructions for a leper who was cleansed are spelled out in intricate detail in Leviticus 14. The whole procedure took more than a week. The man was restored at once to the Hebrew *family*, but he had to wait until the first day of a new week before he could be restored to the *fellowship* of God's people.

It is understandable, perhaps, and not at all unusual, that this newly cleansed man did not do what the Lord commanded. Instead, he began to tell everyone about the transforming miracle in his life. Nowadays we would applaud a new convert for doing that. In this man's case, however, his testimony was counterproductive.

We note, also, *his commission and how it was disregarded:*

> But he went out, and began to publish it much, and to blaze abroad the matter, insomuch that Jesus could no more openly enter into the city, but was without in desert places: and they came to him from every quarter. (1:45)

Jesus sent the newly cleansed leper to the priest, but he went to the people, or, as we would say today, "he went public." Perhaps he was on his way to the priest. Doubtless, he was so thrilled with his cleansing that he was bursting to tell people. Maybe some people recognized him and wanted to know what he was doing out of the leper colony.

In any case, he was sidetracked. Instead of getting out of sight for the prescribed period of inspection, separation, and instruction, he became a flaming evangelist.

The Lord, however, always knows best. This man needed the wonderful teaching inherent in the ritual for the cleansing of the leper. Had he obeyed the Lord, he would have been a wiser man when it was over. As it was, however, the Lord's work was hindered. Such crowds resulted that the Lord Himself could not get into the city, and a "revival" without the Lord was not going to last very long. We would be pleased with such enthusiastic crowds today. We would congratulate ourselves on our success. But the Lord was hindered, and He was not in all of this superficial excitement.

He was hindered but not halted! He retired to "desert places." The people now had to seek Him on *His* terms. And so they did. They came to Him from all over. And there in the calm stillness of the wilderness, He carried on His work.

In Mark's account, it did not take long for opposition to the Lord to begin to surface. His critics soon found fault with His *method* (2:1–12), His *men* (2:13–28), and His *ministry* (3:1–6).

Mark 2 begins with the Lord back "in the house," presumably Peter's house. At once the house was mobbed by people, eager to hear the Lord's teaching and hoping, no doubt, to see some more miracles. Peter's house had never been so popular! The crowds filled his living room, jammed the doorway, spilled over into his yard, and thronged the street so that only with the greatest difficulty could anyone move.

And hemmed in by this heaving mass of people was Jesus. Not much can be done with a mob, even a friendly one, but Jesus took advantage of the presence of the crowd to preach. "He preached the word unto them" (2:2). Peter doesn't seem to remember what He preached—at least Mark doesn't tell us. Perhaps He told them a story from their Old Testament Scriptures. Perhaps He told about Moses and his multitudes, or about Elijah and his multitudes on Mt. Carmel. Or maybe He borrowed the language of the prophet and talked about those multiplied multitudes "in the valley of decision" (Joel 3:14). In any case, we can be sure that He looked with compassion on those multitudes and saw them "as sheep not having a shepherd" (Mark 6:34) and loved them and taught them the Word of God from a full heart.

    B. The Servant's work belittled (2:1–3:6)
        1. Finding fault with His method (2:1–12)
           a. The situation (2:1–5)
              (1) A packed place (2:1–2)
                  (a) The people (2:1–2a)
                  (b) The Preacher (2:2b)
              (2) A peculiar performance (2:3–4)
                  (a) The paralytic (2:3)
                  (b) The problem (2:4a)
                  (c) The pragmatists (2:4b)
              (3) A pardoned patient (2:5)
           b. The scribes (2:6–12)
              (1) Their thoughts exposed (2:6–8)
                  (a) Their secret animosity cherished (2:6–7)
                      i. Why? (2:6–7a)
                      ii. Who? (2:7b)

(b) Their secret animosity challenged (2:8)
    i. What the Lord discerned (2:8a)
    ii. What the Lord demanded (2:8b)
(2) Their thoughts expanded (2:9–12)
    (a) The question He asked (2:9)
    (b) The question He answered (2:10–12)
        i. The importance of His claim (2:10a)
        ii. The implementation of His claim (2:10b–12a)
        iii. The impact of His claim (2:12b)

2. Finding fault with His men (2:13–28)
  a. His publican friends (2:13–17)
    (1) The multitude (2:13)
      (a) Where they were (2:13a)
      (b) What they wanted (2:13b)
    (2) The man (2:14)
      (a) His secular calling (2:14a)
      (b) His spiritual call (2:14b)
    (3) The Master (2:15–17)
      (a) Where He went (2:15)
      (b) Why He went (2:16–17)
        i. His critics' scorn (2:16)
        ii. His critics silenced (2:17)
  b. His personal friends (2:18–28)
    (1) A challenge concerning fasting (2:18–22)
      (a) The critics (2:18)
      (b) The Christ (2:19–22)
        i. His question asked (2:19a)
        ii. His question answered (2:19b–22)
           a. The case of a wedding (2:19b–20)
              1. When the bridegroom was abiding with them (2:19b)
              2. When the bridegroom was absent from them (2:20)
           b. The case of a wardrobe (2:21)
           c. The case of a wineskin (2:22)
    (2) A challenge concerning feasting (2:23–28)
      (a) The action of the disciples described (2:23)

                i. The day (2:23a)

              ii. The deed (2:23b)

         (b) The action of the disciples decried (2:24)

              i. The obscurantists (2:24a)

              ii. The objection (2:24b)

         (c) The action of the disciples defended (2:25–28)

              i. A biblical reference (2:25–26)

                  a. A deep need (2:25)

                  b. A dire necessity (2:26)

              ii. A basic reason (2:27)

            iii. A blinding revelation (2:28)

    3. Finding fault with His ministry (3:1–6)

      a. The synagogue (3:1a)

      b. The sufferer (3:1b)

      c. The Sabbath (3:2)

      d. The Savior (3:3–6)

        (1) A legal regulation (3:3–4)

        (2) A lightning revelation (3:5)

          (a) Of a redeeming heart (3:5a)

          (b) Of a religious heart (3:5b)

        (3) A lasting restoration (3:5c)

        (4) A lethal reaction (3:6)

C. The Servant's work blessed (3:7–19)

    1. The Servant and the cheering multitudes (3:7–12)

      a. How He held them (3:7–8)

        (1) The place (3:7a)

        (2) The people (3:7b–8)

          (a) The regions from whence they came (3:7b–8a)

          (b) The reasons for which they came (3:8b)

        (3) The plan (3:9)

      b. How He healed them (3:10–12)

        (1) His abundant ability (3:10)

        (2) His absolute authority (3:11–12)

          (a) Demonic testimony rendered to Him (3:11)

          (b) Demonic testimony rejected by Him (3:12)

    2. The Servant and His chosen men (3:13–19)

      a. Their call (3:13–14a)

        (1) How He sought them (3:13)

        (2) How He taught them (3:14a)

    b. Their commission (3:14b–15)

        (1) How He employed them (3:14b)

        (2) How He empowered them (3:15)

           (a) To deal with disease (3:15a)

           (b) To deal with demons (3:15b)

    c. Their company (3:16–19)

        (1) A muster (3:16–19a)

           (a) The triad (3:16–17)

               i. The one He newly named (3:16)

               ii. The ones He nicknamed (3:17)

           (b) The team (3:18)

           (c) The traitor (3:19a)

        (2) A move (3:19b)

D. The Servant's work blasphemed (3:20–35)

  1. Opposition from His friends (3:20–21)

    a. The enormous crowds (3:20)

    b. The erroneous conclusion (3:21)

        (1) What they decided (3:21a)

        (2) What they declared (3:21b)

  2. Opposition from His foes (3:22–30)

    a. A blatant rejection of Christ (3:22)

        (1) Some notable visitors (3:22a)

        (2) Some new vindictiveness (3:22b)

    b. A blistering rebuttal by Christ (3:23–30)

        (1) His undisputed wisdom (3:23–27)

           (a) The parable (3:23–26)

               i. The question asked (3:23)

               ii. The question answered (3:24–26)

                   a. In the secular realm (3:24–25)

                       1. A monarch and his domains (3:24)

                       2. A man and his domestics (3:25)

                   b. In the satanic realm (3:26)

           (b) The point (3:27)

               i. The strongman's possessions (3:27a)

               ii. The stronger man's power (3:27b)

         (2) His undiluted warning (3:28–30)

           (a) A twofold reality (3:28–29)

       i. An unfailing Savior (3:28)
       ii. An unforgiven sin (3:29)
     (b) A terrible reason (3:30)
   3. Opposition from His family (3:31–35)
    a. His natural family (3:31–32)
     (1) Their arrival was intentional (3:31)
      (a) Their relationship (3:31a)
      (b) Their resolve (3:31b)
     (2) Their arrival was ignored (3:32)
    b. His new family (3:33–35)
     (1) Whom the Lord disowned (3:33)
     (2) What the Lord declared (3:34)
      (a) Regarding His present disciples (3:34)
      (b) Regarding His prospective disciples (3:35)

—⚙—

B. The Servant's work belittled (2:1–3:6)
 1. Finding fault with His method (2:1–12)
  a. The situation (2:1–5)

And again he entered into Capernaum after some days; and it was noised that he was in the house. And straightway many were gathered together, insomuch that there was no room to receive them, no, not so much as about the door: and he preached the word unto them. And they come unto him, bringing one sick of the palsy, which was borne of four. (2:1–3)

The crowds were definitely in the way for the small procession that was now approaching. A few friends were coming, carrying a sick man on a stretcher. They wanted to bring him to Jesus. They had elbowed their way successfully through the crowd to the door of the house, but that was as far as they could get; there was no budging anyone from there. Undaunted by the obstacle, the four men climbed up onto the flat roof of the house and hauled up their friend. Then they tore a large hole in the roof and boldly lowered the sick man down into the room below, where the Lord, also hemmed in by the crowd, was seated.

And when they could not come nigh unto him for the press, they uncovered the roof where he was: and when they had broken it up, they let down the bed wherein the sick of the palsy lay. (2:4)

We can picture Peter's surprise and consternation as the blows, aimed at making a big hole in the roof, began to resound through his house! But he was hemmed in too! He would have found it as hard to get out to put a stop to this attack on his property as these men had found it to get in. All he could do was stand there and witness the breakup of his roof. We can imagine the wry humor with which he told the story in later years to his young colleague, Mark. Doubtless, too, the Lord Himself watched the proceedings, appreciating the humor of it. Peter's face must have been a study!

Jesus saw the faith of this man's friends, but He saw more; He saw the sick man's physical and spiritual needs. To everyone's astonishment, He greeted the invalid with the most unorthodox words, as Mark recorded:

When Jesus saw their faith, he said unto the sick of the palsy, Son, thy sins be forgiven thee. (2:5)

That was not what the man was hoping to hear. The Lord, however, could read this man's soul. Paul reminds us of a day when the Lord will "judge the secrets of men" (Rom. 2:16). The secrets of this man's soul were as open and obvious to the Lord as the sickness of his body. To His mind, the man's sins were far more serious than his palsy, so He dealt with them first.

"Son, thy sins be forgiven thee!" Here we have the two most wonderful words of the gospel: *son* and *forgiven!* The first word put the man in the *family* of God; the second word put him in the *fellowship* of God (1 John 1:7–10). We are reminded of the repentant prodigal (Luke 15). He had already made up his mind what to say to his father, but when he got to the part "I am no more worthy to be called thy son," the floodgates of the father's love were opened, and the wayward boy was restored to the family and the father's fellowship with a ring, a robe, shoes, and a place at the table. "Son!"

Forgiven! What a blessed word for a sin-burdened soul! The debt discharged! The guilt gone! The conscience cleansed! The past pardoned! The record removed! Forgiven!

But that was by no means the end of the story. Critical eyes and ears were watching, listening, waiting, and disapproving.

b. The scribes (2:6–12)

Note how *their thoughts were exposed:*

> *But there were certain of the scribes sitting there, and reasoning in*
> *their hearts, Why doth this man thus speak blasphemies? who can*
> *forgive sins but God only? And immediately when Jesus perceived*
> *in his spirit that they so reasoned within themselves, he said unto*
> *them, Why reason ye these things in your hearts? (2:6–8)*

The scribes were educated men. After the Babylonian captivity, they were the leaders of the Jewish nation. Ezra was a scribe. Their task was to copy the Scriptures. They were also professional interpreters of the Mosaic Law and administered both its religious and its civil codes. The scribes determined how the details of the law should be applied to everyday life. In time, they became the custodians of the so-called "oral law," which, by Jesus' day, was already replacing the written law as the rule of life. The scribes were regarded as the authorities on historical and doctrinal matters. They were the nation's teachers, each scribe having a number of disciples around him. Their power increased after Malachi closed the Old Testament canon and prophecy ceased. The Sanhedrin had a number of them among its membership. They were bitter enemies of Christ, sitting in judgment of Him and finding fault with almost everything He did and said.

Jesus knew that some of the scribes were in the crowd. He knew, too, what their reaction would be when He declared the palsied man's sins to be forgiven! Sure enough! They mentally accused Him of blasphemy, of arrogating to Himself the ability to do things that only God could do. But had He not done that already in cleansing the leper and in the numerous other miracles that He had performed there in Capernaum? Of course, He had! It is typical of unbelief that it conveniently overlooks awkward facts.

The Lord knew about their hostility. The instant the accusing thoughts entered their minds, He knew it.

He "perceived in his spirit," Mark says. They, by contrast, "reasoned in their hearts," that is, in their souls. The unregenerate person has to rely on his reasoning power. The Lord Jesus did not have to reason out what would be the response of these men to His statement. He was aware of it instantly. Before they could say a word, He challenged them: "Why reason ye these things in your hearts?" It was not a question that required an answer. He knew the answer, anticipated it, and annulled it.

Note how *their thoughts were expanded* (2:9–12):

> *Whether it is easier to say to the sick of the palsy, Thy sins be for-given thee; or to say, Arise, and take up thy bed, and walk? (2:9)*

"Which is easier to *say?*" Well, of course, both are equally easy to *say*. If, how-ever, one is a quack and wants to get a reputation for power without either proof or performance, then, obviously, it is easier to say, "Thy sins are forgiven thee" than it is to say, "Arise, and take up thy bed, and walk." Who can say whether the sins have been forgiven? But whether the needy one takes up his bed and actually walks is the real test.

"Thy sins be forgiven thee!" Jesus said. "Arise, and take up thy bed, and walk!" Caustic were the words of Thomas Aquinas to the pope of his day. The pope was in his counting house counting out his money. "You see, Thomas," said the pope, "the church no longer has to say, 'Silver and gold have we none.'"

"True, Holy Father," said Aquinas, "and neither can it say to the sick, 'Take up thy bed, and walk.'"

> *But that ye may know that the Son of man hath power on earth to forgive sins, (he saith to the sick of the palsy,) I say unto thee, Arise, and take up thy bed, and go thy way into thine house. (2:10–11)*

The Lord Jesus was quite prepared to put His reputation on the line. If the man continued to lie there sick of the palsy, it was all over. In that case, the Lord Jesus, all of His claims to be the Son of God notwithstanding, would be exposed as just another religious charlatan. So we can well imagine how keenly the audi-ence watched to see what would happen. The Lord Himself had no doubt as to the outcome. He not only knew that the man would get up but also gave him some directions as to his immediate future steps. He was to get up and go home. No doubt his loyal quartet of friends would march with him in a triumphant procession every step of the way.

A profound truth is embedded in the Lord's words: "That ye may know that the Son of man hath power on earth to forgive sins." If our sins are to be forgiven, it must be while we are still *on earth*. It will be too late once we are dead because both character and destiny are fixed at death. The solemn pronouncement is, "He that is unjust, let him be unjust still: and he which is filthy, let him be filthy still: and he that is righteous, let him be righteous still: and he that is holy, let him be holy still" (Rev. 22:11). So much for Rome's purgatory, endless masses said for dead men's souls, and the vain hope of eventual beatification and canonization. The Bible knows no such teaching. The Bible offers no hope of redemption beyond the grave. Both the rich man and Lazarus knew that in the afterlife their condition was fixed beyond change. Between them was "a great gulf fixed" (Luke 16:19–31). A path runs from earth to heaven, and a path runs from earth to hell, but no path runs from hell to heaven. Purgatory is a myth. We get our sins forgiven on earth—or not at all. And the One who has power on earth to forgive sins is the Son of Man alone. He has delegated hat power to no one else.

And immediately he arose, took up the bed, and went forth before them all; insomuch that they were all amazed, and glorified God, saying, We never saw it on this fashion. (2:12)

Immediately the man got up, picked up his bedroll, and marched out of the house, elbowing his way through the crowds. Did he come back later to help Peter mend his roof? Did the former carpenter take that task in hand? It would be interesting to know.

The impact on the people present was immediate. Amazed, they glorified God. "We never saw it like this before!" they said.

The rabbis and the scribes, the Pharisees and the Sadducees, the priests and the Levites, and all of the religious establishment had never demonstrated such power and authority, in either what they preached or what they practiced, either individually or collectively. This was new! Here was a Man who spoke with authority. He could command that sins be forgiven, and He could command that sickness be healed.

Who can forgive sins but God? they asked themselves. Well, who could command sickness to flee but God? Having proved His ability to command instant healing of a man who was obviously in a very bad way, so ill that he could not even get off his bed, He proved His ability to forgive sins and, therefore, proved to them that He was God.

At this point, the hostility of the official Jewish establishment had not yet hardened into fixed opposition. Before long, however, they would become so accustomed to seeing Him do the most extraordinary things that they would become hardened. They would find some plausible explanation for the Lord's amazing power, one that would not force them to face His deity. They would say that He was in league with the Devil.

> 2. Finding fault with His men (2:13–28)
>   a. His publican friends (2:13–17)

And he went forth again by the sea side; and all the multitude resorted unto him, and he taught them. And as he passed by, he saw Levi the son of Alphaeus sitting at the receipt of custom, and said unto him, Follow me. And he arose and followed him. (2:13–14)

Jesus now went down to the lakeside, and the multitudes, eager to see more miracles, hastened after Him. "He taught them," Mark says. The message was more important than the miracles. Just as He taught the disciples on the road to Emmaus from all of the Scriptures "the things concerning himself" (Luke 24:27), so He taught these Galilean crowds. The rabbis wrote the graffiti of their own man-made traditions all over the wall of the Word of God. Jesus took the people back to the splendid, pristine truth of the Word of God and showed them its rich colors, its divine texture, and its matchless worth.

Then He moved on. He had His eye now on a new recruit, Levi, the son of Alphaeus, better known to us as Matthew. He was busy when Jesus called him. Most Jews would have had nothing to do with him. Because of the disreputable profession he had chosen to follow, they would have held him in the utmost contempt.

We do not know whether Alphaeus, the father of Levi (Matthew), was the same Alphaeus who was the father of James the less, another of the Lord's disciples, but he became one of the most famous of the Lord's disciples.

He lived in Capernaum and must have been well known to Peter and his business partners. He was evidently of the tribe of Levi, the tribe set apart by God to minister to the other tribes in sacred things. By the time of Christ, many of the Levites were the nation's lawyers. It must have been a bitter disappointment to his parents when young Matthew (whose name means "gift of Jehovah") turned his back on the legal profession to get rich quickly, at any cost, even at the cost of losing his character by becoming a publican. The publicans collected taxes for the Roman government, and the Jews regarded them as traitors and extortioners.

They grew rich by padding the tax assessments that they were to collect. Matthew likely was a customs official with a tax office by the lake; he was responsible for collecting customs duties on the lucrative fishing trade.

Matthew had no doubt seen some of the Lord's miracles. He had heard Him preach, and his heart had been touched. He was ready when the Lord called.

How did the other disciples react to the call of a *publican?* Doubtless, their feelings were harrowed at first, and they looked askance at their new colleague. But Matthew was used to that look, and he was not thin-skinned. He would never have made it as a publican if he had been susceptible to sneers and hostile glances.

> *And it came to pass, that, as Jesus sat at meat in his house, many publicans and sinners sat also together with Jesus and his disciples: for there were many, and they followed him. (2:15)*

The scene now changes to Matthew's house. Evidently, Mark is describing a gala occasion, one that made a deep impression on Peter's mind. Matthew arranged to bring all of his old friends to meet all of his new friends. He especially wanted all of his old friends to meet Jesus. Matthew was probably rich and possibly had a large house. He might also have had many friends among the lower classes. The religious world classified the kind of people with whom Matthew associated simply as "publicans and sinners" and would have nothing to do with them. Jesus, however, received them gladly. His followers received them because He received them, but one suspects that they received them grudgingly.

Were it not for Jesus, the meeting would have been impossible. The world of the publicans and sinners was far removed from the world of such loyal subjects, such honest businessmen, such moral and religious worthies as Peter, James, and the Zebedee brothers. To this point, the two groups had despised each other and had nothing for each other but hard names, ill feelings, and caustic comments. Even supposing that some well-meaning person had wanted to effect a reconciliation between the two groups and had arranged a gathering of as many of them as possible, from both sides of the tracks, for dialogue and an exchange of ideas, how many would have come? What would they have found to talk about with each other? Most of us have attended functions, such as weddings, at which people from quite opposite social, political, religious, cultural, and moral poles are thrown together at a reception. In such situations, people tend to gravitate toward their own kind. Any cross-conversation is shallow and forced and entered into only when necessary.

That's how it was at Matthew's gala, too, because Matthew's popularity was with his own crowd. Jesus made the difference; *both* sides were interested in *Him*. He was the common center around which they all gathered. They could all talk about Him. His disciples could share some of their experiences. The publicans and sinners could express their astonishment and pleasure that He would come so willingly to a gathering convened by one of their own kind. We can picture Matthew's beaming at the success of his daring venture. The only sour note came from outside, and it wasn't long in coming.

> *And when the scribes and Pharisees saw him eat with publicans and sinners, they said unto his disciples, How is it that he eateth and drinketh with publicans and sinners? (2:16)*

When He forgave the palsied man's sins, the scribes had objected, albeit silently. Now the Pharisees joined them, and they voiced their criticism audibly. Even at that, however, their objection was cautious. They approached the disciples, not the Lord Himself; they still were somewhat in awe of Him. The scribes were the custodians of the *text* of Scripture; the Pharisees were the custodians of the *traditions* of Scripture. They were meticulous in keeping the countless man-made rules and regulations that had evolved around the basic 613 commandments of the Mosaic Law. Their idea of a holy man could be summarized in the word *separation*. A good man would not want to be contaminated by associating himself with traitors. He would not want to be compromised socially or have his reputation ruined by such association.

"Publicans! Sinners!" We can hear the horror and contempt in their voices. We can see the disgust on their faces. Why, such people were moral lepers. They were outcasts, untouchables. Not one of the members of the religious establishment would even so much as dream of having his name linked with such people.

Yet, here was this young prophet from Nazareth attending a party convened by the scum of the neighborhood. They could not gainsay His miracles, but now they began to question His morals. They challenged His disciples to explain this very peculiar behavior of their prophet. Surely a prophet's task was to denounce and damn such people, not to dine with them. The Lord, however, did not need His disciples to make excuses for Him. He was well able to explain Himself. Mark says,

When Jesus heard it, he saith unto them, They that are whole
have no need of the physician, but they that are sick: I came not
to call the righteous, but sinners to repentance. (2:17)

A lot of noise must have been going on all around. Dozens of people were there. Many of them were old friends or colleagues. On such occasions, the buzz of conversation soon becomes a roar. But the Lord's ears missed nothing, even as His eyes saw everything. He saw the disciples, who were evidently keeping pretty well to themselves, as the scribes and Pharisees approached with their scarcely veiled criticism. He heard what they said, as He hears all that is said.

Before the embarrassed disciples could blurt out some inadequate reply, He took the floor. He drew a simple but obvious parallel. "It's not healthy people who need a doctor but sick people," He said. "It's not good people who need a Savior but bad people."

The Lord's critics, of course, thought themselves to be good people, and they classified publicans and harlots as bad people. They brought into focus one great fact of the gospel—no one is too bad for the Lord Jesus to save, but many people think themselves to be too good to need salvation.

People who imagine themselves to be too good to need to be saved judge themselves and others on a scale of relative values. They put sin in various categories and grade it according to differing degrees. Therefore, the Prodigal Son's sins would be much more wicked to them than the sins of his older brother. On their scale, a harlot would be much worse than a hypocrite and a murderer much worse than a murmurer. But God has a different scale—His own absolute goodness. That leaves everyone in the same category. We are *all* lost sinners in need of a Savior.

   b. His personal friends (2:18–28)
        (1) A challenge concerning fasting (2:18–22)

Note, first, *the critics:*

And the disciples of John and of the Pharisees used to fast: and
they come and say unto him, Why do the disciples of John and of
the Pharisees fast, but thy disciples fast not? (2:18)

We are now introduced to some strange bedfellows. The Pharisees, as a group, rejected the ministry of John the Baptist. John, in turn, denounced the Pharisees as "a generation of vipers" (Matt. 3:7). But here the disciples of John and the disciples of the Pharisees, who are at odds about most things, find that they have something in common—fasting. The disciples of John fasted evidently because they thought it to be a proof of their repentance; the Pharisees fasted because they considered it part of their religion.

To the surprise of the Pharisees and the followers of John, the disciples of Jesus did not fast at all. The disciples of *John* must have looked upon this avoidance of such an obvious help to holiness with considerable *surprise*. John himself was a thoroughgoing ascetic, whose life of rigorous self-denial had set him apart from the whole nation. The *Pharisees* and their disciples must have looked upon this avoidance of fasting with considerable *skepticism*. So much for *Jesus'* supposed prophetic status if He and His disciples neglected the most obvious duty of a holy man—to fast, and the longer and the more often the better.

Note, now, *the Christ* (2:19–22):

> *And Jesus said unto them, Can the children of the bridechamber fast, while the bridegroom is with them? as long as they have the bridegroom with them, they cannot fast. But the days will come, when the bridegroom shall be taken away from them, and then shall they fast in those days. (2:19–20)*

As Solomon had said, there is a time and place for everything (Eccl. 3:1–8). Fasting during a wedding feast would be most inappropriate. The Bridegroom had come! It was a time for laughter, not lamentation; a time to feast, not a time to fast. After all, the ultimate goal of all such self-denial had been reached. The Lord of Glory had come! It was a time to rejoice and be glad. A new day had dawned. A new age had been born. Holiness now no longer went hand in hand with heaviness; it went arm in arm with happiness.

The Lord, however, foresaw a change ahead. The Bridegroom was to be taken away. Then there would be time enough for fasting.

Thus, early in His ministry, the Lord knew where it all would end. He would be rejected and would return to His home on high. A long, impenetrable silence would be heaven's answer to man's wickedness. The children of the bride chamber would then have plenty of reasons to fast.

Fasting has its place. It can put an edge on our prayers. It is a difficult tool to use, however. It can impart a false feeling of sanctity. It can make the user feel that he can force God's hand. It can become habit-forming and degenerate into a formality. It can make a person self-righteous and critical of others. It can become a substitute for genuine holiness. And it can be legalistic.

On the other hand, Jesus fasted. He fasted for forty days during the time of His encounter with the Devil in the wilderness. In answering the question that the Pharisees and John's disciples raised, He did not depreciate true fasting. He simply explained why His disciples did not fast *then*. To do so would have been wholly out of character with the times.

> *No man also seweth a piece of new cloth on an old garment: else the new piece that filled it up taketh away from the old, and the rent is made worse. (2:21)*

The new piece of cloth was what we now call Christianity. The old garment, patched and worn out, was Judaism, with its feasts and fasts and rules and regulations and sacrifices and ceremonies. What the disciples of John and the Pharisees themselves had to realize was that the advent of Christ had changed everything. He had come to bring in something new and different. He had not come to patch up Judaism, which had already served its purpose and outlived its usefulness. Trying to sew Christianity onto Judaism would not work. Judaism was obsolete and was to be replaced altogether.

> *And no man putteth new wine into old bottles: else the new wine doth burst the bottles, and the wine is spilled, and the bottles will be marred: but new wine must be put into new bottles. (2:22)*

The wine is the Holy Spirit. The wineskins represent the believer. Christ came to make us new, fit vessels for the indwelling Holy Spirit. Thus, all begins now with a new birth, with "the new man," to use one of Paul's favorite expressions. We have new life in Christ. The Holy Spirit could not and cannot be poured into an old life. He would tear it to pieces. The Lord did not come to improve our old nature; He came to provide us with a new nature capable of handling the baptism, indwelling, filling, and anointing of the mighty Spirit of God. This is the message of Pentecost. The coming of the Spirit in this new way was accompanied by flames of fire and a mighty, rushing wind—forces capable of tearing a person apart. No wonder a new birth and a new man were needed! All things were made new—new bottles for new wine.

(2) A challenge concerning feasting (2:23–28)

And it came to pass, that he went through the corn fields on the sabbath day; and his disciples began, as they went, to pluck the ears of corn. (2:23)

Before long, however, the critics found something else to criticize.

On every hand were fields of tossing, golden grain. Here was the Lord, and there were the disciples. The disciples were hungry, and because the Mosaic Law allowed the passerby to take a cob, they did so. The *Lord of the Harvest* Himself was with them. He had created the seed that had been sown. He had sent the rain and even provided the soil. He had commanded His beaming sun to smile upon the fields and farms, and now the whole land was full of grain, bowing to acknowledge its Creator.

Were the disciples hungry? Well, let them take advantage of the provision in the law. His was the hand that had written on the tablets of stone that Moses had carried down from the mount. His was the voice that had dictated to Moses the provision for the poor. Let them take a little of the teeming bounty that was at hand.

And so they did, with His blessing—but it was the Sabbath. "The better the day, the better the deed," as we would say. He saw no hindrance in its being the Sabbath. The Sabbath was His provision for the benefit and blessing of His own. He was the *Lord of the Sabbath* as well as the Lord of the Harvest.

And the Pharisees said unto him, Behold, why do they on the sabbath day that which is not lawful? (2:24)

The Pharisees had been narrowed by the rabbis and had become steeped in the so-called "oral law." They attacked the Lord, not because His disciples ate some corn from a nearby field but because they did it on the Sabbath. Indeed, nothing stirred them to wrath more than the Lord's attitude toward the Sabbath. The rabbis had built enormous bulwarks around the Sabbath. They had hedged it in with a thousand man-made rules and regulations, most of them ridiculous. They had made the Sabbath a burden, whereas God had intended it to be a blessing. In their view, plucking an ear of corn was equivalent to reaping; rubbing away the husk was the same as threshing. So, according to the Pharisees' traditions, the disciples had violated the Sabbath and broken the law.

"Behold!" they said. It was obvious. It needed no explanation. Surely, even the most ignorant Jew knew that what the Lord's disciples were doing constituted a violation of the law. Was He blind?

> *And he said unto them, Have ye never read what David did, when he had need, and was an hungred, he, and they that were with him? (2:25)*

The Lord had His Bible ready for them. Had they not read what David did when he was hungry? Of course, they had read it. They knew those Old Testament stories by heart. So did the Lord. But He saw things in the Bible that they never saw. They were too busy with trivia to see truth, even when it stared them in the face. They were too fond of allegorizing and legalizing and dissecting the sacred text, debating it and distorting it and devaluating it by their pontifical traditions. They failed to see the obvious. To them, what the fathers had said was more important than what the Father had said. But Jesus ignored all of their endless rabbinical discussions, all of their footnotes and marginal notes, all of their rabbinical interpretations, and all of their traditions and *ex cathedra* pronouncements. He went right to the heart of every chapter, every verse, and every line of the sacred text.

> *How he went into the house of God in the days of Abiathar the high priest, and did eat the shewbread, which is not lawful to eat but for the priests, and gave also to them which were with him? (2:26)*

For good measure, the Lord reminded them of how David had gone into the tabernacle in the days of Abiathar, the high priest, and had partaken of the shewbread, something that was reserved, by the Mosaic Law, for only the priests. Moreover, he had given some of that consecrated bread to his companions too. They were just as hungry as he was (1 Sam. 21:1–6). That passage was an extraordinarily apt passage of Scripture to quote because it dealt with the very thing about which the Pharisees were complaining—eating what they said was not lawful to eat.

The table of shewbread stood in the Holy Place of the tabernacle. Once a week, the officiating priest placed twelve loaves of bread on the table, one loaf for each tribe of Israel. The bread that was removed to make room for the fresh loaves was sacred and could be eaten by only the priests. This consecrated bread was that which Abiathar, contrary to the letter of the law, gave to David and his men when they were fleeing from King Saul. The obvious lesson is that God is not a legalist and that His laws are not only wise but also benevolent.

The Pharisees would have considered it high treason against God Himself if a mere layman had presumed to go into the temple and, just because he was hungry, eat one of the loaves on the sanctuary table. But, for all intents and purposes, that was what David did. Abiathar was caught between a rock and a hard place when David made his demand. He was afraid of Saul, afraid of David, and afraid of breaking the law. But David's common sense prevailed.

Thus, with the Word of God as His weapon, the Lord argued for common sense. The Sabbath restrictions, invented by the rabbis, ignored the fact that human hunger was a more real issue than rabbinical rules.

> *And he said unto them, The sabbath was made for man, and not man for the sabbath. (2:27)*

The Lord had a parting shot for His critics. "The sabbath," He said, "was made for man, and not man for the sabbath." A wise and benevolent heavenly Father had planned for the Sabbath to be a weekly blessing to His own. One day in seven was to be a holiday from work. The body could have its quota of rest, and the soul and the spirit could be restored by the worship of God.

The Sabbath itself predated the Mosaic Law by some twenty-five hundred years, depending on the date of Genesis 1. It had its roots in creation because God Himself, after working in creative activity for six days, rested on the seventh day.

He who knows our frame and who remembers that we are but dust instituted the Sabbath for our good. The Sabbath was made for man. By the time the rabbis had finished adding all of their prohibitions to it, however, it became an intolerable burden. They seemed to think that man was made for the Sabbath. One word of common sense from the Lord blew away all of the countless petty rules and restrictions that they had erected allegedly to protect it.

> *Therefore the Son of man is Lord also of the sabbath. (2:28)*

As the Lord of the Sabbath, He could do what He liked with it. In fact, He intended to abolish it. The Sabbath always fell on the seventh day of the week. After Calvary, however, things happened on the first day of the week. Jesus rose from the dead on the first day of the week. The Day of Pentecost fell on the first day of the week. The Holy Spirit came on the first day of the week. The early church met for worship on the first day of the week (Acts 20:7). Now our rest is not in a day but in a Person. Now the law is replaced by the Lord. Our rest is in Him. The whole subject is spelled out in Hebrews 4, where the discussion revolves around the whole subject of *rest*—creation rest, Canaan rest, and Calvary rest.

So the Son of Man, who perfectly understands us, is Lord of the Sabbath just as He is Lord of everything else.

3. Finding fault with His ministry (3:1–6)

And he entered again into the synagogue; and there was a man there which had a withered hand. (3:1)

Again we are back in the synagogue on the Sabbath. And, sure enough, there was another sufferer, this time a man with a paralyzed hand. Jesus had a special place in His heart for the handicapped; His heart went out to them. The failure of any member of the body to function throws a burden on the rest of the body. Usually, especially in ages past, when people did not have access to modern surgery, mechanical limbs, motorized wheelchairs, and all of the other wonders of modern medicine, the handicapped person was unable to work. He had to subsist on charity.

This man's handicap was a withered, or paralyzed, hand. He could do nothing with it. He could make shift with the other one, but there were a hundred things he couldn't do. Nonetheless, he could attend the synagogue, and that was where Jesus found him.

Jesus had been in this Capernaum synagogue many times. The last time, as recorded by Mark, He had healed a demoniac. It had been a Sabbath day. Even so, the response of the people had been enthusiastic (1:21–28). Now, however, the mood had changed. A new critical spirit was taking root. The disciples had been criticized for plucking a few ears of corn on the Sabbath. They had been ably defended by the Lord and the critics put to silence.

And they watched him, whether he would heal him on the sabbath day; that they might accuse him. (3:2)

Now they were keeping an eye on Him. He had taken them by surprise when He healed the demoniac on the Sabbath. He had taken them by storm in His flawless defense of His disciples. But from now on the Lord's enemies would be ready for Him.

Three things set the Jews apart from the rest of the world. These three things kept them separate from the Gentiles and, on the purely human level, helped them keep their racial purity in spite of their being scattered far and wide, century after century, throughout the Gentile world. The three distinctives were the rite of circumcision, the strict Levitical dietary law, and the weekly observance of the Sabbath. All three distinctives have been abolished in Christ. The Jewish leaders of Christ's day, however, were not about to let this young prophet from Nazareth imperil their survival as a nation by a lax attitude toward the Sabbath, one of their bulwarks against assimilation. They had strengthened this particular bulwark over the centuries by adding countless supporting rules and regulations to buttress the simple, unadorned ordinance of the Mosaic Law. Any compromise about the Sabbath (as hedged about by their rules and regulations) was bound to be suspect.

So they watched Him. They were just waiting for one more irregularity, and they would accuse Him. Under the Mosaic Law, profaning the Sabbath was a capital offense (Num. 15:30–41).

> *And he saith unto the man which had the withered hand, Stand forth. (3:3)*

The Lord was not intimidated. He could have suggested to the man that he come around to Peter's house once the service was over, or that he come for healing on the morrow. But the Lord did no such thing. He had long since written off the rabbinical Sabbath restrictions as nonsense, so He boldly told the man to come forward where everyone could see him.

> *And he saith unto them, Is it lawful to do good on the sabbath days, or to do evil? to save life, or to kill? But they held their peace. (3:4)*

The answer was obvious—at least it was obvious that it was not lawful to do evil or commit murder on the Sabbath day or any other day. As far as *that* went, the Sabbath was no different than any other day. That was the point. Conversely, when it came to doing good or to saving a life, the Sabbath day was equally no different from any other day.

Must a man stand by and watch his neighbor's house burn down without lifting a finger to help just because it is the Sabbath? Was that what God intended?

Must a doctor refuse to administer aid to a child who has fallen and broken his leg just because it is the Sabbath? Must a man stand on the bank and watch someone drown, when he could rescue him, just because it is the Sabbath?

The problem, as the Lord knew full well, was not with the law of the Sabbath but with their ignorance of the *Lord* of the Sabbath.

"But they held their peace." They neither could refute His point nor would admit their error. They responded like the elder brother in the Lord's parable (Luke 15), which ends with the father still pleading and with the elder brother wrapped in a stubborn silence. It was an eloquent silence. It was a silence of rejection and unbelief.

> *And when he had looked round about on them with anger, being grieved for the hardness of their hearts, he saith unto the man, Stretch forth thine hand. And he stretched it out: and his hand was restored whole as the other. (3:5)*

Jesus was angry and grieved. Not one other person there had any sympathy or feeling for the crippled man. They were too wedded to their precious religious traditions. Their silence said that it was better for a man to lose his house, for a child to lose his limb, and for a drowning man to lose his life than for someone to break a rabbinical rule. No wonder Jesus was both angry and grieved. Their hardness was what moved His own heart so. He knew where that hardness would take them—to a lost eternity.

Then, in open defiance of their unspoken but bitter opposition, He healed the poor fellow who had been standing there, no doubt on pins and needles, wondering, perhaps, whether Jesus would bow to their rules. The Lord's heart went out to the needy man. As Mark tells the story, all of the initiative in this case was with Jesus. The man had simply been there, a passive member of the congregation. He had not appealed to Christ for healing. Perhaps he was too afraid to risk the wrath of the rabbis by breaking their religious taboos.

But now he had to decide on whose side he was. "Stretch forth thine hand!" That was impossible; it was withered. That was imprudent; it might mean his excommunication. But that voice had authority to overwhelm the imprudence, and that voice had power to overcome the impossible. The man responded and was healed instantly—and no doubt he spent the rest of his life telling the wonderful tale.

> *And the Pharisees went forth, and straightway took counsel with the Herodians against him, how they might destroy him. (3:6)*

Surely, we have here two of the most terrible statements in human language—"against him" . . . "destroy him." *Him!* The One who came from glory. The only begotten of the Father, full of grace and truth! He who went about doing good! Who healed their sick, gave sight to their blind, cleansed their lepers, raised their dead, and fed their hungry multitudes! They were *against* Him. Why? Because they could not pour Him into their religious mold. Such is false religion.

Worse still, they wanted to destroy Him. *Him!* The Eternal, uncreated, self-existing second person of the Godhead, the Ancient of Days, He who was from everlasting to everlasting, hymned by the highest archangels of glory, the theme of the seraphs' song, the Creator and Sustainer of the universe, God over all, blessed forevermore, omnipotent, omniscient, omnipresent! They wanted to destroy *Him!* They would have had a better chance of trying to destroy the galaxy. But such is false religion.

And how did these little men, these village "holy men," propose to accomplish this gigantic task? With allies, of course. They thought at once of the Herodians, another group of little men who imagined themselves to be very big men indeed.

The Herodians were more than a religious party and less than a religious sect. The group seems to have been organized to serve Herod the Great. It was prepared to offer homage to Roman power in return for political and religious favors. The Pharisees had had little in common with them—until now. Now they instinctively turned to them as natural allies against this unwanted Messiah. In this new alliance came together the most deadly of all combinations—the union of religion and politics. And this volatile union was against Christ. When religious fanatics join forces with political extremists, let others beware.

C. The Servant's work blessed (3:7–19)
    1. The Servant and the cheering multitudes (3:7–12)

The enemies of the gospel *belittled* the work of God's perfect Servant, but the fact remained that it was *blessed.* The multitudes were still full of enthusiasm for this amazing Messiah.

> *But Jesus withdrew himself with his disciples to the sea: and a great multitude from Galilee followed him, and from Judaea, And from Jerusalem, and from Idumaea, and from beyond Jordan; and they about Tyre and Sidon, a great multitude, when they had heard what great things he did, came unto him. (3:7–8)*

The multitudes came from all parts of the country. They came from the south, from Idumea, the area south of Judea and the Dead Sea. They came from Judea and Jerusalem, from the capital itself. They came from the north, from all over Galilee. They came from the east, from beyond the Jordan. And they came from the west, along the coastline of the Mediterranean Sea. So much for the Pharisee-Herodian coalition!

The mention of a Jerusalem contingent here might explain why the local religious leaders in Capernaum were so upset. The Lord not only had profaned the Sabbath, in their view, but also had done so to their embarrassment. The local provincial leaders were always intimidated by the more sophisticated leaders from Judea and Jerusalem.

Prudently, the Lord removed Himself from this vicinity, where plots against His life were being hatched. The multitudes followed Him. From that time, the Capernaum clerics had the synagogues, but Jesus had the crowds. His fame spread far and wide, and people came in droves from near and far. Even the nation's capital was ringing with His exploits. They came from Edom and Transjordan and even from the ancient Phoenician coastal cities of Tyre and Sidon. In one sweeping embrace, Mark gathers up the whole land. The entire country was agog with excitement.

The conspiracy against Christ was too small and too soon. It was the wrong time and the wrong place for it to succeed. However, as oncoming events cast their shadows before them, so this conspiracy was the harbinger of more serious conspiracies to come. Thus, however, early in the Lord's ministry, did serious opposition develop—and that in His own adopted hometown of Capernaum.

And he spake to his disciples, that a small ship should wait on him because of the multitude, lest they should throng him. (3:9)

So great were the crowds now thronging the lakeshore that Jesus asked His disciples to find a small boat that He could use as a platform. He was in danger of being crowded into the lake. The sensible thing was to have a boat available to pick Him up should that happen—and anyone else, for that matter, who found themselves pushed into the water by the throng. Not that He needed a boat to secure His safety. As God, a word from Him, and the waters would have parted, giving Him a wide path to the other side. Or, He could have done what He did on another occasion—simply walk on the water. But that was not His way. His miracles had a sort of prodigality about them, yet they exhibited a strict economy too. He never did for others what they could do for themselves. For example, He fed the five thousand but told the disciples to gather up the leftovers for later. Moreover, He never performed a miracle for His own benefit. He refused instantly the Devil's suggestion that He turn stones into bread to feed Himself. He never performed a miracle just to impress people. Thus, He refused the Devil's suggestion that He throw Himself down from the pinnacle of the temple just to be spectacular.

No! A boat would do well enough in this situation. So that was what He ordered.

> *For he had healed many; insomuch that they pressed upon him*
> *for to touch him, as many as had plagues. (3:10)*

Mark makes clear that it was the miracles that drew the multitudes. Wonderful, wonderful Jesus! All they had to do was touch Him, and their diseases fled! No wonder they crowded upon Him. This was His answer to His rejection in the synagogue. He didn't go away in a rage, as Naaman did. He didn't sulk, as Jonah did. He did not argue with the authorities or cover them with scorn as Elijah did. He simply moved a little way along the lake and made Himself available to one and all.

> *And unclean spirits, when they saw him, fell down before him,*
> *and cried, saying, Thou art the Son of God. And he straitly charged*
> *them that they should not make him known. (3:11–12)*

These evil beings did not try to touch Him. For them, His touch would have been like the tormenting touch of fire. They had no difficulty recognizing Him, and down on their faces they went before Him, proclaiming His deity. Moreover, as always, the Lord silenced them. He wanted and needed no testimony from the likes of them.

2. The Servant and His chosen men (3:13–19)

> *And he goeth up into a mountain, and calleth unto him whom*
> *he would: and they came unto him. (3:13)*

The scene changed. The critics in the synagogue and the crowds along the seashore vanish. Jesus went away to a nearby mountain, where He faced realistically

His rejection in the synagogue. The enmity would increase until it ended in His death. The time had come for Him to appoint a special group of men who could become not only disciples but also apostles, men who could carry on after He had gone.

Luke tells us that He spent the night in prayer. By morning, He was ready to choose the dozen men to whom He would eventually entrust the greatest enterprise in the history of the universe. He chose with great care from the ranks of the many who had become His followers those few with whom He intended to spend most of His time for the next year or so. He called; they came. This balance always exists in God's dealings with men. God will woo, but He will not ravish. He will invite, but He will not invade.

> *And he ordained twelve, that they should be with him, and that he might send them forth to preach, And to have power to heal sicknesses, and to cast out devils: (3:14–15)*

Never in the annals of history has there been an age like it. There they go! A dozen men clothed with godlike power, marching here and there throughout that little land, a microcosm of the whole wide world, to spread the word that the kingdom of God was at hand.

Note that He sent them forth first and foremost to preach; healing was secondary. Physical healing is undoubtedly important. The entire world of medicine—so vast, complex, expensive, and needful—pays tribute to the natural desire of a hurting person to be made well. But healing of bodies must take second place to saving of souls. Keeping people out of hospitals is not nearly as important as keeping them out of hell. Casting out demons, too, was a secondary priority. Undoubtedly, a great deal of demonic activity occurs in the world today. Demons are real foes and must be fought. Still, we must not degenerate into animism, which sees a demon under every bush and in every tree, haunting church buildings and hiding in the baptistery. Preaching must come first.

> *And Simon he surnamed Peter; (3:16)*

Mark now gives us the list of the apostles, beginning with his hero, Peter. This passage is one of a number of lists of the apostles. Peter comes first in all of the lists. He seems to have been a born leader—impulsive, outspoken, warmhearted, and devoted to Christ.

Mark thought a lot of Peter. Mark's gospel comprises the essence of what Mark had so often heard Peter preach. Mark had known Peter a long time. The early Jerusalem church met, at first, in the home of Mark's mother. Doubtless, Mark had many long talks with Peter. After his debacle with Paul (Acts 13:13), Mark traveled for a while with his uncle Barnabas, but later he seems to have attached himself to Peter. He probably found Peter to be far less demanding than Paul. Peter had been in on the movement from the very beginning. Since the Day of Pentecost (Acts 2), Peter's reputation as an apostle had been well established throughout Palestine. The Jewish churches generally revered him; as a result of his reputation, the Gentile churches honored him too. He was a "living epistle," a walking encyclopedia of the knowledge of Christ. Peter had an enormous fund of goodwill among the Gentile churches, and they lionized him.

But all of this esteem was in the future. After a night of prayer, the Lord placed at the top of His list of apostles the name of Peter. The name means "a stone," literally a pebble (Matt. 16:13–20), and it was given to Simon after his great confession of Christ. But that, too, was in the future.

> *And James the son of Zebedee, and John the brother of James; and*
> *he surnamed them Boanerges, which is, The sons of thunder. (3:17)*

Peter, James, and John formed a trio, a kind of inner circle among the apostles. The Lord chose them on several occasions to receive special glimpses of Christ that were not shown to the other apostles. The Lord gave descriptive names to all three men. James and John were brothers and were likely the Lord's cousins. On one occasion, the pair wanted to call down fire on the Samaritans to avenge a slight, and the Lord had to rebuke them (Luke 9:54–55). He called them "sons of thunder!" They were martyr material. James was the first of the apostles to die, martyred by Herod Agrippa I (Acts 12:1–2), perhaps because he was too outspoken. John was the last of the apostles to die, but he experienced persecution, exile, and incarceration along the way. He gave us a gospel, three epistles or memos, and the great Apocalypse. He was somewhat of a mystic. Time greatly mellowed him, and his writings breathe a spirit of love.

> *And Andrew, and Philip, and Bartholomew, and Matthew, and*
> *Thomas, and James the son of Alphaeus, and Thaddaeus, and*
> *Simon the Canaanite, (3:18)*

Here we have a string of eight names listing most of the apostles. A few of these leap to prominence, but some never emerge from the shadows. Thus it has ever been with men and nations in both the world and the church. Note the strong family ties that united a number of the Lord's disciples both to each other and to Himself. Doubtless, Jesus had known some of these men since childhood and had observed them over many years.

The first four in the list (Peter, James, John, and Philip) all came from the nearby fishing village of Bethsaida on the Sea of Galilee near the Jordan. Peter and Andrew were brothers and business partners with James and John, the sons of Zebedee and Salome. Thomas and Matthew (sometimes called Levi) are often paired together in the Gospels. The name *Thomas* (or Didymas) means "a twin." Then there was James the less (or James the Little, as he is sometimes called, perhaps on account of his short stature). The apostle Jude was either a brother or a son of James of Alphaeus. (Jude is called Thaddaeus here, and he is also called Lebbaeus elsewhere.) After the defection of Judas Iscariot, the name Jude, or Judas, took on such an ill odor that it is not surprising that the Evangelists made every effort to distinguish the faithful Jude from the faithless Judas.

A look back over the list shows that it seems likely that half of the disciples were related, in one way or another, to the Lord. Add to that the fact that Philip grew up in Bethsaida and was possibly a good friend of the Zebedee brothers and their partners. Bartholomew (or Nathaniel, as John calls him) was a close friend of Philip, who introduced him to Christ.

That brings us to Simon the Canaanite (Simon the Zealot). Nothing is known of him beyond the fact that he had been a member of the Jewish patriotic party.

> *And Judas Iscariot, which also betrayed him: and they went into*
> *an house. (3:19)*

The last one named was the traitor, Judas Iscariot. He is always named last, and the reason is always given. He was the only Judean, and he was a traitor. He was the only apostle who held office, being the company's treasurer, and he was a traitor. He comes last, although he doubtless aspired to be first. He probably saw himself clothed with power and majesty in the messianic kingdom. He imagined that wealth and honor would be his. Perhaps he dreamed of ruling over the royal tribe of Judah, the predominant tribe. The tribes of Israel would rule the world, but Judah, with Judas at the head, would rule them all. We can well believe that such were his thoughts. The expected glitter and glamour of it soon turned to dust and ashes. To Judas, Jesus was a disappointment.

Judas must have been astonished when the Lord refused to accept the offer of the crowd to make Him a King. He must have been appalled when the Lord talked about such things as a new birth and turning the other cheek. He must have been horrified, too, when Jesus antagonized the powerful religious establishment. He could make no sense of it when Jesus talked, not of global empire but of a church, of a kingdom not of this world, and when He spoke, not of a crown but of a cross.

Judas was soon thoroughly disillusioned with the nature of the enterprise that he had joined. Well! He would salvage what he could from the wreckage of his dreams. He pilfered money from the bag to feather a little nest that he was preparing for the future. Then, when he saw a chance to get a lump sum, he sold out. So he who would have liked to be first became last. And he lost his soul in the bargain.

The selection of the Twelve was completed, and Jesus went into a house. What an ordinary thing to do! He wanted to relax and rest, have a meal, and, perhaps, be alone for an hour or so. Some people might have expected that the Lord would have sent Judas to Jerusalem to look for a suitable building to be the temporary headquarters for the new Messianic Mission. Others might have expected Him to endow His disciples at once with authority over the old tribal territories and send them forth, armed with might and miracle to prepare the clans for the King. But no! He went into a house. We can almost see Him as He shut the door on the outside world, took off His shoes, loosened His belt, had something to eat, and went to bed. He had the nucleus of the church. He had made initial preparation for changing history for the next two thousand years. So—He went into a house. Come to think of it, that was what the church did so well in its early days. The believers simply went from house to house. And the church multiplied and grew.

D. The Servant's work blasphemed (3:20–35)
   1. Opposition from His friends (3:20–21)

Opposition to the Lord Jesus now took on a more virulent and serious form. It came from friends, foes, and family alike.

> *And the multitude cometh together again, so that they could not*
> *so much as eat bread. (3:20)*

If crowds are a yardstick of a preacher's success, then this was success. Doubtless, the disciples thought so. Judas must have been delighted. Maybe the tide was coming in after all. Here were the beginnings of a mass movement; it would spread, and soon Judea would be inundated. Eventually, the world would own its King.

Meanwhile, the crowd was rather a nuisance. It was always there, clamoring for attention. Why did there have to be so many sick people, so many lepers and demoniacs? Why could they not allow the disciples a few minutes' peace to eat their supper? Crowds presented disadvantages. The Lord, of course, had just demonstrated that fact. He had not recruited battalions of men to march in a mass movement; He had called only a dozen individuals. He had no intention of founding a kingdom on popular mass appeal.

> And when his friends heard of it, they went out to lay hold on
> him: for they said, He is beside himself. (3:21)

They thought that He was (literally) out of His senses—just because He was too busy to eat. His family and friends never did understand Him. Perhaps, too, they sensed trouble coming from the establishment. As much as the Sanhedrin resented Rome, its members did not want some mass movement, over which it had no control, to rock the boat. The Romans were ruthless when it came to putting down budding insurrections.

But Jesus was not out of His senses. The accusation came from His friends, who were anxious about His welfare. He was the sanest person who ever lived. People who are sold out to a cause, or to God, are often looked on as fanatical by their contemporaries.

When I first joined the staff of Moody Bible Institute, a young student on the campus was like that. He was consumed by a passion to win people to Christ. I picked him up one day to take him somewhere in my car. The road was a busy one with an intersection and a traffic light every few hundred yards. Impatient of delay, whenever I was stopped in a line of cars, held up by a traffic light, he jumped out of the car, rushed to the head of the line, and worked his way back to where I was. He knocked on car windows and shoved tracts through the openings when startled motorists rolled down their windows! Some people thought that he was a fanatic. He was simply on fire for God.

2. Opposition from His foes (3:22–30)
   a. A blatant rejection of Christ (3:22)

> *And the scribes which came down from Jerusalem said, He hath*
> *Beelzebub, and by the prince of the devils casteth he out devils.*
> *(3:22)*

This accusation was the cold, caustic criticism of the sophisticated Jews from the capital. They refused to accept the fact that He was God and that He cast out demons by the power of God. The implications of that reality were more than they were willing to face. It meant that God had invaded history and that everything must change. The establishment, of which they were leading members, would have to change. They themselves would have to change.

Oh, no! It was simpler to explain away the remarkable miracles of Jesus and to ignore or deny the evidence of His sinless life. No one could deny that the supernatural was involved in the Lord's ability to perform miracles. Only one explanation was possible: He was in league with satanic powers. They could not have conceived a greater insult. Not content with accusing Him of being under the influence of fallen Lucifer, they accused Him of being in league with Beelzebub, the lord of the flies, the lord of filth. It was a foul and wicked thing to say, the belching forth of the hot lava of the pit itself from the seething volcano of their wicked hearts.

b. A blistering rebuttal by Christ (3:23–30)

The Holy Spirit records *His Undisputed Wisdom* (3:23–27):

> *And he called them unto him, and said unto them in parables,*
> *How can Satan cast out Satan? (3:23)*

He neither responded with His emotions nor reacted with anger, sarcasm, or scorn. He appealed calmly to their common sense. These men were scribes, the nation's intelligentsia, men learned in the law and religious tradition. Some of them were very clever. Moreover, they were not provincial men but members of the elite Jerusalem religious establishment, influential men, educated men. What they had just said did not come from their intellects but from their darkened hearts. Their unbelief was deliberate. They had no excuse for it, given His countless, marvelous, and undeniable miracles. What they said came from men with mean and malicious hearts.

He called them unto Him. They stood before Him, wrapped in their self-righteousness. They stared sullenly at this "Messiah" from a despised province and from an even more despised town. Hatred and hostility were written all over them. The text draws our attention to *them* and to *Him;* the contrast could hardly be greater. He was dressed in homespun, they in costly robes. He was young; they were old. He was not the product of their schools and seminaries, whereas they were steeped in the oral law and the traditions of the rabbis. He loved them although they loathed Him. So, there they stood, face-to-face.

He simply asked them a question followed by three more questions. "How can Satan cast out Satan?" He asked. He appealed to their reason. He ignored the "what" (i.e., that they had accused Him of being in league with a foul friend) and focused on the "how." They had made a serious accusation, so He asked them to prove it. "How can Satan cast out Satan?" He asked. Then He went on to demonstrate the folly of their assertion.

> *And if a kingdom be divided against itself, that kingdom cannot stand. (3:24)*

He gave an illustration from *the secular world.* No worse tragedy can befall a nation than for it to be rent by civil war, brother fighting brother. Even when the upheaval comes to an end, the old resentments continue to smolder. And all of the time the nation's weakened condition invites interference by a foreign power.

> *And if a house be divided against itself, that house cannot stand. (3:25)*

He gave an illustration from *the social world.* What chance do the children have in a home in which the parents are constantly at each other's throats? What hope do parents have of support and security in their old age if they have rebellious children? What bond remains for mutual help and encouragement if brother hates brother? Such a family soon descends into chaos. The Bible gives ample illustrations. For example, the situations in Jacob's family and in David's family show what happens when family ties are torn. By contrast, the pagan world soon learned that an attack upon Lot was also an attack upon Abraham because ties were strong in Abraham's family (Gen. 14).

> *And if Satan rise up against himself, and be divided, he cannot stand, but hath an end. (3:26)*

He gave an illustration from *the spirit world*—and He knew a lot more about Satan and his sphere than His critics did. Satan had once been known as Lucifer, the highest and the most beautiful, powerful, and gifted of all created beings. A third of the heavenly host followed him in his rebellion. Satan organized those fallen angels to help him rule over our conquered planet. In the spirit world are ranks and hierarchies: principalities and powers, thrones and dominions, rulers of this world's darkness, and wicked spirits in high places, as well as countless hosts of demons. Sin is a divisive force in the universe. Satan makes full use of that fact, but woe betide him if he allows that to weaken his authority and power! He uses all of his skill and genius to prevent the divisive force of sin from tearing apart his own empire. He knows that if he once lost control of his fellow conspirators, his end would be in sight.

> *No man can enter into a strong man's house, and spoil his goods,*
> *except he will first bind the strong man; and then he will spoil his*
> *house. (3:27)*

It all comes down to a question of naked power. Satan is the strongman. He has organized and kept his "house," the sphere where he puts forth all of his power, organization, influence, and diabolical brilliance. And what a vast "house" it is. It embraces much of the unseen world; beings of enormous power, of vast and malignant intelligence, and of unimaginable wickedness own his sway. The world is part of his house, and it lies in the lap of the Wicked One.

So he keeps his "goods." Mere men are virtually powerless against him. The disciples, in themselves, were powerless against him (Matt. 17:21). They triumphed only when the Lord Himself commissioned and empowered them.

Jesus, by contrast, plundered the strongman's house at will. Even the most ferocious demons fled at His word. That could only mean that He was stronger than Satan and all of his countless millions of evil spirits. He had bound the strongman. Satan, as strong as he was, was no match for the incarnate Son of the living God—and he knew it.

The Holy Spirit also records *His undiluted warning* (3:28–30):

> *Verily I say unto you, All sins shall be forgiven unto the sons of*
> *men, and blasphemies wherewith soever they shall blaspheme:*
> *But he that shall blaspheme against the Holy Ghost hath never*
> *forgiveness, but is in danger of eternal damnation: Because they*
> *said, He hath an unclean spirit. (3:28–30)*

The Lord concluded with a terrible warning against blaspheming the Holy Spirit—an unforgivable sin.

God is not only a living God but also a forgiving God. Well He knows the terrible ravages that sin has wrought in our souls. Even as men spiked Him to the tree, He would pray, "Father, forgive them for they know not what they do." So much of sin is rooted in our ignorance and so much of the rest of it in our impotence. Much of human wickedness results from human weakness. The Lord has pity on us. He forgives us, pardons us, and provides salvation for us. No matter what we have done or said, Calvary covers it all. That, of course, was why He came to earth in the first place.

Blasphemy against the Holy Spirit, however, is something else. Nobody can commit that sin today. It was a sin peculiar to those who lived when He lived and who heard His marvelous teaching for themselves. It was a sin reserved for those who saw His many matchless miracles, those who had looked into His eyes, experienced His grace, and felt His power. It was the sin of those who then—out of sheer malice, envy, hatred, and determined wickedness—accused Him of conspiring with the Evil One. Such a sin revealed a state of soul beyond the possibility of redemption, so it was unpardonable.

That was how Caiaphas and his crowd conspired against Jesus. They bought Judas and then brought the Son of God before their judgment seat. They mocked Him, abused Him, and falsely accused Him. They hired perjurers to distort His teachings. They condemned Him to death because He claimed to be who He was. They handed Him over to the Romans to be crucified. Then Caiaphas and his cronies sealed up His tomb—just in case. Worse still, when confronted with His resurrection, they bribed the guard to lie about that monumental, historic event and persecuted His disciples for proclaiming the truth that Jesus was alive from the dead and mighty to save.

Such was the sin of blasphemy against the Holy Spirit.

3. Opposition from His family (3:31–35)

There came then his brethren and his mother, and, standing without, sent unto him, calling him. (3:31)

His mother! Mark doesn't tell us much about His mother. We have to go to Matthew and Luke for information about the Lord's mother and for the circumstances of His birth. Although Mark devotes little space to the Lord's mother, he doubtless had met her.

The picture we get of Mary from the Gospels reveals a pure-minded, spiritually sensitive, and deeply exercised woman. She was a constant source of joy to the Lord. She alone, of all people on this planet, knew the full and wondrous story of His birth; His earliest and fondest memories were linked with His mother. But even she was not perfect. Once, upon the outset of His ministry, she ventured to advise Him and was gently but firmly rebuffed (John 2). We learn now that the "friends" (v. 21), who thought that He was "beside himself," included His family. How He must have been saddened to find His own mother standing in that group.

His brothers! He had long since taken the measure of His half brothers. They were not bad men; they simply did not understand Him or, as yet, believe in Him. Their unbelief must have pained Him. Surely they knew the circumstances of His birth—unless that was one of the things that Mary hid in her own heart (Luke 2:51). In any case, they had the evidence of His absolutely sinless life. They probably reacted against that the way Joseph's brothers reacted against his goodness. Something about genuine goodness either attracts or repels a sinful person. The Lord's immaculate goodness was matched by His infinite grace—which would doubtless have added a great deal of charm to His character. With it all, He was perfectly human. Probably His brothers simply did not know what to make of Him. James, for one, probably resented the Lord's attitude toward official, Talmudic Judaism and the traditions of the elders.

Well, there they were, outside, calling for Him. They were "standing without," Mark recalls. They were on the outside. For many years they had been on the inside. They had seen Him and known Him as no others in the world had known Him. They had memories of Him that could have filled volumes. Now between Him and them was a distance. Familiarity with holy things is always dangerous because it tends to breed contempt. But what must have saddened Him most was that His mother was there, standing with His brothers. So, sadly and momentarily, the same measure of distance existed between Him and her.

And the multitude sat about him, and they said unto him, Behold, thy mother and thy brethren without seek for thee. (3:32)

The throng was nearer to Him than His own family. Even they could see that. They "sat about him." His family was "without." Moreover, He was very obviously ignoring His mother and His brothers. The crowd could not understand it. Family came first in those days. The Lord, however, knew what He was doing.

He was putting mother and brother alike in their place. He knew why they had come; they thought that He was "beside himself." They had come to take Him home. With the best of intentions, they had come to take over. They thought that He was going too far. Moreover, He was putting Himself (and them) in danger, or so it seemed to them. They were sadly out of touch with both Him and His work. Mary, at least, should have known better. Years earlier, old Simeon had foretold that her Son would be attacked and that she, too, would feel the stab of pain (Luke 2:34–35).

> *And he answered them, saying, Who is my mother, or my brethren? (3:33)*

Now He put an eternity of distance between Himself and His natural family. The distance had always been there, of course, given the extraordinary circumstances of His birth, given who He was and who His Father was, and given the fact that, although He was truly human, He was at the same time God. His natural family had now given Him the opportunity to put an end to the mere family connection.

> *And he looked round about on them which sat about him, and said, Behold my mother and my brethren! (3:34)*

It was a cryptic statement. He took in those who sat about Him, drinking in His words, awed by His works, and eager for more, and He said, "Behold my mother and my brethren." At that moment, He felt closer to those who were willing at least to give Him a hearing than He did to those who were simply related to Him by the natural ties of birth.

However, He did not leave it at that. He opened a breathtaking door of opportunity to one and all. The natural family was being replaced by the new family.

> *For whosoever shall do the will of God, the same is my brother, and my sister, and mother. (3:35)*

Anybody could become related to Him in a family tie that was nearer and dearer than any forged by natural birth. Natural ties would be swallowed up in spiritual ties. Henceforth, He would regard anyone who had the same relationship with His Father as He had as being in the new family. His relationship to the

Father, while here on earth as a Man among men, was one of obedience (Heb. 10:7). All who were willing to accept the yoke of obedience would be kin to Him!

By natural birth, we are "children of disobedience." We are children of Adam, of whom it is written that it was by one man's disobedience that sin entered and death by sin. To become, instead, children of obedience calls for a new birth, a spiritual birth (John 1:11–13), as the Lord explained to Nicodemus (John 3:3). The Lord did not elaborate to His listeners on the "how," just on the "what." The principle of obedience, which characterizes the new family and its relationships, is illustrated in the conversion of Saul of Tarsus. The moment his eyes were opened, he enthroned Jesus as Lord. He said, "Lord, what wilt thou have me to do?" (Acts 9:6).

Section 2: The Servant's Words (4:1–5:43)

  A. They were exact in purpose (4:1–34)

    1. The parabolic mystery (4:1–20)

      a. The message (4:1–9)

        (1) The setting (4:1)

          (a) The innumerable people (4:1a)

          (b) The innovative platform (4:1b)

        (2) The story (4:2–9)

          (a) The sower (4:3)

          (b) The soil (4:4–8)

             i. The poor soil (4:4–7)

               a. The hopeless soil (4:4)

               b. The hypocritical soil (4:5–6)

               c. The handicapped soil (4:8)

             ii. The productive soil (4:8)

          (c) The sequel (4:9)

      b. The meaning (4:10–20)

        (1) A word of exhortation (4:10–13)

          (a) A question (4:10)

          (b) A quotation (4:11–13)

             i. A sad condition (4:11)

             ii. A scriptural confirmation (4:12)

             iii. A sobering consideration (4:13)

        (2) A word of explanation (4:14–20)

          (a) The seed (4:14)

          (b) The soil (4:15–20)

             i. The disappointing response to the Word (4:15–19)

               a. The Word and the infernal foe (4:15)

                  1. The Word initially delivered (4:15a)

                  2. The Word instantly devoured (4:15b)

               b. The Word and the internal foe (4:16–17)

                  1. No root (4:16–17a)

                  2. No fruit (4:17b–c)

                     (i) Serious things arise (4:17b)

                     (ii) Second thoughts arise (4:17c)

             ii. What he does (4:29b)

         (4) Growing (4:30–32)

            (a) A question asked (4:30)

            (b) A question answered (4:31–32)

                i. The mustard plant (4:31–32b)

                   a. Its seed (4:31)

                   b. Its size (4:32a–b)

                     1. Its growth (4:32a)

                     2. Its greatness (4:32b)

                ii. This mustard plant (4:32c–d)

                   a. The branches (4:32c)

                   b. The birds (4:32d)

     b. The extent of this method (4:33–34)

         (1) He employed parables frequently (4:33–34a)

            (a) Extensively (4:33)

            (b) Exclusively (4:34a)

         (2) He explained parables fully (4:34b–c)

            (a) Personally (4:34b)

            (b) Privately (4:34c)

B. They were executive in power (4:35–5:43)

   1. Triumphing over disaster (4:35–41)

     a. The time (4:35a)

     b. The trip (4:35b–36)

         (1) The proposal (4:35b)

         (2) The preparation (4:36a–b)

            (a) The crowd (4:36a)

            (b) The Christ (4:36b)

         (3) The postscript (4:36c)

     c. The tempest (4:37–38)

         (1) The terrible storm (4:37)

         (2) The tranquil Savior (4:38)

     d. The transformation (4:39–40)

         (1) The furious storm rebuked (4:39)

         (2) The fearful sailors rebuked (4:40)

     e. The terror (4:41)

         (1) The reality of their terror (4:41a)

         (2) The reason for their terror (4:41b)

   2. Triumphing over demons (5:1–20)

a. Confrontation (5:1–5)
    (1) The arrival of the Master (5:1–2a)
    (2) The arrival of the madman (5:2b–5)
        (a) His dwelling (5:2b–3a)
        (b) His defiance (5:3b–4)
            i. His demoniac strength (5:3b–4a)
            ii. His demoniac savagery (5:4b)
        (c) His distress (5:5)
            i. He was homeless (5:5a)
            ii. He was hopeless (5:5b–c)
                a. His terrible cries (5:5b)
                b. His terrible cuts (5:5c)
b. Contradiction (5:6–8)
    (1) His coming (5:6)
        (a) With haste (5:6a)
        (b) With homage (5:6b)
    (2) His cry (5:7–8)
        (a) What he declared (5:7)
            i. His testimony to Jesus (5:7a)
            ii. His terror of Jesus (5:7b)
        (b) What he dreaded (5:8)
c. Confession (5:9)
    (1) The demon's name (5:9a)
    (2) The demon's number (5:9b)
d. Consternation (5:10–12)
    (1) The voice of the demoniac (5:10)
        (a) The insistent nature of his plea (5:10a)
        (b) The insidious nature of his plight (5:10b)
    (2) The voice of the demons (5:11–12)
        (a) What they beheld (5:11)
        (b) What they besought (5:12)
e. Condemnation (5:13)
    (1) What the unclean spirits possessed (5:13a)
    (2) What the unclean swine preferred (5:13b)
f. Consultation (5:14–17)
    (1) The report (5:14–16)
        (a) The information that was conveyed (5:14a)
        (b) The investigation that was conducted (5:15b–16)

           i. Visual confirmation of the report (5:14b–15)

           ii. Verbal confirmation of the report (5:16)

       (2) The response (5:17)

   g. Consecration (5:18–20)

       (1) The healed man's impassioned request (5:18)

       (2) The healed man's important responsibility (5:19)

          (a) The plea that was denied (5:19a)

          (b) The plan that was described (5:19b–c)

             i. Where he should testify (5:19b)

             ii. What he should testify (5:19c)

       (3) The healed man's immediate response (5:20)

          (a) The scope of his ministry (5:20a)

          (b) The success of his ministry (5:20b)

 3. Triumphing over disease (5:21–34)

   a. Jairus and his introduction (5:21–24)

       (1) The ruler (5:21–23)

          (a) His approach (5:21–22)

             i. How public it was (5:21–22a)

             ii. How passionate it was (5:22b)

          (b) His appeal (5:23)

             i. His fervor (5:23a)

             ii. His faith (5:23b)

       (2) The response (5:24)

          (a) It was immediate (5:24a)

          (b) It was impeded (5:24b)

   b. Jesus and the interruption (5:25–34)

       (1) The woman who sought (5:25–28)

          (a) Her condition (5:25–26)

             i. Its duration (5:25)

             ii. Its devastation (5:26a–b)

                 a. All medical recommendations had now failed (5:26a)

                 b. All material resources had now failed (5:26)

             iii. Its deterioration (5:26c)

          (b) Her coming (5:27)

             i. She heard of Jesus (5:27a)

             ii. She hurried to Jesus (5:27b–c)

                 a. Her determination (5:27b)

     b. Her deed (5:27c)
    (c) Her confidence (5:28)
   (2) The wonder He wrought (5:29–34)
    (a) How He healed her body (5:29–32)
     i. Her immediate healing (5:29)
      a. It was complete healing (5:29a)
      b. It was conscious healing (5:29b)
     ii. Her immediate horror (5:30–32)
      a. What Jesus said (5:30–31)
       1. The Lord's demand (5:30)
        (i) He asked, "Why?" (5:30a)
        (ii) He asked, "What?" (5:30b)
       2. The Lord's disciples (5:31)
        (i) And the throngs (5:31a)
        (ii) And their thoughts (5:31b)
      b. Who Jesus sought (5:32)
    (b) How He sealed her belief (5:33–34)
     i. Her public confession (5:33)
     ii. Her personal confirmation (5:34)
      a. A wonderful new relationship (5:34a)
      b. A wonderful new reassurance (5:34b)
 4. Triumphing over death (5:35–43)
  a. The tidings for Jairus (5:35)
   (1) Sad words (5:35a)
   (2) Skeptical words (5:35b)
  b. The tenderness of Jesus (5:36–43)
   (1) A word of peace (5:36)
   (2) A word of perception (5:37–40)
    (a) A choice (5:37)
    (b) A challenge (5:38–39)
     i. What He saw (5:38)
     ii. What He said (5:39)
    (c) A charge (5:40)
     i. Their scorn voiced (5:40a)
     ii. Their scorn vetoed (5:40b)
   (3) A word of power (5:41–42)
    (a) His tenderness (5:41)
     i. A tender touch (5:41a)

            ii. A tender tone (5:41b)
       (b) His triumph (5:42)
   (4) A word of precaution (5:43)
      (a) A proposed silence (5:43a)
      (b) A practical suggestion (5:43b)

—⚂—

Section 2: The Servant's Words (4:1–5:43)
  A. They were exact in purpose (4:1–34)
    1. The parabolic mystery (4:1–20)
      a. The message (4:1–9)

Mark's emphasis turns now from the Savior's *works* to His *words,* words that he shows to be both *exact in their purpose* and *executive in their power.* He reminds us that "Never man spake like this man" (John 7:46).

We note, first, *the setting:*

> *And he began again to teach by the sea side: and there was gathered unto him a great multitude, so that he entered into a ship, and sat in the sea; and the whole multitude was by the sea on the land. (4:1)*

Evidently, the Lord had been in someone's house when His mother and brothers arrived. Now, having put them in their place, He came out of the house and went down to the shore of the lake. He borrowed a boat and made it His pulpit.

We can picture His sitting in that little vessel with His face toward the shore. Before Him stretched the multitudes, spread out over the hillside and eager to listen to His words.

Many years ago, when I was a soldier in the British army in Palestine, I went on a chaplain-conducted tour of Galilee. I remember the padre telling us all to sit down on the slopes above the lake. There was a busload of us, and we were seated at least fifty yards from the lake itself.

The chaplain took out a pocket Testament and opened it to this chapter. He handed it to me and told me to go down to the lake, turn around at the water's edge, face the sitting soldiers, and read aloud the first nine verses. He told me to read in a conversational tone of voice and not to raise my voice at all. I did as I was instructed. The still waters of the lake behind me acted as a sounding board. Every syllable was caught up and amplified and heard clearly by the men sitting on the hillside. The whole area turned out to be a natural amphitheater, and the acoustics were remarkable. A microphone was unnecessary. The lake was its own amplifier. The Lord knew all about the acoustical qualities of the area and took advantage of them to address vast crowds with ease.

Did His mother and brothers stay? We can certainly hope that they did. It would be pleasant to picture their sitting there with all of the other people, part of that colorful spectacle, interested observers to the arrangements being made on the boat. Did His brothers pass the natural comment to their neighbors— "He's our Brother, you know?" Or did they add to His cup of sorrows that, put out by His words, they wrapped themselves in their offended dignity and went back home?

We note, now, *the story* (4:2–9):

> *And he taught them many things by parables, and said unto them in his doctrine, (4:2)*

The Lord now taught the people in parables. The parables of Jesus were simply earthly stories, each with a heavenly meaning. The Lord was fond of using these homespun illustrations, and He drew them from the everyday events of life. Most of them were about people, the way they were, and the things they did and said. They conveyed great truths. They immortalized His doctrine. Although many of us are familiar with them and read them almost as a matter of course, without any sense of wonder, they are very profound utterances. Nor are they always easy to interpret, especially the "mystery" parables and the kingdom parables.

We must keep three strands of truth from becoming tangled in our minds when we study the Lord's parables: salvation truth, church truth, and kingdom truth. Failure to discern the differences between these differing truths leads to error. Many of the wrong teachings current today are based on or bolstered by a wrong interpretation of a parable. Sometimes a parable contains a certain amount of "window dressing" to provide a setting for the truth that it is intended to convey. Much foolish exegesis has resulted from trying to force a meaning on every item in a parable. Normally, a parable contains one central truth. Any interpretation of a parable must be consistent with what is taught elsewhere in the Bible. Moreover, a knowledge of everyday life in Bible times is often needed, along with a knowledge of God's dispensational dealings with the human race and an acquaintance with the Holy Spirit's use of symbolic language, if one is to understand properly the Lord's parabolic teaching.[1]

Hearken; Behold, there went out a sower to sow: (4:3)

The Lord began with the parable of the sower, the seed, and the soil. In all likelihood, the seated multitudes could actually see a plowed field not far from where they sat. It was a familiar enough scene. An ox or a couple of asses would be harnessed to a primitive plow. The farmer could be seen breaking up the soil in preparation for planting. Or, perhaps, the sower could be seen, a corner of his work robe gathered up to make a pocket. They could see him dip his hand into the seed and scatter it about him as he made his way down the furrow.

The initiative was always with the sower. A certain amount of waste was bound to occur, but he was prepared for that. The experience of a hundred generations taught him that he must sow liberally. Not all of the seed sown would return a harvest. If the sower waited for a guarantee of a full return on his investment, he would wait forever; the Fall had put an end to that (Gen. 3:17–19).

And it came to pass, as he sowed, some fell by the way side, and the fowls of the air came and devoured it up. (4:4)

The crowd would smile and nod their heads. They had seen it happen. Perhaps it was happening before their eyes even as Jesus spoke. There they were, flocks of birds, drawn from here, there, and everywhere, flying noisily behind the sower and descending in clouds upon the furrows, greedily eating the seed before it could even sink into the soil. They were the bane of the farmer's life. Sometimes he would turn and shake his fist at them or try to chase them away. It was hopeless. As soon as he turned back to his sowing, down they came again. Bitter experience taught the sower to expect the birds to get a third, if not half, of his precious seed. It was a fact of life. His only recourse was to sow plentifully.

And some fell on stony ground, where it had not much earth; and immediately it sprang up, because it had no depth of earth: But when the sun was up, it was scorched; and because it had no root, it withered away. (4:5–6)

---

1. See John Phillips, *The Bible Explorer's Guide* (Grand Rapids: Kregel, 2002).

Next, the Lord spoke of the stony ground. Again, the people would look wise. They had seen that too. As for the farmer, he knew all about that part of his field. His plow had made heavy work of it. A stony ledge there was covered by just a few inches of soil. Past experience had taught him not to expect much from that area.

This soil was worse than the wayside soil. Wayside soil had been trampled down and compacted by the coming and going of people, but the stony soil was hard by nature. It was deceptive, too, because the underlying rock had a covering of soil. It was all the more disappointing for that very reason. The seed came up with initial promise. On previous occasions, the sower had inspected the sprouts of wheat, dried up by the sun, from that part of the field. The depth of the soil there was insufficient to allow the seed to take root. The seed germinated, so nothing was wrong with the seed, but the ground was incompatible. It was as hard as a rock underneath.

> *And some fell among thorns, and the thorns grew up, and choked it, and it yielded no fruit. (4:7)*

Next came the weed-infested soil, plagued with choking thorns. Again the people would agree. A curse was on the land. It took plowing and planting, fertilizing and cultivating to produce a crop of corn, but weeds would grow anywhere! They were tough, hardy, useless, and militant. The people had often cursed the weeds that grew in their own gardens at home, especially the thorns that fought back, tearing at one's hands and clothes. Good seed had no chance once thorns took over. Thorns would compete for every inch of soil.

> *And other fell on good ground, and did yield fruit that sprang up and increased; and brought forth, some thirty, and some sixty, and some an hundred. (4:8)*

Finally, there was the good soil, but even this failed to yield a full harvest. The people would agree again. They had seen this very thing. Even good, responsive soil produced a varied crop. Even soil that was not trodden into a thoroughfare by the feet of passersby and that was not hindered by rocks or weeds responded in varying degrees. The harvest was never uniform. At best, only a percentage of what was sown reached the highest potential at harvest time.

> *And he said unto them, He that hath ears to hear, let him hear. (4:9)*

He left the interpretation of the parable up to them. They had enjoyed the story. Now let them figure out its significance.

In Matthew's gospel, this parable is the first in a series (Matt. 13) of what we call "mystery" parables. This kind of parable was a new technique in the Lord's method of teaching. He had been rejected officially. Foes, family, and friends alike had failed to respond to the obvious facts of His life. Now He would teach in parables of a new sort—parables that were patently obvious as to the story part but mystical and hidden as to their significance. People would not grasp their meaning, and even His disciples would need coaching to interpret them. These parables, as we learn from studying Matthew's collection, were parables of the kingdom of heaven. Throughout, failure is evident. Yet, God pursues His kingdom purpose, sublimely and sovereignly, despite all seeming setbacks and hindrances.

b. The meaning (4:10–20)

First, comes *a word of exhortation* (4:10–13):

> *And when he was alone, they that were about him with the twelve asked of him the parable. (4:10)*

Even the Lord's disciples were as mystified by these parables as those who were afar off. It was a good story—or, rather, it was an excellent summary of observable agricultural facts. But, so what? Everybody knew about sowers, about seed, and about soil. There had to be more to it than that! They asked Him to explain.

> *And he said unto them, Unto you it is given to know the mystery of the kingdom of God: but unto them that are without, all these things are done in parables: (4:11)*

He had deliberately adopted a method of teaching, He told them, designed to reveal and conceal at the same time. It was part of the genius of the Lord's teaching that He could use such simple, everyday things to accomplish so profound and complex a goal. Just trying to invent half a dozen original parables will soon convince one of the Lord's genius. It is not likely that He gave these parables on the spur of the moment. He probably had been thinking about these things for thirty years.

Matthew gives us the fullest account of the "mystery" parables (chap. 13). All of them record failure and a mixture of good and bad. All of them were designed to deal with the now evident Jewish rejection of Christ. The nation had failed. Now what would happen to God's eternal plan to establish a kingdom on this planet? Well, that purpose was now to be postponed for an unspecified period of time. Israel would be set aside temporarily, and God would introduce on this planet something entirely new—the church. The church would carry forward God's wider purposes until those purposes were complete and God could resume His dealings with the nation of Israel. When that time came, a new generation of messengers once again would proclaim that the kingdom was at hand (Matt. 24:14; Rev. 11). The long-awaited millennial age would come at last.

Meanwhile, God's kingdom purposes underwent a change. A new phase was introduced—the "mystery" phase, heralded by the "mystery" parables (Matt. 13). All of this was about to be revealed by the Lord. His own would come to understand all of this; the unsaved never would.

The present age of grace (the church age) fills the period between the postponement of the kingdom and the inauguration of the kingdom. The church looks forward to the kingdom and prays, "Thy kingdom come, Thy will be done on earth as it is in heaven."

Mark does not go into all of the details. They would be of more interest to a Jewish audience (such as Matthew had in mind) than to a Roman audience (which Mark kept in view). Mark, however, does give this one sample of the Lord's teaching in mystery form. The Lord now expounded the parable of the sower.

> *That seeing they may see, and not perceive; and hearing they may hear, and not understand; lest at any time they should be converted, and their sins should be forgiven them. (4:12)*

This is a quotation from Isaiah 6:9–10. The Lord quoted this famous Old Testament passage to explain why He was now teaching in mysteries. The Old Testament context of Isaiah's words is significant. The prophet Isaiah had been convicted and cleansed and then called to the ministry (Isa. 6:1–8). From the outset, he had been warned that his preaching would produce no lasting results. The nation of Israel was so apostate that nothing was left but judgment. The nation of Judah was not much better. So serious was the apostasy of Israel in Isaiah's day that God intended to have the nation of Israel deported. Judicial blindness would seize upon the apostate people, and they would become deaf and blind to Isaiah and the truth that he taught.

Israel's rejection of Christ and the unpardonable apostasy of its leaders were now going to bring about an even greater and longer deportation. As before, judicial blindness would herald the coming judgment (Rom. 11:25); hence, both the mystery parables and the Lord's use of Isaiah 6:9–10 here.

Paul later quoted this same prophecy (Acts 28:25–27) when it became evident that the Jews of both the homeland and the Diaspora had rejected not only the *Son of God* but also the *Spirit of God* (Heb. 10:26–31). The punishment of the Jewish nation could no longer be delayed.

Ordinarily, God speaks to be understood. At times, however, He speaks only to seal the blindness, deepen the deafness, and confirm the hardness of those to whom the message is sent. It is the first step in setting the stage for judgment. Thus, Noah preached—in vain—right up to the day he entered the ark. Thus, the men of Sodom were smitten with blindness, even as their doom was about to fall from the skies. The people of the Lord's day had *seen* a most amazing and countless display of miracles. They had *heard* the most gracious and glorious teaching ever given. Yet, they had rejected Christ. The nation of Israel confirmed its rejection of Christ by its subsequent rejection of the church. The hardening process began. Their blasphemy of the Holy Spirit had put them in a category apart. For such there was no healing, only hardening, no salvation, only judgment. The world is entering a similar phase of increasing apostasy in our own day, especially in lands that have been singularly blessed by the gospel.

> *And he said unto them, Know ye not this parable? and how then will ye know all parables? (4:13)*

These words were addressed to the disciples, those who were not smitten with the general blindness. They should have been able to understand the parable of the sower. It was the simplest of all of the mystery parables. But they were still learners and failed to grasp many things. The fact, for instance, that the Lord must die by crucifixion and that He must be buried and rise again was quite beyond their grasp in those days. Peter was horrified when the Lord first declared that He was going to the cross, and he objected strenuously (Matt. 16:21–23). He did not conceive a Messiah acting thus, especially not One who could command the very forces of nature! Later, the Lord would open the eyes of their understanding so that they would comprehend all of His teachings (Luke 24:44–45; John 20:9, 22). At this point in their spiritual education, however, the deeper meaning of the parable of the sower escaped them. So the Lord explained it to them.

Note, then, *the word of explanation* (4:14–20). First, He referred to *the seed* (4:14):

> *The sower soweth the word. (4:14)*

He made one simple statement, and all of the rest was plain. The seed symbolized the Word of God. The sower, in the first instance, was the Son of God. Subsequently, the servants of God became sowers. The gospel is told forth, the Good News is scattered far and wide within the hearing of all kinds of people. We do not manufacture seed; God provides it. It contains the secret of life, and it reproduces after its kind. God makes Himself responsible for the mysterious and complex process whereby a seed germinates in the soil and grows and for the way the Word of God germinates in a human heart. Our responsibility is to sow the seed.

The Lord turned next to *the soil* (4:15–20):

> *And these are they by the way side, where the word is sown; but when they have heard, Satan cometh immediately, and taketh away the word that was sown in their hearts. (4:15)*

Satan wastes no time. The key word here is *immediately*. He, or (because he is not omnipresent but a finite being) one of his agents, is there every time the gospel is proclaimed. He is there to seize the seed before it can germinate. If he cannot prevent its being sown, he will do his best to snatch it away once it is sown. We see it happen at every service. The moment the benediction is given, there is a buzz of conversation, and what was said in the sermon is forgotten. By the time we get to the car, the conversation has turned to lunch or the size of Mrs. Baldy's hat or whether to go for a drive. In any case, the seed is gone.

The word *wayside* also provides a clue. The wayside is a place where people come and go, where there is constant movement. Traffic passes by there all of the time. The ebb and flow of the multitudes, bent on business or pleasure, keeps the ground hard and packed so that the enemy can snatch away the seed. Satan and his companion "powers of the air" have great success in such places.

> *And these are they likewise which are sown on stony ground; who, when they have heard the word, immediately receive it with gladness; And have no root in themselves, and so endure but for a*

time: afterward, when affliction or persecution ariseth for the word's sake, immediately they are offended. (4:16–17)

With the stony soil the initial response was encouraging. The seed germinated and showed promise. Again, nothing was wrong with the seed; it was always the soil that was the problem. This time, the soil was deceptive. It was shallow because a hidden ledge of rock ran just beneath the thin layer of soil. There was just enough soil to give promise but not enough to give performance.

What is depicted for us here is mere profession of faith rather than true possession of Christ. People who exhibit this kind of response to the gospel often have only an emotional experience of some sort. Sometimes people give only an intellectual assent to the truth. In neither case is there more than a superficial stirring of the soul.

The condition described is illustrated in the case of Orpah. Both Ruth and Orpah initially responded to Naomi's testimony. However, as soon as Orpah was confronted with the hard facts involved, she went back on her profession and returned to Moab. Ruth went all of the way. "Two walked the aisle," so to speak, "but there was only one wedding."

The seed sown on stony soil depicts those who seem to do well at first, but then they run into persecution. The opposition that confronts them is solid, real, adamant, and unyielding. At once, they abandon their profession of faith, thereby proving it to have been worthless. The opposition, moreover, is directed specifically toward the Word that they profess to have believed. The world soon shows itself to be the enemy of God's Word. The test invariably comes soon after a profession of faith is made.

And these are they which are sown among thorns; such as hear the word, And the cares of this world, and the deceitfulness of riches, and the lusts of other things entering in, choke the word, and it becometh unfruitful. (4:18–19)

This time a variety of problems arise. The Lord points to three common hindrances—worry, wealth, and wants. Each hindrance focuses attention on this world to the exclusion of the world to come.

Again the problem was with the soil. This time the soil was deep enough and fertile enough, but it was also full of thorns. Thorns are the very emblems of the curse (Gen. 3:17–18). They need no cultivation, they like the soil, they are plants of hardy growth, and they choke out the good seed.

The Adamic nature produces an abundant, perennial crop of weeds, things that prevent the gospel from bearing fruit, even though it germinates in the heart and shows initial promise. The Lord indicated three of these weeds.

The first He calls "the cares of this world," just the plain grind of poverty—the common lot of most people in this world. The Lord knew all about it because He Himself was poor. He came from the working class. A thousand cares exist to occupy the mind of the poor. Worry is a daily ingredient of their lives. The Devil uses worry to focus our attention on this world. The gospel, which focuses attention on the next world, is often crowded out, despite its "exceeding great and precious promises," by preoccupation with the pressures of life.

The second weed is what the Lord calls "the deceitfulness of riches." Wealth, like worry, focuses attention on this world. This time the weed that chokes the Word is not poverty but plenty. Wealthy people tend to be independent and self-sufficient. Money insulates them from most of the harsh realities of life, so they do not feel the need for the gospel. They can take care of themselves. The gospel, with its call for sacrifice and hearty generosity, does not appeal to them—as the story of the rich young ruler makes plain (10:17–24).

The third kind of weed the Lord calls "the lusts of other things." Most people have a lengthy "want" list. As soon as they acquire this, they want that. Solomon said that the horse leech had two daughters. These daughters represented insatiable appetite and unappeasable lust. They had one constant and continuous cry: "Give! Give!" The Lord calls this "the lusts for other things," all sorts of things, from lewd things to legitimate things.

All three hindrances to the development of the Word in a human heart are aspects of worldliness, of whatever focuses our attention on this world rather than on the world to come.

> *And these are they which are sown on good ground; such as hear the word, and receive it, and bring forth fruit, some thirtyfold, some sixty, and some an hundred. (4:20)*

The seed that falls on good ground has the best chance of producing a crop. Here is a soul that is receptive to the gospel. It hears. It heeds, holds the Word in the heart, and, mixed with faith, it germinates. It takes hold, and Satan cannot snatch it away. No thoroughfare of human activity tramples it, no rocky ledge obstructs, no hostility is allowed to prevail, and no carnal or worldly longings are allowed to halt the steady growth in the soul in the knowledge of

Christ. The Word prevails and proves its presence by the production of fruit. Christ is to be seen in the believer's life—in some more than in others, but Christ *is* seen.

  2. The parabolic method (4:21–34)
    a. The examples of the method (4:21–32)

Glowing! (4:21–23):

> *And he said unto them, Is a candle brought to be put under a bushel, or under a bed? and not to be set on a candlestick? (4:21)*

The parable about *life* is now followed by a parable about *light*. A candle is a remarkable invention. It is a simple instrument for dispelling darkness. Darkness, with all of its power to frighten and bewilder, is no match for the light. The faintest gleam will dispel darkness. The function of a candle is to provide the light that dispels the darkness. A candle does that at great expense to itself. It has to give itself up to the flame and be consumed. The light of the sun and the stars is provided on the same principle.

In the spiritual realm, the Lord Jesus is the Light that dispels the darkness. The light that He brings has been provided at infinite cost. When we come to Him, He kindles that light in us—which brings us to the point of His parable. The fact that we are now light bearers means that we, too, must pay the price of shining. Our light is not to be hidden. It is to be placed where it will be seen of men. Many people hate and resent the light and will try to extinguish it. On the other hand, many other people will be drawn to it. The light itself is the miracle; we are just candles.

> *For there is nothing hid, which shall not be manifested; neither was any thing kept secret, but that it should come abroad. (4:22)*

Then, too, every hidden thing will be revealed. God knows all about us. Paul affirms that God will "judge the secrets of men" (Rom. 2:16). The world loves darkness. Men love their sins, many of which are committed under cover of darkness. At the Great White Throne (for sinners) and the judgment seat of Christ (for saints), all hidden things will be exposed—as Reuben (Gen. 49:3–4), Aachan (Josh. 7:1–26), and Ananias and Sapphira (Acts 5:1–11) discovered.

If any man have ears to hear, let him hear. (4:23)

Again the Lord's challenge rings forth. He has used these very words before (4:9). It is a phrase often repeated. In writing from glory to the seven churches of Asia, the Lord uses the expression over and over again (Rev. 2–3). Shakespeare borrowed the expression and used it in a different form when recounting Mark Anthony's speech to the Romans attending Caesar's funeral: "Friends, Romans and countrymen, lend me your ears." The words are a challenge to us to pay attention to what is being said. That is important when listening to any communication. When the speaker is God, it is vital.

Showing! (4:24–25):

> *And he said unto them, Take heed what ye hear: with what measure ye mete, it shall be measured to you: and unto you that hear shall more be given. (4:24)*

First, there is a word of *caution*. We are to take heed what we hear. We must be careful about that to which we listen. There are many voices. We hear false words, foolish words, and filthy words spoken. There are fanciful words and fiendish words. Some words flatter. Some are fierce. We would do well to censor the books we read, the programs we watch, and the voices we hear.

Then there is a word of *counsel*. We are to measure out to others wholesome words that come our way. We are particularly responsible to pass on divine truth. There is something reciprocal about it. The more we pass on to others, the more we will have passed on to us.

Then there is a word of *clarification*. Those who hear what God has to say will want to hear more. In the Lord's encounter with the woman at the well, we see the rapid growth of a soul in the knowledge of Christ. First, she called Him "a Jew." Then she said, "Sir." Then she called Him "a prophet." Finally, she confessed Him as Messiah and as "Christ" (John 4:7–29).

> *For he that hath, to him shall be given: and he that hath not, from him shall be taken even that which he hath. (4:25)*

It is a basic law of economics: the man who has money is in a position to make more and more money. He can invest in this and buy into that. He can enlarge his capital and increase his fortune. The man who is in debt finds his debt increasing. He has to pay more and more for less and less. He mortgages his home. He loses his car. In olden days, debtors prison awaited him; nowadays it is the bankruptcy court.

It is a law of the spiritual realm too. One man grows in grace and increases in the knowledge of God. Another man neglects the things of God, shrivels, and becomes a worldly, carnal Christian, a spiritual pauper. The Lord's parable of the talents (Matt. 25) tells us much the same thing. So does the parable of the pounds. We either *use* or *lose* what we are given.

Sowing! (4:26–29):

> *And he said, So is the kingdom of God, as if a man should cast*
> *seed into the ground; (4:26)*

The Lord turns now from the necessity of spiritual growth to the mystery of spiritual growth. Spiritual growth is divided into two parts—our part and God's part. We cannot do very much. All we can do is take the seed and sow it. Anyone can do that. Nobody needs a degree in agriculture to be able to take handful after handful of seed and throw it on the soil. However, the marvel and wonder of what follows ought never to cease to amaze us.

> *And should sleep, and rise night and day, and the seed should*
> *spring and grow up, he knoweth not how. (4:27)*

Having sown his seed, the farmer waits. What else can he do? He can water and fertilize the ground, but he cannot make the seed germinate or grow. All is now up to God. He alone has the ultimate secret of life. The biologist can dissect the seed and expose and name its various parts. The geneticist can go even deeper into the structure of things and define the seed's genetic code. He can clone and produce identical plants. He can breed and produce hybrid plants. But if no life is there, it is all in vain. The law of biogenesis states, "There can be no life without antecedent life." Ultimately, all life comes from God. The most zealous believer can no more convert a soul than he could create a star. Life, especially spiritual life, remains a mystery.

> *For the earth bringeth forth fruit of herself; first the blade, then*
> *the ear, after that the full corn in the ear. (4:28)*

After the passing of time, the farmer, who has been going about his other affairs, comes back to look at his field. The miracle has happened. It shows green. Little blades of corn are poking through the soil. He comes back often now to observe the miracle of growth. The plant takes on stature. It matures. The ear appears and then, the crowning wonder, the cob, bursting with kernels of corn, the promise of more crops to come.

But how does it all happen? The farmer does not know. He knows only that it does. It is almost a commonplace occurrence, one that he often takes for granted, but the fact remains—it is a miracle. Every growing stalk in the farmer's field is a miracle. The farmer owes it all to God. He might be a clever and intelligent farmer; but, without God, he can produce nothing.

> *But when the fruit is brought forth, immediately he putteth in the sickle, because the harvest is come. (4:29)*

Now it's up to the farmer again. God works the miracle of creating a crop, but now it is the farmer's responsibility to reap and conserve the harvest. God does not do for us what we can do for ourselves.

The law of growth operates in the spiritual realm. We can sow the seed of Scripture but, after that, it is up to the Spirit of God. He causes the seed to germinate. He superintends the various stages of its growth. We can water it with our tears and prayers, but we can no more force spiritual growth than we can arrange for a plant to grow. But we can reap the harvest when the process is complete and anticipate a reward at the judgment seat of Christ for playing our little part both in the sowing end and the mowing end of things.

Growing! (4:30–32):

> *And he said, Whereunto shall we liken the kingdom of God? or with what comparison shall we compare it? (4:30)*

Matthew also records this next parable (of the mustard seed) and others that Mark does not mention (Matt. 13). There is a different emphasis in Matthew's "kingdom" parables and similar parables in the other Synoptic Gospels. John does not mention any of them. In Matthew, the emphasis is on the *kingdom of heaven,* and the interpretation is *dispensational.* In the other Gospels the emphasis is on the kingdom of God, and the interpretation is *devotional.*

Here we see the Lord casting about in His mind for an illustration. To what could He liken the kingdom of God? It is a kingdom quite unlike earthly kingdoms, where often evil men sit in the seat of power, wage war with their neighbors, and oppress their own people. The greatest approach to an ideal king in the Old Testament was David, but we know how badly he sinned and how arbitrarily he abused his power to cover up his guilt. The nearest approach to an ideal kingdom was Solomon's. It won the admiration of both the Queen of Sheba and Hiram, King of Tyre. It was marked by peace, prosperity, and power. But Solomon failed badly, and his kingdom fell apart after his death.

The typology of all of this is clear enough. When the Lord returns, He will reign, as David reigned and put down all of His foes. Then He will reign as Solomon reigned in prosperity and peace. The Lord, however, does not look to either David or Solomon for His illustration. He wanted something much more spiritual than was to be found in the kingdoms of Israel's two most illustrious sovereigns. Not even David's wonderful songs or Solomon's wise sayings were enough to offset their failures. So the Lord turned from the national realm to the natural realm and gave another illustration from the world of nature.

It is like a grain of mustard seed, which, when it is sown in the earth, is less than all the seeds that be in the earth: (4:31)

Imagine the astonishment of the disciples when they heard that! The Lord was about to describe the kingdom of God. They had visions of a global empire. They doubtless pictured an ivory palace, a majestic throne, a glittering court, ambassadors from earth's remotest bounds waiting in long lines for an audience, and an invincible army at the command of a powerful, magnificent king. They waited eagerly for the Lord's description of such a kingdom, one in which they would be high ministers of state. Then came the shock.

"The kingdom of God," He said, "is like a grain of mustard seed." They must have stared blankly at Him in astonishment. A grain of mustard seed? Why, that was nothing! You could hardly see it; it was so small and insignificant.

Ah! But it had life! It would grow! The point of the parable lies in the contrast between the size of the seed when it is sown and the size of the plant when it is grown. In each case, the Lord used hyperbole for emphasis. The kingdom of God seems small and insignificant in men's eyes. In the Lord's day, such was the people's contempt for it that they murdered its King. But when it is fully grown, when it reaches its full potential, they will be awed by it then!

> *But when it is sown, it groweth up, and becometh greater than*
> *all herbs, and shooteth out great branches; so that the fowls of the*
> *air may lodge under the shadow of it.* (4:32)

People have a poor opinion of God's work in this world, but it actually is vast. It reaches into many lands. On the Day of Pentecost alone, five thousand souls were born into that kingdom. Who can tell how many people have been saved every day since that day? The Holy Spirit Himself superintends the work, and He cannot fail, no matter what people think. The kingdom of God on earth in our day is represented by the church, the body of Christ (1 Cor. 12:12–13).

Everywhere the kingdom of God has gone, it has brought with it hospitals and schools; truth, morality, and ethics; decency and compassion; and, above all, salvation. Wherever the gospel has gone, it has abolished cannibalism, child sacrifice, the immolation of widows, polygamy, demonism, slavery, and a thousand other such ills. It has built orphanages and asylums, cared for the sick, comforted the bereaved, and helped the infirm. In many lands, even secular governments have taken color from its creeds. Even the unsaved have found shelter beneath its branches and found comfort and a better lifestyle in its shade.

b. The extent of this method (4:33–34)

> *And with many such parables spake he the word unto them, as*
> *they were able to hear it.* (4:33)

Illustrations! What an integral part of His teaching they were! He told stories; used metaphors; and drew parallels from the fields, the sky, the sea, the kitchen, the hedgerow, and the marketplace. They said, "Never man spake like this man." Even so, He had to proceed at their pace.

Sin has so thoroughly blinded our minds, corrupted our hearts, and weakened our wills that we can take in only a little of the truth at a time. Often, the gospel encounters prejudice, preconceived ideas, entrenched traditions, false philosophies, and hostile religions. Just as a child has to learn to count, then learn how to do simple arithmetic, and then move on to fractions and long division before it can go on to algebra and calculus and trigonometry, so the Lord had to begin with very basic spiritual truths, and even these, His disciples found hard to grasp.

But without a parable spake he not unto them: and when they were alone, he expounded all things to his disciples. (4:34)

The Lord performed countless miracles, but only about three dozen of them are recorded in the Gospels. Similarly, He told countless parables, but not all of them, we can be sure, have been preserved. Nevertheless, enough of them have been recorded for us to marvel at His wisdom and His words. He was a prolific illustrator. Mark says that He never spoke without using illustrations. Not content with that, He would often explain His teaching at greater length to His disciples privately. Some of the deeper and more profound teachings of Jesus were recorded in the writings of the apostle John. John wrote for the third generation at a time when the church was well established and much of its doctrine had been written in the Epistles. It took a more mature age to grasp the more mature truths that John taught.

B. They were executive in power (4:35–5:43)
   1. Triumphing over disaster (4:35–41)

And the same day, when the even was come, he saith unto them, Let us pass over unto the other side. (4:35)

What a day it had been! He had faced and healed a fierce demoniac (Matt. 12:22). He had dealt with the opposition of both His friends (3:20–21) and His foes (Matt. 12:24). He had preached. He was tired.

"The other side" lay across about six miles of water. Several of the disciples were veteran boatsmen who had fished this lake for years. They had grown up on its banks, its shore had been their boyhood playground, and they knew its every curve, current, and mood. These men were handy with oars and sails. The Lord was in safe hands when He boarded that boat. Rather, they were in safe hands once *He* stepped on board. Still, they thought that this was their realm. He could leave the sailing to them.

And when they had sent away the multitude, they took him even as he was in the ship. And there were also with him other little ships. (4:36)

It had been a busy day with crowds of people, and He had loved every minute of it, just as He loved every one of the people. But the day was done, and it was time to go home for rest. Even the most popular preacher with the most enthusiastic and appreciative of crowds comes to the moment when the crowds have to be sent away.

The thronging people were gone at last, the ship was ready, and the attendant craft were pulling away from shore. So He stepped on board—"as he was," Mark says.

This same Jesus is willing to come on board our little vessels too. But we must receive Him *as He is*. He is not going to change, but He will change us. That's the way He is. He is loving, wise, strong, and holy. We are mean, foolish, weak, and sinful. What He is and what we are cannot coexist. One of us will have to change. He is not going to change. He is "the same yesterday, and today, and for ever" (Heb. 13:8). We receive Him *as He is*. We should be more careful to tell people that when we proclaim the Good News. Zacchaeus received Him as He was, and Zacchaeus was changed. Peter received Him as He was, and Peter was changed. With some people, the change is sudden, swift, and sure. With other people it takes more time. We take Him aboard our lives, however, as He is because He wants to make us as He is (1 John 1:17).

> *And there arose a great storm of wind, and the waves beat into the ship, so that it was now full. (4:37)*

The presence of Christ on board does not guarantee a smooth passage. On the contrary, the enemy will do his best to stir up a storm. Some preachers proclaim what they call a "prosperity gospel": accept Christ and be rewarded with wealth, health, and happiness. It is a false gospel. The Beatitudes, which begin the Sermon on the Mount, ought to convince us of that fact (Matt. 5:1–12). Believers are not exempt from sickness, poverty, natural disasters, bereavement, death, and various ills of life. What He promises is not His protection *from* the storm but His presence *in* the storm.

The Sea of Galilee is notorious for its sudden and fierce squalls that come from the surrounding hills and whip the waters into frenzy. It was bad enough on board the ship where Jesus was. What must it have been like on the other "little ships" that did not have Him on board! Life's sudden disasters shake even God's own people. What must it be like to be caught in one of the disasters of life without a Savior?

The waves beat into the boat, and soon it was full. Any other boat would have gone to the bottom. Not that one! As the old hymn "Master the Tempest Is Raging" by Mary A. Baker puts it,

No waters can swallow the ship where lies
The Master of ocean, and earth, and skies.

And he was in the hinder part of the ship, asleep on a pillow: and
they awake him, and say unto him, Master, carest thou not that
we perish? (4:38)

The disciples had found a spot for Him in the stern where He could go to sleep. They also gave Him a pillow. Soon He was sound asleep. It is all so very natural, so very human. Although Jesus was God in the absolute sense of the word, He was also truly Man. He knew what it was like to be hungry and thirsty, to become weary with His journey, and to go to sleep.

Evening shadows deepened into night. The waves lapped against the boat. The air was calm and cool. The men pulled at the oars in skillful unison. The motion of the waves and the lullaby of the breeze rocked Jesus gently. All was well. The Lord of Glory slept. Incidentally, this is the only occasion when we read of Jesus sleeping. The whole scene underlines His humanity.

Suddenly, the storm was upon them because Satan had seen his opportunity. The Lord was asleep! He was vulnerable! All Satan had to do was sink that boat! The wind howled, the waves arose, and the boat was tempest tossed. The disciples were drenched to the skin and at the mercy of the raging wind.

Then they thought of Jesus. They woke Him up. "Carest thou not that we perish?" they asked. What impertinence! We can forgive them for their rudeness because they were panic-stricken. But at least they knew where to turn. They must have been astonished that Jesus could sleep on in such imminent danger, totally unconcerned, while their world was being torn apart. He was Man, and exhaustion demanded its due. Besides, He was in His Father's care, and He knew full well that it was not His Father's will that He be drowned. Moreover, it was not time for Him to die. So He slept. The storm had no terror for Him. Behind the tempest's awful voice was the voice of the Evil One, but not even that voice, with all of its hatred and malice urging on the wind and the waves, could disturb Him. He was greater than either Satan or the storm. So He slept.

And he arose, and rebuked the wind, and said unto the sea, Peace,
be still. And the wind ceased, and there was a great calm. (4:39)

Note the difference between what He said to the wind and what He said to the sea. He rebuked the wind because the wind was what stirred up the waves, but He spoke "peace" to the waves. Evidently, there was more to it than that. The wind itself is often at the mercy of other forces—the whole complex of high pressures and low pressures, of high temperatures and low temperatures—that create the forces that give rise to hurricanes, tornadoes, cyclones, and breezes, forces that we understand only partially. He knew them all. He created them. One word from Him, and they would do His will.

There was even more to it than that, however. Perhaps there always is. The Bible indicates that sometimes demonic forces are involved when storms wreak havoc on the world (Rev. 7:1–3; 8:1–6). Behind the waves was the wind, but behind the wind was the Evil One himself, the "prince of the power of the air" (Eph. 2:2); hence, the rebuke. Having rebuked the wind, the Lord spoke to the waves. "Peace," He said, "be still." That was all. At once, the wind was hushed, and the waves sank to rest. The shrieking, howling wind and the tumultuous, heaving waves were replaced by total, instant calm.

> *And he said unto them, Why are ye so fearful? how is it that ye have no faith? (4:40)*

Faith and fear cancel each other out. If we have fear, we have no faith; if we have faith, we have no fear. Their terror proved their lack of trust.

Faith! But not faith in the abstract, not faith in a vacuum. Faith always has an object. It is linked to something or someone. We exercise faith in the pilot when we step on board a plane. We have faith in the bank when we hand over our deposit. The Lord asked His disciples why they had no faith—in *Him*.

D. L. Moody once met a man who told him that he could not trust. Mr. Moody was very blunt with him. He said, "Young man, *whom* can't you trust?" It is an insult to tell someone we cannot trust him. How much more serious it is to say that we cannot trust God.

So Jesus challenged them. "Why did you fear? Why don't you have any faith? Why could you not *trust* Me—*Me?*" He asks the same question of us all.

> *And they feared exceedingly, and said one to another, What manner of man is this, that even the wind and the sea obey him? (4:41)*

They now transferred their fear from the storm to the Savior. They were tongue-tied at His question, "Why did you fear?" Suddenly, they were afraid of *Him*. They had seen a hundred miracles, but all of them paled into insignificance before this One. Suddenly, they realized that this Jesus of Nazareth, their wise Teacher, their wonderful Friend, was as far removed from them as the remotest star.

"What manner of man is this?" they asked. They knew the answer; that is why they feared exceedingly. He was the Creator Himself. It was the same with the soldiers who crucified Christ. Matthew recalls that when they saw the earthquake and the other attendant miracles that "they feared greatly" (Matt. 27:54).

2. Triumphing over demons (5:1–20)

First, we have *confrontation* (5:1–5):

> *And they came over unto the other side of the sea, into the country of the Gadarenes. (5:1)*

The country of the Gadarenes was on the eastern shore of the lake, opposite Magdala and five miles from the point where the Jordan emptied into the Sea of Galilee. A short distance south of the city was a spot where the steep hills came down close to the water.

It had been a wild and stormy night. Now it was to be a wild and stormy morning. Jesus had just dealt with bad weather. Now He is confronted by blatant wickedness.

In this chapter, the Lord Jesus dealt with demons, disease, and death—the three great terrors of mankind. He delivered, in turn, a man, a woman, and a child. What a Savior!

> *And when he was come out of the ship, immediately there met him out of the tombs a man with an unclean spirit, Who had his dwelling among the tombs; and no man could bind him, no, not with chains: (5:2–3)*

The man was the terror of the neighborhood. Satan had just tried to drown the Lord; now, he tried to have Him killed by this ferocious demoniac. What the disciples thought when this fearsome savage appeared we are not told. They must have been frightened, to say the least. This demented man was not merely in the grip of ungoverned passion and rage. Nor was he victimized by the delusions of one who was criminally insane. Nor was he an ordinary demoniac, possessed by an evil spirit. This was Satan's prize exhibit, a man tormented and driven by a vast number of fearful evil spirits.

The people who lived in this vicinity tried to protect themselves from this fearful man. They had chained him. They had driven him into the wilds. He now lived with the dead in some nearby tombs—a poor, lost, lonely man who was hated, shunned, and feared by all.

We do not know how he got into his condition. Demon possession is a mysterious but very real condition, as any missionary working in pagan lands or among heathen tribes can testify. Idolatry and demon possession are often twins. Tampering with the occult, getting involved with drugs, flagrant immorality, and cultic vegetarianism are all means whereby evil spirits get hold of people, invade their bodies, and control their souls. Jesus saw beyond the terrible wreckage of a demented and dangerous individual. He saw, way down beneath all of the conflict and confusion, a lost and desperate man.

> *Because that he had been often bound with fetters and chains,*
> *and the chains had been plucked asunder by him, and the fetters*
> *broken in pieces: neither could any man tame him. (5:4)*

The ordinary or even the harshest restraints imposed by society had failed. Locking him up was of no use. He had demonic strength, and no prison could hold him. Nowadays people would try psychology on him, but no amount of analysis and corrective therapy would do him the slightest bit of good. No man could tame him. This was not a case of mental aberration or ordinary madness; this was outright demon possession. And psychology, whether the primitive kind of olden times or the sophisticated kind of modern times, cannot cure demon possession.

So the man was left to roam the graveyard, and sensible people left him alone and gave him a wide berth.

> *And always, night and day, he was in the mountains, and in the*
> *tombs, crying, and cutting himself with stones. (5:5)*

At least people knew where he was; they could hear him. He howled through the surrounding hills like a wolf. Long, long ago, his pitiful cries had reached the heart of God and touched the heart of Christ. Just as once "he must needs go through Samaria," so now He made His deliberate way to Gadara. He had come to meet this hopeless derelict as purposefully as He had gone to meet the woman at the well.

Next, comes *contradiction* (5:6–8):

> *But when he saw Jesus afar off, he ran and worshipped him, (5:6)*

Amazing! What a sight he must have been. His body was covered with self-inflicted wounds and old scars, his hair and beard were long and tangled, and his eyes were ablaze. He was unwashed and either naked or arrayed in a ruin of rags.

When anyone came along the way that led near the tombs, the demon-possessed man would fall on him violently to do him harm. When Jesus came, however, he fell down before Him and worshiped Him.

> *And cried with a loud voice, and said, What have I to do with*
> *thee, Jesus, thou Son of the most high God? I adjure thee by God,*
> *that thou torment me not. (5:7)*

Now it was the demon speaking. The voice of the Evil One was easily recognizable. It confessed Christ to be the Son of God and then immediately slandered Him and accused Him of being a tormentor.

Throughout the gospel narratives, we consistently see demons recognizing the Lord Jesus instantly and confessing His deity as well as owning themselves bound to obey Him. The Lord habitually commanded them to be silent and refused to accept witness from them. To this day, evil spirits, masquerading as the Holy Spirit, cannot confess that Jesus Christ is come in the flesh—consequently, this criteria has become the Holy Spirit's own required test for the presence of a demon (1 John 4:1–3).

The demons that inhabited the body of this wretched man paid tribute to the deity of Christ. They also knew His name—Jesus—and insolently addressed Him as such, although they hated and feared that name and dreaded His humanity as much as His deity. "Ye call me Master and Lord," Jesus said to His disciples, "and ye say well; for so I am" (John 13:13). There is a proper form of address to be used when approaching Him. We are to give Him His titles. In the New Testament, only demons addressed Him as Jesus. We are not to "take His name in vain."

> *For he said unto him, Come out of the man, thou unclean spirit.*
> *(5:8)*

Perhaps that was how the demons, who were tormenting this poor man, knew who had arrived on the scene—by the ring of divine authority in the command. The demons, now terrified themselves, stalled for a few moments. They knew well enough, however, that they could no more resist that command than a snow-flake could defy a flame.

"Come out of the man!" They were usurpers. They had not the slightest claim to the body and soul of this man. They had fastened upon him by the thousands, as bacteria fasten upon an individual. But they were intruders and invaders. They had no legitimate claim to the house they tenanted. They knew it, and Jesus knew it. They could scoff at the poor attempts of the local people to "tame" this man, but they could not scoff at Christ. The strongman armed might be able to keep his stolen goods, but now that One who was stronger than he had come, and their time was up.

Then we have *confession:*

> *And he asked him, What is thy name? And he answered, saying,*
> *My name is Legion: for we are many. (5:9)*

Here we see an extreme case of the confusion of identity of the demented. Split personalities are not at all uncommon. In the book *The Three Faces of Eve,* one young woman exhibited three totally different identities, each self-contained. The puzzle was to decide which of the three was the real woman. Her counselors tried to find a psychological explanation. The Bible would give a spiritual diagnosis and point to demon possession.

In the case of the Gadarene, the man was possessed with a legion of demons, thousands of them. The man's answer to the Lord's question as to his name and identity is revealing: "*He* answered, . . . Legion: for *we* are many." The Lord's presence had already helped him to unravel some of the confusion of his being. It was the man himself who said "Legion"; it was probably the demons who added "for we are many."

Next, we see *consternation* (5:10–12):

> *And he besought him much that he would not send them away*
> *out of the country. (5:10)*

Evidently, the man now became the spokesman for all of the demons. If so, it suggests that he had grown so accustomed to the companionship of these evil spirits that he could not imagine life without them. Either that or they took over complete control of his voice and answered the Lord's questions themselves.

We wonder why they did not want to be sent away out of the country. We learn from the book of Daniel that fallen angels rule over the affairs of fallen men. Satan's agents in the spirit world rule over designated territories. Thus, Gabriel told Daniel about the princes of Persia and Greece (satanic beings) and told him that the archangel Michael was the God-appointed angel who presided over the affairs of the Hebrew people (Dan. 10:11–21). These are some of those "principalities" of which Paul speaks. He also refers to "powers" and "the rulers of the darkness of this world" and "spiritual wickedness in high places" (Eph. 6:12). Satan's organization of his unseen empire likely includes the demons, and they, too, are given territorial spheres in which to operate. If so, then these demons were, for some reason, terrified of being ejected from "the country" where they lurked. We do not know if they were terrified of their overlords in Satan's empire, or, perhaps, they feared being sent directly to Tartarus by Christ.

> *Now there was there nigh unto the mountains a great herd of swine feeding. And all the devils besought him, saying, Send us into the swine, that we may enter into them. (5:11–12)*

T. H. Huxley, in his utter contempt for the Word of God, called what happened next "The Gadarene Pig Affair." Much he knew about it! This time it was the demons who spoke, adding their legion of voices to that of the demoniac. The demons, fearing to be again disembodied, craved permission to enter the bodies of some swine, rather than be totally disembodied. Even to take up that abode, however, they needed Christ's permission.

Next comes *condemnation:*

> *And forthwith Jesus gave them leave. And the unclean spirits went out, and entered into the swine: and the herd ran violently down a steep place into the sea, (they were about two thousand;) and were choked in the sea. (5:13)*

So the demons were swiftly disembodied after all. The swine preferred death to demon possession. In the Roman army, a legion consisted of six thousand men. That would mean that each of the "about two thousand" pigs was seized upon by three evil spirits. That was more than enough for them. They precipitated themselves headlong down the steep slopes into the lake, where they were drowned.

Then we have *consultation* (5:14–17):

> *And they that fed the swine fled, and told it in the city, and in the country. And they went out to see what it was that was done. (5:14)*

Under the Mosaic Law, the swine was classified as an unclean animal. These people, then, were engaged in an unclean and illegal business. The Lord has been criticized for destroying other people's property. He did nothing of the kind. He was the rightful King of the country and had every right to clean it up as He saw fit. On two occasions, He took a whip of cords to rid the temple courts of profane traffic. Do we complain when police seize and burn stockpiles of cocaine?

The swine herdsmen took to their heels, however, when the hogs took to theirs! They went into town to report to the owners of the swine what had happened to both the demoniac and the swine. A crowd soon gathered at the scene, looking first at the lake and then at the Lord. Far and wide the shores of the lake were littered with the carcasses of the dead animals. As for the former demoniac, he was sitting calmly. They stared from the one to the other. Then they looked at Jesus.

> *And they come to Jesus, and see him that was possessed with the devil, and had the legion, sitting, and clothed, and in his right mind: and they were afraid. (5:15)*

What an astonishing thing! They were afraid! They had feared the demoniac when he was worse than a raving lunatic. Now they were afraid at the sight of him, but now a transformed man, sitting at Jesus' feet. Here was power beyond their understanding. It filled them with awe and dread. They were up against transparent, awesome goodness, impeccable holiness, supernatural power, and invincible love. And they didn't like it. They recoiled from it. They feared it. Perhaps the transformation in the former demoniac's life made them think of their own need for the same regeneration. Some of them were doubtless angry over the demolition of their business and the loss of their liquid assets. They had invested a lot of money in those pigs. But fear was the predominant emotion.

And they that saw it told them how it befell to him that was
possessed with the devil, and also concerning the swine. (5:16)

Doubtless, these eyewitnesses were the swineherds. Or maybe it was another
party of men from the town coming out to try binding the man one more time. In
any case, the disciples were there, and their testimony would doubtless be heard.

And they began to pray him to depart out of their coasts. (5:17)

They asked Him to go away. Such is the human heart. Faced on the one hand
with the Lord of Glory and the evidence of a transformed life and on the other
hand with the challenge to their own lives and the loss of a herd of pigs, that was
their verdict—"Please go away." How very sad, but how often repeated.

Finally, we have *consecration* (5:18–20):

And when he was come into the ship, he that had been possessed
with the devil prayed him that he might be with him. (5:18)

The Lord acceded to their pitiful request and prepared to leave. But the freed
demoniac ran to the boat and prayed to be allowed to go with Him.

This was a different kind of prayer, the prayer of a grateful heart. The con-
verted man wanted to be with Jesus, to become one of His disciples, to abide
with Him, henceforth to sit at His feet. So one man from Gadara that day was
full of wonder and gratitude.

As for the Lord, doubtless He was used to the sparse response to His efforts.
He had already proclaimed the fact that the gate to heaven was narrow, and so
was the path that led to life, and few would find it—in contrast to the multitudes
who enter in at the wide gate and tread the broad way to destruction (Matt.
7:13–14). The Lord's kingdom parables (Matt. 13) told the same story, and when
He cleansed the ten lepers, only one returned to give thanks (Luke 17:17).

Howbeit Jesus suffered him not, but saith unto him, Go home to
thy friends, and tell them how great things the Lord hath done for
thee, and hath had compassion on thee. (5:19)

The Lord denied the man's plea. He was to become a home missionary to
his family, his neighbors, and his friends. He who had been a terror to every-

body was now to give his testimony to one and all: once he had been bound, body and soul, but now he was free. All because he met the Lord Jesus Christ! The Lord had been asked to leave, but the people could hardly ask that of this man, who had lived there all of his life. He was to live Christ among them, so that when Jesus came back that way, as He did, they would be ready to receive Him.

> *And he departed, and began to publish in Decapolis how great things Jesus had done for him: and all men did marvel. (5:20)*

Decapolis was a loose association of ten cities on the main highway that ran from Damascus to Arabia along the edge of the desert and along the three roads that connected that thoroughfare with Esdraelon. Gadara was one of those ten cities. The population was heavily Greek in composition, the Greeks having come long ago in the wake of Alexander's conquests.

The transformed man did not limit his testimony to his hometown but carried the evangel through the whole area. The Lord had done great things for him. He had the scars on his body that testified to the days when he had mutilated himself in his frenzies and to the times when he had been bound with chains. He was a living epistle to the love of Christ and the power of God. He had been forgiven much, and He loved much. And people marveled. There could be no denying that a mighty miracle had been wrought in his life.

> 3. Triumphing over disease (5:21–34)
>> a. Jairus and his introduction (5:21–24)

We note, first, *the ruler* (5:21–23):

> *And when Jesus was passed over again by ship unto the other side, much people gathered unto him: and he was nigh unto the sea. (5:21)*

The Lord did not stay where He was not wanted. He returned to the west side of the lake and went on back to Capernaum, where He made His home. Soon He had the crowds again. "He was near the lake," Mark notes. Probably the people saw the boat coming and spread the word. They liked His teaching, so simple yet so sublime. They liked His miracles even more. They also liked the authority with which He spoke and rebuked His critics. He was the most popular preacher of the day.

> *And, behold, there cometh one of the rulers of the synagogue,*
> *Jairus by name; and when he saw him, he fell at his feet, (5:22)*

Now came Jairus, one of the rulers of the synagogue. The ruler of the synagogue was a man whom the Jews respected. It is not at all unlikely that this man had been a member of the Jewish delegation that had pleaded the cause of the Roman centurion who had built the Capernaum synagogue and whose servant Jesus had miraculously healed. So the ruler knew firsthand the Lord's power to save. When the ruler of the synagogue arrived where Jesus was, he instinctively flung himself at His feet in utter abasement. He was conscious of a need, desperate almost beyond words, a need that only Jesus could meet.

> *And besought him greatly, saying, My little daughter lieth at the*
> *point of death: I pray thee, come and lay thy hands on her, that*
> *she may be healed; and she shall live. (5:23)*

He had no doubt that Jesus had the power to heal because he had seen Him heal others. Somehow he entertained the notion that Jesus had to be present to heal.

Those who have seen a cherished little one fall desperately ill, resist all of the skill of the physicians, and grow weaker and weaker until the very shadow of death creeps across the dearly loved countenance know the anguish of this father. Doubtless, Jesus, who had been to the Capernaum synagogue numerous times, knew this little girl. She was twelve years of age (v. 42).

Note, next, *the response* (5:24):

> *And Jesus went with him; and much people followed him, and*
> *thronged him. (5:24)*

The Lord Jesus responded at once, without comment, taking the path to Jairus's house. The multitudes, with a well-developed appetite for miracles, came along, pushing and jostling, each one eager to be close so as to get the best view. Everyone knew Jairus and his little girl—at least everyone in Capernaum and all those who attended the synagogue.

b. Jesus and the interruption (5:25–34)
   (1) The woman who sought (5:25–28)

We note her condition (5:25–26):

And a certain woman, which had an issue of blood twelve years,
(5:25)

However, there was about to be an interruption, one that would drive poor Jairus
to distraction. Yet, the woman who caused the interruption was desperate too. Jairus
had enjoyed twelve years of delight; this poor woman had endured twelve years of
despair. Under the Mosaic Law, her affliction rendered her untouchable, if not an
actual outcast (Lev. 12:4–8; 15:19–33). Her disease was defiling and debilitating. It
cut her off from society and from the sanctuary. And it had gone on for twelve years.

And had suffered many things of many physicians, and had spent all
that she had, and was nothing bettered, but rather grew worse, (5:26)

She had suffered embarrassment, pain, disappointment, and financial ruin.
The doctors could not diagnose her condition or heal her. They prescribed their
useless remedies, collected their fees, then gave up on her when they could get no
more money from her. In spite of everything, her condition got worse.

It was indeed a sad tale of hopeless despair. Now, bleeding, broken, and bank-
rupt, she turned to Jesus.

We note, also, *her coming:*

When she had heard of Jesus, came in the press behind, and touched
his garment. (5:27)

Someone told her the good news about Jesus. She heard and she came. That is
the way it works. Like the aristocratic Nicodemus, however, she decided to come
to Jesus secretly. In her case, she was tired of being poked and prodded by doctors, tired of the unwelcome publicity that clung to her and made her an object
of rejection. One can hardly blame her. In any case, she came.

We note, moreover, *her confidence:*

For she said, If I may touch but his clothes, I shall be whole. (5:28)

Such was her confidence in Christ. She thought that even His garments exuded power. Nor was she far wrong. On the Mount of Transfiguration His garments became white and glistening. They partook of His glory. Why should they not partake of His power? After all, our garments partake of our diseases. Who would want to don the dress of a leper? So this woman's faith soared. She stands alone in her expression of utter confidence in Christ.

(2) The wonder He wrought (5:29–34)

Note *how He healed her body* (5:29–32):

> *And straightway the fountain of her blood was dried up; and she felt in her body that she was healed of that plague. (5:29)*

Her faith was not misplaced. Her reasoning was absolutely sound. Her cure was instantaneous and complete. She had begun with *fact.* The Lord's power was so absolute, He was so mighty to save, that a touch would do, even a touch of His robe, even a touch of its hem. Fact had been followed by *faith.* She came! She touched! It worked! It was faith, her personal faith in Christ, that distinguished her from all of the others who thronged Him. They touched Him, too, but nothing happened to them. Even today, many people brush up against Him, but they go away the same as they came. Finally, she had *feelings.* Many people want the feelings to come first. Salvation, however, is not based on feelings. Feelings are the result of a transformed life. She knew, deep down inside her, that something wonderful had happened to her. She felt it in her body. She would never be the same again.

> *And Jesus, immediately knowing in himself that virtue had gone out of him, turned him about in the press, and said, Who touched my clothes? (5:30)*

He knew at once that power had gone forth from Him. He knew that His garment had been touched by the hand of faith. He knew whom! But what He was after now was a public confession for the woman's own good. Otherwise, she might carry with her a gnawing fear that her blessing, having in a sense been gained by stealing, might not last. The Lord did not want her to exchange a tormented body for a tormented mind.

So He stopped and turned around, and the multitude came to a lumbering halt with people still pressing up against Him. "Who touched my clothes?" He asked. Only one person in that throng knew why He asked that, and she froze in her tracks. Her heart stood still.

> *And his disciples said unto him, Thou seest the multitude thronging thee, and sayest thou, Who touched me? (5:31)*

His disciples were astonished. The Lord had been hardly able to walk toward poor Jairus's house because of the throng! What kind of a question was that? The Lord, however, wasn't talking to them. Between Him and them, disciples though they were, was a great gulf fixed. It had been the same when He talked to the woman at the well, when He commentated on the disappointed hopes of the rich young ruler, when mothers brought their little ones to Him, when He talked about the bread of heaven, and when they quarreled among themselves as to who was to be the greatest even with Calvary just hours ahead. It was the same when He told them that, far from being crowned, He was going to be crucified. Indeed, they seem to have understood very little at all. It is the same with us; we question His ways with us all of the time.

Note, too, how He sealed her belief (5:33–34):

> *And he looked round about to see her that had done this thing. (5:32)*

His was no idle question. He began to look here and there to find the woman. Even as He looked, she was making up her mind. She had faith enough to come, but would she have courage enough to confess? Secret disciples are weak disciples. We are to "confess with [our] mouth the Lord Jesus" as well as "believe in [our] heart that God hath raised him from the dead" (Rom. 10:9).

> *But the woman fearing and trembling, knowing what was done in her, came and fell down before him, and told him all the truth. (5:33)*

He already knew the whole story, of course, but He wanted to hear it from her lips. Many years before, Jacob had tried to steal a blessing. It had brought him nothing but years of exile and strife. The Lord was not going to let this woman make Jacob's mistake.

As for the woman, faith and feelings had now given way to fear. Of what was she so afraid? Did she think that the Lord was going to punish her? Surely she knew Him better than that! Did she fear the gossip of the people, some of whom, doubtless, were her neighbors? Whatever it was that she feared, she came and poured her heart out to Jesus. She told Him the whole sad story. Twelve years of misery! Hopeless doctors! All of her money gone! Her condition—so unclean, so debilitating, so embarrassing, and so socially damning—was only getting worse and worse. She told how she had heard Him and seen Him at work. Her new hope! Her little scheme! And now she was completely cured! But now she had a new set of fears lest, having stolen her cure, it might be taken away from her.

> And he said unto her, Daughter, thy faith hath made thee whole;
> go in peace, and be whole of thy plague. (5:34)

No blame! Only bliss! "Daughter!" He said, as He put her in His family and *sealed her faith*, "thy faith hath saved thee. Go in peace!" He *stilled her fears*. "Be whole!" He said and *secured her future*. Just a dozen and a half words, but they set the joy bells ringing in her soul.

Meanwhile, Jairus had been standing by on pins and needles because of this delay. His daughter was dying. Why couldn't this woman have waited another half an hour? Why was Jesus taking so long?

4. Triumphing over death (5:35–43)
   a. The tidings for Jairus (5:35)

> While he yet spake, there came from the ruler of the synagogue's
> house certain which said, Thy daughter is dead: why troublest
> thou the Master any further? (5:35)

Now came bitter news for Jairus. His daughter was dead. Bad news, indeed, and bluntly spoken. Spoken, too, by those who little knew the Lord. "Why troublest thou the Master any further?" they asked—as though any needy one could be a trouble to Him! As though, while He could doubtless perform miracles of healing, no one, not even He, could do anything about the dead. Jairus himself gave way to despair. His one hope—of getting Jesus to his daughter's bedside in time—was dashed.

Oh why, oh why, had Jesus gone across the lake, where He could not be reached in this hour of need? Why had that woman come just then? Why had Jesus stopped and spent all of this time with her when his own case was so dire? And now it was too late. His precious child was dead.

b. The tenderness of Jesus (5:36–43)

First, comes *a word of peace:*

> *As soon as Jesus heard the word that was spoken, he saith unto the ruler of the synagogue, Be not afraid, only believe. (5:36)*

Faith and fear pull in different directions. The Lord saw utter desolation and despair sweep over the face of Jairus. His little girl was dead! It was all over! All that was left was the funeral and an empty chair at table, an empty bed in the corner, an empty house, and an empty heart.

Nobody could raise the dead. Jairus had been to too many funerals. While there had been life, there had been hope. Now there was nothing. Who could do anything about the dead? Of course, the Bible had stories about Elijah and Elisha raising the dead, just as it had stories about Moses turning Egypt's water to blood and about Daniel in the lions' den. But that was in Bible times. That was a long time ago. It couldn't happen now.

But why not? Hadn't Jesus, just this very moment, healed a woman who had been afflicted with an incurable disease for twelve long years? Twelve years! She had begun to bleed the same time his little girl was born. It had been twelve years of horror for her, twelve years of happiness for him. And Jesus had healed her. Surely *that* fact should have spoken to him. But no! Not even Jesus could do anything now. His little one was dead.

Jesus read the whole brief struggle in the man's face and saw despair win. "Be not afraid," He said, "only believe." He had just preached on that text. "Thy faith hath made thee whole," He had said. "Now then, Jairus, you had enough faith to come. Get a fresh hold on it, man. Believe! Look at *Me* and believe. One greater than Moses, Elijah, Elisha, or Daniel is here."

Then comes *a word of perception* (5:37–40):

> *And he suffered no man to follow him, save Peter, and James, and John the brother of James. (5:37)*

The Lord, now about to perform one of His mightiest miracles, took His three closest disciples with Him into the death chamber where the little corpse lay.

This was to be a family affair. Jesus was no stage magician, no modern "faith healer" playing to an audience. This miracle, one of His greatest, was to be done privately. This was as much out of concern for Jairus and his very personal grief as for anything else. Still, the dread power of death was about to be challenged. Something that had rarely happened since the death sentence had been pronounced on Adam and Eve was about to transpire, so witnesses were desirable. All twelve of the disciples would be too many. Already the professional mourners were crowding into Jairus's house. Because the law required that "two or three witnesses" be present to establish truth, Jesus chose His three closest friends, ones who had been with Him from the beginning.

> *And he cometh to the house of the ruler of the synagogue, and seeth the tumult, and them that wept and wailed greatly. (5:38)*

It was not the first time that He had seen genuine heartbreak mingled with the professional wailing of hired mourners. That people would pay other people to come and howl at a funeral seems odd to us. Funeral customs, like wedding customs and birth and puberty celebrations, differ widely around the world and have differed throughout the ages. The Lord did not go along, however, with custom for custom's sake. He soon distinguished between those who wept real tears and those who wailed for pay.

> *And when he was come in, he saith unto them, Why make ye this ado, and weep? the damsel is not dead, but sleepeth. (5:39)*

He said much the same thing when He heard that His friend Lazarus was dead (John 11:11–13). Sleep here does not refer to the soul, which never sleeps; it refers to the body. Thus, the Lord viewed the death of a child and of a believer as no more terrifying or unnatural than sleep. Who's afraid of sleep? We court sleep. "He giveth his beloved sleep," says the psalmist (127:2).

Sleep is a strange phenomenon. We get tired, begin to yawn, seek our beds, and fall asleep. Sometimes sleep comes easily; at other times, we toss and turn before it comes. There are even times when we fight it. We drift off, at last, and the observer sees the body, its eyes closed, lying on the bed "dead to the world." But it is not dead. A mysterious process of rejuvenation is taking place as the body renews itself for a new day.

The Lord, however, saw a parallel between sleep and death. Sleep is an illustration, drawn by the hand of God, to remind us of our mortality and of the certainty of a glorious morning yet to dawn and of a wondrous awakening to a new, eternal day.

> *And they laughed him to scorn. But when he had put them all out, he taketh the father and the mother of the damsel, and them that were with him, and entereth in where the damsel was lying. (5:40)*

They laughed Him to scorn. What fools they were! He took charge at once. Some people were cast out; other people were brought in. It is always that way. The scoffers received short shrift; out they went. It must be a dark and dreadful state of soul that would cause someone to scoff at the Son of God. Well, such people have their day, then out they go. How sudden was their change from weeping to ribald laughing! How total and complete was their expulsion. How complete, on a coming day, will be the swift change from mocking to weeping and wailing and gnashing of teeth!

In my library is an illustrated copy of *The Pilgrim's Progress*. One of the full-color plates depicts Atheist. He is a well-dressed, prosperous, old man standing on the edge of a precipice. He is not looking where he is going. Indeed, the walking stick that he has in his hand and on which he is about to put his weight is poised over the gulf. He has a sneering, mocking look on his face. His whole demeanor is one of contempt. He is unaware that he is only a heartbeat from death.

So, at the house of Jairus, some people were put out, and some people were taken in. No wonder God calls the atheist a fool (Ps. 14:1)! Just five people saw what happened next—the child's parents and the Lord's three dearest earthly friends.

Now comes a word of *power* (5:41–42):

> *And he took the damsel by the hand, and said unto her, Talitha cumi; which is, being interpreted, Damsel, I say unto thee, arise. (5:41)*

He addressed the dead child in her native Aramaic. The word *Tali* is the word for a body; the word *Talitha* is the word for a girl. The word *cumi* means "Arise!" That was all He had to do and say—take her by the hand and tell her to get up!

Two words and the soul is snatched from the maw of that old lion, death. The child's pale cheeks blushed red with new life. Her eyelids fluttered. She opened her eyes, saw Jesus, and sat up! Just like that! That's healing New Testament style!

> *And straightway the damsel arose, and walked; for she was of the age of twelve years. And they were astonished with a great astonishment. (5:42)*

She soon left her bed! In a moment, she was up and about. Five of the seven people in the room stared and stared. Soon the little girl was running from one to another, the very picture of health and strength. Here was no gradual recovery! Here was no long convalescence! Here was a child who was very much dead, indeed, one moment, and very much alive the next. Nor was there any danger of a relapse. Here was divine healing indeed! No mass meetings, no showmanship, no tricks or gimmicks, no hype or hoopla, no offerings, and no failure were involved.

Mark adds the interesting note that the girl was twelve years old. Jesus, gazing at her, would doubtless remember when He Himself had been twelve. That was the age when He knew exactly who He was, who His Father was, and what His business was. Raising that twelve-year-old girl was part of His Father's business.

And, finally, there is *a word of precaution:*

> *And he charged them straitly that no man should know it; and commanded that something should be given her to eat. (5:43)*

There had been enough commotion already. The last thing that the little girl needed was for her privacy to be invaded by the sensation-seeking crowds. The paid mourners and the people thronging the gate—let them all stay there. They would make a clamor to get in if once they knew what had happened. They would want to ask a thousand questions and touch the miracle child. No! Keep them outside. Instead, give the child something to eat. After all, her sickness had depleted her reserves. Now let life go on as normal. Put something on the table for the child to eat! What practical common sense! It set the stage for life to go on as normal, although it could never be quite the same as it had been before.

What did she have for breakfast? Did Jesus bless and break the bread? He probably did not. Doubtless, He and His friends slipped away, leaving the reunited family to enjoy their miracle. Doubtless, many curious eyes watched them as they left. Doubtless, too, many people wanted to know what had happened. They were left to wonder. Jesus simply went away.

Section 3: The Servant's Ways (6:1–8:26)

A. The attitude of others toward God's Servant (6:1–29)

  1. The attitude at home (6:1–13)

    a. Rejection expressed by the hometown congregation (6:1–6)

      (1) The setting (6:1)

      (2) The synagogue (6:2a)

      (3) The sneers (6:2b–3)

        (a) A critical review (6:2b–3a)

          i. They knew His fame (6:2b–c)

            a. The fame of His wisdom (6:2b)

            b. The fame of His works (6:2c)

          ii. They knew His family (6:3a)

        (b) A crucial rejection (6:3b)

      (4) The Savior (6:4–6)

        (a) His first reaction (6:4–5)

          i. He conveyed a message (6:4)

          ii. He curtailed His ministry (6:5)

        (b) His further reaction (6:6)

          i. He marveled (6:6a)

          ii. He moved (6:6b)

    b. Rejection expected on the homeland crusade (6:7–13)

      (1) The commission (6:7)

        (a) Their enlistment (7:7a–b)

          i. The Twelve (6:7a)

          ii. The twos (6:7b)

        (b) Their enablement (6:7c)

      (2) The commands (6:8–11)

        (a) Those who would receive them (6:8–10)

          i. Living by faith (6:8–9)

          ii. Living with families (6:10)

        (b) Those who would reject them (6:11)

          i. A symbolic deed (6:11a)

          ii. A severe doom (6:11b)

      (3) The campaign (6:12–13)

        (a) The message (6:12)

      (b) The miracles (6:13)

          i. Cleansing the demoniacs (6:13a)

          ii. Curing the diseased (6:13b)

2. The attitude of Herod (6:14–29)

  a. Herod's conscience (6:14–16)

    (1) The ghost that haunted him (6:14–15)

      (a) His personal view about Jesus (6:14)

          i. What he heard (6:14a)

          ii. What he held (6:14b)

      (b) His people's view about Jesus (6:15)

    (2) The guilt that haunted him (6:16)

      (a) The murder that tormented him (6:16a)

      (b) The man who terrified him (6:16b)

  b. Herod's crime (6:17–29)

    (1) The arrest of John the Baptist (6:17–20)

      (a) Herod's reasons (6:17–18)

          i. A weak will (6:17a)

          ii. A wicked woman (6:17b)

          iii. A warning word (6:18)

      (b) Herod's reactions (6:19–20)

          i. Where he drew the line (6:19)

          ii. Why he drew the line (6:20)

    (2) The assassination of John the Baptist (6:21–29)

      (a) The day (6:21)

      (b) The dance (6:22–23)

          i. The performance (6:22)

          ii. The promise (6:23)

      (c) The demand (6:24–25)

          i. Who she asked (6:24)

          ii. What she asked (6:25)

      (d) The dismay (6:26)

      (e) The deed (6:27)

      (f) The dish (6:28)

      (g) The disciples (6:29)

—m—

Section 3: The Servant's Ways (6:1–8:26)
   A. The attitude of others toward God's Servant (6:1–29)
      1. The attitude at home (6:1–13)
         a. Rejection expressed by the hometown congregation (6:1–6)

And he went out from thence, and came into his own country; and his disciples follow him. (6:1)

He was coming home after a spectacular and successful tour of ministry. For some time now, the Lord had made Capernaum His headquarters, but on this occasion He was going back to Nazareth to visit His family and the friends of His boyhood and early manhood days. As a rule, one has a sense of anticipation about going home, especially to a place where one has had a happy childhood. Home is a place where one is loved, known, and accepted at face value, a place where one can take off one's shoes and snoop around, looking for something to eat. Home is the place of a thousand memories. Home is where one walks down the street and sees old familiar sights and greets neighbors and acquaintances at every turn. There's the milkman! And there's the village baker! And there's the carpenter's shop! How small it all seems to have become!

And when the sabbath day was come, he began to teach in the synagogue: and many hearing him were astonished, saying, From whence hath this man these things? and what wisdom is this which is given unto him, that even such mighty works are wrought by his hands? (6:2)

The Sabbath found Him in the synagogue in His usual seat and invited to teach. Of course, His fame had preceded Him. Even so, the people were not prepared for what they heard. They sat with their mouths open—His brothers and His sisters, perhaps all grown up and married now and likely with children of their own, and there's the milkman, the local butcher, the metalworker, and some of the local farmers.

They listened to the Lord Jesus as they had never listened to Him before. It slowly dawned on them that He was famous. Moreover, He taught with insight and authority. He presented old truths in a new light and stripped them of all of the encrusted tradition of the ages that the rabbis so loved. His teaching was full of illustrations drawn from everyday life. It appealed to the heart, the mind, the will, and the conscience. They had never heard such teaching before.

But, to them, He was still just a local boy. They knew the small village school that He had attended. They knew the local rabbi who had taught Him the basics of Hebrew and Scripture. He certainly had not acquired His knowledge, understanding, and wisdom from *him*. So from where did this wisdom and power come? How did He know so much? Where did He learn to speak like that? And, judging by the stories circulating about Him all over Galilee, how was He, the former village carpenter, able to do these miracles?

> *Is not this the carpenter, the son of Mary, the brother of James, and Joses, and of Juda, and Simon? and are not his sisters here with us? And they were offended at him. (6:3)*

They called Him "the carpenter." What right had a village carpenter to become a preacher? What made Him think that He was better than His brothers and sisters? They rattled off His siblings' names.

Humanly speaking, the Lord had at least four younger brothers and two younger sisters. None of them was out of the ordinary. How did He come to be so different? It offended their pride and stirred their jealousy and resentment that He was so different. What right did He have to rise above His station in life? Once a carpenter, always a carpenter! That was their philosophy. They took small-minded offense at Him.

They did not mention His Father. They referred to His mother, however. Mark does not tell us what they thought about the circumstances of His birth, but that was the ultimate explanation of the whole thing. His mother, Mary, was one of the village girls of royal descent to be sure but nonetheless a peasant—and He had no human father.

He was the Son of God. *That* was the answer to their question. That was the source of His marvelous words and mighty works. Surely it ought to have been obvious.

"They were offended at him." Why? What had He done except good? What had He said except truth? In their opinion, it was just that He was only the village boy whom they had known, some of them for thirty years. In their opinion, He should have remained a villager and been content to be the local carpenter.

> *But Jesus said unto them, A prophet is not without honour, but in his own country, and among his own kin, and in his own house. (6:4)*

What a revelation that is of the home life of the Son of God! His own natural-born brothers and sisters could not see the obvious, that He was different from them. He never quarreled, never lost His temper, never told lies, and never acted selfishly. He was never disobedient, never discourteous, and never moody. They were so accustomed to His absolute goodness and its marvelous unobtrusiveness that they failed even to see it.

As for the village itself, it was like any other village, filled with all kinds of people, including its quota of small-minded and parochial local characters. The local boy who goes out and makes a tremendous impact on the business, academic, political, or religious world is often resented as much as He is admired among the local folks where He was born and raised. The Lord's answer to the small-mindedness of the townsfolk of Nazareth was to quote them a proverb, the English equivalent of which would be, "Familiarity breeds contempt."

> *And he could there do no mighty work, save that he laid his hands upon a few sick folk, and healed them. (6:5)*

Their unbelief hindered His doing much of anything at Nazareth. He healed a few sick people, that is all. Who were they? we wonder. And why just those few and no others? It was just enough to silence the skeptics. Maybe the people whom He healed appealed to His pity because of their age, the burden that their illnesses laid on their families, or perhaps because they were the exception to the rule and saw in Him what others failed to see.

> *And he marvelled because of their unbelief. And he went round about the villages, teaching. (6:6)*

There could not have been many things at which He could marvel. There was nothing for Him to marvel at in the stars, as awesome as they are. He knew them all by number (Ps. 147:4) and by name (Isa. 40:26). There was nothing for Him to marvel at, either, in that which awed the psalmist, the amazing complexity of our physical frames (Ps. 139:14–16). He had made us Himself and understood fully the nature of the cell and the mysteries of the genetic code. There was nothing for Him to marvel at in general human spiritual blindness. He knew far better than anyone did the totality of the Fall. He had known Adam both before and after his fall.

What made Him marvel was *their* unbelief. He had lived among them for thirty years. He had exhibited before them His perfect humanity. They had heard from all over Galilee stories of His deity and of the outpouring of supernatural power in miracle after miracle. Many of them had seen some of these miracles for themselves. Yet, when He stood before them, ready and willing to demonstrate His deity in many mighty works, they stared Him down in cold, critical, and caustic unbelief. He marveled at that fact, at the hostility of His own hometown.

b. Rejection expected on the homeland crusade (6:7–13)

So He went elsewhere—to small, backwoods villages—and He concentrated on teaching, a far more lasting and profitable task than performing miracles. Note *the commission:*

> *And he called unto him the twelve, and began to send them forth*
> *by two and two; and gave them power over unclean spirits; (6:7)*

If Nazareth would have no part of Him, well, there was still the whole country to be reached. Let Nazareth nurse its nastiness. He would multiply Himself by sending out the Twelve, armed with might and miracle, to blanket the entire land with the good news of the gospel.

It was a good and wise plan to send the disciples out in pairs. "Two are better than one," said the wise man of old (Eccl. 4:9–12), and so they are. They can encourage one another, support each other's testimony (Deut. 17:6), and strengthen each other's hand in God. It would be interesting to know whom He chose to go with whom! Whom did He send with Simon the Zealot, for instance? And who went with Judas? If we were choosing the couples, whom would we match together? And why? Would the ones whom *we* would choose to be pairs be the same ones whom *He* chose? Surely He matched them according to their strengths and weaknesses and their relative dispositions, abilities, and faith. In any case, He made no mistakes, we can be sure of that.

He gave them power over unclean spirits. That was the particular fact that caught Mark's interest. There seems to have been a massive incursion of demons into the land at that time, as Satan gathered all of his agents together to fight the threat that the Lord Jesus posed to his kingdom. The disciples were empowered to confront all of the power of the enemy with His almighty power. And so they did.

Note, also, *the commands* (6:8–11):

*And commanded them that they should take nothing for their jour-
ney, save a staff only; no scrip, no bread, no money in their purse:
But be shod with sandals; and not put on two coats. (6:8–9)*

There they were, standing around Him in their everyday clothes, quite unpre-
pared as they were to be sent off then and there on a nationwide mission. "Off
you go!" He said as He paired them, "Just as you are."

It must have been a startling moment! Later, when the nation turned against
Him and He began to prepare for a global mission, He changed all of this (Luke
22:35–38). But at that time and in that place, these original marching orders
were appropriate. Countless homes would be opened to them, and hundreds of
people would contribute to their material needs. All they needed was power over
the enemy—and that He gave them in full.

*And he said unto them, In what place soever ye enter into an
house, there abide till ye depart from that place. (6:10)*

In every place someone—rich or poor, artisan or aristocrat—would be waiting for them, glad for the opportunity of extending hospitality to them. They
were not to change their lodgings, even if they felt that they were being a burden
to someone or because some more affluent or influential citizen offered them
more comfortable accommodations.

Both Elijah and Elisha had been accommodated in this way at various periods
in their ministry. The Lord Himself was content to live thus during His traveling
years. It was a system that gave the disciples an opportunity to develop their faith
and that gave others an opportunity to have practical fellowship with the Lord's
servants. It was to be an enriching experience for both groups of people.

*And whosoever shall not receive you, nor hear you, when ye depart
thence, shake off the dust under your feet for a testimony against
them. Verily I say unto you, It shall be more tolerable for Sodom
and Gomorrha in the day of judgment, than for that city. (6:11)*

Not everyone would receive them with open arms. Already the forces of reaction were at work. The Jewish religious establishment had made up its mind
against Him. To this day, not everyone is glad to hear the gospel or is appreciative
of its ministers.

It is a serious matter, however, to reject the Lord's ambassadors, more serious in God's sight, in fact, than the heinous sins of Sodom. The messenger, in his ready-made suit and his modest coat, might not look important to the worldly-wise, but he is the envoy of heaven. Woe to those who reject and abuse him; a day of reckoning is coming. Pharaoh made this mistake when Moses and Aaron confronted him. They seemed to him to be a couple of contemptible shepherds. The people of Sodom made this mistake when the two "men" passed through their gates and they sought to abuse them. The antediluvians made this mistake when they ignored the testimony of Enoch and Noah.

Note, too, *the campaign* (6:12–13):

> *And they went out, and preached that men should repent. (6:12)*

That fact must always come first. The first great work of the Holy Spirit in a human heart is to produce conviction of sin. As Jesus said, a man must know that he is sick before he will seek a doctor. It is conviction of sin, a sense of guilt and shame that leads to repentance. A man could be healed of a hundred physical ailments, but what good will it do in the end? In the end, he dies. But, if he repents and turns to Christ, he will live forever. So, while the Lord armed His disciples with might and miracle, He sent them out primarily to preach that men should repent.

> *And they cast out many devils, and anointed with oil many that were sick, and healed them. (6:13)*

Their mission resulted in outstanding success. They found that the mighty power of the Lord went with them. They made a threefold frontal attack on Satan's kingdom: *darkness* was expelled, and people repented; *demons* were cast out, and people were set free from nightmare bondage; and *disease* was eradicated, and people experienced, even on the physical level, newness of life. Many people would like to reverse the order; many prayer requests are for physical healing, but few are for salvation and sanctification.

2. The attitude of Herod (6:14–29)
   a. Herod's conscience (6:14–16)

Note, first, *the ghost that haunted him* (6:14–15):

And king Herod heard of him; (for his name was spread abroad:)
and he said, That John the Baptist was risen from the dead, and
therefore mighty works do shew forth themselves in him. (6:14)

Herod Antipas heard of the fame of Jesus. He had his own explanation: John the Baptist, he said, had come back from the dead. That was his guilty conscience speaking. Herod Antipas was the son of Herod the Great. He was the tetrarch of Galilee and Perea from 4 B.C. until he was banished in A.D. 39. Like all of the Herods, he was a thoroughly evil person.

Shakespeare says that conscience makes cowards of us all. Conscience will often lie dormant, seemingly sound asleep. Then, suddenly, the sight of a certain face, the sound of a certain voice, the mention of a certain name, a visit to a certain place, and suddenly conscience is wide awake, baying at the door of memory, or growling angrily over some deed, long dead and buried but now horribly raised and crying out for vengeance.

The name of Jesus was mentioned—brought by someone, perhaps a wife or a courtier, or an acquaintance or a friend—and Herod was reminded of somebody else—John! John the Baptist was a man whose memory Herod had been trying to forget for many months. He tried to forget the haunting memory of John the Baptist by making merry, traveling, keeping busy, and going to bed late and getting up early.

"Jesus?" Herod asked. "Maybe that's what they call him *now*. But I know who he really is. He is John, dead and buried, his head chopped off and his carcass rotting in the grave. This man is not called Jesus; he is John—John alive from the dead. He did no miracles before, but he has come back to do them now." And Herod trembled on his throne, his angry conscience snarling; his memory painting ghastly, guilty pictures; and his face white now with fear or red with shame.

Others said, That it is Elias. And others said, That it is a prophet,
or as one of the prophets. (6:15)

Unenlightened human views of Jesus are worthless. Many people are willing to pay lip service to the humanity of Christ. They will call Him a great man, a good man, or an outstanding teacher, One whose example we should emulate. They will view Him as a model and as a martyr, but they will not own Him as the Son of God. The Jews were willing to put Him on a par with the great men of their world. They would acknowledge Him as a prophet, even as a prophet come back from a bygone age, even Elijah, the wonder-working prophet of old. Today, people will equate Him with Confucius, Buddha, and Mohammed, and, in so doing, expose their unbelief because between Him and the greatest of men of Adam's ruined race is a great gulf fixed. They were men; He is God.

Note, too, *the guilt that haunted him:*

> But when Herod heard thereof, he said, It is John, whom I be-
> headed: he is risen from the dead. (6:16)

Herod was not satisfied with any of the popular speculations of his day. He had his own. It shouted down all of the others. Everywhere he looked, he saw the stern face of John. Everywhere he went, he heard the accusing voice of John. He was haunted; he lived with a ghost. He was guilty. He lived with an accusing conscience. "It is John," he said, "John, whom I beheaded."

b. Herod's crime (6:17–29)
(1) The arrest of John the Baptist (6:17–20)

> For Herod himself had sent forth and laid hold upon John, and
> bound him in prison for Herodias' sake, his brother Philip's wife:
> for he had married her. (6:17)

John the Baptist had roundly and publicly denounced Herod Antipas for his immoral behavior. Herod had conceived a guilty passion for Herodias, the wife of his brother, Herod Philip. To marry Herodias, a veritable New Testament Jezebel, Herod Antipas divorced his legal wife, the daughter of Aretas of Arabia. He then stole his brother's wife and married her. He had taken on a bad one! Herodias soon spurred Antipas to commit one act of wickedness after another, just as Jezebel had spurred Ahab to commit wicked acts. Herodias was ambitious. The promotion of her brother Agrippa to be a *king* excited her envy. She prevailed on Antipas to go with her to Rome to ask for a crown. Caligula refused to grant her the crown and banished the worthless tetrarch. So much for Herodias's ambition! So much for Herod's stolen wife! She was a woman who nursed resentful spite against John.

> For John had said unto Herod, It is not lawful for thee to have
> thy brother's wife. (6:18)

With all of the boldness of an Old Testament prophet, John had denounced Herod's marital juggling. That boldness would cost John his life. Herodias was furious, never forgave him, bided her time, and stoked the fire of her wrath. Herod was not provoked at John the Baptist to the same extent as Herodias was because he half admired and half feared the man. In any case, the people popularly regarded John as a prophet; therefore, he was able to command enormous crowds. Moreover, Herod had made an implacable enemy of his former father-in-law, Aretas, who was now mobilizing his army for war against him. To infuriate the friends and followers of John under these threatening circumstances would be madness. So Herod prevaricated, and Herodias plotted.

> *Therefore Herodias had a quarrel against him, and would have killed him; but she could not: (6:19)*

For the time being, at least, although he was besotted with Herodias, Antipas managed to ward off her furious demand that John be executed at once. He compromised. He gave orders for John to be arrested and incarcerated, but he would not kill him. Moreover, Herod stood unexpectedly firm, and Herodias fumed and nursed her desire for revenge. Revenge would be sweet.

> *For Herod feared John, knowing that he was a just man and an holy, and observed him; and when he heard him, he did many things, and heard him gladly. (6:20)*

John was a far stronger man than Herod Antipas was. Herod, like King Agrippa with Paul, was fascinated by John. John drew him as a candle draws a moth, and, like a moth, Herod danced in John's orbit. He feared him too. Tragically, however, he did not fear him half enough. Nonetheless, he took every opportunity to hear what John had to say. Perhaps he hoped that John might court him, apologize to Herodias, and plead for clemency. John, however, was uncompromising when it came to sin. Herod cleaned up some peripheral areas of his life, awed as he was by John's holiness. But if he was afraid of John and fascinated by him, he was even more fascinated by Herodias and even more afraid of her. Reform is not regeneration. Going partway but not all of the way in repentance only compounds guilt.

(2) The assassination of John the Baptist (6:21–29)

> *And when a convenient day was come, that Herod on his birth-*
> *day made a supper to his lords, high captains, and chief estates of*
> *Galilee; (6:21)*

Then came what Mark calls "a convenient" (opportune) day—what Shakespeare calls "a line by us unseen which crosses every path; the hidden boundary between God's mercy and His wrath." Herod did not die that day, but he forfeited his last hope of salvation.

It had all begun with a party. Parties are dangerous affairs. It was at a party that Ahasuerus, having tried to debase his wife, Vashti, decided to divorce her. It was at a party that Belshazzar's doom was read to him. Many a person has lost his soul at a party, when drinks are flowing, bawdy jokes are flying, passions are inflamed, morals are lowered, and restraints are removed.

> *And when the daughter of the said Herodias came in, and danced,*
> *and pleased Herod and them that sat with him, the king said*
> *unto the damsel, Ask of me whatsoever thou wilt, and I will give*
> *it thee. (6:22)*

Then came Salome's provocative dance, a dance that inflamed the passions. Forgotten now, drowned by drink and buried at last by lust, was all thought of John. The lascivious dance that Salome performed had all of the men lusting and applauding. Herod himself was carried away by the performance. Even as his guests were clapping and cheering and banging their wine glasses on the table and shouting for more, Herod spoke. "Half of the kingdom," he said, "anything you want, Salome. Just ask!" Where was John now? In his stark, lonely prison, pondering his lot and praying for grace to finish well.

> *And he sware unto her, Whatsoever thou shalt ask of me, I will*
> *give it thee, unto the half of my kingdom. (6:23)*

That set the foolish, drunken promise in concrete. It was as silly a promise as Jephthah's vow (Judg. 11:30–40) with equally tragic results—for someone else. Vows are all very well, although we should take even the best of them sparingly, and foolish vows ought to be discontinued. When the Jews of Babylon came to Zechariah asking if they should keep the fasts that they had vowed to keep, Zechariah annulled them at once. God had not commanded those vows;

rather, the Jews had taken them upon themselves during the Captivity to keep fresh in their memories their recent tragic history. Zechariah promptly canceled these burdensome fasts and self-imposed vows and read them a lesson in true spirituality.

Herod was now trapped by his oath, and the trap was soon to be sprung.

> *And she went forth, and said unto her mother, What shall I ask?*
> *And she said, The head of John the Baptist. (6:24)*

Herodias was Herod's Jezebel. She hated the truth as Jezebel hated it and was moved with malice toward John as Jezebel was toward Elijah. The only difference was that Herod had bowed to his wife and put John in prison, whereas Jezebel never could get Ahab to lay his hands on Elijah. Also, Elijah was armed with might and miracle, whereas John did no miracles.

Salome might as well have gone to a black widow spider for advice as to Herodias! Salome must have had much of her mother about her or she surely would have shrunk in horror at her mother's terrible reply. "What shall I ask?" Back came the instantaneous response: "The head of John the Baptist."

> *And she came in straightway with haste unto the king, and asked,*
> *saying, I will that thou give me by and by in a charger the head of*
> *John the Baptist. (6:25)*

"Straightway!" "With haste!" "At once!" We detect behind these words the urgent prompting of Herodias. "Hurry, girl. Don't wait. He'll change his mind. Run!" Thus was this young woman, a Herod to the core of her being, precipitated on her way. It was a terrible demand that she made quite apart from the fact that John was "a prophet and more than a prophet," and, as Jesus said, "the greatest man born of a woman." That fact only aggravated Salome's sin. She was without shame, as her obscene dance had just confirmed. She was without conscience, as her hurrying on such an errand and delivering her demand with such determination and in such detail testified. But then, the Herods made a specialty of murdering their consciences.

> *And the king was exceeding sorry; yet for his oath's sake, and*
> *for their sakes which sat with him, he would not reject her.*
> *(6:26)*

The king was caught, and he knew it. He must either lose face in front of all of his noble guests or execute a man he both respected and feared. It did not take him long to make up his mind. He would rather be a murderer than a perjurer. "Execute him," he said to a soldier. "Then bring his head here on a dish." Now perhaps Herodias would be quiet. Maybe he had silenced Herodias. He had certainly silenced God. God never spoke to him again (Luke 23:8–11). But his murdered conscience rose from the dead to haunt his dreams. Thus it was that when he heard of Jesus, his conscience told him that it was John, risen from the dead. When, at last, Jesus did stand before him, He refused to speak to him. Herod responded by jeering at Him. So, having first murdered John, Herod ended up mocking Jesus.

"Sorry!" Is that what Mark says? No, he says, "*Exceeding* sorry!" Which only proves that remorse is not repentance. We can be sorry and then go on to do worse. "Sorry is as sorry does," says the proverb. Herod was sorry that his drunken tongue had landed him in such an awkward situation. But he was not sorry enough to do what was right. He was not sorry about his sin; he went on to commit worse ones. He was only sorry that he had said what he'd said and that he had no way out of his predicament, except to confess himself in the wrong. But with the curious eyes of his guests upon him, the implacable eye of Herodias in his thoughts, and the mocking eye of Salome challenging him, he forgot all about the all-seeing eye of God.

> And immediately the king sent an executioner, and commanded
> his head to be brought: and he went and beheaded him in the
> prison, (6:27)

Herod did not take long to make up his mind. A nod to the executioner, and the dreadful deed was done. Down in the depths of the dreadful dungeon John heard the sound of approaching feet. Had the Messiah moved at last? Had Herod decided to loose him and let him go? The key turned in the lock. The light, held high by one of the guards, fell full on the grim form of the executioner standing there, axe in hand. And, in an instant, it was all over. John was dead, and Herod was damned. John took his place on high in the ranks of the martyrs of the faith, along with Abel, Isaiah, Zechariah, and countless others besides. He was at once both the last prophet to die in the Old Testament age and the first one to die in the New Testament age. "He was the greatest." That was the Lord's own assessment of John. That was the man whom Herod murdered to still the tongue of his wanton wife.

*And brought his head in a charger, and gave it to the damsel: and
the damsel gave it to her mother. (6:28)*

A dreadful pause ensued while the executioner departed on his errand. Then
came the sound of returning footsteps and, ah! the first glimpse of the grisly
token. With what shrinking horror, we wonder, did this young woman receive
the proffered dish? Were the eyes of the fearless prophet open, staring blindly at
her from the plate? Did she ever rid herself of the sight of that head?

Eugene Sue, in his book *The Wandering Jew,* imagined the daughter of Herodias,
driven from all human kind, condemned to wander the world, age after age,
doing endless penance for her deed until the coming again of Christ. It is a
fanciful notion, but it catches the seriousness of the young woman's sin. There
might be some excuse for her. Perhaps she made the request flushed with the
excitement of the occasion and spurred on by that diabolical woman, her mother.
Then, too, she was a Herod, heir to "all sin," aggravated by the lawlessness of that
demon brood.

But neither Herod nor Herodias had an excuse. The girl wasted no time in
handing her gruesome prize to her mother. Perhaps even Herodias herself was
daunted by the sight of that blood-bespattered head and ordered it to be taken
away. Perhaps, ever afterward, her dreams became nightmares and her nights
haunted by the memory of her crime. Or perhaps not. Perhaps her conscience
had already been seared as with a hot iron.

*And when his disciples heard of it, they came and took up his
corpse, and laid it in a tomb. (6:29)*

Thus ended a noble chapter in the story of God's invasion of our sin-cursed
planet. It was not the ending that John or his disciples had expected. On the
contrary, it looked as though Satan had won another victory. Unknown to most
people, a fierce battle was raging, and Satan would not yield. He would fight on,
using all of the weapons in his power. Nor would he rest until he had won an
even greater victory at a place called Calvary and the Lord's disciples would take
up *His* lifeless body and lay it, also, in a tomb.

Much good might that do the Devil! Satan's victories are hollow victories at
best. Napoleon once said of Britain, "Britain loses every battle except the last."
Satan might win one tactical victory after another in "the holy war" now being
waged, but he has already lost the strategic battle. Calvary was his biggest blunder

because the Man of Calvary is now seated in splendor on high, "from henceforth expecting till his enemies be made his footstool" (Heb. 10:13).

B. The attitude of God's Servant toward others (6:30–8:26)
    1. What was wrought (6:30–56)
        a. He met the needs of hungry people (6:30–44)
            (1) The move (6:30–31)
                (a) The disciples (6:30)
                    i. Their return (6:30a)
                    ii. Their report (6:30b)
                (b) The desert (6:31)
                    i. The proposal (6:31a)
                    ii. The pressure (6:31b)
            (2) The multitude (6:32–33)
                (a) Their deduction (6:32–33a)
                (b) Their determination (6:33b)
            (3) The Master (6:34)
                (a) His coming (6:34a)
                (b) His compassion (6:34b–c)
                    i. His recognition of their lostness (6:34b)
                    ii. His response to their lostness (6:34c)
            (4) The men (6:35–38)
                (a) A needless observation (6:35)
                (b) A natural obligation (6:36–38)
                    i. A revealing exclamation (6:36a)
                    ii. A ready excuse (6:36b–38)
                      a. How it was expressed (6:36b)
                      b. How it was exposed (6:37–38)
                        1. Give! (6:37)
                        2. Go! (6:38)
            (5) The miracle (6:39–44)
                (a) A simple precaution (6:39–40)
                (b) A supernatural provision (6:41–44)
                    i. Its source (6:41a)
                    ii. Its scope (6:41b–44)
                      a. A staggering feat (6:41b–43)
                      b. A statistical fact (6:44)

    b. He met the needs of helpless people (6:45–52)
        (1) A great desire (6:45–46)
            (a) For solitude (6:45–46a)
                i. He dismissed His companions (6:45)
                ii. He dismissed the crowds (6:46a)
            (b) For supplication (6:46b)
            (c) For silence (6:47)
        (2) A great dismay (6:48–50a)
            (a) What the tender Savior saw (6:48)
                i. Their serious situation (6:48a)
                ii. His simple solution (6:48b–c)
                    a. What He indicated (6:48b)
                    b. What He intimated (6:48c)
            (b) What the terrified sailors saw (6:49–50a)
                i. An approaching form (6:49)
                ii. An appalling fear (6:50a)
        (3) A great discovery (6:50b–51)
            (a) The Lord's comforting presence (6:50b)
            (b) The Lord's compelling power (6:51a)
        (4) A great disappointment (6:51b–52)
            (a) Their amazement expressed (6:51b)
            (b) Their amazement explained (6:52)
    c. He met the needs of hurting people (6:53–56)
        (1) Where He went (6:53)
        (2) Who He was (6:54)
        (3) What they wanted (6:55)
        (4) What He wrought (6:56)
2. What was taught (7:1–23)
    a. The crisis (7:1–4)
        (1) A delegation (7:1–2)
            (a) It was an official delegation (7:1)
            (b) It was an officious delegation (7:2)
        (2) A description (7:3–4)
            (a) Their occupation with hygiene (7:3)
            (b) Their obsession with hygiene (7:4)
    b. The criticism (7:5–13)
        (1) Questions from the critics (7:5)

        (a) Their view of the Law's demands (7:5a)

        (b) Their view of the Lord's disciples (7:5b)

    (2) Quotations by the Christ (7:6–13)

        (a) The first quotation (7:6–8)

            i. An appeal to Scripture (7:6–7)

                a. The hypocrites whom Isaiah denounced (7:6a)

                b. The hypocrisy that Isaiah denounced (7:6b–7)

            ii. An application of Scripture (7:8)

                a. What the hypocrites rejected (7:8a)

                b. What the hypocrites respected (7:8b)

        (b) The further quotation (7:9–13)

            i. An appeal to Scripture (7:9–10)

                a. Their first love (7:9)

                b. Their forsaken law (7:10)

                    1. The great prophet (7:10a)

                    2. The great precept (7:10b; Exod. 20:12)

            ii. An application of Scripture (7:11–13)

                a. Their evasive tactic described (7:11–12)

                b. Their evasive tactic denounced (7:13)

  c. The commentary (7:14–23)

    (1) Expressed for the multitudes (7:14–16)

        (a) A call to hearken (7:14–15)

            i. The summons (7:14)

            ii. The summary (7:15)

                a. A false view of defilement (7:15a)

                b. A factual view of defilement (7:15b)

        (b) A call to hear (7:16)

    (2) Explained to His men (7:17–23)

        (a) The request (7:17)

        (b) The rebuke (7:18)

        (c) The reason (7:19–22)

            i. The material side of life (7:19)

            ii. The moral side of life (7:20–22)

                a. The source of defilement (7:20–21a)

                b. The substance of defilement (7:21b–22)

        (d) The recapitulation (7:23)

3. What was thought (7:24–37)

    a. Abasement (7:24–30)
        (1) The site (7:24a)
        (2) The secret (7:24b)
        (3) The suppliant (7:25–26)
            (a) Who she was (7:25)
            (b) What she wished (7:26)
        (4) The Savior (7:27–30)
            (a) How He rebuffed her (7:27–28)
                i. His negative response (7:27)
                ii. His noble reply (7:28)
            (b) How He rewarded her (7:29–30)
                i. The decree (7:29)
                ii. The deliverance (7:30)
    b. Astonishment (7:31–37)
        (1) The move (7:31)
        (2) The man (7:32)
        (3) The miracle (7:33–35)
            (a) The contact (7:33)
            (b) The command (7:34)
            (c) The cure (7:35)
        (4) The mandate (7:36a)
        (5) The multitude (7:36b–37)
            (a) The astonishment of the people (7:36b)
            (b) The assessment of the people (7:37)
 4. What was naught (8:1–9)
    a. There was nothing for the multitudes (8:1–3)
        (1) What Jesus discerned (8:1)
        (2) What Jesus declared (8:2)
        (3) What Jesus deplored (8:3)
    b. What was nothing to the Master (8:4–9)
        (1) The size of the problem (8:4–5)
            (a) The requirement assessed (8:4)
            (b) The resources assessed (8:5)
        (2) The solution to the problem (8:6–9)
            (a) The command (8:6a)
            (b) The Christ (8:6b–7)
                i. The first miracle (8:6b)

    ii. The further miracle (8:7)

   (c) The comment (8:8–9)

    i. The abundant supply (8:8)

    ii. The abounding surprise (8:9)

5. What was sought (8:10–12)

 a. The site (8:10)

 b. The sign (8:11–12)

  (1) The sign demanded (8:11)

   (a) Interrogation (8:11a)

   (b) Incitement (8:11b)

  (2) The sign denied (8:12)

   (a) The Lord's emotional response (8:12a)

   (b) The Lord's intellectual response (8:12b)

   (c) The Lord's volitional response (8:12c)

6. What was fought (8:13–21)

 a. The disciples and their consternation (8:13–14)

  (1) The departure (8:13)

  (2) The discovery (8:14)

 b. The disciples and their confusion (8:15–21)

  (1) A blunt remark (8:15)

   (a) Beware of those who make religion a matter of pretense (8:15a)

   (b) Beware of those who make religion a matter of politics (8:15b)

  (2) A bewildered reply (8:16)

  (3) A biblical response (8:17–21)

   (a) The questions (8:17)

   (b) The quotation (8:18–20)

    i. An appeal to the prophetic word (8:18a)

    ii. An application of the prophetic word (8:18b–20)

     a. Their short memories (8:18b)

     b. His sublime miracles (8:19–20)

      1. His first miracle of supply (8:19)

      2. His further miracle of supply (8:20)

   (c) The quietus (8:21)

7. What was brought (8:22–26)

 a. The blind man's condition (8:22)

      (1) The place (8:22a)

      (2) The plea (8:22b)

   b. The blind man's cure (8:23–26a)

      (1) The partial cure (8:23–24)

         (a) Where Jesus took him (8:23a)

         (b) Where Jesus touched him (8:23b–24)

            i. An unusual act (8:23b)

            ii. An unusual fact (8:24)

      (2) The perfect cure (8:25–26a)

   c. The blind man's commands (8:26b–c)

      (1) Where he was to go (8:26b)

      (2) What he was to do (8:26c)

—⚬⚬—

B. The attitude of God's Servant toward others (6:30–8:26)

   1. What was wrought (6:30–56)

     a. He met the needs of hungry people (6:30–44)

Note, first, *the move* (6:30–31):

> *And the apostles gathered themselves together unto Jesus, and told him all things, both what they had done, and what they had taught. (6:30)*

Mark abruptly drops the story of John to continue with the story of Jesus. He picks it up at the point where the disciples came back in triumph from their preaching tour (6:7–13). What stories they had to tell of victory after victory over all of the power of the enemy! Satan had been allowed his nasty little triumph over John, but now he had to contend with Jesus, and he was no match for Him.

> *And he said unto them, Come ye yourselves apart into a desert place, and rest a while: for there were many coming and going, and they had no leisure so much as to eat. (6:31)*

The popular enthusiasm for the Lord now reached its peak. The Lord, sensing the pressure, suggested to His disciples that they take a holiday. It was a sensible suggestion. The Lord "knoweth our frame" (Ps. 103:14). We can become too busy, even in the Lord's work. God, however, is never in a hurry; neither does He expect us to be constantly on the run. After He had poured out His energy in six days of creative activity, He "rested" the seventh day—obviously, not because He was tired. A God who can lock enough energy into an atom to destroy a city and who can power a hundred billion stars in a hundred billion galaxies evidently is not a God who gets tired. He ceased from His activity because He had finished what He set out to do and because He wanted to enjoy the fruits of His labor. The Hebrew ideas of a weekly Sabbath, a Sabbath of years, and a Sabbath of Sabbaths are inherent in the Genesis account of creation. It is not a time division, however, that we derive from the nature of the universe by means of *observation*. Our days, months, and years are derived from the movement of the earth, the moon, and the sun. The idea of a *week* with its Sabbath is derived, not from deduction but from revelation. It is the *Bible* that divides our days into weeks, each week comprising six days for work and one day for rest. It is the wise provision of a loving God, One who knows how we are made and who makes provision for us to rest not only between each day but also one day out of seven.

One reason Elijah became overwrought when he fled from Jezebel was that he was worn out. "The journey is too great for thee," the angel said as he made provision for the exhausted prophet's physical and emotional needs (1 Kings 19:4–8).

So, when the disciples came back, flushed with excitement, from the triumphant missionary tour, the Lord told them that they needed a rest.

Note, too, *the multitude* (6:32–33):

> *And they departed into a desert place by ship privately. (6:32)*

So, off they went, across the lake by boat, for a little holiday. How very human Jesus was! Mark shows us the Lord Jesus, as God's Servant, busy from morning to night. He also tells us how He took a holiday.

Holidays are a great idea. How we look forward to them! Some of our happiest memories are linked to our holidays. A holiday usually is associated with a change of location and a change of occupation.

God is a great believer in holidays. He took one Himself, when He had completed His work of creation, to enjoy the fruits of His labor. In the Mosaic Law, He instituted various feasts and Sabbaths for the benefit and blessing of His people. Several of the feasts called for joyous pilgrimages to Jerusalem. So, we are not surprised to learn that Jesus and the disciples went off on a holiday.

And the people saw them departing, and many knew him, and
ran afoot thither out of all cities, and outwent them, and came
together unto him. (6:33)

It turned out to be a very short holiday indeed! Word that Jesus and His disciples were heading across the lake spread like wildfire. From all over the area, the people flocked out of their villages, ran for all they were worth to where they expected the boat to dock, and—there they were! They were not going to let this wonder-working Messiah out of their sight for a single day.

We note, also, *the Master:*

And Jesus, when he came out, saw much people, and was moved
with compassion toward them, because they were as sheep not hav-
ing a shepherd: and he began to teach them many things. (6:34)

Many of their religious leaders were false shepherds. Most of the rest were no better than sheep themselves. Sheep without a shepherd soon cease to be a flock. They wander off in all directions and become easy prey for predators. This very thing had happened to the chosen people. They were scattered and dispersed into all parts of the world, prey for all manner of religious parties and philosophies. Many of those who claimed to be their shepherds were deluded men, more concerned with the religious traditions than with divine truth. The Lord's heart went out to these lost sheep of the house of Israel and to those other sheep not of this Jewish fold (John 10:16). He would be their shepherd. So He taught them "many things," Mark said.

Then we note *the men* (6:35–38):

And when the day was now far spent, his disciples came unto
him, and said, This is a desert place, and now the time is far
passed: (6:35)

But now it was getting late. The disciples reminded the Lord of the time and the bleak nature of the place. Doubtless, the truth of the matter was that they were tired and hungry themselves. Their holiday had been ruined. As for the teaching, they had heard it all before. About now, too, they must have been heartily sick of demanding crowds. The evening shadows were lengthening. They had nowhere to get provisions. Many of these people had a long way to go;

besides, many women and children were among them. It all added up to a good excuse to get rid of them. That way, at least, the disciples could look forward to a quiet evening with the Lord and a decent night's rest.

> *Send them away, that they may go into the country round about,*
> *and into the villages, and buy themselves bread: for they have*
> *nothing to eat. (6:36)*

So they suggested to the Lord that He send the multitudes away to get something to eat in the villages round about. Blunt and practical advice—as if the Lord could not figure that out for Himself. Everybody was tired and hungry. Some of them had run halfway around the lake. The Lord Himself had been teaching all day. He could hardly go on all night. So, why not quit now while there was still sufficient daylight left for the people to go home?

It all seemed very sensible. But the Lord had a better idea.

> *He answered and said unto them, Give ye them to eat. And they*
> *say unto him, Shall we go and buy two hundred pennyworth of*
> *bread, and give them to eat? (6:37)*

This was a conservative estimate. A man would work all day for a penny in those days. The businessmen among the disciples had done some mental arithmetic. They dismissed from their minds any thought of their being of any help. Where were they going to raise something like ten thousand dollars (in today's equivalent)? It was quite out of the question.

> *He saith unto them, How many loaves have ye? go and see. And*
> *when they knew, they say, Five, and two fishes. (6:38)*

The total available supply was one little lad's lunch—five small "loaves" (pieces of pocket bread, perhaps) and a couple of little fishes—what the young boy's mother had thoughtfully provided for him.

From looking at the *demand,* which the disciples considered to be outrageous, the disciples looked at the *supply,* which they decided was equally ridiculous. The hungry boy would have polished off the whole meal in a matter of minutes. The Lord, however, was not thinking in terms of the law of supply and demand. It was not mathematics that He had in mind but a miracle!

Finally, we come to *the miracle* (6:39–44):

> *And he commanded them to make all sit down by companies*
> *upon the green grass. And they sat down in ranks, by hundreds,*
> *and by fifties. (6:39–40)*

There was to be no pushing and shoving, no scrambling or squabbling once food became available. In preparation, the Lord had everyone sit down in orderly fashion, in groups, with space enough between the groups for the disciples to walk back and forth. A ripple of happy anticipation doubtless ran through the people as they sorted themselves out and looked to the Lord.

> *And when he had taken the five loaves and the two fishes, he*
> *looked up to heaven, and blessed, and brake the loaves, and gave*
> *them to his disciples to set before them; and the two fishes divided*
> *he among them all. (6:41)*

Then followed one of the Lord's greatest miracles and the only one recorded in all four Gospels. Even John, who habitually left out of his gospel what the others recorded in theirs, included this miracle.

"He looked up to heaven." From the very beginning, the Lord had been looking beyond this world's sources of supply. The world soon exhausts what it has to offer. The Lord lived all of His life, from the cradle to the grave, with His eye on heaven.

The miracle of multiplying by dividing and of adding by subtracting began. The Lord of the atom, the Creator of the genetic code, simply bypassed all of the usual means whereby loaves and fishes are made and went into the business of doing the humanly impossible. Loaves and fishes multiplied in His hands as easily as water transformed itself into wine at His look. Given an omnipotent God, who is able to create everything—from subatomic particles to sprawling galaxies—from nothing is incredible about this miracle. It is exactly what one would expect were God to be present, manifest in flesh.

> *And they did all eat, and were filled. (6:42)*

They were hungry! Fish sandwiches! They disappeared as fast as they were produced, and still there was more, a never failing supply of energy-rich proteins and carbohydrates.

So much for vegetarianism! The Lord of glory, Creator of the universe, with all of the resources of Deity at His disposal, who just as easily could have produced baskets of fruit and vegetables, provided bread and fish. The Lord knows what is best for us. He was no vegetarian. He ate meat. He ate it in His preincarnate form when He visited Abraham (Gen. 18:1–8). He ate it at the Passover. He ate it in His resurrection body in the Upper Room. A meat diet was divinely ordained for our race after the Flood (Gen. 9:3–5) and was endorsed by the dietary code of the Mosaic Law. It was also endorsed by the vision given to Simon Peter (Acts 10:9–16). Peter was not scandalized because the net contained animals but because some of them were classified as "unclean" by Levitical law, and he was told to eat *them* as well. Peter was not scandalized at the thought of eating *meat*. After His resurrection the Lord provided a breakfast for a group of His disciples on the shore of the lake. The meal included fish. Obviously, then, the Bible does not advocate a vegetarian diet.

> *And they took up twelve baskets full of the fragments, and of the fishes. And they that did eat of the loaves were about five thousand men. (6:43–44)*

Mark gives the figure of five thousand men. Matthew adds the note that women and children were also there (Matt. 14:21). It was a notable miracle. So-called "liberal" theologians (although why such persistently narrow-minded materialists should be called "liberal" is hard to say) deny that the miracle ever happened.

In spite of the wild guesses of agnostic theologians, the four Evangelists agree that the Lord Jesus manufactured that meal miraculously. There was enough food for everyone, with plenty left over besides. John and Matthew, the Evangelists, were both there when it happened, so theirs is a reliable eyewitness account—far better than the speculations of skeptical theologians.

The *Lord* now proposed to send the multitudes away. A great deal of messianic fervor was in the air. The well-fed multitudes were disposed to force the pace, acclaim Him King, mobilize Galilee, and march on Jerusalem. They wanted bread and miracles to become a permanent thing.

The Lord dismissed the disciples first, lest they should join the rising clamor. He had no intention of either founding the kind of kingdom that the crowd had in mind or of being stampeded into accepting a crown by popular demand. The Romans had a saying, *vox populi, vox Dei:* "The voice of the *people* is the voice of God." Jesus did not think so. He listened moment by moment to the voice of *God.* He did not recognize the still, small voice of God in a clamorous majority vote.

b. He met the needs of helpless people (6:45–52)

Hard on the heels of the feeding of the five thousand came an even greater miracle.

First, we have *a great desire* (6:45–46):

> *And straightway he constrained his disciples to get into the ship, and to go to the other side before unto Bethsaida, while he sent away the people. And when he had sent them away, he departed into a mountain to pray. (6:45–46)*

Night descended on mountain and lake, and the last voice died away. Finally, He was alone with His Father in heaven. They had much to talk over, and although the Lord Jesus was tired after such a strenuous day, He did not allow that to interfere with His necessary quiet time alone with God.

He needed to review with His Father the growing enthusiasm of the multitudes, over whom He yearned as a Shepherd. There was also the dullness of His disciples in grasping spiritual truth. Then, too, there was the disciples' current location in the middle of the lake with a storm coming on. Beyond all of that was the mounting opposition from the establishment. He also needed to review His personal, human needs. He prayed into the night.

Then came *a great dismay* (6:47–50a):

> *And when even was come, the ship was in the midst of the sea, and he alone on the land. (6:47)*

The scene shifts suddenly to the disciples. He was here; they were there. Well He knew their mounting peril. Distance made no difference to Him. It often seems as though we are here and He is there—far, far away, removed from us and unaware of our pressing needs. But neither demons, nor disease, nor death made any difference to Him. Nor did distance, nor seeming disaster. He is Lord!

> *And he saw them toiling in rowing; for the wind was contrary unto them: and about the fourth watch of the night he cometh*

> *unto them, walking upon the sea, and would have passed by*
> *them. (6:48)*

The fourth watch of the night was from three o'clock at night until six o'clock in the morning. So they had been having a night of it. "He saw." The darkness could not conceal them from Him any more than could the distance. He saw! He always does! "Thou God seest me," was the lesson that poor Hagar learned when, for the first time in the Old Testament, the Jehovah angel ("the angel of the LORD") appeared to a human being (Gen. 16:13). The recognition of this truth changed her life.

The Evangelists record the most amazing miracles in a nonchalant, matter-of-fact way. They jot down the bare facts and leave it at that. They offer no hyperbole and make no attempt at sensationalism; they just present a bare record of what happened.

He "would have passed by them," Mark says. Jesus never intrudes. "Jesus of Nazareth passeth by" was the word that aroused the blind man (Luke 18:37). "He made as though he would have gone further," Luke says in recording the Emmaus road experience. The Lord awaited an invitation from these two before entering their home (Luke 24:28). "Ye took me not in" will be part of the indictment in the Judgment Day (Matt. 25:43).

So, there He went, walking on the waves as though they were solid pavement beneath His feet! His course would have taken Him right past the tempest-driven disciples. All of the resources of Deity were His to command, but there had to be some response from them before it could be of any benefit to them. It was terrifying to the disciples to see that One out there walking on the tossing sea. It was even more tragic that He "would have passed by them." We must never allow that to happen.

> *But when they saw him walking upon the sea, they supposed it*
> *had been a spirit, and cried out: For they all saw him, and were*
> *troubled. (6:49–50a)*

Their terror of the storm was swallowed up by an even greater terror. They thought that they were seeing a ghost. No mortal man could walk on waves. Well they knew that the little lake, for all its beauty and bounty, was given to sudden tempests such as the one that then had them in its grip. Moreover, it was a demon-haunted spot. It was on the shores of this lake that He had cast out a legion of demons from the Gadarene. Where did they go? The legion of demons that had possessed the Gadarene had entered into the bodies of the swine, which, preferring death to devilry, had thrown themselves into this very lake. In Capernaum, too, on the shore of this same lake, the Lord had cast out many evil spirits. It is not surprising, therefore, that the disciples should have imagined that it was a ghost that they saw walking eerily upon the angry deep.

But then comes *a great discovery* (6:50b–51):

> *And immediately he talked with them, and saith unto them, Be of good cheer: it is I; be not afraid. (6:50b)*

He had their attention now. The ghostly vision horrified them because it was contrary to all experience and beyond all human explanation. The voice hushed them. Their fears dissolved instantly. It was the Lord! All was well! If it was the Lord out there, approaching through the storm, then farewell, fear. It was the sound of His voice that did it—and the cheerful word, ten simple monosyllables: "Be of good cheer!"—a word to their *emotions;* "It is I!"—a word to their *minds;* "Be not afraid!"—a word to their *wills.* Courage can be commanded. Terror can be overcome. His nearness makes the difference.

> *And he went up unto them into the ship; and the wind ceased; and they were sore amazed in themselves beyond measure, and wondered. (6:51)*

Mark, no doubt, reflecting Peter's influence, and not wishing to hurt Peter's feelings, does not tell the story of Peter's adventure (Matt. 14:22–32; John 6:15–21). He moves directly to the stilling of the storm and the effect that this miracle had on the disciples.

The storm stopped! Total calm succeeded total chaos. And there, in the boat with them, was the One who had wrought the change. He could not only bestride the heaving waves and brave the howling winds but also hush the very forces of nature to instant sleep. No wonder the disciples were "sore amazed," or awestruck! Their amazement was "beyond measure"! They were beside themselves with astonishment.

There follows *a great disappointment* (6:51b–52):

> *For they considered not the miracle of the loaves: for their heart was hardened. (6:52)*

They should not have been astonished. Indeed, their astonishment now becomes their indictment. Had they not seen Him an hour or so ago, as Lord of the harvest, multiply a boy's picnic lunch into a banquet for ten thousand people? Why should they be astonished because the winds and the waves obeyed Him? The Holy Spirit attributes that astonishment to chronic unbelief. The word for "hardened" suggests that they had grown "calloused," "dull," "void of understanding." We sometimes speak of those who have been raised under the sound of the gospel, and yet who remain in their sins, as being "gospel hardened." The disciples had become *glory* hardened. They had become so used to seeing miracles that they no longer saw them; and even when they saw them with their outward eyes, they failed to grasp their significance. Mark's emphasis is on the sad fact (and doubtless Peter told him this) that their dullness had become a settled state of mind. They ought to have known and anticipated that the Lord, having sent them on their way, would see them through, come what may.

c. He met the needs of hurting people (6:53–56)

And when they had passed over, they came into the land of Gennesaret, and drew to the shore. And when they were come out of the ship, straightway they knew him, (6:53–54)

As they drew the boat up onshore at Gennesaret on the northwest shore of the lake, it took only a moment or two for the people to recognize Him. Jesus had come! A thrill of excitement and anticipation ran through the surrounding communities. Preachers today can come into town with all kinds of advance advertisement and preparation. They can mobilize the crowds, hold meetings and conduct services. Sometimes a little stir of blessing occurs, but, usually, nothing out of the ordinary happens. The preacher says his farewells and leaves town. The vast majority of the people in that place are unmoved. Most of them do not even know that he has come and gone. Not so when Jesus came! When He came, things happened.

And ran through that whole region round about, and began to carry about in beds those that were sick, where they heard he was. (6:55)

Mark paints a picture of widespread hustle and bustle as people from all over gathered up their sick folk and carried them off to wherever He was. It was an opportunity not to be missed. Jesus was in town!

> *And whithersoever he entered, into villages, or cities, or country,*
> *they laid the sick in the streets, and besought him that they might*
> *touch if it were but the border of his garment: and as many as*
> *touched him were made whole. (6:56)*

It made no difference whether He showed up in some sizeable town, some little village, or some place in the countryside, instantly the place where He was was carpeted with sick people, begging to be allowed just to touch the mere hem of His garment—so great was their faith in His unfailing power to heal.

This was probably the high-water mark of His popularity and acclaim. If these are the things that mark pastoral success—enormous crowds, popular applause, and unfailing results—then He had it. He was now famous, but how long would it last?

2. What was taught (7:1–23)
   a. The crisis (7:1–4)

> *Then came together unto him the Pharisees, and certain of the*
> *scribes, which came from Jerusalem. (7:1)*

This seems to have been a committee of inquiry from the religious establishment. The officials in the capital were becoming increasingly angry with this Galilean Messiah. His fame was already in every town and village throughout the country. Moreover, this was becoming a popular messianic movement, and reports of a recent move in Galilee to crown Him King alarmed them. Nothing was to be allowed that might attract the attention of Rome, and certainly no movement in which the Sanhedrin was denied a leading role.

So some of the Pharisees and the scribes from Jerusalem came to see for themselves what all of the excitement was about. Doubtless, also, they wanted to find out if this new north country preacher was a solid supporter of rabbinical Judaism and a zealous upholder of both the written and the oral law.

For the moment, these Pharisees and scribes were just observers. Given their peculiar mind-set, however, and their devotion to the traditions of the elders, it would not take them long to find something to criticize. They soon found what they wanted.

> *And when they saw some of his disciples eat bread with defiled,*
> *that is to say, with unwashen, hands, they found fault. (7:2)*

That was the specialty of the Pharisees and scribes—making mountains out of molehills. Here was One who could walk upon the raging deep, and "they found fault." Here was One who could feed people by the thousands with next to nothing, and "they found fault." Here was One who "went about doing good," who spoke as never any man spoke before, and "they found fault." They found fault over a trifle, over the failure of a few of His disciples to wash their hands before eating—something that transgressed their traditions and rules!

> *For the Pharisees, and all the Jews, except they wash their hands oft, eat not, holding the tradition of the elders. And when they come from the market, except they wash, they eat not. And many other things there be, which they have received to hold, as the washing of cups, and pots, brasen vessels, and of tables. (7:3–4)*

Mark elaborates for the sake of his Gentile readers. Gentiles often observed the Jews' preoccupation with physical cleanliness. Nothing was wrong with that, nor with the lengths to which they took it. What *was* wrong was their disdain of the Gentiles because they were not equally obsessed with ritual cleanliness. Also, the religious Jews were satisfied with mere physical cleanliness, ignoring the need for inner cleanliness. Legalism often substitutes outward forms for true holiness.

b. The criticism (7:5–13)

First, we have *questions from the critics:*

> *Then the Pharisees and scribes asked him, Why walk not thy disciples according to the tradition of the elders, but eat bread with unwashen hands? (7:5)*

They had something on Him at last! He allowed His disciples to eat with dirty hands! And for this they would eventually crucify Him. Never in the history of the race had such a prophet arisen. He spoke with authority, He acted with power, and He fulfilled the things that the Scriptures foretold. He taught as no man ever taught. He performed hundreds of startling, authenticated miracles. He was good beyond all goodness. Wisdom, love, and power shone in all of His ways. But He did not make His disciples wash their hands before lunch, so He was not of God!

They picked a fight with Him over it. Such is legalism. As for their rules and regulations, they were man-made, burdensome, endless, unauthorized, and uninspired. They were not part of the inspired Scriptures and, therefore, not binding on anyone. Often, their traditions went beyond the laws of common sense. They put the emphasis on the wrong issues. They had so many man-made rules that they were impossible to remember, much less keep. They were based on false exegesis of the Scripture, and they specialized in trivia. They magnified the outward ritual rather than the inward reality. In short, the "tradition of the elders" was just that—man-made tradition, set in concrete, and more important to the Pharisees and the scribes than revealed truth, truth that not only was written in the Scriptures but also stood before them as the incarnate Christ.

Then we have *quotations by the Christ* (7:6–13):

> *He answered and said unto them, Well hath Esaias prophesied of you hypocrites, as it is written, This people honoureth me with their lips, but their heart is far from me. Howbeit in vain do they worship me, teaching for doctrines the commandments of men. (7:6–7)*

The Lord was ready for them. He had long anticipated this day. His sword was in His hand in a flash. He had Isaiah and all of the rest of the Scriptures memorized in His head, enthroned in His heart, and ready on His lips. The Pharisees and the scribes pointed to their tradition; He pointed to God's inspired truth (Isa. 29:13).

Nor did He spare their feelings. They were hypocrites, religious play actors. They were all talk. Their religion was outward, and their hearts were completely estranged from God.

That is the essence of all false religion. God, however, will be worshiped only on His terms. When the Lord talked with the Samaritan woman at the well, she raised a point of long-standing controversy. The Samaritans had once had a temple on Mount Gerizim, but it had been destroyed long ago by the Jews. The Jews, however, still had their temple in Jerusalem. Although their temple was gone, the Samaritans still believed that the mountain where it had stood was sacred. Said the woman at the well to Jesus, "Our fathers worshipped in this mountain; and ye say, that in Jerusalem is the place where men ought to worship" (John 4:20).

The Lord bluntly told her that salvation was of the Jews and that the Samaritans did not know God. However, He sought to lift her thoughts higher than mere religion with its temples and traditions. "Believe me," He said, "the hour cometh, when ye shall neither in this mountain, nor yet at Jerusalem, worship the Father. . . . But the hour cometh, and now is, when the true worshippers shall worship the Father in spirit and in truth: for the Father seeketh such to worship him" (John 4:21, 23).

The Jews had fallen into the same trap as the Samaritans whom they despised. They had set aside God's Word for their traditions. God refused to be worshiped on their legalistic terms. Their worship was vain.

> *For laying aside the commandment of God, ye hold the tradition*
> *of men, as the washing of pots and cups: and many other such like*
> *things ye do. (7:8)*

The Jews elevated their traditions above the Torah. They substituted their oral law, with its endless haggling over minutia and its burdensome rules and regulations, for the Word of God. They set aside the magnificent spiritual concepts of the Old Testament and taught the people to be preoccupied with pots and pans—as, for instance, in their endless rules regarding not seething a kid in its mother's milk.

The heart of unregenerate man always seems to lean in the same direction. The Roman Catholic Church cherishes the same love for the traditional teachings of the Fathers as do the Jews. Romanism is concerned with feasts and fasts, pilgrimages and penance, robes and rituals, and icons and images. The simple truth of the Word of God is buried beneath it all. Not that Protestant churches are much better. We develop our own outward forms and traditions. People can remain in our fellowship as long as they conform to our little rituals. That is often all that we expect of them. But Christianity is not a matter of foot washings, head coverings, infant baptism, and such things. Judging by the zeal with which their advocates defend these things and insist on them, one would think that it was all there was to being a Christian.

> *And he said unto them, Full well ye reject the commandment of*
> *God, that ye may keep your own tradition. (7:9)*

That is where legalism always ends. Our creeds become more important than God's commandments. Our interpretations, based on human cleverness, are more important than illumination by the Holy Spirit. God's law ceases to be a standard; it becomes a system that we manipulate and control until our traditions and teachings take the place of God's Word.

> *For Moses said, Honour thy father and thy mother; and, Whoso*
> *curseth father or mother, let him die the death: (7:10)*

The Lord cites a case in point. He refers them to the fifth commandment, which had to do with honoring one's parents and with the appended blessing of long life (Exod. 20:12). The rule regarding a rebellious son, who was to be put to death, was added to this commandment later (Deut. 21:18–21). The law was clear and uncluttered. A child could read it and understand it. On the one hand, parents honored; on the other hand, parents dishonored. On the one hand, the prospect of long life; on the other hand, the prospect of swift and sudden death. Nobody needed pages of rabbinical interpretation to understand that commandment. God's moral law was written for everyone to understand. But the rabbis were not content to leave it at that.

> *But ye say, If a man shall say to his father or mother, It is Corban,*
> *that is to say, a gift, by whatsoever thou mightest be profited by*
> *me; he shall be free. And ye suffer him no more to do ought for his*
> *father or his mother; (7:11–12)*

This was a lawyer's trick. A son could say to a parent, whom it was his duty to support in his old age, "I have dedicated to God that which would relieve your need." This let him off the hook as far as his parents were concerned. It was more important, in the view of the scribes and the Pharisees, that a man pay his tithes and temple taxes than that he support his needy parents. A man could even say, "I have dedicated all that I have to God," thus giving him a rabbinical loophole for evading his most obvious and basic duty—to care for his aged parents.

> *Making the word of God of none effect through your tradition,*
> *which ye have delivered: and many such like things do ye. (7:13)*

The religious leaders rendered God's Word null and void by such manipulation of the law. The Lord drew a sharp line between the written law—the law given in writing to Moses at Sinai, which He calls "the word *(logos)* of God"—and the "oral law," which the rabbis developed over many years. The Lord bluntly labels these commentaries "your traditions." All of His life He had heard the rabbis expound these traditions. They were the beginnings of the Talmud. They would grow and grow, century after century, until they were as voluminous as the

Encyclopedia Britannica. The rabbis carried these oral teachings for centuries in their incredibly capacious memories. These "traditions" set as hard as concrete and became more important to the Jews than the Bible itself. But the Lord swept all of this traditional teaching onto the rubbish heap. The authorities hated Him accordingly and plotted His destruction.

c. The commentary (7:14–23)

Note *what He expressed for the multitudes* (7:14–16):

> *And when he had called all the people unto him, he said unto them, Hearken unto me every one of you, and understand: (7:14)*

Now He turned from the scribes and the Pharisees to the multitudes. There was little hope for the leaders of the establishment; they were already set in their ways. But the rank and file was not so wedded to this legal pettifogging as to be beyond reason. Therefore, He invited them to hear and understand.

> *There is nothing from without a man, that entering into him can defile him: but the things which come out of him, those are they that defile the man. If any man have ears to hear, let him hear. (7:15–16)*

They had accused the disciples of eating with unwashed hands. It ought to have been obvious to anyone that what is expelled from the body is more unclean than that which might enter the body—a few germs, perhaps, or traces of soil and dirt from a person's hands. The body's natural defenses take care of most of that.

The expression "he that hath ears to hear, let him hear" are the Lord's alone. He employed it seven times while on earth and eight times after His ascension. He always used the expression to call particular attention to what He was saying. The use of the expression as recorded here is the sixth occasion that the Lord used it. He wanted His hearers to heed His words.

Note, also, *what He explained to His men* (7:17–23):

> *And when he was entered into the house from the people, his disciples asked him concerning the parable. (7:17)*

The Lord now turned His back on crowds and critics alike and took refuge in the house. At once, the disciples took advantage of the respite to ask Him to explain "this parable." They, at least, had discernment enough to realize that the Lord had more in mind than mere physical defilement from without and within. Even so, they failed to get the point.

> *And he saith unto them, Are ye so without understanding also?*
> *Do ye not perceive, that whatsoever thing from without entereth*
> *into the man, it cannot defile him; Because it entereth not into*
> *his heart, but into the belly, and goeth out into the draught, purging*
> *all meats? (7:18–19)*

All of this was just a natural physical function. What and how we eat does not affect our souls, only our physical well-being. Moreover, the body has its own way of disposing of its impure waste products. In any case, all ceremonial rules regarding "clean" and "unclean" meats were only temporary. Mark's expression "purging all meats" ("making all meats clean"—as in Acts 10:15) shows that the Lord anticipated the change in dispensations that would result from Pentecost. The entire ritual law, inherent in the Mosaic Law, was to be abolished, including the strict rules on eating "clean" and "unclean" animals. Peter was among the first to learn this truth (Acts 10:15), and doubtless he told his friend Mark about it. In any case, Peter's experience in the house of Simon the tanner soon became public knowledge. Mark shows that the Lord, in His own mind, had already dismissed the Hebrew dietary laws as irrelevant to spiritual life and a hindrance to the spread of the gospel in the church age.

> *And he said, That which cometh out of the man, that defileth the*
> *man. (7:20)*

The Lord now enlarged on His "parable" by focusing attention on the heart.

> *For from within, out of the heart of men, proceed evil thoughts, adul-*
> *teries, fornications, murders, Thefts, covetousness, wickedness, deceit,*
> *lasciviousness, an evil eye, blasphemy, pride, foolishness: (7:21–22)*

What a catalog of horrors! And to think that we carry all of them around in our hearts. Truly, as the prophet said, "The heart is deceitful above all things, and desperately wicked" (Jer. 17:9). No less than thirteen items are in this terrible list. In the Greek text, the first seven are in the plural; the remaining six are in the singular. All thirteen are listed in the form of an *asyndeton,* one following right after the other in rapid sequence and hurrying us on to the climax of the sentence.

The Lord looks into everyone's heart. Everywhere He looks, He sees these dreadful things. We have only to look within our own hearts to see them for ourselves. Restraints are imposed upon us by society, family, friends, conscience, the church, and the Holy Spirit, but all of these things are there just the same. Only God's grace keeps us from expressing them. No wonder Jesus told Nicodemus that we need to be born again (John 3:3).

> *All these evil things come from within, and defile the man. (7:23)*

That is the climax of the argument. This is real uncleanness, the uncleanness that destroys, and not mere ritual uncleanness. The Lord went to the heart of the matter. And how terribly defiling these things are! These are the things that wreck homes and ruin lives and start wars and spread disease. These are the things that, in their appalling and incalculable sum, were to be placed upon the Lord Jesus at Calvary and for which He would have to die.

3. What was thought (7:24–37)
   a. Abasement (7:24–30)

> *And from thence he arose, and went into the borders of Tyre and*
> *Sidon, and entered into an house, and would have no man know*
> *it: but he could not be hid. (7:24)*

The Lord's Galilean ministry was now drawing to a close. Mark tells us that He left the Sea of Galilee and moved over to the seacoast, to the vicinity of the old Phoenician strongholds of Tyre and Sidon, cities with an illustrious, though pagan, past.

The Lord seems to have had two reasons for this move. Opposition was on the rise, fanned by the arrival of the Jerusalem scribes and Pharisees. Also, the Lord still felt His need to get away from the crowds that thronged Him everywhere. He sought seclusion in the home of someone who had a house near the sea.

"He could not be hid" is Mark's terse comment! He never can be! Moses could be hid (Exod. 2:1–3), and Elijah could be hid (1 Kings 17:2–3), but Jesus cannot be hid. The commencement of His public ministry thrust Him into the limelight, and there He will remain forever.

> *For a certain woman, whose young daughter had an unclean*
> *spirit, heard of him, and came and fell at his feet: (7:25)*

The word for "young daughter" is *thugatrion*. It is a diminutive, meaning "a little daughter." Evil spirits are no respecters of age. We can well imagine the heartache of this mother when faced with the totally irresponsible behavior of her little girl. This was not ordinary badness, the kind that can be curbed and corrected by reason or by the rod. This mother realized that her little one was demon possessed.

> *The woman was a Greek, a Syrophenician by nation; and she*
> *besought him that he would cast forth the devil out of her daugh-*
> *ter. (7:26)*

She was not a Hebrew but a Gentile. The Lord's ministry, however, was still restricted at this time to "the lost sheep of the house of Israel." In the not-so-distant future—not far from these Phoenician cities, on the same stretch of seacoast, in the Roman city of Caesarea—Peter would open the door of the church to the Gentiles. But that time had not yet come. At the time of this incident, this woman's Gentile background was a handicap to her.

> *But Jesus said unto her, Let the children first be filled: for it is not*
> *meet to take the children's bread, and to cast it unto the dogs.*
> *(7:27)*

Just the same, the Lord's heart was deeply moved by this poor woman's plight. His seeming hardness toward her was just a test, that was all. And she was a woman well able to pass the test—as doubtless the Lord knew full well, just as He knew everything else about her.

The Lord did not refuse her request outright. He just posed the question of propriety—was it fitting to take food off a child's plate to feed the dogs under the table? In effect, and perhaps to the disciples' astonishment, He called this woman a dog! This was a common Jewish epitaph for the Gentiles, but we certainly would not have expected Jesus to use it. It was part of the test. The woman was not to be put off.

> *And she answered and said unto him, Yes, Lord: yet the dogs under the table eat of the children's crumbs. (7:28)*

"Yes, Lord!" She refused to be diverted by taking offense at being called a dog. She accepted the insulting title. But even dogs have their rights. All she wanted was a few crumbs. Surely those could be spared. Dogs were allowed to have what the children threw away.

There was a kindness in the Lord's words that caught the attention of this desperate mother. The word the Lord used for "dogs" was *kynarion*. It was not the pariah, scavenger dogs of the city streets to which He referred but to the little dogs, the puppies, that were domesticated as pets. The woman seized on that usage, claiming, as it were, domestication within the household of faith. She would gladly be a "doggie" if that would give her access to a crumb.

> *And he said unto her, For this saying go thy way; the devil is gone out of thy daughter. (7:29)*

The Lord did not offer to go to her house and perform the requested miracle, although His very soul had been stormed by this woman's tenacious trust. He did not have to go! Faith as strong as hers needed no more than His bare word. And His word was enough for this woman. If the Lord said that her daughter was set free, that was all she needed to hear. It ought to be enough for us.

> *And when she was come to her house, she found the devil gone out, and her daughter laid upon the bed. (7:30)*

Evidently, a violent demon had possessed her little daughter. The word for *laid* means "thrown." The demon departed, because it had to. The voice of the Son of God had reached it, and that voice could not be denied. Just the same, as happened so often when a demon was evicted by the Lord, this one vented its spite. It flung the child on the bed in a convulsion as it left.

b. Astonishment (7:31–37)

First, we note *the move:*

> *And again, departing from the coasts of Tyre and Sidon, he came*
> *unto the sea of Galilee, through the midst of the coasts of Decapolis.*
> *(7:31)*

The Lord was now drawn back again to the chief scene of His labors, the shores of Galilee. Decapolis (the Ten Cities) was located on the east side of the lake. The cities so named included Scythopolis, Hippos, Gerasa, Dion, Canatha, Raphana, and Damascus. Alexander the Great had built most of these cities although they now displayed a strong Roman influence. The Lord was putting distance between Himself and Jewish Galilee. The last time He had been on the east side of the lake, the people of Gadara had asked Him to go away. He had left the cleansed demonic there, however, to bear testimony to the great thing that the Lord had done for him. This man had done his work well because the people were willing enough now to receive the Lord into their midst.

Next, we note *the man* (7:32):

> *And they bring unto him one that was deaf, and had an impedi-*
> *ment in his speech; and they beseech him to put his hand upon*
> *him. (7:32)*

We see no indication that the man was born deaf. Possibly he became deaf, and his speech impediment was a natural result of his deafness. The Greek word that Mark used is *mogilalon*. The word suggests that the man stammered so badly that he was practically dumb. People had the greatest difficulty making out what he was trying to say. The people themselves were very sorry for this man and took the initiative in asking the Lord to heal him.

Then comes *the miracle* (7:33–35):

> *And he took him aside from the multitude, and put his fingers*
> *into his ears, and he spit, and touched his tongue; (7:33)*

The crowd always tends to intrude between the individual and Christ. Our own particular crowd, especially, often becomes an obstacle. Jesus pried the man loose from those people who were pressing around, eager, as much as anything, just to see a miracle.

We do not know why Jesus spat, probably into His hand, and then poked His fingers into the man's ears and mouth. The word that Mark uses is a strong one. It literally means "to thrust." The Lord has many ways of performing His miracles in people's lives. Possibly He was indicating to the man, who could neither hear nor speak properly, what He was about to do—heal his afflicted members.

The spitting is most interesting. Just a few verses earlier, Mark records the Lord's words: "the things which come out of him, those are they that defile a man." Such was not the case with the Lord of Glory. Even His saliva was pure and charged with power. Later, men would spit on Him, demonstrating their utter loathing and contempt. When He spat, however, it was out of compassion and with the intent to heal.

> *And looking up to heaven, he sighed, and saith unto him,*
> *Ephphatha, that is, Be opened. (7:34)*

That was "the word of his power" (Heb. 1:3). He sighed. Literally, "He groaned." And He looked up to heaven, to His Father. There was the deepest and closest communion between them. He was in touch with heaven at all times. Faced with fresh evidence of the ravages of the Fall, He shared His burden with His Father. He did not need to speak. The upward glance was enough.

Then He spoke the word. It was the first word that the poor sufferer had heard for a long time. "Be opened!" The man's ears and his mouth were both locked by some invisible force, probably demonic. But no longer!

> *And straightway his ears were opened, and the string of his tongue*
> *was loosed, and he spake plain. (7:35)*

The case was similar, in some ways, to that of the crippled woman whom the Lord healed in one of the synagogues on a Sabbath day. Luke describes that particular case with care. The woman had been bent double for eighteen years and was "bowed together." It was a long-standing condition. She "could in no wise lift herself up." The Lord "loosed" her from her infirmity, Luke says. When the ruler of the synagogue objected because the Lord healed her on the Sabbath, the Lord told the man that he was a hypocrite. He did explain, however, just exactly what He had done. The woman was "a daughter of Abraham," He said, and Satan had bound her all of this long time. It was appropriate that she be "loosed from this bond on the sabbath day" (Luke 13:10–16).

Satan had tied this man's tongue, too, it would seem. Jesus loosed him. All it took was a touch and a word, and Satan's power in this man's life was broken. Next, we have *the mandate* (7:36a):

> *And he charged them that they should tell no man:*

And we have *the multitude* (7:36b–37):

> *but the more he charged them, so much the more a great deal they published it; (7:36b)*

The human heart is all too eager to do the opposite of what the Lord commands. Possibly the Lord wanted to protect the man whom He had healed from the clamor, noise, and excitement of publicity. He would be besieged by requests to tell his story. The Lord sought to protect his privacy, but it was not to be. The more the Lord urged the people to keep quiet about this miracle, the more they blazed it abroad. Keeping quiet about such an astounding miracle made no sense to them at all.

> *And were beyond measure astonished, saying, He hath done all things well: he maketh both the deaf to hear, and the dumb to speak. (7:37)*

So the wave of His popularity crested again. His praise rang all along that eastern shore of Galilee. But the applause of the crowd does not last. Nonetheless, for just a little while longer, the Lord rode the tidal wave of human popularity.

4. What was naught (8:1–9)
   a. There was nothing for the multitudes (8:1–3)

> *In those days the multitude being very great, and having nothing to eat, Jesus called his disciples unto him, and saith unto them, (8:1)*

The Gospels record only about thirty-six miracles of the Lord, although He performed many more than that. At times, the Evangelists lump many healing miracles together in a blanket statement, as when John says that the world itself could not contain all of the books that could have been written about the things the Lord did (John 21:25).

This miracle is similar to the feeding of the five thousand, which Mark has already recorded. How many other times, we wonder, did He perform this kind of miracle? On this occasion, fewer people and smaller statistics were involved. A slightly bigger supply and a somewhat smaller demand were also involved. Therefore, we tend to overlook this miracle. We think that it was inferior to the other one. Away with such thoughts! Here was another stupendous miracle. Who but Jesus, in the history of the world, ever did the like?

> *I have compassion on the multitude, because they have now been*
> *with me three days, and have nothing to eat: (8:2)*

Here was a truly hungry crowd. Any supplies they might have bought would have long since been consumed. This crowd obviously did not want to miss anything that this astonishing Messiah said or did. They were willing to stay even though they had nothing to eat.

The Lord did not divorce His teaching from His compassion. He had not failed to note that the people, by now, were very hungry. Perhaps, too, He was getting hungry Himself. In any case, His heart was full of compassion for them all.

> *And if I send them away fasting to their own houses, they will*
> *faint by the way: for divers of them came from far. (8:3)*

That people would come from long distances to hear Him is, in itself, a compliment. No doubt, many from near and far flocked to the Lord's meetings, because they longed to hear the Word of God taught properly. The husks and slops that so many of the local preachers served satisfied nobody.

Well, they had feasted to the full on the Word of God; now they were physically hungry. For some of them, it was a long way to go home. The Lord recognized that fact. He, Himself, knew what it was to be hungry, thirsty, and weary.

b. What was nothing to the Master (8:4–9)

Note, first, *the size of the problem* (8:4–5):

> *And his disciples answered him, From whence can a man satisfy*
> *these men with bread here in the wilderness? (8:4)*

What amazing shortsightedness and what astounding unbelief! Why He had already fed similar hungry multitudes with a little lad's lunch! And it was a bigger crowd than this at that! How deep-seated is our unbelief! How slow we are to learn! Thus it was with Abraham, who, having denied Sarah before Pharaoh (Gen. 12:10–20), turned around later and denied her before Abimelech (Gen. 20:1–18). Thus it was with Elijah when he complained to the Lord about being the only believer left and then (1 Kings 19:9–10), a little later, repeated the complaint in the same words, even though the Lord had freshly restored and reassured him (1 Kings 19:13–18). And these were mature saints!

> *And he asked them, How many loaves have ye? And they said, Seven. (8:5)*

Was this a gentle hint? Was He reminding them of the feeding of the five thousand? If so, it does not seem to have provoked any response. More loaves and fewer people were on hand, but, to the disciples, it was still a meager supply and an enormous crowd. They seem to have forgotten that any demand that He made on them was ultimately a demand upon Himself, and no demand on Him can possibly be a demand that He is unable to meet. All of the infinite resources of Deity are His.

Note, also, *the solution to the problem* (8:6–9):

> *And he commanded the people to sit down on the ground: and he took the seven loaves, and gave thanks, and brake, and gave to his disciples to set before them; and they did set them before the people. And they had a few small fishes: and he blessed, and commanded to set them also before them. (8:6–7)*

Note the *methodical* way He went about resolving the situation. He knew how to control the crowd. He prevented a stampede by, first of all, having the people sit.

Note, also, the *miraculous* way He multiplied the loaves and fishes into a banquet for thousands. Only He could do that.

Note, furthermore, the *ministerial* way He arranged to get the food to the people. He put the disciples to work, ministering to the people by taking the loaves and fishes to them. That was something they could do. The Lord never does for us what we can do for ourselves. The disciples could not multiply loaves and fishes, but they could wait on the hungry multitudes. We can no more save souls than we can create stars, but we can convey the gospel to those around us. He has committed the ministry of reconciliation to us.

> *So they did eat, and were filled: and they took up of the broken meat that was left seven baskets. (8:8)*

That was not as many as the last time, but, just the same, there was "bread enough and to spare," a bounteous feast for both the disciples themselves and the multitude. Note, also, that the word for "baskets" used when the Lord fed the five thousand is *kophinos,* indicating small wicker baskets. Here, however, the word used is *spuris,* meaning a large hamper.

The story illustrates the divine superlative. Our God is not a stingy God. Jabez prayed not just that the Lord would bless him but that He would bless him *indeed* (1 Chron. 4:10). When Moses sang on the salvation side of the sea, he did not simply say, "the LORD hath triumphed!" He sang, "the LORD hath triumphed *gloriously*" (Exod. 15:1). The Lord did not simply promise to make us free. He said, "Ye shall be free *indeed.*" In the creation account, we do not simply read that "the waters brought forth," we read that the waters brought forth *"abundantly"* (Gen. 1:20). We see this divine prodigality in all of nature. We see it in all of redemption. The Lord does not offer us mercy, but *tender* mercy (Ps. 69:16); not just kindness, but *loving* kindness (Ps. 25:6). The Lord Jesus did not die for the sins of just the elect, but for "the sins of the *whole world*" (1 John 2:2). The blood of Jesus Christ, God's Son, does not cleanse us from only *some* sins; it cleanses us "from *all* sin" (1 John 1:7).

So "they were *filled,*" Mark says. Of course, they were. Look who provided the feast!

> *And they that had eaten were about four thousand: and he sent them away. (8:9)*

And surely He watched them heading off in all directions. They were full of food for thought from all that He had taught them. They were full of good food, too, and full of amazement at His miracle. Surely His heart was full as well. As He said to the disciples, after He had just won the trust of the Samaritan woman, when the disciples urged Him to eat something, "I have meat to eat that ye know not of" (John 4:32).

5. What was sought (8:10–12)

*And straightway he entered into a ship with his disciples, and
came into the parts of Dalmanutha. (8:10)*

Dalmanutha is thought to have been a place on the western shore of the Sea of
Galilee near Magdala or Tiberias. In any case, the Lord was now back on the side
of the lake where He lived and where He had performed countless miracles.

*And the Pharisees came forth, and began to question with him,
seeking of him a sign from heaven, tempting him. (8:10)*

His old enemies were back, entrenched now in their unbelief, demanding a
sign from heaven—as though He had not already given them signs enough on
earth. A sign from heaven had already been given many years earlier. When He
was born, God put a new star in the sky. When He died, God would give them
another sign from heaven—He would put out the sun. People who demand
signs, however, are rarely satisfied when they get one; they want more.

It would have been easy enough for Him to give them signs from heaven. He
could have summoned twelve legions of angels. They were there, all about Him,
with drawn swords. How would they have liked that? He could have called down
fire and brimstone from heaven, as He once had done to destroy Sodom. How
would they have liked that? He could have made the sun stand still until one side
of the earth was reduced to a desert and the other side into an arctic waste. How
would they have liked that?

*And he sighed deeply in his spirit, and saith, Why doth this gen-
eration seek after a sign? verily I say unto you, There shall no sign
be given unto this generation. (8:12)*

The word for "sighed deeply" conveys the thought of a deep groan rising from the
very depths of His being. Doubtless, the Lord heard, in this demand for a sign, the
voice of Satan. Right from the start, Satan had tempted Him to do something spectacular to prove Himself to be the Son of God. He urged Him to throw Himself
down from the pinnacle of the temple to be miraculously preserved by the angels
(Matt. 4:5–7). The Lord resolutely refused to respond to any such temptation. The
Evil One had taken over the hearts of these Pharisees, and it was his voice that He

heard. Later, mighty signs would be given at Calvary (Matt. 27:45, 51–53), but that "wicked and adulterous" generation soon forgot and ignored these signs.

6. What was fought (8:13–21)

And he left them, and entering into the ship again departed to the other side. (8:13)

How solemn! And how sad! He simply turned on His heels and left them to themselves and to their sinful unbelief. He had no more to say to them. That is a serious state of soul. It was the same when He stood before Herod. Jesus had nothing to say to him. The man who had murdered John the Baptist was quite ready to mock at Jesus, so Jesus, who read the man's heart, ignored him. The silence of God in such cases is evidence of His mercy because had He spoken, it would have been in judgment.

Now the disciples had forgotten to take bread, neither had they in the ship with them more than one loaf. (8:14)

This loaf would not be the kind of loaf with which we are familiar, capable of being cut up into slices, but the small, round pocket bread of the Middle East, one being hardly enough for one man, let alone all of the disciples. The disciples had been too busy, it would seem, to do their ordinary housekeeping tasks. But who should worry? They had with them One whose hands could make one small loaf go a very long way indeed!

And he charged them, saying, Take heed, beware of the leaven of the Pharisees, and of the leaven of Herod. (8:15)

They had just been given a sample of the leaven of the Pharisees. Leaven in Scripture is uniformly used as a symbol of evil, especially of evil doctrine. The leaven of the Pharisees was dead fundamentalism and religious hypocrisy. The leaven of Herod refers to the philosophy of the Herodians. Their leaven was worldly compromise, coming to terms with the *status quo* for the sake of material gain. The Herods were a wicked lot, but they held power and could dispense patronage. The Herodians could not see any sense in doing things that would provoke retaliation. A man such as John the Baptist would seem to them to be a very dangerous man because he denounced Herod. That was bound to make Herod angry, and an angry Herod was a danger to everyone.

> *And they reasoned among themselves, saying, It is because we have no bread. (8:16)*

The disciples were almost as bad as the Pharisees. The mention of leaven raised their thoughts no higher than bread—as if the Lord was all that concerned by their failure to lay sufficient provisions on board!

> *And when Jesus knew it, he saith unto them, Why reason ye, because ye have no bread? perceive ye not yet, neither understand? have ye your heart yet hardened? Having eyes, see ye not? and having ears, hear ye not? and do ye not remember? (8:17–18)*

Throughout the Gospels, we find this sad inability of the disciples to discern when the Lord was speaking to them in symbolic language. He spoke of leaven; they immediately thought of bread. He was referring, however, to the mind-set of the Pharisees upon whom He had just turned His back. The disciples thought that He was rebuking them for having only one loaf of bread.

The Lord was grieved at their inability to raise their thoughts beyond the material to the spiritual. Why would He, who had all power at His command, be concerned about such a paltry matter as the number of loaves they had? Sadly, He brought His teaching down to their level.

> *When I brake the five loaves among five thousand, how many baskets full of fragments took ye up? They say unto him, Twelve. And when the seven among four thousand, how many baskets full of fragments took ye up? And they said, Seven. (8:19–20)*

So much, then, for their dismal preoccupation with material things. One loaf of bread, in His hands, would have fed them all, with bread enough and to spare. *That* was what they should have been thinking, even on the low level of concern about material things.

> *And he said unto them, How is it that ye do not understand? (8:21)*

He took them back to His original statement: "Take heed, beware of the leaven of the Pharisees, and of the leaven of Herod." All of the miracles that the Lord had performed were lost on the Pharisees. All of the Lord's claims to be the Messiah were lost on the Herodians. Were these things to be lost on His disciples as well? Let them beware indeed.

7. What was brought (8:22–26)

And he cometh to Bethsaida; and they bring a blind man unto him, and besought him to touch him. (8:22)

Bethsaida was where the Lord had performed some of His greatest miracles. It was near there that He had fed the five thousand. It was to this place that the Lord retired upon being told of the murder of John the Baptist by Herod. Now He was back, and the people were eager for another miracle.

And he took the blind man by the hand, and led him out of the town; and when he had spit on his eyes, and put his hands upon him, he asked him if he saw ought. (8:23)

Scofield points out the significance of the Lord's taking the blind man out of the city to heal him. The Lord had already pronounced coming judgment on the city of Bethsaida because of its chronic unbelief (Matt. 11:21–24). So He would not now either perform a miracle in that city or allow further witness there (v. 26). Nevertheless, although His blessing had been withdrawn from the community, He would show kindness to individuals.

The Lord's method of healing this man was unusual. He spat on the man's eyes and then touched him, which is what the people had asked Him to do. Even the Lord's saliva seems to have had healing properties. Just the same, it seems an unusual thing for Him to do. It might, perhaps, be linked somehow to the curse under which the people of Bethsaida now lived.

And he looked up, and said, I see men as trees, walking. (8:24)

That was an improvement. Before, he could see nothing.

We are not told why the Lord healed this particular man in stages. Perhaps an unusual satanic hindrance was present; after all, the people of Bethsaida were under sentence of impending judgment. Perhaps the man himself only half believed. The Lord had been unable to do many mighty works in His hometown of Nazareth because of hindering unbelief (Luke 4:16–30; Mark 6:1–6). Or maybe the Lord wanted to teach a deeper lesson, namely, that spiritual illumination often comes gradually. Even the best and most mature believer really sees only partially (1 Cor. 13:12). The Lord's own disciples could barely grasp the simplest lessons and failed even the simplest tests, as they had only just proved. The Lord had only minutes before had to say to even them, "Perceive ye not? . . . Having eyes, see ye not? . . ." (vv. 17–18). Later, He would have to tell them that although He still had many things to teach them, they were in no condition to receive them; they would have to await the coming of the Holy Spirit to be fully enlightened (John 16:12–13). Even at that, He had to convert and commission an outsider (Saul of Tarsus) to be His vehicle for writing a major section of the Epistles and for revealing Christianity's profoundest truths.

> *After that he put his hands again upon his eyes, and made him look up: and he was restored, and saw every man clearly. (8:25)*

When the outlook is none too bright, it is always a good idea to look up. Having taught the lessons that He intended to convey in healing this man's blindness in stages, the Lord swept aside all obstacles, put forth His hand, and touched the man again, exerting His mighty power and healing him fully.

> *And he sent him away to his house, saying, Neither go into the town, nor tell it to any in the town. (8:26)*

He had no more to say or to show the people in that place. The coming storm clouds were now beginning to build upon the horizon. The forces of the foe were to become increasingly evident. The Lord could now see Calvary clearly on the skyline.

Evidently, this blind man did not actually live in Bethsaida. We can imagine the wonder with which he looked at everything that he saw as he made his way to wherever he lived.

Section 4: The Servant's Worth (8:27–9:13)

A. How it was recognized (8:27–38)

  1. The confession (8:27–30)

    a. Where He was (8:27a)

    b. What He wanted (8:27b–30)

      (1) The first question (8:27b–28)

        (a) The question asked (8:27b)

        (b) The question answered (8:28)

          i. John the Baptist: he must be a resurrected man (8:28a)

          ii. Elias: he must be a raptured man (8:28b)

          iii. A prophet: he must be a returned man (8:28c)

      (2) The further question (8:29–30)

        (a) The question asked (8:29a)

        (b) The question answered (8:29b–30)

          i. What the Lord enjoyed (8:29b)

          ii. What the Lord enjoined (8:30)

  2. The cross (8:31–38)

    a. A cross for the Christ (8:31–33)

      (1) The revelation (8:31)

        (a) His coming rejection (8:31a–b)

          i. Who was behind it (8:31a)

          ii. What was before Him (8:31b)

        (b) His coming resurrection (8:31c)

      (2) The rebuke (8:32–33)

        (a) How Peter rebuked the Lord (8:32)

        (b) How the Lord rebuked Peter (8:33)

    b. A cross for the Christian (8:34–38)

      (1) The cross extended (8:34)

      (2) The cross explained (8:35–37)

        (a) The logic of Calvary (8:35)

        (b) The logic of Christ (8:36–37)

      (3) The cross exonerated (8:38)

        (a) A present repudiation of Christ (8:38a)

        (b) A prospective repudiation by Christ (8:38b)

B. How it was revealed (9:1–13)

1. The pledge (9:1)
2. The place (9:2)
3. The plan (9:3–7)
    a. The vision (9:3)
    b. The visitors (9:4)
    c. The voices (9:5–7)
        (1) The silly voice (9:5–6)
            (a) What Peter said (9:5)
            (b) Why Peter spoke (9:6)
        (2) The silencing voice (9:7)
            (a) The cloud (9:7a)
            (b) The command (9:7b)
4. The person (9:8–9)
    a. The look (9:8a)
    b. The Lord (9:8b)
    c. The lesson (9:9)
        (1) What Jesus required of them (9:9a)
        (2) What Jesus revealed to them (9:9b)
5. The problems (9:10–13)
    a. The first problem (9:10)
    b. The further problem (9:11–13)
        (1) The question about Elijah asked (9:11)
        (2) The question about Elijah answered (9:12–13)
            (a) In relation to the Lord's coming to reign (9:12a)
            (b) In relation to the Lord's coming to redeem (9:12b–13)
                i. The forecast (9:12b)
                ii. The forerunner (9:13)

—⚹—

Section 4: The Servant's Worth (8:27–9:13)
A. How it was recognized (8:27–38)
  1. The confession (8:27–30)

And Jesus went out, and his disciples, into the towns of Caesarea Philippi: and by the way he asked his disciples, saying unto them, Whom do men say that I am? (8:27)

Caesarea Philippi was at the most eastern and most important of the two sources of the Jordan. The city was located in a valley at the base of Mount Herman, twenty miles north of the Sea of Galilee. Herod Philip enlarged it. He named it after Caesar but added his own name to distinguish it from Caesarea on the coast. The place also represents the northernmost limit of the Lord's travels. The time of this visit was just a week before the Transfiguration.

As the Lord and His disciples wended their way north, He asked them a question: "Whom do men say that I am?" The answer we give to that question reveals us fully. All kinds of answers are given, including the most blatant and blasphemous unbelief and the most patronizing platitudes.

> And they answered, John the Baptist: but some say, Elias; and others, One of the prophets. (8:28)

Jesus called John the Baptist the greatest man born of a woman (Matt. 11:11). John risen from the dead—that was one view that people had of Christ. Others believed that He was Elijah returned from heaven. Still others thought that He was one of the other prophets—Moses, Daniel, Jeremiah, or Ezekiel—alive from the grave. About one thing they all agreed, however: the mighty miracles performed by Jesus could be performed only by someone living in resurrection power. Thus, they equated Him with the greatest men of their history, both recent and remote.

> And he saith unto them, But whom say ye that I am? And Peter answereth and saith unto him, Thou art the Christ. (8:29)

The answers of the multitude, even those who ranked Him with their greatest prophets, were wholly inadequate. He is not to be compared with men of genius, giants though they might have been. To equate Him with Buddha, Confucius, or Muhammad is a mark of spiritual blindness. After all, those were mere men, and sinful men at that. Jesus is not to be compared with them. Between Him and them is a great gulf fixed.

The Lord gave His disciples an opportunity to give their verdict. Peter spoke for them all: "Thou art the Christ," he said. He saw Him as the Messiah, the Anointed One—Prophet, Priest, and King—the long-awaited, often-promised Kinsman-Redeemer, Son of Man and Son of God. That set Him poles apart from the rank and file of this world's great ones. And the Lord accepted Peter's statement at its face value because that is exactly who He is—the Christ—with all that is implied in that title!

And he charged them that they should tell no man of him. (8:30)

Sufficient testimony had already been given to that generation as to whom He really was. They were demanding more proofs—signs from heaven, indeed. He refused to give them any such signs. And He refused to give them any more statements. They had already made up their minds. His foes accused Him of being in league with the Evil One. Even those who were inclined to give Him full credit came far too short in their assessment of Him. After all, what prophet ever performed a tithe of the miracles that He wrought or promulgated a tithe of the truth that He taught? No! Leave them alone. Tell them nothing more. Later generations would believe. That generation had been given wonders and words enough.

2. The cross (8:31–38)

First, we have *a cross for the Christ* (8:31–38):

> *And he began to teach them, that the Son of man must suffer many things, and be rejected of the elders, and of the chief priests, and scribes, and be killed, and after three days rise again. (8:31)*

Peter's confession opened the door. He and the others, at least, had come to know just who He was. Now He could lead them on to deeper, more awesome truth. Ahead awaited—a *cross*. They had been expecting a crown.

The Evangelists give us only a summary statement. He began to teach them about the "many things" that He must suffer. Perhaps He took them through the types and shadows of the Old Testament and by way of the numerous direct prophecies such as Psalm 22; Psalm 69; and Isaiah 53. Perhaps He expounded to them the spiritual significance of the Passover and the Day of Atonement and showed them His suffering foreshadowed in all of the sacrifices of the Levitical law.

One thing was certain: that recent confrontation with the sign-seeking Pharisees at Dalmanutha showed all too clearly which way the wind was now blowing. Official Judaism had made up its mind that He was not the Christ. By what miracle of unbelief they arrived at that conclusion, only those who know their own dark depths of doubt and disbelief can say.

The "elders" comprised the original governing body of the Sanhedrin. This body had its roots in the council of seventy men Moses associated with himself by divine decree to govern Israel (Num. 11:16). The Sanhedrin came into prominence during the days that followed the Greek conquest of Palestine. In New Testament times, it consisted of the chief priests (the heads of the two dozen courses into which the priesthood was divided), the "elders" (men of age, experience, and influence), and the scribes (lawyers learned in Jewish law). It had seventy-one members, the high priest, as a rule, being the president. When in session, the members sat in a semicircle. In Jesus' day, the Sanhedrin was the Jewish supreme court. Its primary responsibilities were to guard against error and to try those who deceived the people. This group of men, as a body, now rejected Jesus, just as they had rejected John the Baptist.

"The Son of man," Jesus assured His stunned disciples, "must be killed."

"Killed?" Impossible! "*Must* be killed?" Incredible!

This is one of the mysterious "musts" of the Bible. Earlier, Jesus had reminded Nicodemus, "As Moses lifted up the serpent in the wilderness, even so *must* the Son of man be lifted up" (John 3:14). Shortly after that, John wrote, "He *must* needs go through Samaria" (John 4:4). Or, as He reminded His mother and Joseph, "Wist ye not that I *must* be about my Father's business?" (Luke 2:49).

"Must be killed!" As Peter later reminded the Jews on the Day of Pentecost, the Lord Jesus was "delivered by the determinate counsel and foreknowledge of God" (Acts 2:23). It had all been settled in heaven countless ages ago. A Kinsman-Redeemer would have to be found for the lost people of Adam's ruined race.

But His being killed would by no means end the story. "And after three days rise again," Jesus added. And possibly here He reminded them of "the sign of the prophet Jonah" (Matt. 12:39; 16:4) and the story of Abraham and Isaac on Mount Moriah (Heb. 11:17–19).

> And he spake that saying openly. And Peter took him, and began
> to rebuke him. (8:32)

The word for "openly" conveys the idea of plain, unmistakable speaking. Here were no vague hints or allusions. Here was blunt, open speech. There could be no mistaking His meaning.

It was too much for Peter. He took the Lord aside from the other disciples, as the original suggests, and began to "rebuke" Him. The word used means to remonstrate with someone. Peter had just owned Jesus to be the Christ, with all that implied in terms of unlimited wisdom and power. Now he, a mortal man, took Him aside to rebuke Him!

> *But when he had turned about and looked on his disciples, he*
> *rebuked Peter, saying, Get thee behind me, Satan: for thou*
> *savourest not the things that be of God, but the things that be of*
> *men. (8:33)*

Peter thought to shield the Lord from the embarrassment of his rebuke by taking Him apart from the others. "Not so the Lord!" Peter's offense was very serious inasmuch as he had just owned Jesus to be both Lord and Christ. The Lord turned His back on Peter and deliberately faced the disciples. Then He rebuked Peter publicly before them all. The word for "rebuked" in this case is the same word that had just been used of Peter. Peter did not realize how serious and presumptuous his action had been. The Lord saw beyond Peter's blundering, ignorant action and saw the Evil One lurking in the shadows. It was he who had prompted Peter to speak with such worldly carnality. Satan himself, the great enemy, had tried once before to get Christ to accept the crown without the cross (Matt. 4:8–10). Peter had no idea that Satan was there, still less that he had become his very instrument.

The words must have come as a shock: "Get thee behind me, Satan!" We can see now why Jesus turned His back on Peter. He did not want Peter to think for even one moment that the Lord was calling *him* Satan. No indeed! The Lord knew exactly where Satan was. He exposed him and expelled him. The shock of realizing that he had actually become Satan's tool was punishment enough for Peter.

Then, too, we have *a cross for the Christian* (8:34–38):

> *And when he had called the people unto him with his disciples*
> *also, he said unto them, Whosoever will come after me, let him*
> *deny himself, and take up his cross, and follow me. (8:34)*

The Lord now enlarges His audience and speaks to all who would follow Him, not just to His immediate disciples. The time had come for plain speaking to them too. If a cross was prepared for Him, as He had just told His disciples, a cross was also prepared for everyone who would follow Him.

So much for the so-called "prosperity" gospel! The "name it, claim it" religion is far removed from true Christianity. If the world offered Him, the Lord of Glory, a cattle shed in which to be born and a cross on which to die, why should we expect that it would offer us anything else?

The world is enemy territory. Satan goes around about it "as a roaring lion, . . . seeking whom he may devour" (1 Peter 5:8). People think it strange that Christians suffer the same horrors and hardships as other people do and that they are often so bitterly persecuted, even to the death. It is not so strange. This is a God-hating, Christ-rejecting world. It would be stranger, by far, if the Lord's people were not hated by the world.

> *For whosoever will save his life shall lose it; but whosoever shall lose*
> *his life for my sake and the gospel's, the same shall save it. (8:35)*

It is all a matter of perspective. If this life is all there is, then certainly the lot of suffering saints hardly seems worth the candle. But if a greater, grander life lies ahead, well then, as Paul puts it, the sufferings of this present time are not worth comparing with the glory yet to be revealed (Rom. 8:18).

> *For what shall it profit a man, if he shall gain the whole world,*
> *and lose his own soul? Or what shall a man give in exchange for*
> *his soul? (8:36–37)*

The issues are now broadened to include one and all. It all boils down to this: for which world are we living? The greatest commentary on this question is the divinely inspired book of Ecclesiastes, which Solomon wrote in his old age as he looked back over a misspent life. The key word in the book is *vanity*. The idea behind that word, as used in the Old Testament, is that of emptiness. Having made a terrible shipwreck of his own life, and having set the course unalterably for the shipwreck of his kingdom, Solomon had nothing to anticipate but judgment to come. In his early years upon the throne, he had lived for the world to come. Then his roving eye became taken up with women, all sorts of women, including pagan and idolatrous women. He married them by the hundred. At last, these women stole his heart completely away from God. He began to live for the wrong world, and he almost lost his soul in the process. He certainly lost his godlike wisdom and invincible power.

God brings out His scales. On the one side, He puts the whole world—something that no one has ever possessed, although many people have tried. Nimrod tried to possess it. Nebuchadnezzar tried. Napoleon tried. All failed. The Antichrist will try to gain the whole world and will, indeed, rule a global empire for a few short, shaky years. But then his rickety empire will fall apart under the judgment of God, and he himself, laden down with sins, will be plunged headlong into a lost eternity.

On the other side of the scales, God puts a human soul. The world stands revealed at once. It is too light, too flimsy a thing, when eternity's values are in view for which to give one's soul—even if there was some prospect of getting it. He is a fool who throws away his own soul in a vain effort to control even the whole world, let alone the tiny portion that is offered to him as bait by Satan, in whose lap the whole world lies (1 John 5:19).

> *Whosoever therefore shall be ashamed of me and of my words in this adulterous and sinful generation; of him also shall the Son of man be ashamed, when he cometh in the glory of his Father with the holy angels. (8:38)*

For a while, right now, Satan is the prince of this world, but his time is running out. He can bully and browbeat believers; he can mock them and martyr them. But Jesus is coming again, in glory and power and backed by the armies of heaven.

Satan has his men in our schools and colleges; sitting in the seat of the scornful; and intimidating, threatening, and seeking to bully the believer. He has his men in the business world and the world of education, men who wield power, men who curse and blaspheme and take the name of the Lord Jesus in vain, men who link that precious name to the foulest words that can be dredged from the dark sewers of the unregenerate mind. Such men try to cow the believer into silence. Satan has his men in government where they can pass laws against Christianity and threaten Christians with imprisonment, torture, and painful deaths. But Satan's time is running out.

The Lord puts it all into perspective. We are to get our eyes on *Him.* Once we see Him and remember who He is and where He is, then we shall not be ashamed of Him. And He will not be ashamed of us. As the old hymn puts it:

> Ashamed of Jesus, that dear Friend,
> On whom my hopes of heaven depend?
> Ashamed of Jesus, sooner far
> Should evening blush to own a star![1]

---

1. J. Grigg, "Ashamed of Jesus," in *Sacred Songs and Solos,* comp. Ira D. Sankey (London: Marshall, Morgan and Scott, n.d.), no. 905.

B. How it was revealed (9:1–13)

Note, first, *the pledge:*

> *And he said unto them, Verily I say unto you, That there be some*
> *of them that stand here, which shall not taste of death, till they*
> *have seen the kingdom of God come with power. (9:1)*

He was talking particularly about Peter, James, and John. The kingdom of God is not the same as the kingdom of heaven. The expression "kingdom of heaven" is Matthew's phrase, and it refers to the millennial kingdom. The kingdom of heaven is temporal. It refers to the rule of the heavens over the earth (Dan. 4:26). It embraces all kinds of people, many of whom will have to be weeded out of it. The "mystery" parables (Matt. 13) have to do with the kingdom of heaven. The kingdom of God, by contrast, is eternal and spiritual and can be entered only by means of the new birth (John 3:3, 5). In his introduction to the story of the Transfiguration, Matthew avoids his usual technical use of the expression "kingdom of heaven" and simply says, "till they see the Son of man coming in his kingdom" (Matt. 16:28).

The Lord taught His disciples to pray, "Thy *kingdom* come" (Matt. 6:10). It was the *church* that came in grace and power at Pentecost. The disciples wanted to know if the Lord was about to set up the millennial kingdom (Acts 1:6). No indeed! That was now postponed by some two thousand years. He was about to bring into being a *church.* Soon now, the church age will be over, and the time will come for the kingdom to be set up. It will come in power and glory at the Second Advent. The church age will be over, and the Rapture will have removed church-age believers from the earth. A regenerated Hebrew people will have the kingdom restored to them (Matt. 24:30–31). It is to *this* event that the Transfiguration looks.

The Lord was about to be dishonored. He was to be betrayed and given a mock trial before three earthly courts. He was to be insulted, beaten, derided, scourged, crucified, and slain—all of this on our planet. Surely, that cannot possibly be the end of it! The day must come when, right here, on this earth, the scene of such outrageous atrocities, "this same Jesus" will be owned and crowned as Sovereign, Lord, and King.

The Transfiguration was a foreshadow of that event. Only Peter, James, and John saw it. Those three men saw, in miniature, "the kingdom of God come with power." The Lord wanted His disciples to realize that the only reason the powers of darkness would be able to arrest, try, and crucify Him would be because He would let them do so (John 19:10–11).

Note, also, *the place:*

> *And after six days Jesus taketh with him Peter, and James, and John, and leadeth them up into an high mountain apart by themselves: and he was transfigured before them. (9:2)*

This remarkable incident took place on Mount Hermon on the northeast border of Palestine. The mountain towers above the old border city of Dan. Hermon is the most conspicuous and beautiful mountain in Palestine. Even in the heat of summer, one can see white bands of snow on its hoary head. It rises to a height of some ten thousand feet. The city of Caesarea Philippi was not far away. It was to this isolated spot that the Lord now led His closest earthly friends.

There He was transfigured! The word comes from the Greek *metamorphoō*, which means "to change the form or appearance." The word is used of the transformation that is to take place in the believer's behavior down here. It involves both a crisis (Rom. 12:1–2) and a process (2 Cor. 3:18).

Note, next, *the plan* (9:3–7):

> *And his raiment became shining, exceeding white as snow; so as no fuller on earth can white them. (9:3)*

All about them lay the virgin snows of Hermon. Suddenly, His very garments rivaled the driven snow for whiteness and purity. Such whiteness in a human garb had never been seen on earth.

In Bible times, the process of fulling (cleansing) clothes consisted of trampling the garments with the feet or pounding them in tubs of water to which some alkaline chemical was added. Nitre (Prov. 25:20) and soap (Matt. 3:2) are mentioned. The whitening process included rubbing the garments with chalk or earth of some kind. The process seems to have been unpleasant, causing offensive odors, and it required space for drying the clothes. For these reasons, the trade was usually carried on outside the city.

No fuller could have produced whiteness to compare with the dazzling splendor of the Lord's transfigured peasant robe. That robe without, ablaze with light, was a reflection of His stainless character within.

And there appeared unto them Elias with Moses: and they were
talking with Jesus. (9:4)

Suddenly Moses and Elijah appeared. Moses represented the law, Elijah the prophets. Both were men of might and miracle in their day. Moses died and God buried him on Mount Nebo. He represents the resurrected saints at the Rapture. Elijah was caught up living into heaven. He represents raptured saints, caught up alive into heaven at the Rapture.

Peter (whose view of the Transfiguration Mark is recording here) does not tell us about what Moses, Elijah, and the Lord Jesus were talking. Peter was too busy talking himself. Luke, however, tells us that they "spake of his decease which he should accomplish at Jerusalem" (Luke 9:31). Doubtless they reviewed all of the Old Testament Scriptures that spoke of Calvary, its cause, its cost, and its consequences. The Lord could have stepped from the Mount of Transfiguration straight into glory because the Transfiguration was God's vindication of His immaculate, peerless life. But then Moses and Elijah would have had to remain on earth, Elijah to die in due course and Moses to die again. There would have been no Rapture and no return, no church age and no kingdom.

And Peter answered and said to Jesus, Master, it is good for us to
be here: and let us make three tabernacles; one for thee, and one
for Moses, and one for Elias. (9:5)

Peter "answered." Nobody had been talking to him, but he had been listening to the conversation. Now he simply had to blurt out the muddled thoughts of his own carnal mind and offer his opinion of what ought to be done.

What he said on the mount was as bad as what he had said a week before when he had rebuked the Lord. Now he was guilty of making the same mistake as the unregenerate multitudes, who equated the Lord with John the Baptist, Elijah, and others of the prophetic order. Peter now put the Lord on a par with Elijah and Moses. He thought that it would be a good idea to stay on the mountain. The word *us* actually implies that he exhorted the Lord Jesus to join him and the others in this utterly inappropriate project.

For he wist not what to say; for they were sore afraid. (9:6)

In fact, Peter and his companions were terrified. The word *afraid* implies that they were thrown into a violent fright. The only other place where the word is found in the New Testament is in describing Moses' terror on Sinai (Heb. 12:21). Motivated by sheer terror, Peter blurted out the first nonsensical thing that came into his head.

> *And there was a cloud that overshadowed them: and a voice came*
> *out of the cloud, saying, This is my beloved Son: hear him. (9:7)*

Peter's words jarred so completely on the vision that it was withdrawn. It was replaced by the voice of the Father in open rebuke of Peter. It gave God's complete endorsement of the matchless life of the Lord Jesus and focused attention on the Lord as the only One who needed to be heard.

That voice had been heard before, at the Lord's baptism (1:11). It was to be heard again as the Lord, rejected by Israel, anticipated the day when the Gentiles would respond to Him (John 12:28).

The overshadowing cloud screened the departure of Moses and Elijah back to heaven.

Note, furthermore, *the person* (9:8–9):

> *And suddenly, when they had looked round about, they saw no*
> *man any more, save Jesus only with themselves. (9:8)*

It was all over, but Jesus was still there. It would have been all over, indeed, had Jesus been the One to go! What need was there for Moses when *He,* the Lord, was the One who fulfilled the law? What need was there for Elijah when *He,* the Lord, was the One of whom all of the prophets spoke? Far better to have Jesus than Moses, who was kept out of the Promised Land for losing his temper, or Elijah, whose ministry was terminated because he persisted in being depressed. As great as these men were, they were merely men. Jesus was the Son of God. Neither Moses nor Elijah could bring in the promised kingdom in their day, although they tried. Jesus can and will bring it in when He comes to earth again.

> *And as they came down from the mountain, he charged them*
> *that they should tell no man what things they had seen, till the*
> *Son of man were risen from the dead. (9:9)*

The Mount of Transfiguration was the high point in the Lord's earthly pilgrimage. From now on, His path led directly to the cross. The opposition would grow and become more bitter and better organized; hence, the command that Peter, James, and John keep the vision on Mount Hermon a closely guarded secret.

Note, finally, *the problems* (9:10–13):

> *And they kept that saying with themselves, questioning one with another what the rising from the dead should mean. (9:10)*

The Lord had already begun to warn the disciples that He was to be killed, and Peter had already resisted that revelation and been rebuked for his consequent behavior. The additional truth that the Lord was to rise again from the dead had not sunk in—nor would it until after it happened, and even then, some of them would be convinced only after the Lord had given them "many infallible proofs." Indeed, apart from Mary of Bethany (John 12), only the Lord's enemies seem to have taken His teaching about His resurrection seriously; even at that, they did not really believe it (Matt. 27:62–66).

Possibly Peter and the others had heard Moses and Elijah talking with the Lord about not only His death but also His resurrection. Elijah had once raised a person from the dead (1 Kings 17:17–24), and the truth of the Lord's resurrection was embedded in Moses' writings (Gen. 22:5; Heb. 11:17–18, for instance; Lev. 14:1–7).

> *And they asked him, saying, Why say the scribes that Elias must first come? (9:11)*

The word for "asked" is in the imperfect tense, meaning that they kept on asking Him.

The Old Testament ends with a prophecy of the coming of Elijah (Mal. 4:5–6). The disciples might have thought that the sudden appearance of Elijah on the Mount of Transfiguration was a fulfillment of that prophecy. If so, it was not a very satisfactory one because, in that case, the Lord would have appeared before His appointed herald! The disciples were perplexed, as many people are, over specific details of Bible prophecy, especially over the chronological sequence of events. The Lord seems reluctant to go into prophetic details at this time. The disciples were in no condition to grasp all of the intricacies of interwoven prophecies relating to the two comings of Christ. Indeed, truth about a *second* coming was not yet openly revealed.

> *And he answered and told them, Elias verily cometh first, and restoreth all things; and how it is written of the Son of man, that he must suffer many things, and be set at nought. (9:12)*

The disciples seem to have asked two questions, one about the prior appearance of Elijah, which the Lord is now about to answer (v. 13), and another question about prophecies concerning the sufferings of the Messiah as the Son of Man.

They appealed to things already written. Mark does not say to what written sources they referred, nor does he record the Lord's answer to this question. All such questions would be answered in due time. Such Scriptures as Psalm 22; Psalm 69; Isaiah 53; and Zechariah 13 would be familiar to all of them.

> *But I say unto you, That Elias is indeed come, and they have done unto him whatsoever they listed, as it is written of him. (9:13)*

The Lord was referring to John the Baptist who, although not the literal Elijah, came in the spirit and power of Elijah to call the nation back to God before the proclamation that the Christ had come (Matt. 11:14). Had the nation accepted Jesus as Messiah, then John's ministry would have made him Elijah by proxy.

The crime of Calvary, and the Jews' subsequent rejection of the Holy Spirit, necessitated an agelong postponement of the promised messianic, millennial kingdom. The stage will have to be reset for the second coming of Christ.

After the rapture of the church, the Lord will send two witnesses to call the Jewish people back to God before the return of Christ (Rev. 11:3–13). These will win 144,000 Jewish converts, who will, in turn, take the gospel of the kingdom to all nations (Rev. 7). One of the two witnesses will doubtless be Elijah himself. Probably his companion will be Enoch, the only other man to be raptured to heaven without dying.

Section 5: The Servant's Will (9:14–29)

A. The tragic development (9:14–16)
  1. What Jesus discerned (9:14)
    a. The crowd (9:14a)
    b. The critics (9:14b)
  2. What Jesus displayed (9:15)
  3. What Jesus demanded (9:16)

B. The terrible demon (9:17–27)
  1. A sad father (9:17–18)
    a. His need unmasked (9:17–18a)
      (1) How his son was possessed by the demon (9:17)
      (2) How his son was persecuted by the demon (9:18a)
    b. His need unmet (9:18b)
  2. A sobering failure (9:19)
    a. The Lord's grievous intimation (9:19a)
    b. The Lord's gracious invitation (9:19b)
  3. A satanic fiend (9:20–22a)
    a. Its perception (9:20a)
    b. Its passion (9:20b)
    c. Its persistence (9:21)
    d. Its paroxysms (9:22a)
  4. A serious fault (9:22b–24)
    a. The *if* of the man (9:22b)
    b. The *if* of the Master (9:23–24)
      (1) The rebuke (9:23)
      (2) The response (9:24)
  5. A saving Friend (9:25–27)
    a. The Lord's command (9:25)
      (1) When He spoke (9:25a)
      (2) What He said (9:25b)
    b. The Lord's compassion (9:26–27)
      (1) A terrible torment (9:26)
      (2) A tender touch (9:27)

C. The troubled disciples (9:28–29)
  1. An exclamation (9:28)
  2. An explanation (9:29)

—ᴡ—

Section 5: The Servant's Will (9:14–29)
A. The tragic development (9:14–16)

> *And when he came to his disciples, he saw a great multitude*
> *about them, and the scribes questioning with them. (9:14)*

It was a dramatic change of scenery and situation. A short while before, they had been up above, partaking of the heavenly vision, witnesses of the glory of Christ, looking in awe at visitors from the past and listening to the voice that spoke out of the cloud.

Now they had come down from the mount to a waiting world, a world in Satan's iron grip, a world that challenged and mocked and warred below. And there the other disciples were locked in futile wrangling with the scribes while a skeptical, rootless multitude milled around. Even at this first glance, it was evident that the disciples, without Christ, were out of their depth. How often we have been as powerless as they were.

> *And straightway all the people, when they beheld him, were greatly*
> *amazed, and running to him saluted him. (9:15)*

The Lord had come! All was well! But there was something about Him that filled them with awe. They were "greatly amazed." The word used means to be greatly astonished. Only Mark uses it. It occurs only here and in two other places—in Gethsemane (14:33) and at the empty tomb (16:5–6).

Something of the awesome glory of His transfiguration must have still lingered about the person of the Lord.

> *And he asked the scribes, What question ye with them? (9:16)*

But, as would soon be discovered, that was by no means all of it, for the poor father had the right idea. He would bring the boy to Jesus! The disciples were a poor substitute for Him, as much as they loved Him, as long as they had been with Him, and as often as they had seen Him cast out demons with a word. Not one of us is any substitute for Him.

B. The terrible demon (9:17–27)

We begin with *a sad father* (9:17–18):

> *And one of the multitude answered and said, Master, I have*
> *brought unto thee my son, which hath a dumb spirit; And*
> *wheresover he taketh him, he teareth him: and he foameth, and*
> *gnasheth with his teeth, and pineth away: and I spake to thy*
> *disciples that they should cast him out; and they could not.*
> *(9:17–18)*

Truly, the boy was in desperate need. It is all so graphic and vivid. The demon, said the distraught father, "taketh him." The word is *katalambanō*, from which we get our English word *catalepsy*, and it means "to seize hold of someone or something so as to make it one's own."

"He teareth him," the father continued. The word is *rhēgnumi*. The idea is that the fierce demon would dash the poor boy on the ground. It means "to distort" or "to convulse."

Then, too, the boy foamed at the mouth like a mad dog. And he gnashed with his teeth. The word is *trizō*. It suggests a shrill cry accompanied by the grinding of the teeth. As a result of these hideous contortions and sufferings, the lad was pining away. The word is *xērainō*. It means to waste away, to wither. It is used of the withering of the grass. In addition, the wretched boy was unable to speak, unable to say a word to his parents, unable to express his intolerable sufferings.

The boy's father had, at last, thought of Jesus and, unable to find Him, did the next best thing. He brought the demon-possessed boy to the Lord's disciples only to find that he might just as well have stayed at home for all they were able to do.

Next, we have *a sobering failure:*

> *He answereth him, and saith, O faithless generation, how long shall*
> *I be with you? how long shall I suffer you? bring him unto me. (9:19)*

The Lord had recently given His disciples authority over unclean spirits, and they had exercised it (6:7), so they were really without excuse. Moreover, time was getting short because the Lord knew that He would not be here much longer. He exclaimed over the terrible unbelief that lurks in even the most devoted follower's heart.

"Bring him unto me," He said. That must have been music to the father's ears. As for the scribes, they were as powerless as the disciples. They might as well hold their peace.

We look next at *a satanic fiend* (2:20–22a):

> *And they brought him unto him: and when he saw him, straight-*
> *way the spirit tare him; and he fell on the ground, and wallowed*
> *foaming. (9:20)*

This was an especially defiant and daring demon. Usually, evil spirits cried out in terror when confronted by Christ, but this one put on an exhibition of his malice and power.

"The spirit tare him," Peter recalled, as reported by Mark. He made his last malicious attack. The word used tells us that the demon completely convulsed him, so much so that the poor boy fell wallowing on the ground. The word that Mark used paints a picture of the boy's rolling over and over on the ground. Also, he was foaming at the mouth. It was just as the boy's father had described it.

> *And he asked his father, How long is it ago since this came unto*
> *him? And he said, Of a child. (9:21)*

What a childhood! How the Lord's heart must have gone out in compassion to this poor little boy. No doubt, the Lord already knew all about it. Nonetheless, He asked this question, perhaps because He wanted to impress upon the disciples, the scribes, and all of the gathered people just how long this behavior had been going on and how hard and stubborn a case of demon possession this one was. It must have been of some consolation to the disciples to know that, if they had failed, the case involved mitigating circumstances.

> *And ofttimes it hath cast him into the fire, and into the waters to*
> *destroy him: (9:22a)*

The demon, not content with inflicting this child with dumbness and tearing him with terrible convulsions, tried more than once to kill him by throwing him into the fire and into the water. It was indeed an evil spirit.

Then we have *a serious fault* (9:22b–24):

> *but if thou canst do any thing, have compassion on us, and help*
> *us. (9:22b)*

The unhappy father, disappointed in the disciples and discouraged by their failure, his faith shaken to the core, said, "If thou canst do any thing . . ."

> *Jesus said unto him, If thou canst believe, all things are possible to*
> *him that believeth. (9:23)*

He threw the man's *if* back to him. Also, He contrasted the man's *anything* with His own *all things*. With Jesus, all things are possible. One who could create a hundred billion galaxies, each composed of a hundred billion stars, was not to be daunted by the antics of a demon.

> *And straightway the father of the child cried out, and said with*
> *tears, Lord, I believe; help thou mine unbelief. (9:24)*

The word used here for "help" means literally to run to the cry of those in danger. The father confessed that he needed help not only for himself but also for his boy. The word for "child" here is a diminutive. It tells us, at last, that the boy was only a little boy, a mere infant. How utterly pitiless evil spirits are! It was sad enough for the disciples to have seen a grown man, gripped by a legion of demons, terrorize a whole community (5:1–5), but it was far worse to see a helpless child tormented as this small boy was.

But now we see *a saving Friend* (9:25–27):

> *When Jesus saw that the people came running together, he rebuked*
> *the foul spirit, saying unto him, Thou dumb and deaf spirit, I*
> *charge thee, come out of him, and enter no more into him. (9:25)*

Word had got around that Jesus was about to perform another miracle. Unlike sensation-seeking "healers" today, Jesus did not make a display of His healing powers. As soon as He saw the crowds come running, He instantly cast out the demon and made an end of it before a crowd could gather.

"I charge thee," he said, and the *I* is emphatic. This wicked spirit was not up against Matthew the publican, Thomas the doubter, James the less, and Jude the obscure now. He was up against the omnipotent Christ.

The spirit is described as a "foul" spirit. The word used is *akathartos*. It means corrupt, unclean, foul indeed. The spirit is also described as a "dumb and deaf" spirit, probably because it had the power to inflict both deafness and dumbness on its victim.

Demons are incorrigible, beyond all hope of reformation. This particular demon had already demonstrated its tenacity and defiance. The Lord slammed the door on the thought that the foul thing seemed to have cherished of reclaiming its victim once the Lord was gone. "Enter him no more," He said. What a relief it must have been, too, to the boy's father, to know he would never have to worry about a fresh outbreak.

> *And the spirit cried, and rent him sore, and came out of him:*
> *and he was as one dead; insomuch that many said, He is dead.*
> *(9:26)*

It was the last savage, spiteful act of this ferocious fiend. Having done his worst, the demon left the boy for dead—or so it hoped. If it couldn't have him, nobody would. Well, now it was gone, and the poor boy lay still at last. Many of the people believed the worst. They thought that the boy was dead.

> *But Jesus took him by the hand, and lifted him up; and he arose.*
> *(9:27)*

It was something that the boy would remember the rest of his life—the strong, capable hand of Jesus gently lifting him up and steadying him upon his feet to walk now in newness of life.

C. The troubled disciples (9:28–29)

> *And when he was come into the house, his disciples asked him*
> *privately, Why could not we cast him out? And he said unto them,*
> *This kind can come forth by nothing, but by prayer and fasting.*
> *(9:28–29)*

This kind! We know so little about the demon world. Evidently, different kinds of spirits exist. Their whole history is shrouded in mystery. From where do they come? Why, in contrast with fallen angels, do they crave to possess human bodies?

Why do some of them tremble at the presence of Christ? Why was this one so defiant and determined? Why did "this kind" need special prayer and fasting as a condition for the ability to expel him? Spirits of such power and wickedness evidently are quick to assess the spiritual condition of those with whom they have to do.

Section 6: The Servant's Wisdom (9:30–10:52)
A. Perfect wisdom (9:30–50)
    1. A solemn prophecy (9:30–32)
        a. A secret trip (9:30)
        b. A sad truth (9:31–32)
            (1) The prophecy of the Master (9:31)
                (a) His coming rejection (9:31a)
                (b) His coming resurrection (9:31b)
            (2) The perplexity of the men (9:32)
                (a) Their failure (9:32a)
                (b) Their fear (9:32b)
    2. A simple perspective (9:33–37)
        a. The big debate (9:33–34)
            (1) The searching question (9:33)
            (2) The sudden quiet (9:34)
        b. The big difference (9:35–37)
            (1) Illumination (9:35)
            (2) Illustration (9:36–37)
                (a) The child (9:36)
                (b) The challenge (9:37)
    3. A sectarian problem (9:38–41)
        a. The sectarian act reported (9:38)
            (1) What the Lord's disciples had seen (9:38a)
            (2) What the Lord's disciples had said (9:38b–c)
                (a) Their reaction (9:38b)
                (b) Their reason (9:38c)
        b. The sectarian act repudiated (9:39–41)
            (1) The Lord's policy (9:39)
            (2) The Lord's perspective (9:40)
            (3) The Lord's postscript (9:41)
    4. A sobering possibility (9:42–50)
        a. The exclamation (9:42)
            (1) The crime of stumbling a child (9:42a)
            (2) The consequences of stumbling a child (9:42b)
        b. The exhortation (9:43–48)
            (1) Working amiss (9:43–44)

(4) The tenderness that was conveyed (10:16)
2. Jesus and materialism (10:17–31)
   a. The sorrow of the rich man (10:17–22)
      (1) His desire (10:17)
         (a) His haste (10:17a)
         (b) His humility (10:17b)
         (c) His hope (10:17c)
      (2) His declaration (10:18–20)
         (a) The challenge of the Lord (10:18)
         (b) The challenge of the law (10:19–20)
            i. The Mosaic commandments (10:19)
            ii. The mistaken comment (10:20)
      (3) His discovery (10:21)
         (a) The Master's great love (10:21a)
         (b) The man's great lack (10:21b–c)
            i. Of practical compliance with the law (10:21b)
            ii. Of personal commitment to the Lord (10:21c)
      (4) His departure (10:22)
         (a) His sadness (10:22a)
         (b) His snare (10:22b)
   b. The sermon on the rich man (10:23–31)
      (1) A word of astonishment (10:23–27)
         (a) The great impediment (10:23–25)
            i. An illuminating principle (10:23–24)
               a. A general rule (10:23)
               b. A genuine reason (10:24)
            ii. An illustrating parable (10:25)
         (b) The great impossibility (10:26–27)
            i. An exclamation (10:26)
            ii. An explanation (10:27)
      (2) A word of assessment (10:28–31)
         (a) The question asked by Peter (10:28)
         (b) The question answered for Peter (10:29–30)
            i. Relinquishments (10:29)
               a. What we surrender (10:29a)
               b. Why we surrender (10:29b)
            ii. Rewards (10:30–31)

   a. The earthly prospect (10:30a–b)

    1. Provisions we can expect (10:30a)

    2. Persecutions we can expect (10:30b)

   b. The eternal prospect (10:30b–31)

    1. The fact (10:30b)

    2. The footnote (10:31)

C. Practical wisdom (10:32–52)

 1. A repeated prediction (10:32–34)

  a. A noted direction (10:32a)

  b. A new dread (10:32b–c)

   (1) They were awed (10:32b)

   (2) They were afraid (10:32c)

  c. A necessary disclosure (10:32d)

   (1) A deliberate disclosure (10:32d)

   (2) A detailed disclosure (10:33–34)

    (a) The trials (10:33)

     i. The Hebrew trial (10:33a)

     ii. The heathen trial (10:33b–34a)

    (b) The triumph (10:34b)

 2. A resented petition (10:35–45)

  a. A kingly setting (10:35–44)

   (1) The two disciples (10:35–40)

    (a) Their approach (10:35)

    (b) Their appeal (10:36–40)

     i. Their appeal described (10:36–37)

     ii. Their appeal discussed (10:38–39)

      a. The cup (10:38)

      b. The claim (10:39a)

      c. The clue (10:39b)

     iii. Their appeal denied (10:40)

      a. A divine limitation (10:40a)

      b. A divine legislation (10:40b)

   (2) The ten disciples (10:41–44)

    (a) Their displeasure stated (10:41)

    (b) Their displeasure studied (10:42–44)

     i. This world's way (10:42)

     ii. That world's way (10:43–44)

    a. The ministry of a servant (10:43)
    b. The ministry of a slave (10:44)
  b. A key Scripture (10:45)
   (1) The Lord gives His life in service (10:45a)
   (2) The Lord gives His life in sacrifice (10:45b)
 3. A resolute person (10:46–52)
  a. The man (10:46–47)
   (1) Where he was (10:46a)
   (2) What he was (10:46b–47)
    (a) He was a blind man (10:46b)
    (b) He was a beggar man (10:46c)
    (c) He was a believing man (10:47)
  b. The multitude (10:48)
   (1) Its displeasure ignited by Bartimaeus (10:48a)
   (2) Its displeasure ignored by Bartimaeus (10:48b)
  c. The Master (10:40–52)
   (1) The call (10:49–50)
    (a) The Master's call heralded (10:49)
    (b) The Master's call heeded (10:50)
   (2) The cure (10:51–52)
    (a) It was an individual cure (10:51)
    (b) It was an instantaneous cure (10:52a)
    (c) It was an incontrovertible cure (10:52b)

—⁓—

Section 6: The Servant's Wisdom (9:30–10:52)
 A. Perfect wisdom (9:30–50)

We begin with *a solemn prophecy* (9:30–32):

> *And they departed thence, and passed through Galilee; and he*
> *would not that any man should know it. (9:30)*

Now the Lord was on the move again, heading back toward home, seeking to keep His movements as secret as possible. The miracle-hungry crowds created interruptions that He wanted to avoid. His chief goal now was to teach His disciples as much as possible. As unpromising material as they doubtless seemed to be at this state, the future of the church and of God's program for the next two millennia were in their hands. It was far more important that He teach them than that He heal a few dozen more sick people.

> *For he taught his disciples, and said unto them, The Son of man*
> *is delivered into the hands of men, and they shall kill him; and*
> *after that he is killed, he shall rise the third day. But they under-*
> *stood not that saying, and were afraid to ask him. (9:31–32)*

"He taught." The imperfect tense is used. It is a continuation of "he began to teach" (8:31), taking us back to the previous occasion a week or so earlier when He had, at Caesarea Philippi, first broached the subject of His impending death. "The Son of man is delivered," He said. He used the present tense to indicate the imminence of His predicted sufferings. His enemies were mobilizing. The traitor, as yet unrevealed, was in their midst, possibly angry at being left with the others when Peter, James, and John had gone up the mount with Jesus, and angry, too, at being unable to cast out the deaf and dumb demon. And now all of this talk about being killed and rising again three days later! What kind of talk was *that?*

Not only Judas but also all of the other disciples were getting confused and discouraged by the Lord's word about a cross—a gallows. Not even the favored three, who had only just recently heard Elijah and Moses conversing with Jesus about His forthcoming decease—which they described as something that He would "accomplish"—understood.

Moreover, they were afraid to ask Him. Doubtless, the Lord's sharp rebuke of Peter at Caesarea Philippi made them afraid of voicing their thoughts. So they trudged along, unhappily nursing their doubts and difficulties while, all the time, the Lord taught them and would willingly have answered their questions if only they had put them into words.

Next, we have *a simple perspective* (9:33–37):

> *And he came to Capernaum: and being in the house he asked them,*
> *What was it that ye disputed among yourselves by the way? (9:33)*

They arrived back home and gathered in a house, probably Peter's. They had been unwilling to ask Him the question that they had been debating among themselves on the journey home, so He now gives them their opportunity. Evidently, they had had quite a discussion among them at some point between Lebanon and Capernaum, and the Lord's keen ears had caught the tone and tenor of it. The word for "asked" here can be rendered "kept on asking" because they were reluctant to tell Him what it was about which they had been arguing.

> *But they held their peace: for by the way they had disputed among*
> *themselves, who should be the greatest. (9:34)*

The word used can be phrased "kept on being quiet." Suddenly, they were ashamed of themselves.

We can well imagine the kind of things that they had said. Doubtless, Peter would have claimed the primacy. After all, he was the one who had made the great declaration. He was the one whose name the Lord had changed in consequence. James and John, "the sons of thunder," would have disagreed. If anyone stood highest in the Lord's favor, it was they. After all, were they not the Lord's cousins? Matthew's bid would have been universally scorned because when all was said and done, he had been a publican. Judas would have staked his claim on the grounds that he was a Judean; moreover, he was the only one to hold office. He was the treasurer. And so it would have gone on. The Lord, with Calvary now ever before His eyes, had heard it all. Now they were too ashamed to speak.

> *And he sat down, and called the twelve, and saith unto them, If*
> *any man desire to be first, the same shall be last of all, and ser-*
> *vant of all. (9:35)*

In one short sentence, He turned upside down their whole scale of values, and ours as well. The way to true greatness in the Master's service is to become the servant of all.

All about us the opposite philosophy prevails. We see men pushing their way up the corporate ladder, eager to get to the top, where prosperity and power beckon, heedless of those whom they hurt or ruin on the way up. In the political arena, we see people jockeying for position, verbally abusing each other, glad for someone else's failure, weakness, or vulnerability, which they can turn to their own advantage. We also see it in the professing church.

> *And he took a child, and set him in the midst of them: and when*
> *he had taken him in his arms, he said unto them, Whosoever*

shall receive one of such children in my name, receiveth me: and
whosoever shall receive me, receiveth not me, but him that sent
me. (9:36–37)

The principle that the Lord now proclaims reaches right up to the very throne of God. Who can read the biography of George Müller, for example, and not see the truth of it? George Müller became the servant of all. A poor, humble man, he went after the orphans of Bristol and gathered them into his home to feed, house, clothe, educate, and put them into gainful employment. There were thousands of them. Kind, gentle, meek, a servant of all, a Christlike man, Müller won the heart of the city itself. When he died, all of Bristol went to his funeral.

When the Lord took that little child in His arms and presented to the disciples the great lesson, *children* were the furthest thing from their thoughts.

Next comes *a sectarian problem* (9:38–41):

And John answered him, saying, Master, we saw one casting out
devils in thy name, and he followeth not us: and we forbad him,
because he followeth not us. (9:38)

Was that a deliberate attempt to change the subject? The idea of ministering to children and other helpless and handicapped people did not much appeal to the disciples. Perhaps John hoped to earn a word of praise for his denominational spirit. Twice he said, "he followeth not us." He was jealous for the exclusiveness, the honor, and the uniqueness of the apostolic circle to which he belonged. How dare anyone who was not of their circle use the name of Jesus to exorcise demons? To add to John's ire was the fact that this outsider was apparently successful at what he was doing, whereas the disciples themselves had but recently covered themselves with embarrassment over their failure to cast out an evil spirit.

But Jesus said, Forbid him not: for there is no man which shall
do a miracle in my name, that can lightly speak evil of me. For he
that is not against us is on our part. (9:39–40)

This party spirit has kindled the fires of persecution down through the centuries, and professional jealousy often is at the bottom of it. The Lord wanted no part of it. They should have left the man alone. The mere fact that he was using the Lord's name to cast out evil spirits was, by no means, an endorsement of either his moral character or his spiritual life. At the same time, while the man was doing that, he could not be regarded as an enemy—and the Lord had plenty of those. In any case, John did not say, "We stopped him because he does not follow *You*." He said, "We stopped him because he does not follow *us*." The Lord's word is that we should leave all such people to *Him*.

> *For whosoever shall give you a cup of water to drink in my name, because ye belong to Christ, verily I say unto you, he shall not lose his reward. (9:41)*

We are to help people, not hinder them. The thought flows smoothly from the Lord's correction of the disciples for interfering in the activities of one who did not belong to their particular crowd.

A cup of cold water! What is in view here is not the material value of the gift, which is minimal, but the spiritual value, the sharing, the encouragement, the reviving. All is made much more significant because the person thus aided belongs to Christ. The whole concept is lifted to millennial significance in the Lord's later parable of the sheep and the goats (Matt. 25:31–46).

The Lord introduces here the subject of rewards. He has in view the judgment seat of Christ. We shall discover, when standing there, that no helping hand extended to a fellow believer will go either unnoticed or unrewarded. The disciples had been thinking in terms of importance and greatness—greatness as envisioned by ambitious men. The Lord's scale of values embraced even the humblest, lowliest, most insignificant acts.

Then our attention is drawn to *a sobering possibility* (9:42–50):

> *And whosoever shall offend one of these little ones that believe in me, it is better for him that a millstone were hanged about his neck, and he were cast into the sea. (9:42)*

The word for "offend" means "to cause to stumble." The Lord might have had in mind the man whom the disciples had rebuked (v. 38) and whose faith they might have harmed. We can, of course, simply take the words at their face value. It is a serious thing to cause a child to stumble, especially one of His own children. How fearful is the punishment for those who rob a child of its innocence, who tamper with its fragile guilelessness, who are guilty of luring them into child pornography, who befoul a child to gratify their own outrageous lusts, who undermine a child's simple faith, or who betray its trust. And what about those more sophisticated destroyers who occupy the halls of learning, who sit in the seat of the scornful in schools and colleges, or who occupy professors' chairs in theological institutions and who systematically set about undermining the belief of their students in the Word of God? Surely God has a special millstone for the necks of those people.

> *And if thy hand offend thee, cut it off: it is better for thee to enter into life maimed, than having two hands to go into hell, into the fire that never shall be quenched: Where their worm dieth not, and the fire is not quenched. And if thy foot offend thee, cut it off: it is better for thee to enter halt into life, than having two feet to be cast into hell, into the fire that never shall be quenched: Where their worm dieth not, and the fire is not quenched. And if thine eye offend thee, pluck it out: it is better for thee to enter into the kingdom of God with one eye, than having two eyes to be cast into hell fire: Where their worm dieth not, and the fire is not quenched. (9:43–48)*

The word for "offend" here means constantly to cause one to stumble. *Hand! Foot! Eye! Better! Hell! Fire! Worm! Not quenched!* Could language be more forceful, more solemn? We can in no way dilute these words, phrases, and sentences. With each repetition, they are underlined, emphasized, and affirmed. To seek refuge from them because they are couched in symbolical language does not help. The use of pictorial language only makes more vivid the truth that is taught. Jesus clearly, unequivocally, and repeatedly taught that there is not only a heaven to be gained but also a hell to be shunned. Indeed, He actually spoke more about hell than He did about heaven, and He declared both to be literal realities.

So, like a man driving a stake into the ground with repeated hammer blows, the Lord drove home His warning. Don't dare tamper with His little ones!

> *For every one shall be salted with fire, and every sacrifice shall be salted with salt. (9:49)*

The focus is still on the judgment to come. In the Old Testament, offerings were salted to aid in the burning (Deut. 29:33). Our conduct is to be thoroughly tested at the judgment seat of Christ. Paul warns, "Now if any man build upon this foundation gold, silver, precious stones, wood, hay, stubble; Every man's work shall be made manifest: for the day shall declare it, because it shall be revealed by fire; and the fire shall try every man's work of what sort it is" (1 Cor. 3:10–15).

Salt is good: but if the salt have lost his saltness, wherewith will ye season it? Have salt in yourselves, and have peace one with another. (9:50)

Saltless salt! It is a contradiction in terms. The Lord had already told His disciples that they were the salt of the earth (Matt. 5:13). Before the days of refrigeration, salt was used as a preservative and an antiseptic. In the world, the believer is to act as a wholesome restraining influence on a corrupt society. Saltless salt represents profession without reality. "Have salt in yourselves, and have peace one with another," Jesus concludes, taking the disciples back to the acrimonious rivalry and carnal pushing and shoving for position that had occurred among them on the way from Hermon to Capernaum.

B. Penetrating wisdom (10:1–31)
   1. Jesus and marriage (10:1–16)
     a. The permanence of a legal oath (10:1–12)

And he arose from thence, and cometh into the coasts of Judaea by the farther side of Jordan: and the people resort unto him again; and, as he was wont, he taught them again. (10:1)

This chapter records what is usually called the Perean ministry of Christ. Mark leaves out several months of chronology to concentrate on the Lord's later ministry in Judea and on the east side of the Jordan. Galilee has now been left behind. The Lord has no more either to do or to say in that greatly blessed area where He had lived and taught for so long and performed so many of His miracles. Now Calvary looms ahead, its shadowy outline becoming clearer and clearer every day.

The people, as always, dogged His steps, and as He always did, He taught them.

And the Pharisees came to him, and asked him, Is it lawful for a man to put away his wife? tempting him. (10:2)

This was a loaded question, and well He knew it. Two matters are put side by side in this chapter—the question about divorce and the incident with the children. The two events, put thus so close together, give a picture of the Lord's ideal for the family—its essential sanctity and the need for parents to bring their children to Jesus.

Two schools of thought existed among the Jews on the subject of divorce. The rabbi Shammai espoused the narrow view, which restricted it to moral transgressions, indeed, exclusively to unchastity. Actually, however, Jewish law allowed divorce on almost any grounds. The rabbi Hillel espoused the liberal view, which allowed divorce for almost anything. A woman could be divorced for spoiling her husband's dinner, for going outside the house with her head uncovered, for being quarrelsome, for being childless, or even if the husband found some other woman more attractive.[1] The Pharisees doubtless hoped to make the Lord take sides on this controversial issue, thus alienating Him from many people on one side or the other. They were "tempting" Him. The word used means "to put to the test." They wanted to force Him to commit Himself on a highly controversial issue.

> *And he answered and said unto them, What did Moses com-*
> *mand you? And they said, Moses suffered to write a bill of di-*
> *vorcement, and to put her away. (10:3–4)*

The Law of Moses to which they referred is found in Deuteronomy 24:1–4. A man who discovered something shameful or offensive in his wife could dismiss her from his house with a writ of divorcement. Such ground of divorce obviously had to be something other than adultery because adultery very speedily dissolved the marriage by means of death. A great deal was left to the discretion of the husband; the wife had few rights. The Pharisees knew all about the Mosaic Law and the body of rabbinical traditional teaching that had developed around it.

> *And Jesus answered and said unto them, For the hardness of your*
> *heart he wrote you this precept. (10:5)*

In other words, somewhere in every case of divorce is hardness. Often, it is a leading cause of divorce in the first place. Sometimes it is a subsequent factor that

---

1. Alfred Edersheim, *The Life and Times of Jesus the Messiah* (Grand Rapids: Eerdman's, 1959), 2:333–34.

becomes evident when positions become cemented into place and unfairness and acrimony develop.

> *But from the beginning of the creation God made them male and female. (10:6)*

The Lord now sidesteps both the narrowness of Shammai and the liberalism of Hillel. He circumvents, also, the concession to human hardness found in the Mosaic Law. He takes His questioners back to God and His original intent in creating people male and female. Obviously, the plan was for the two to supplement and complement each other in love and harmony. Marriage, after all, was God's ideal for the human race. A happy human home is a place about as close to heaven as will ever be found on earth. Paul says that the relationship that God planned was to be similar to that ordained between Christ and His church. Adam's paradise was not complete until God introduced him to Eve.

> *For this cause shall a man leave his father and mother, and cleave to his wife; And they twain shall be one flesh: so then they are no more twain, but one flesh. (10:7–8)*

The Lord was precise in His choice of words here. The word for "leave" is a very strong one—*kataleipō*. It is "to leave behind," "to depart from," or "to forsake." When a couple get married, they must not have as an unspoken option or reservation in their minds the possibility of running back to Mom and Dad. No! The old ties are broken, and a new bond is forged.

The word for "cleave" is *proskollaō*. It means literally "to glue," or "to cement." God intends for the bond formed by marriage to be strong and permanent, one that is not easily dissolved. The two become one.

> *What therefore God hath joined together, let not man put asunder. (10:9)*

When a couple nowadays begin to talk of the possibility of a divorce, they do not begin here, but this is where God begins. In our permissive society today, people are all too willing to break their marriage vows. God says that these vows are sacred and strong and not to be easily set aside. Indeed, from the divine point of view, no man has any right to break apart a marriage once God has welded the two into one. Only great pain, loss, wreckage, and ruin can result from trying to force asunder what God has forged together.

> *And in the house his disciples asked him again of the same matter. (10:10)*

The disciples themselves were far from satisfied by this answer, so doubtless the Pharisees certainly were not happy with it either.

> *And he saith unto them, Whosoever shall put away his wife, and marry another, committeth adultery against her. And if a woman shall put away her husband, and be married to another, she committeth adultery. (10:11–12)*

In Mark's account are no *ifs, ands,* or *buts.* Matthew gives the fuller account, the exception the Lord acknowledges, the inability of some people to accept these absolutes, and the various options in terms of remarriage (Matt. 19:3–12).

Mark simply records the ideal. He shows us marriage, divorce, and remarriage from God's standpoint. The divine standard calls for perfection and allows for nothing less. Those who take Mark's account alone do not get the full picture, but they do get a view of the permanence, perfection, and purity of marriage and the general unacceptability of divorce from the standpoint of heaven. Mark does not look at the other side of the issue—that we are imperfect people living in a sinful environment. Matthew does consider that other side, and it is a mistake to isolate Mark's teaching from Matthew's teaching.

b. The preciousness of a little one (10:13–16):

> *And they brought young children to him, that he should touch them: and his disciples rebuked those that brought them. (10:13)*

The disciples seem to have been fond of doing that kind of thing! A little while back, they had forbidden a man to cast out demons in Jesus' name because he didn't belong to their group. Now they were officiously bullying some mothers for wanting to have their children blessed by Jesus. Doubtless, they thought it part of their calling to shield Jesus from His own public, especially from His having to be bothered with mere children. How little they knew Him!

The verb *brought* is in the imperfect tense, implying that they kept on bringing their children. The word for children is *paidion,* a diminutive, implying young children and infants, although the word does not exclude older children. Probably the children were of all ages.

The disciples "rebuked" these mothers. The word used conveys the thought of injustice. It is "to reprimand." It is in the imperfect tense, suggesting that they were not being very successful in driving away these women, who were determined to have their little ones blessed by the Lord.

> *But when Jesus saw it, he was much displeased, and said unto*
> *them, Suffer the little children to come unto me, and forbid them*
> *not: for of such is the kingdom of God. (10:14)*

Much displeased! The word used has been rendered various ways. It means "to feel pain" or "to be indignant" (2 Cor. 7:11). The disciples thought that the Master was far too important to be bothered with small children. Jesus, by contrast, thought that small children were too important *not* to be brought to Him in their tender years. The disciples rebuked the mothers, but the Lord rebuked the disciples. He bluntly told His disciples to stop hindering these little ones from being brought to Him.

Statistics gathered over many years have shown that, generally, more people are saved when they are children than at any other time of life. A child's heart is tender and impressionable. Children are great believers. They have not yet succumbed to the world and its ways.

The classic example of the importance of childhood conversion is Moses. He was born under the sentence of death, but his mother hid him at home for as long as she could. That is the purpose for homes. They should be places of refuge. They should be kept free from all harmful influences and forces of this hostile, hateful world. When Jochebed could no longer hide Moses at home, she put him in a little ark, modeled on Noah's ark. It was to be a place of refuge from the wrath of the prince of this world. Both the ark of Moses and the ark of Noah pictured salvation from wrath, a salvation found only in Christ. Moses' mother received her son back as from the dead to rear him during his most impressionable years. Before Pharaoh's daughter, who adopted him, was able to bring the influence of this world to bear upon Moses, his mother rooted and grounded him in the faith. Indeed, Jochebed did such a thorough job of indoctrinating the young child that, when he grew up, not all of the power, the pleasures, or the prospects of Egypt could tempt him! Such is the power of a godly home.

No wonder Jesus, with a heart full of love, demanded that the little ones be brought to Him! How He longed to bless these children, their mothers, and their homes!

It is surely significant that the incident of the children immediately follows the Lord's teaching on divorce. The family must be protected at all costs. Divorce is a terrible destroyer of children.

> *Verily I say unto you, Whosoever shall not receive the kingdom of God as a little child, he shall not enter therein. And he took them up in his arms, put his hands upon them, and blessed them. (10:15–16)*

We must come to Jesus with all of the simplicity, sincerity, and eagerness of a little child. It is commonplace nowadays to see in our great shopping malls at Christmastime parents bringing their little children to see a dressed-up Santa Claus. Even the most skeptical of children cannot resist the temptation of climbing up on Santa's knee to tell him solemnly all of the things they want for Christmas, while their parents look on full of pride. They take pictures, the children enjoy themselves, and even passersby are attracted. But it is all a solemn farce, and we know it, but we go along with it just the same.

How much more eager we should be to bring our children to that One who gives meaning to Christmas, the One who was born in Bethlehem, who was once a little boy, who went through all of the stages of growing up, the One who alone can truly satisfy the needs and wants of this world's little ones.

We, too—as grown up, sophisticated, and worldly-wise as we are—need to lay everything aside and come with childlike trust to Him.

Those mothers of old were not sent away empty. One after the other, the Lord took their children in His arms and touched them with His holy hands. He blessed them. It was an experience that they would never forget. When they were old themselves, those grown-up children would say to their children and grandchildren, "Yes, He once put His hands on me. I remember. . . ."

2. Jesus and materialism (10:17–31)

We note *the sorrow of the rich man* (10:17–22):

> *And when he was gone forth into the way, there came one run-*
> *ning, and kneeled to him, and asked him, Good Master, what*
> *shall I do that I may inherit eternal life? (10:17)*

We do not know why this man was in a hurry. He ran. He flung himself at Jesus' feet. Evidently, he had been greatly moved by something that Jesus had said or done. "Good Master!" he began. The word he used was *didaskalos,* "Teacher," or to use our modern title "Doctor." The parallel Hebrew term would be "Rabbi."

Luke, in recording this incident, calls the young man by the word *archōn,* "a first one," that is, a man of prominence. The word was used to describe the ruler of a synagogue or an outstanding Pharisee (Matt. 9:18; Luke 14:1; 18:18). It seems also to have been used to designate a member of the Sanhedrin, a great man, or a prince. Evidently, the young man was someone of importance, which makes his homage to the Lord Jesus all the more remarkable. Many people in positions of authority, especially those who were connected with the Jewish establishment, were becoming increasingly hostile to Christ. Even those who were not actively His enemies tended to be patronizing. This young man, however, was eager to learn. As young as he was, as rich, and as influential as he was, he sensed a need in his life and had the good sense to come to Christ. He addressed the Lord as "*Good* Master," and doubtless he was sincere. The goodness of Jesus was self-evident to all who had eyes with which to see and ears with which to hear. It was probably in this very area of goodness that the young man sensed his own lack. He did not come to Jesus seeking some material benefit, as did so many other people. Rather, he came wanting to know what to do to inherit eternal life. He had inherited wealth, position, and influence—all of the things that people covet—but he had not inherited eternal life. So as rich as he was, he was poor, and as great as he was, he was lost.

His basic error is revealed in what he said. "What shall I *do* that I may *inherit. . . .*" A person does not *do* anything to inherit; an inheritance is some-thing that we receive as a bequest from someone else.

> *And Jesus said unto him, Why callest thou me good? there is none*
> *good but one, that is, God. (10:18)*

Jesus stopped the man in his tracks. "What do you mean when you call Me 'good,'?" Jesus asked. In effect, He asked, "Are you talking about *relative* goodness? Goodness as compared with other 'good' men? Or are you talking about *absolute* goodness, the kind of goodness that is found only in God Himself?" In other words, was this young man prepared to stake everything on the absolute goodness of the Lord Jesus, a goodness that recognized Him to be totally apart from all ordinary men and made Him equal with God? If it came, however, to the question of practical human goodness, then the place to go was the law.

> *Thou knowest the commandments, Do not commit adultery, Do not kill, Do not steal, Do not bear false witness, Defraud not, Honour thy father and mother. (10:19)*

These were the comparatively simple commandments to keep—at least outwardly. Paul, in his unconverted days, imagined that he had kept all of these commandments. Not until he came to the tenth commandment—"Thou shalt not covet" (i.e., entertain no lust, have no evil desire) did he realize his utter inability to live a holy life (Rom. 7:7).

> *And he answered and said unto him, Master, all these have I observed from my youth. (10:20)*

How painful and pointed was the young man's willingness to drop the word *good* in his reply. It was no longer "Good Master!" but simply "Master!" Evidently, he was not prepared to own Jesus as God. He also claimed ever since coming of age to have kept conscientiously the commandments that Jesus cited. The Lord now proved to him that he had not kept them at all. But first Mark adds an observation.

> *Then Jesus beholding him loved him, and said unto him, One thing thou lackest: go thy way, sell whatsoever thou hast, and give to the poor, and thou shalt have treasure in heaven: and come, take up the cross, and follow me. (10:21)*

The word used for "beholding" means "to look in," "to fix the eyes upon," or "to look intently." It means to know something or someone by inspection. Jesus read this young man's heart. He saw the turmoil that His next words would bring. His own great heart of love went out to him.

In effect, Jesus said to him, "You lack reality, young man. I quoted to you the seventh, sixth, eighth, ninth, and fifth commandments. These commandments have to do essentially with your behavior toward your fellowmen, with your professed safeguarding of the well-being of others. You want to *do* something to inherit eternal life. This is what you have to do: love poor people as God loves them, as I love them. You say that you have always kept these commandments. Prove it. Invest everything you have in the poor. You will have treasure in heaven.

"Oh, and there is one thing more. I am on the way to a place called Calvary, there to die on a cross. I invite you to come too. 'Take up the cross, and follow me.'" It was very strong medicine indeed.

> *And he was sad at that saying, and went away grieved: for he had great possessions. (10:22)*

It was more than the young man had bargained for. It is more than all of those who are committed to *doing* something bargain for. He came running; he went away broken. Instead of owning Jesus as Lord and investing his all in eternal treasure and eternal life, he turned his back on Jesus and went away.

What happened to him? Did he eventually become the rich man of Luke 12:15–21 and finally the rich man of Luke 16:19–31? The possibility certainly exists.

Then came *the sermon on the rich man* (10:23–31):

> *And Jesus looked round about, and saith unto his disciples, How hardly shall they that have riches enter into the kingdom of God! (10:23)*

Two worlds exist: this one and the one to come. Two systems exist: this world's system, with its promises, prospects, pleasures, possessions, perspectives, and power; and that other world's system, with its totally different set of values. The two worlds appeared suddenly in human history. They surfaced immediately after the Fall. The descendants of Cain (Gen. 4) lived for this world, and the descendants of Seth (Gen. 5) lived for the world to come. There can be no compromise between these two worlds.

Wealth tends to ally itself to this world, which is why materialism is such a deadly enemy of the kingdom of God. Ultimately, God brings people to Calvary, where we learn what this world thinks of Christ and what God thinks of this world. Those who have riches have a greater stake in this world than do those who are poor. That is why it is harder for those who have riches to enter the kingdom of God. Riches tend to blind one's eyes to ultimate, eternal, and spiritual realities by anchoring us to the wrong world.

> And the disciples were astonished at his words. But Jesus answereth again, and saith unto them, Children, how hard is it for them that trust in riches to enter into the kingdom of God! (10:24)

The Lord had just upset an entire system of values. In the Old Testament, the blessing of the Lord promised riches and well-being (Prov. 10:22). Indeed, this was the criterion by which Job's friends judged the stricken patriarch. It was taken for granted, even by the Lord's disciples, that wealth and health were the natural evidences and attributes of a godly life. Bethlehem, Calvary, and Pentecost have changed all of that.

The Lord adds a word here that shows the subtlety of riches. Those who have them come to *trust* in them. They rely on them. Money can buy most things, so they think it can buy spiritual blessings too.

> It is easier for a camel to go through the eye of a needle, than for a rich man to enter into the kingdom of God. (10:25)

The disciples would have easily understood this reference. Their astonishment must have been only increased by this familiar illustration. Apparently, the Lord's reference is to the small door that is fixed in the main door of a walled city. It was there for the convenience of people who wanted access to the city after the big door was closed; there could be no hope of getting *that* door opened once it was bolted and barred for the night. A traveler arriving late with a loaded camel would have a problem. The camel with its load would be too big to get through even the smaller door, which was referred to as "the eye of the needle." The owner of the camel would have to divest the beast of its load before there could be any hope of squeezing it through the small opening.

This, then, was the predicament of the rich man. To gain access to the kingdom of God through that "strait" (narrow) gate, of which Jesus spoke (Matt. 7:13–14), he must first unload the camel, divest himself of what was hindering him from getting into the kingdom of God—his wealth.

> *And they were astonished out of measure, saying among themselves, Who then can be saved? (10:26)*

The notion that prosperity is to be equated with godliness was deeply ingrained. Despite the Lord's blunt denial of this wrong idea, it persists to this day. Those who espouse it ignore the Lord's warnings of rejection, suffering, persecution, want, and woe that the godly can expect in this age. Multitudes believe that they are offered wealth and health, along with long life and happiness, as the birthright of belief. The whole history of the church in a hostile world puts the lie to such fanciful ideas.

> *And Jesus looking upon them saith, With men it is impossible, but not with God: for with God all things are possible. (10:27)*

Salvation is impossible with men, rich or poor, be they as rich as the disappointed young ruler or as poor as the beggar Lazarus. Salvation is beyond purchase; beyond money; beyond price; and beyond all human standards of religion, morality, good works, and self-effort. The disciples should have known from the Old Testament Scriptures themselves that the basic principle of salvation rests on something other than money (Isa. 55:1; Mic. 6:5–8).

But what is impossible with men is possible with God. Salvation is God's idea, planned by Him before even time began, provided by Him at infinite cost and offered to one and all as the gift of His grace.

> *Then Peter began to say unto him, Lo, we have left all, and have followed thee. (10:28)*

Suddenly, Peter saw the other side of the coin. The rich young ruler had not been prepared to give up anything for Christ; Peter and the other disciples had given up everything for Him. Peter, Andrew, James, John, and Matthew had all given up lucrative businesses to become the Lord's disciples. It had never occurred to them, until now, apparently, that there was anything particularly meritorious about their action. At the time, it had seemed the sensible thing to do. They had been more than rewarded by their association with the miracle-working, heartwarming, life-transforming, mind-expanding Son of the living God.

> *And Jesus answered and said, Verily I say unto you, There is no man that hath left house, or brethren, or sisters, or father, or*

mother, or wife, or children, or lands, for my sake, and the gospel's,
But he shall receive an hundredfold now in this time, houses, and
brethren, and sisters, and mothers, and children, and lands, with
persecutions; and in the world to come eternal life. (10:29–30)

Two figures of speech are discernible in this remarkable statement. The first is the *paradiastole* (the repetition of the disjunctives "either, or," or the disjunctives "neither, nor"). The word *or* is repeated constantly to separate each thing that is surrendered from the other things that are surrendered. This figure of speech is used for emphasis. Thus, the Lord particularizes each item. Similarly, the *polysyndeton* is used—the word *and* is repeated constantly to separate each promise, to draw attention to each promise, and to emphasize each promise. Thus, each promise is made independent, important, and emphatic.

The Lord used these figures of speech to draw attention to His appreciation of all that is ever given up for His sake and the gospel's and to show what a sharp eye He keeps on each surrender to ensure subsequent rewards.

Each item in the first list is repeated in the second list, except for *fathers* and *wives*. A disciple of the Lord, cut off from home and hearth, can have any number of sisters and brothers and so on; he is promised ten thousand such. He does not need multiplied fathers because he already has a Father in heaven. It would have been inappropriate to promise him ten thousand wives!

Having listed the marvelous return on one's investment in the cause and work of Christ, the Lord adds "with persecutions"—just in case someone should simply want to get in on only the benefits.

But there is more! There is all this and heaven too!

But many that are first shall be last; and the last first. (10:31)

The Lord now looks ahead to "the crowning day that's coming by and by," when some startling revelations will occur. People we have seen reigning as kings down here will find themselves set aside up there. Many people whom we regard as nobility down here are not known as great aristocrats in heaven. The prophet Samuel discovered this principle when God sent him to choose a king from among Jesse's sons. They were handsome boys. When the oldest, in all of his natural magnificence, was first to stand before him, he thought for sure that here was one who was every inch a king. The Lord said to him, "Look not on his countenance, or on the height of his stature; because I have refused him: for the LORD seeth not as man seeth; for man looketh on the outward appearance, but the LORD looketh on the heart" (1 Sam. 16:7). Eliab would have been no more use in the Valley of Elah than King Saul—who had been chosen by the people to be king of Israel simply because he was so big (1 Sam. 9:1–2; 18:22, 28).

C. Practical wisdom (10:32–52)

First, we have *a repeated prediction* (10:32–34):

> *And they were in the way going up to Jerusalem; and Jesus went before them: and they were amazed; and as they followed, they were afraid. And he took again the twelve, and began to tell them what things should happen unto him, (10:32)*

The highway now led straight toward the goal—Jerusalem, the city that habitually stoned the prophets and killed those whom God sent to it (Matt. 23:37). The Lord knew what He could expect once He appeared in that den of lions. His earthly pilgrimage was drawing to a close. There seems to have been a new, obvious resolution, firmness, and purpose about Him. As the Niagara River seems to quicken its pace and move forward with renewed force as it approaches the falls, so it was with the Lord. Those who followed Him sensed it and were awed by it.

"Up to Jerusalem!" The Jews always referred to it like that. The city stood on the highest point of the backbone ridge of hills that run north and south between the Jordan and the Great Sea. "Up to Jerusalem." It was the only way to go. God had chosen it for that purpose. There the temple stood. It was appropriate that one should be conscious of putting his feet on higher ground when approaching a place like that—"the city of the great king," as it is called (Ps. 48:2; Matt. 5:35).

This was the third announcement of His sufferings. He had mentioned them in Caesarea Philippi after Peter's great confession of faith (8:3), and He had mentioned them again on the way home from the Mount of Transfiguration (9:31). The next time would be the last time (10:45). It was not a truth that the disciples wanted to face.

> *Saying, Behold, we go up to Jerusalem; and the Son of man shall be delivered unto the chief priests, and unto the scribes; and they shall condemn him to death, and shall deliver him to the Gentiles: And they shall mock him, and shall scourge him, and shall*

spit upon him, and shall kill him: and the third day he shall rise
again. (10:33–34)

We note the steady beat of the *polysyndeton*—"And! And! And!" Each individual suffering is marked out for emphasis, right on through death, without a pause in the beat, to resurrection! Men would do their worst. Then God would act. The resurrection of Christ was as inevitable as His death.

The first two announcements had been very brief because that was all the disciples could take at that time: the leaders of the Jewish religious and governing establishment would kill Him, and He would rise again. Now He adds half a dozen more details, each one more horrifying than the one before. The final rejection would take place in Jerusalem, the nation's capital, toward which He was now striding with such resolution. The Sanhedrin would condemn Him to death. Not content with that, they would hand Him over to the Gentiles. He would be mocked and scourged and spit upon and killed—He, the King of Glory (Ps. 24). The disciples simply could not take it in as the next statement shows.

Next, we have *a resented petition* (10:35–45):

And James and John, the sons of Zebedee, come unto him, saying,
Master, we would that thou shouldest do for us whatsoever we
shall desire. And he said unto them, What would ye that I should
do for you? (10:35–36)

"Promise us something," they said. But He was not about to write them a blank check so that they could fill it in for any amount they desired. They were too much out of tune with reality for that.

We learn from Matthew that their mother was behind the request that they were about to make. Salome, their mother, seems to have been a sister of Mary, the Lord's mother. On the human level, then, she was His aunt, and they were His cousins.

They said unto him, Grant unto us that we may sit, one on thy
right hand, and the other on thy left hand, in thy glory. (10:37)

Thus, they ignored what the Lord had been saying about the cross. Their sights were set on the crown. They wanted the crown without the cross. They were still thinking in terms of the kingdom, the power, and the glory (Luke 4:5–

8). In spite of the Lord's repeated references to the cross, they were apparently still expecting that the millennial kingdom was about to appear. This was their version, too, of Peter's mistake at Caesarea Philippi, when he had taken the Lord aside to urge Him not to speak out more about a *cross* (8:31–34). Well, the kingdom, the power, and the glory were not to be canceled; but they were to be postponed—for two thousand years. The Lord knew this. James and John had not yet grasped it.

> *But Jesus said unto them, Ye know not what ye ask: can ye drink*
> *of the cup that I drink of? and be baptized with the baptism that*
> *I am baptized with? (10:38)*

The cup! Oh, that cup! Gazing into it in Gethsemane would bring the blood sweat to His brow. No one but He on earth and His Father in heaven and the Holy Spirit in His heart could know the full horror of that cup.

And that baptism! He had begun His public ministry by being plunged beneath the chilly waters of the Jordan, thus to identify Himself with Adam's ruined race, which He had come to save. Ahead lay a deeper, darker Jordan, the dark river of death. There He would be identified with the sins of the world. There He who knew no sin would be made sin for us. There He, the Lord of life, would taste of death for every man. Whoever it is who wants to know the full terror of that baptism must fathom the depths of His anguished cry, "My God, my God, why hast thou forsaken me?"

The cup spoke of His inward sufferings; the baptism spoke of His outward sufferings. Thus, He challenged James and John and their ambitious mother.

> *And they said unto him, We can. And Jesus said unto them, Ye*
> *shall indeed drink of the cup that I drink of; and with the bap-*
> *tism that I am baptized withal shall ye be baptized: (10:39)*

Theirs was the answer of ignorance. It is comparable to the abysmal folly of Israel when, presented with the law, declared, "All that the LORD hath spoken we will do" (Exod. 19:8). Israel, at that point, had not even heard what the law contained, still less had they questioned their ability to keep its commandments! They foolishly and confidently committed themselves to keep them—all 613 of them.

The Lord read the hearts of James and John. He foresaw their future as clearly as He foresaw His own. Of course, they could not drink the darkest dregs of the cup that was His or plunge beneath the judgment waters that awaited Him. But they could be martyred for His cause. And so they were. James was the first of the apostles to be martyred (Acts 12:1–2). The apostle John lived to a ripe old age, but he knew what it was like to be banished to a penal isle and, it is said, to have been boiled in oil.

> But to sit on my right hand and on my left hand is not mine to
> give; but it shall be given to them for whom it is prepared. (10:40)

There is all the difference in the world between salvation and rewards. Salvation is free; rewards have to be earned. Rewards are offered to believers as an added incentive to holy living. The judgment seat of Christ is to be convened to deal with all of the issues involved in God's assessment of our lives as believers (1 Cor. 3:12–15; Rom. 14:10). Likewise, crowns are offered and set before us as something to be won. Surely, one of the highest honors must be to be seated alongside Christ Himself in the day of His glory.

> And when the ten heard it, they began to be much displeased
> with James and John. (10:41)

Peter was indignant. Judas was angry. Thomas and Matthew were put out. One and all, they had paid little or no attention to the Lord's announcement that He was on His way to the grave. And they had completely forgotten His teaching on being childlike and humble. How all of this must have grieved the Lord. Not only were they engaging in unseemly jockeying for position but also they were turning on each other in recrimination. The Lord remained patient.

> But Jesus called them to him, and saith unto them, Ye know that
> they which are accounted to rule over the Gentiles exercise lord-
> ship over them; and their great ones exercise authority upon them.
> But so shall it not be among you: but whosoever will be great
> among you, shall be your minister: And whosoever of you will be
> the chiefest, shall be servant of all. (10:42–44)

Thus, the Lord sets His kingdom and its rulers apart from all of the kingdoms of this world. Those who aspire to positions of power in the kingdoms of this world vie for advantage. Shakespeare, in his famous play *Julius Caesar,* describes how the conspirators viewed the great Roman dictator, his ambitions, and their own jealous responses. He has Cassius say to Brutus,

> Why man, he doth bestride the narrow world
> Like a Colossus; and we petty men
> Walk under his huge legs, and peep about
> To find ourselves dishonorable graves . . .[2]

The dying Alexander, the great Greek conqueror, was asked by his closest collaborators about his will. How was he going to dispose of his vast empire? His closest followers gathered closer. "To whom do you bequeath your kingdom?" they asked him, eager to learn who would inherit the coveted prize.

"To the strongest," he said. His dying words were a prophecy: "I see a great funeral contest over me," he said, then he closed his eyes forever.[3]

The Lord's Spirit is as different from that of the conquerors, rulers, and power brokers of this world as day is from night. *Service* is the key word, humble service.

> *For even the Son of man came not to be ministered unto, but to minister, and to give his life a ransom for many. (10:45)*

Amazing! He who had ten thousand times ten thousand angelic ministers, each a flame of living fire, to hang upon His words and rush to do His bidding, came down here to *serve!*

Incidentally, this is the key verse in Mark's gospel. In the first part of the gospel, we see the Lord Jesus giving His life in *service*—He came not to be served but to serve. In the second part of the gospel, we see Him giving His life in *sacrifice*—He came to give His life a ransom for many. And what a life it was! It was a *supernatural* life. One glance from Him, and water blushed into wine. One word from Him, and the fiercest demons fled. One touch from Him, and a little lad's lunch becomes a banquet for more than five thousand.

It was a sinless life. Not once—in thought, word, deed, or hidden, secret desire, whether as a babe or as a boy, as a teen or a grown man, whether in the home or in the schoolroom, at the workbench or when tramping the highways and

---

2. Shakespeare, *Julius Caesar* 1.2.
3. Peter Green, *Alexander the Great* (New York: Praeger, 1970), 259.

byways of His native land—did He ever sin. He was holy, harmless, undefiled, and separate from sinners.

It was a *sufficient* life. The Old Testament law said, "A life for a life." Even at that, no man can provide a ransom for his brother because all have sinned. But even if such a one could be found, he could redeem only one life. The life that Jesus laid down on Calvary's cross was no ordinary life; it was an eternal life, an infinite life. Therefore, it could atone for any number of finite lives. That is why the Bible can say of Christ that "He is the propitiation for our sins: and not for ours only, but also for the sins of the whole world" (1 John 2:2).

Finally, we have *a resolute person* (10:46–52):

> *And they came to Jericho: and as he went out of Jericho with his*
> *disciples and a great number of people, blind Bartimaeus, the son*
> *of Timaeus, sat by the highway side begging. (10:46)*

Jericho was a city of great antiquity. It was located five miles west of the Jordan and seven miles northwest of the Dead Sea. It had become an important place under Herod the Great who fortified it and built a number of palaces there. It was where this monster of a man went to die. The Lord restored sight to several blind men at or near Jericho. Here, too, He accepted the hospitality of the publican Zaccheus. The Lord's story of the Good Samaritan was set on the road between Jerusalem and Jericho.

The Lord was making His way through this ancient city when He encountered blind Bartimaeus. Bartimaeus is one of the few people healed by Jesus who is actually named. Lazarus was another such person, as was Malchus.

> *And when he heard that it was Jesus of Nazareth, he began to cry*
> *out, and say, Jesus, thou Son of David, have mercy on me. (10:47)*

Doubtless, Bartimaeus heard the crowd approaching the spot on the road where he habitually begged for bread. The sudden influx of people gave him hope, perhaps, that someone might spare him a coin or two, an unexpected windfall perhaps.

Then he caught a name: Jesus, of Nazareth! Why, this was the opportunity of a lifetime! Jesus of Nazareth was a miracle worker. He would give him his sight. He had no doubt about that at all. It was now or never for him. He raised his voice.

"Jesus, thou Son of David!" he cried. This title is used nine times. The Syrophoenician appealed to Him by this title but received no answer until she changed her appeal and addressed Him as Lord (Matt. 15:21–28). As a Gentile, she had no claim upon Him as "the Son of David." The title owns Him as Israel's rightful king, David's heir, the claimant to David's throne. Bartimaeus voiced his belief in the Lord Jesus as Israel's true Messiah.

> *And many charged him that he should hold his peace: but he cried the more a great deal, Thou son of David, have mercy on me. (10:48)*

People got in his way, told him to be quiet, and did their best to keep him from Christ. But this sensible man—aware of his need, sure of the saving power of Christ, and conscious that it was now or never for him—refused to be intimidated by the crowd. It was indeed his one and only chance. Jesus was on His way to Calvary. He would not be back that way again. The whole story is a vivid picture of salvation.

God does not guarantee us a second chance to be saved. Why should anyone hear the Good News twice before everyone has heard it once? The gospel tidings are so great and glorious, and they come from such an authoritative and reliable source, that God has every right to expect that the news will be believed and received at once. That He has patience with those who hesitate is just another expression of His grace. Blind Bartimaeus was taking no chances as to that.

> *And Jesus stood still, and commanded him to be called. And they call the blind man, saying unto him, Be of good comfort, rise; he calleth thee. (10:49)*

The Lord's ear was open to this poor man's cry. Above all of the hubbub of the crowd, He heard the voice of this one needy man. His call of faith cheered the Savior's heart. He stopped, cut through the clamor, and commanded that the way be cleared. How eager the Lord is to respond to a fervent, effectual prayer.

> *And he, casting away his garment, rose, and came to Jesus. (10:50)*

The garment was a large, heavy, outer garment that doubtless served poor Bartimaeus as his cover from the weather. The poor often slept wrapped up in such a cloak. But it might be an impediment; it might get in the blind man's way in his haste to respond to the Savior's call, so he flung it aside! How different from the rich young ruler! How often, too, it is not so much the evil things that keep people from Christ as the good things and the necessary things.

> And Jesus answered and said unto him, What wilt thou that I
> should do unto thee? The blind man said unto him, Lord, that I
> might receive my sight. (10:51)

After all, the man had not yet actually voiced his need. People come to Christ for all sorts of wrong reasons. Only a short time earlier, James and John had come wanting a place of prominence.

Bartimaeus had no doubt about what he wanted; he wanted to be able to *see*. "Lord!" he said—"Rabboni! My Master!" In just the same way, Mary Magdalene voiced the great hunger of her heart (John 20:16).

> And Jesus said unto him, Go thy way; thy faith hath made thee
> whole. And immediately he received his sight, and followed Jesus
> in the way. (10:52)

And that is what all of those who come to Christ should do. "Go thy way!" Jesus said to him. He soon showed what way that was—Christ's way! His vision restored, he could now see no man save Jesus only. With his eyes fixed on Christ, he had no trouble knowing which way to go! Nor should we.

PART 2

The Servant Gives His Life in Sacrifice

Mark 11:1–16:20

Section 1: Precipitating the Crisis of Calvary (11:1–12:44)

A. What Jesus did (11:1–33)

  1. His coming (11:1–11)

    a. The preparation (11:1–6)

      (1) The arrival (11:1a)

      (2) The arrangements (11:1b–6)

        (a) The commission (11:1b–3)

          i. The two (11:1b)

          ii. The task (11:2–3)

            a. What they would find (11:2)

            b. What they would face (11:3)

        (b) The compliance (11:4–6)

          i. The colt discovered by them (11:4)

          ii. The colt delivered to them (11:5–6)

    b. The presentation (11:7–11)

      (1) His pathway strewn (11:7–8)

        (a) The colt (11:7)

        (b) The coats (11:8a)

        (c) The carpet (11:8b)

      (2) His praises sung (11:9–10)

        (a) The telling look (11:11a)

        (b) The tethered lamb (11:11b)

  2. His curse (11:12–14)

    a. A simple want (11:12–13)

      (1) The Lord's hunger (11:12)

      (2) The Lord's hope (11:13)

        (a) The hope described (11:13a)

        (b) The hope disappointed (11:13b)

    b. A symbolic woe (11:14)

  3. His cleansing (11:15–21)

    a. The Lord's fearlessness (11:15–17)

      (1) The Lord's valiant judgment (11:15–16)

        (a) The merchandisers (11:15a)

        (b) The money changers (11:15b)

        (c) The manhandlers (11:16)

      (2) The Lord's valid justification (11:17)

      b. The Lord's foes (11:18–21)
          (1) Their plots (11:18a)
          (2) Their plight (11:18b–21)
              (a) Their immediate dilemma (11:18b)
              (b) Their impending doom (11:19–21)
                  i. The interval (11:19–20a)
                  ii. The inevitable (11:20b–21)
4. His counsel (11:22–26)
    a. A word about power (11:22–24)
        (1) The need for faith (11:22)
        (2) The nature of faith (11:23–24)
            (a) The example (11:23)
            (b) The exhortation (11:24)
    b. A word about prayer (11:25–26)
        (1) The need for forgiveness (11:25a)
        (2) The nature of forgiveness (11:25b–26)
5. His critics (11:27–33)
    a. How they confronted Him (11:27–28)
        (1) The temple area (11:27a)
        (2) The temple authorities (11:27b–28)
            (a) Their united front (11:27b)
            (b) Their unanimous focus (11:28)
    b. How He confounded them (11:29–33)
        (1) What He decreed (11:29)
        (2) What He demanded (11:30–33)
            (a) Their dilemma (11:30–32)
            (b) Their decision (11:33a)
        (3) What He declined (11:33b)

—◊◊◊—

Section 1: Precipitating the Crisis of Calvary (11:1–12:44)
  A. What Jesus did (11:1–33)
      1. His coming (11:1–11)

First, there was *the preparation* (11:1–6):

> *And when they came nigh to Jerusalem, unto Bethphage and*
> *Bethany, at the mount of Olives, he sendeth forth two of his dis-*
> *ciples, (11:1)*

The two villages named were close to one another. The name *Bethany* means "the house of dates"; the name *Bethphage* means "the house of unripe figs." Bethphage was the larger of the two places, but Bethany was where the disciples would find the colt. Also, at Bethany, Jesus had some very dear friends. From the Mount of Olives, one could see the city of Jerusalem. The end of the journey was in sight.

> *And saith unto them, Go your way into the village over against*
> *you: and as soon as ye be entered into it, ye shall find a colt*
> *tied, whereon never man sat; loose him, and bring him. And*
> *if any man say unto you, Why do ye this? say ye that the Lord*
> *hath need of him; and straightway he will send him hither.*
> *(11:2–3)*

The Lord knew all about it. Just as He knew all about Lazarus (John 11:1–15) and about the man with an upper room (14:12–15). Sometimes the Lord chose to ask questions to elicit information—a demonstration of His humanity; sometimes He demonstrated a perfect knowledge of people and events—a demonstration of His deity. It is impossible for us to tell where the humanity ends and the Deity begins or where the Deity ends and the humanity begins. Nor should we seek to know. It is all part of the "mystery of godliness" (1 Tim. 3:16).

The Lord knew all about that colt. He knew its age, that it had never been broken to the saddle, that it was tied to keep it under restraint, that the disciples would be challenged when they attempted to release it, and that it would be readily made available to Him. He knew all about the owner of the colt and that He was bestowing on him the unique and priceless privilege of ministering to the Master and having a share in the fulfillment of an ancient prophecy. In the years to come, each time this man read this story in the Gospels, he would be able to say, "That's me!" And how great will be his reward in heaven!

> *And they went their way, and found the colt tied by the door*
> *without in a place where two ways met; and they loose him. (11:4)*

The word for "a place where two ways meet" is *amphodon,* which refers to a roundabout road, perhaps winding around a block of buildings. It is likely that the two disciples whom Jesus sent on this mission were Peter and John—they were the two whom Jesus sent to prepare the Passover and secure use of the Upper Room (Luke 22:8–13). Mark's details regarding where the colt was found strongly suggest that the account was that of an actual eyewitness—doubtless Peter, from whom Mark obtained his information.

> *And certain of them that stood there said unto them, What do ye,*
> *loosing the colt? And they said unto them even as Jesus had com-*
> *manded: and they let them go. (11:5–6)*

Sure enough, the disciples were challenged, just as would be expected when they attempted to get hold of the colt. Mention of the Master was sufficient. His name was security enough for any loan.

Next, we have *the presentation* (11:7–11):

> *And they brought the colt to Jesus, and cast their garments on*
> *him; and he sat upon him. And many spread their garments in*
> *the way: and others cut down branches off the trees, and strawed*
> *them in the way. (11:7–8)*

The Lord who heretofore had discouraged any kind of promotion and publicity now deliberately advertised His coming. One word or touch from Him and the unbroken colt not only submitted to His control but also wended its way through cheering crowds of people who waved palm fronds and flung their garments in front of its feet.

The garments of the apostles made a saddle. All kinds of straw, rushes, reeds, and fronds formed a carpet, as it were, to pave His way. This was the Lord's official entry into the capital as "the Son of David," indeed (Bravo, Bartimaeus, for your perception!), the rightful heir to David's throne.

And they that went before, and they that followed, cried, saying,
Hosanna; Blessed is he that cometh in the name of the Lord:
Blessed be the kingdom of our father David, that cometh in the
name of the Lord: Hosanna in the highest. (11:9–10)

The quotations are from Psalm 118:25–26. The word *hosanna* means "praise now!" Psalm 118 is remarkable for its forecast of the Lord's rejection. Even as He was riding the crest of the wave, the deep trough on the other side was waiting to receive Him. Within the week, this same multitude would be howling for His death—as well He knew.

Doubtless, tidings of this triumphant entry were reported immediately to both the Roman governor and the Sanhedrin. So far as the Romans were concerned, sarcastic grins must have been seen when the news came. "A *king,* riding on a baby *donkey?* How silly! What could you expect, anyway, from a king of the *Jews?*"

The Jewish authorities would not have been so quick to scoff. After all, this had been *prophesied:* "Rejoice greatly, O daughter of Zion; shout, O daughter of Jerusalem: behold, thy King cometh unto thee: he is just, and having salvation; lowly, and riding upon an ass, and upon a colt the foal of an ass" (Zech. 9:9). Although the Sanhedrin had no use for a meek Messiah and wanted rather a militant Messiah, one who would make Israel the hub of a new world empire, they were alarmed at the sudden appearing of Jesus of Nazareth in the recognizable role of Messiah.

And Jesus entered into Jerusalem, and into the temple: and when
he had looked round about upon all things, and now the eventide
was come, he went out unto Bethany with the twelve. (11:11)

The long journey from Hermon was over. The Lord was now in Jerusalem. He had come to be the Passover Lamb and, as such, presented Himself in the temple court to be kept under constant observation so that all could see that He was without spot or blemish. Each night, He would go as far as Bethany, where He had friends such as Martha, Mary, and Lazarus; Simon the leper; and the people who had loaned Him their colt.

We see Him entering Jerusalem, at the end of His long trek from the north, just as the evening shadows begin to gather significantly in the sky. We see Him cast that sweeping glance around the temple courts, taking it all in: the priests, the people, the princes of commerce. We see Him retire back to Bethany to prepare Himself for the monumental confrontations ahead.

2. His curse (11:12–14)

And on the morrow, when they were come from Bethany, he was hungry: (11:12)

We are not told where He had spent the night. The fact that He was hungry suggests that He had not been at the home of Lazarus. Martha was far too good a hostess to let such a loved guest get away without breakfast. More than likely, He had spent the night on Olivet in prayer, preparing Himself for the difficult days ahead.

And seeing a fig tree afar off having leaves, he came, if haply he might find any thing thereon: and when he came to it, he found nothing but leaves; for the time of figs was not yet. (11:13)

The luxuriant foliage on the fig tree was promising. This was a healthy tree. The Mount of Olives, in olden times, was famous for its fig trees. The fruit always appears before the leaves so the Lord had every right to expect figs on the tree although, strictly, it was early in the season for fruit. The usual summer crop of fruit is not gathered until May or June, but in Olivet's sunny ravines, fig trees could have ripe fruit some weeks earlier. Therefore, nothing is strange about the Lord's anticipating, as early as Easter, young, edible figs, although that was not the usual time for harvesting the fruit.

And Jesus answered and said unto it, No man eat fruit of thee hereafter for ever. And his disciples heard it. (11:14)

The fig tree had something to say to Christ. It whispered to Him sadly about barrenness. The Lord answered it. This is an extraordinary incident because on this occasion the Lord performed His only judgment miracle. It was clearly a symbolic act; the fig tree symbolized the nation of Israel. The Lord had come to that nation, just as He had now come to the fig tree. The nation was very much alive, carrying on with all of its political, social, religious, and economic activities, but it was devoid of spiritual fruit. It had nothing at all to give to Jesus—except a cross. The cursing of the fig tree symbolized the subsequent cursing of the Christ-rejecting nation itself, a cursing recorded at length by Matthew (chap. 23). Within the lifetime of some people who were alive at that time, the curse fell. In A.D. 70, the Romans destroyed Jerusalem and the temple. In A.D. 135, at the time of the Bar Cochba rebellion, the Romans put an end to Jewish national life.

3. His cleansing (11:15–21)

We note, first, *the Lord's fearlessness* (11:15–17):

> *And they come to Jerusalem: and Jesus went into the temple, and*
> *began to cast out them that sold and bought in the temple, and*
> *overthrew the tables of the moneychangers, and the seats of them*
> *that sold doves; And would not suffer that any man should carry*
> *any vessel through the temple. (11:15–16)*

The background of this incident is Malachi 3:1. The prophet Malachi foretold that a voice would sound, and the messenger (John the Baptist) would appear. Well, he had appeared, and Herod had murdered him. Then a sudden visitation would occur, the Messiah would appear—in His temple.

Jesus had often visited that temple before. He had visited it once as a twelve-year-old boy. He had visited again when He commenced His ministry in the capital (John 1:13–17). Now He visited it, for the last time, to do what He had done once before—to cleanse it.

All about Him was both architectural splendor and spiritual squalor. The high priesthood was represented by the politically minded Sadducee, Caiaphas, and his father-in-law, the corrupt Annas, who had controlled the priesthood one way and another for half a century. Like Caiaphas, Annas was a Sadducee. He was astute, worldly, devious, and full of malice and meanness. At the time of Christ, the Sanhedrin, which controlled the temple, was little better than a collection of time-serving priests dedicated to keeping themselves in power. Annas sanctioned the shops and concessions that carried on the traffic that so moved the Lord. Indeed, he and his clan seem to have founded them; they derived considerable profit from the proceeds of these concessions. By cleansing the temple, Jesus took on this powerful, venal, and corrupt individual. Annas was the man who was chiefly responsible for the Lord's crucifixion. Nothing could have been more calculated to kindle the wrath of Annas and Caiaphas and their colleagues than to throw out of the temple the merchants and money changers whom they themselves licensed and controlled.

The cluster of annual feasts between Passover and Pentecost brought thousands of Jews to Jerusalem from all parts of the Diaspora. Obviously, these visitors could not bring with them the sacrificial animals that they would need. It was appropriate that provision was made for them to purchase these, but it was not necessary that the temple court be used for the purpose. Then, too, Jews were required to pay an annual temple tax, and that tax could not be paid in the profane coins of Gentile lands; it had to be paid in Jewish money. Provision had to be made for the appropriate money exchange to be made, but, again, this financial matter could have been conducted at plenty of other places elsewhere in Jerusalem.

It was completely inappropriate for these transactions to be centered in the temple area. Moreover, these concessions seem to have been set up in the Court of the Gentiles, a fact that only added to the Lord's displeasure. Such use of the Gentile court was in keeping with the Jews' mean-spirited contempt for Gentiles. The Lord, by contrast, loved Gentiles as much as He loved Jews. The last straw was that the merchandise and market racketeering associated with the concessions was done with the full connivance of the religious authorities.

Jesus put an immediate stop to it. He would not even allow the people to make a thoroughfare of the temple. His anger, though real enough, was holy. This fact is evident. He overthrew the *tables* of the money changers, sending them scrambling for the coins that rolled everywhere, and He overturned the *seats* of them that sold doves. By so doing, He did not hurt the helpless innocent creatures in their cages.

> *And he taught, saying unto them, Is it not written, My house shall be called of all nations the house of prayer? but ye have made it a den of thieves. (11:17)*

This composite quotation is from Isaiah 56:7 and Jeremiah 7:11. The Jews had turned God's house into a robbers' den. It was a terrible indictment of the religious leaders who condoned all of this inappropriate activity; but, by His action and pointed teaching, the Lord signed His own death warrant.

We note, also, *the Lord's foes* (11:18–21):

> *And the scribes and chief priests heard it, and sought how they might destroy him: for they feared him, because all the people was astonished at his doctrine. (11:18)*

For the time being, however, He was safe. The politically astute members of the Sanhedrin knew that, for now, the Lord had the ear of the people. It would not be safe for them to move against Him. It might lead to a riot, which would only bring a fresh crackdown by the Roman garrison and a further curtailing of their privileges.

The authorities, therefore, were uncertain how to proceed against this unwanted Messiah. After all, He was armed with might and miracle, and He was popular with the multitudes. So the scribes and chief priests began to look for some way to accomplish His downfall and death without provoking a riot by the people and without risk of this unwanted Messiah's using His extraordinary miracle-working power in self-defense. But, for now, all they could do was watch and wait.

And when even was come, he went out of the city. (11:19)

Presumably, He went back to Bethany. It had been an eventful day. The disciples would have plenty to talk about. The Lord had acted decisively enough, but they doubtless had their reservations as to whether He had been wise to provoke the establishment. Still, His triumphant entry must have encouraged them. Perhaps He was going to begin acting like a real Messiah after all.

> *And in the morning, as they passed by, they saw the fig tree dried up from the roots. And Peter calling to remembrance saith unto him, Master, behold, the fig tree which thou cursedst is withered away. (11:20–21)*

The fig tree died. Of course! It could not exist without the blessing of its Creator. Nor, incidentally, could the nation of Israel. It had already begun to show its Christ-rejecting spirit in the anger, malice, and plots of the scribes and chief priests. That spirit would grow until they would reject not only the Son of God but also the Spirit of God. Then a judgmental spiritual and agelong blindness would descend upon the nation (Rom. 10:1–3; 11:25), a national blindness regarding Christ that has lasted to this day.

However, that was not the point that the Lord now makes in response to Peter's comment.

4. His counsel (11:22–26)

And Jesus answering saith unto them, Have faith in God. For verily I say unto you, That whosoever shall say unto this mountain, Be thou removed, and be thou cast into the sea; and shall not doubt in his heart, but shall believe that those things which he saith shall come to pass; he shall have whatsoever he saith. (11:22–23)

The Lord's answer does not seem to have anything to do with Peter's observation about the fig tree. The dispensational application of Peter's comment is found elsewhere (Matt. 24:32–33). Here the Lord uses the whole incident to underline the critical importance of faith as a means of removing obstacles. No matter how mountainous and monumental those obstacles might seem to be, God can remove them. Faith is the hand with which we reach out to God and that brings about the necessary change of circumstances. Faith does not have to be great because faith "as a grain of mustard seed" (Matt. 17:20) is all that it takes to achieve great ends. But faith has to be genuine and uncontaminated with doubt. And it has to be faith in *God*. God is quite big enough to remove any mountain. Often, He allows obstacles to arise to provide an opportunity for us to exercise faith and to provide a stage on which He can display His power.

Only a few verses earlier, Mark illustrated this truth. The Lord had come down from the mount. In the valley below was a demon-possessed boy, a distraught father, a mocking world, and a powerless "church." The father turned from the evidently impotent and embarrassed disciples to the all-powerful Lord. "If thou canst do anything," he asked falteringly.

"If thou canst believe," was the Lord's instant reply (9:22–23). There is no *if* about it on His part. Mountains in the way are nothing to Him. Because He made them, He can certainly remove them. All of the forces of nature are at His command, and the resources of Deity are His to command. As John Newton puts it in his hymn "Come, My Soul, Thy Suit Prepare,"

> Thou art coming to a King,
> Large petitions with thee bring,
> For His grace and power are such
> None can ever ask too much.

Therefore I say unto you, What things soever ye desire, when ye pray, believe that ye receive them, and ye shall have them. (11:24)

Thus, the Lord encourages us to pray and to believe that God is well able to grant our requests. Prayer is the expression of faith. Not that prayer is some kind of a magic wand. Prayer has rules just like everything else. The Lord now states one of them. He reminds us (by linking the statement in v. 24 with the statement in v. 25–26) that no text of Scripture can be taken at face value apart from its context.

> And when ye stand praying, forgive, if ye have aught against any:
> that your Father also which is in heaven may forgive you your
> trespasses. But if ye do not forgive, neither will your Father which
> is in heaven forgive your trespasses. (11:25–26)

An unforgiving spirit is a great hindrance to effective prayer. So are our many other trespasses. An unforgiving spirit hinders God's forgiving us our own fallings and failures and so blocks the answer to our prayers.

Forgiveness is not the same as justification. Forgiveness is a plea based on acknowledged guilt. A person who is justified takes his stand upon different ground altogether. A believer is acquitted of wrongdoing on the basis of his identification with Christ. This identification is so perfect and complete that God sees only the righteousness of Christ when He sees the believer. Forgiveness is conditional—God repeatedly makes it depend on our willingness to forgive others (Matt. 6:12; 18:21–35)—but justification is unconditional.

So, while the Lord gives us here a very broad and sweeping promise, indeed, "What things soever ye desire," the assumption is that the person, so approaching heaven with such a large request, will be exercising a faith rooted in a humble, Christlike spirit and that he will be observing all of the usual laws associated with prayer.

5. His critics (11:27–33)

> And they come again to Jerusalem: and as he was walking in the
> temple, there come to him the chief priests, and the scribes, and
> the elders, (11:27)

We now have before us an official inquiry conducted by representatives of the three bodies that made up the Sanhedrin. These men were the religious leaders of Israel. They saw themselves as the custodians of orthodoxy, the defenders of the faith, including all of the multitudinous rabbinical traditions. They seem to have decided that the time had come to challenge this unorthodox Messiah who had now stationed Himself in their city and who treated their temple as though it belonged to Him. They confronted Him with all of the dignity and majesty that they could muster. He must be made to recognize their authority.

> *And say unto him, By what authority doest thou these things?*
> *and who gave thee this authority to do these things? (11:28)*

He might have asked them the same question. The Sanhedrin, as it was constituted in Israel at that time, was an institution of comparatively recent vintage. Authority to speak and act in the name of God, as all of the prophets recognized, was derived not from some self-appointed or state-appointed religious body but from the Word of God and the Spirit of God.

> *And Jesus answered and said unto them, I will also ask of you one*
> *question, and answer me, and I will tell you by what authority I*
> *do these things. The baptism of John, was it from heaven, or of*
> *men? answer me. (11:29–30)*

Well they knew that Jesus was infinitely greater than John the Baptist. John had performed no miracles, but the whole country, from Dan to Beersheba, rang with stories of Christ's countless, marvelous, and fully authenticated miracles. John had preached repentance, but, great preacher and renowned prophet that he was, he was not to be compared with Jesus. No man ever spoke like Him.

What caused these men to be so hostile to Jesus was His recent triumphant ride into Jerusalem. He claimed to be the Messiah, a Messiah whom they had not endorsed or authenticated. They were enraged, too, by His even more recent cleansing of the temple. That this Galilean, from Nazareth of all places, should ignore their authority and that He should expose and denounce them in the bluntest possible language infuriated them (Matt. 23).

John the Baptist had done the same, but Herod had conveniently murdered him. Jesus was a much tougher proposition. They rejected Him with the same hostility and unbelief with which they had rejected John, but they were more than a little afraid of Jesus. A Man who could blast a barren fig tree with a word was no One to be trifled with. Moreover, He was very much more clever than John the Baptist. His question regarding the authority of John's baptism proved that. He had them on the horns of a dilemma with His question, and they knew it.

> *And they reasoned with themselves, saying, If we shall say, From heaven; he will say, Why then did ye not believe him? But if we shall say, Of men; they feared the people: for all men counted John, that he was a prophet indeed. (11:31–32)*

John had been born to the priesthood! He had been an Elijah for boldness and bluntness, appearing in the wilderness to break the silence of centuries. He had been rejected by the Sanhedrin, feared by Herod, hated by Herodias, and loved by the common people. He had arrayed himself in rough clothing. He had been a lonely ascetic. In the popular mind, he was all that a prophet should be. He had declared himself to be the forerunner of the Messiah. He had been filled with the Spirit and had preached repentance without fear or favor. He had attracted vast and responsive crowds. So, how dare they say that his ministry was merely of men? No! No! They dared not do that.

But admit that the baptism of John was of God? No precedents for John's baptism existed in the Old Testament. Elijah and Elisha baptized no one. Isaiah, Jeremiah, and Daniel baptized no one. Ezekiel baptized no one. The Minor Prophets baptized no one. Even the postexilic prophets, the prophets closest to John's time, baptized no one. The law provided for washings of various sorts, but none of them approximated baptism. Moses baptized no one the way John did— although Paul would see a picture of baptism in Israel's crossing of the Red Sea (1 Cor. 10:1–2), and Peter would come to see a picture of it in Noah's ark (1 Peter 3:18–22).

So, where did John get his authority to baptize his converts? Obviously, he got it from God. The Lord Himself had endorsed it by submitting to it Himself. The Father and the Holy Spirit had endorsed it, too, at the same time (Matt. 3:13–17). These things were common knowledge. How could they dare to say that John had no authority outside of his own imagination for doing what he did? On the other hand, how could they dare admit that John's ministry was received from God and blessed of God? The Lord had these men well cornered.

> *And they answered and said unto Jesus, We cannot tell. And Jesus answering saith unto them, Neither do I tell you by what authority I do these things. (11:33)*

What would have been the point in telling them? They had already made up their minds. Their wicked hearts were obdurate in determined unbelief. Now they had rejected Him as surely and as culpably as they had rejected John. He did not argue with them. He did not seek to enlighten them. They had passed beyond mere unbelief into apostasy—and God always leaves the apostate to work out his own doom. He has nothing to say to such—then or now.

   B. What Jesus declared (12:1–44)
      1. A daring parable (12:1–12)
        a. Its national appeal (12:1–9)
          (1) The owner of the vineyard (12:1)
            (a) His diligence (12:1a–c)
               i. How he planted the vineyard (12:1a)
              ii. How he protected the vineyard (12:1b)
             iii. How he provisioned the vineyard (12:1c)
            (b) His departure (12:1d)
          (2) The overseers of the vineyard (12:2–9)
            (a) The servants who were sent (12:2)
               i. The first attempts to get a return from the vineyard (12:2–5a)
                 a. The servant who was smitten (12:2–3)
                 b. The servant who was stoned (12:4)
                 c. The servant who was slain (12:5a)
              ii. The further attempts to get a return from the vineyard (12:5b)
            (b) The son who was sent (12:6–9)
               i. A word about the son (12:6)
                 a. His nearness (12:6a)
                 b. His dearness (12:6b)
              ii. A word about their sin (12:7–9)
                 a. Their conspiracy (12:7)
                 b. Their crime (12:8)
                 c. Their condemnation (12:9)
                   1. The fate of the vinedressers (12:9a)
                   2. The future of the vineyard (12:9b)
         b. Its natural application (12:10–12)
          (1) The question (12:10a)

        (2) The quotation (12:10b–12)

2. A deliberate provocation (12:13–34)

    a. In terms of the secular (12:13–17)

        (1) The plot formed (12:13)

            (a) Its instigators (12:13a)

            (b) Its intention (12:13b)

        (2) The plot furthered (12:14–15a)

            (a) Their subtlety (12:14a)

            (b) Their subject (12:14b)

            (c) Their snare (12:15a)

        (3) The plot foiled (12:15b–17)

            (a) What He recognized (12:15b)

            (b) What He requested (15:15c)

            (c) What He replied (12:16–17)

               i. A simple illustration (12:16)

              ii. A stunning implication (12:17)

                 a. His Word (12:17a)

                 b. Their wonder (12:17b)

    b. In terms of the social (12:18–27)

        (1) What the Sadducees denied (12:18)

        (2) What the Sadducees declared (12:19–23)

            (a) The appeal to law (12:19)

            (b) The appeal to logic (12:20–23)

               i. The parable they unfolded (12:20–23a)

              ii. The point they underlined (12:23b)

        (3) What the Sadducees discovered (12:24–27)

            (a) The Lord's mastery in the situation (12:24–25)

               i. What He exposed (12:24)

                 a. Their ignorance of God's inspired revelation (12:24a)

                 b. Their ignorance of God's infinite resources (12:24b)

              ii. What He explained (12:25)

            (b) The Lord's mastery of the Scriptures (12:26–27)

               i. His confident appeal to the Scriptures (12:26–27a)

                 a. A familiar text (12:26)

                 b. A fabulous truth (12:27a)

        ii. His cutting application of the Scriptures (12:27b)

  c. In terms of the spiritual (12:28–34)

    (1) What the Scripture said (12:28–31)

      (a) The scribe's question asked (12:28)

          i. His perception (12:28a)

         ii. His precaution (12:28b)

      (b) The scribe's question answered (12:29–31)

          i. The supreme commandment of the law (12:29–30)

            a. A revelation of God (12:29)

            b. A response to God (12:30)

         ii. The supplementary commandment of the law (12:31)

            a. A great text (12:31a)

            b. A great truth (12:31b)

    (2) What the scribe said (12:32–33)

      (a) A word of commendation (12:32a)

      (b) A word of commentary (12:32b–33)

          i. A restatement of the first commandment (12:32b–33a)

         ii. A reinforcement of the further commandment (12:33b)

    (3) What the Savior said (12:34)

      (a) His comment (12:34a–b)

          i. The man's perception (12:34a)

         ii. The man's position (12:34b)

      (b) His critics (12:34c)

3. A dramatic punch line (12:35–40)

  a. A word of wisdom (12:35–37)

    (1) The Christ (12:35–37a)

      (a) The temple (12:35a)

      (b) The truth (12:35b–37a)

          i. A proper quotation (12:35b–36)

            a. What the scribes said (12:35b)

            b. What the Scripture said (12:36)

         ii. A puzzling question (12:37a)

    (2) The crowds (12:37b)

> b. A word of warning (12:38–40)
>> (1) The duplicity of the scribes (12:38–40a)
>>> (a) Their craving (12:38–39)
>>>> i. The robes they display (12:38a)
>>>> ii. The respect they desire (12:38b–39)
>>>>> *a.* On the street (12:38b)
>>>>> *b.* In the synagogue (12:39a)
>>>>> *c.* At their socials (12:39b)
>>> (b) Their crimes (12:40a–b)
>>>> i. Their heartless robberies (12:40a)
>>>> ii. Their hypocritical religion (12:40b)
>> (2) The damnation of the scribes (12:40c)
> 4. A deathless principle (12:41–44)
>> a. Where He sat (12:41a)
>> b. Who He saw (12:41b–42)
>>> (1) The wealthy (12:41b)
>>> (2) The widow (12:42)
>> c. What He said (12:43–44)
>>> (1) His evaluation (12:43)
>>> (2) His explanation (12:44)

—m—

> B. What Jesus declared (12:1–44)
>> 1. A daring parable (12:1–12)
>>> a. Its national appeal (12:1–9)

We begin with *the owner of the vineyard:*

> *And he began to speak unto them by parables. A certain man planted a vineyard, and set an hedge about it, and digged a place for the winevat, and built a tower, and let it out to husbandmen, and went into a far country. (12:1)*

The Lord had no message for these men who were plotting against Him, except one of judgment to come. The moment He mentioned the vineyard, their thoughts would go back to Isaiah 5:1–7 and the great Old Testament evangelical prophet's parable of the vineyard. The vineyard, so prepared and protected and provisioned, was the nation of Israel. The owner was God. The vineyard rewarded all of God's care with sour grapes. Consequently, it was handed over to the Gentiles for destruction. The "beloved" of Isaiah's prophecy sets forth the doom of the vineyard—destruction and deportation, first at the hands of the Assyrians and then at the hands of the Babylonians. That doom was about to be repeated at the hands of the Romans. The Lord depicts in His parable the doom of the apostate husbandmen. Appropriately, Isaiah's "song" was followed by a series of terrible "woes" (Isa. 5:8, 11, 18, 20–22). Similarly, the Lord's parable to the vineyard was accompanied by an equally terrible series of "woes" (Matt. 23:13–39).

So the Lord directs the attention of these wicked men to the vineyard, the vineyard that they were supposed to care for and cultivate for God. Three plants in the Bible symbolize the nation of Israel—the fig, the olive, and the vine. The vine represents the nation as it was in Old Testament times, down to the time the nation rejected Christ. The olive (Rom. 11) represents Israel as it will be in a coming day when the veil of unbelief will be removed from their eyes and the Hebrew people as a nation finally recognize and receive Jesus as Savior and Lord and go on into the millennial kingdom. In between, Israel is viewed as the fig tree—a tree that often is associated with sin and failure (Gen. 3:7; Matt. 24:32–34; Mark 11:13–21).

The members of the Christ-rejecting Sanhedrin stood there, knowing full well what this parable of the vineyard portended. It was a sentence of doom issued by the very One whom they had come out to challenge and check.

Next attention is drawn to *the overseers of the vineyard* (12:2–9):

> *And at the season he sent to the husbandmen a servant, that he might receive from the husbandmen of the fruit of the vineyard. (12:2)*

God had grown this vine to maturity in Egypt, where the Hebrew family developed into a populous nation. He had then picked up this vine, carried it across the sands of Sinai, and planted it in the fair and fruitful land of Canaan. He had hedged it about and protected it, giving the leaders of Israel a sure means of defense against all possible foes—Himself. The soil was fruitful for the growth of the vine, and the climate was favorable. Every provision was made for the nation of Israel to flourish into a mighty kingdom. All God wanted was a fair return on His investment in the vineyard, the nation of Israel. He wanted their loyalty and love, but it was not to be.

> *And they caught him, and beat him, and sent him away empty.*
> *And again he sent unto them another servant; and at him*
> *they cast stones, and wounded him in the head, and sent him*
> *away shamefully handled. And again he sent another; and*
> *him they killed, and many others; beating some, and killing*
> *some. (12:3–5)*

From the beginning, the Hebrews were stubborn, stiff-necked, and hostile to the claims of Jehovah, their God, the true owner of the vineyard. The hostility increased and the violence escalated as time went on.

From the time of Moses to the time of Elijah, continuous rebellion and apostasy occurred. When Elijah appeared on the scene, Ahab put out a warrant for his arrest, and Jezebel longed to get her hands on him. Poor Naboth brought things to a head when, significantly enough, he refused to sell his vineyard to Ahab. Jezebel murdered him for his integrity (1 Kings 21:1–26).

Likewise, Ahaziah tried to molest Elijah but had no success because of Elijah's habit of calling down fire from heaven on his foes (2 Kings 1:1–12). When he did succeed in bringing the indomitable prophet before him, Elijah calmly read his doom to him (13–18).

After the translation of Elijah and the death of Elisha, things went from bad to worse. The persecution of God's prophets culminated in the cold-blooded and atrocious murder of Isaiah, who is generally thought to have been sawn asunder by order of King Manasseh (Heb. 11:37).

With the demise of the northern kingdom of Israel, the mantle of apostasy and persecution fell upon the shoulders of Judah. The sufferings of Jeremiah are an eloquent testimonial to the persistent wickedness of the Jews at this period.

Nor was it much different after the return from the Babylonian captivity. Zechariah was murdered between the temple and the altar by the repatriated Jews—as the Lord was soon going to remind His enemies (Matt. 23:33–35). Zechariah was the last martyr of the Old Testament. After him, God spoke only once more, through Malachi, and then He retreated into silence.

Such was the history of the husbandmen, a history now to be climaxed in the worst apostasy of all.

> *Having yet therefore one son, his wellbeloved, he sent him also*
> *last unto them, saying, They will reverence my son. (12:6)*

The son in the story must have known that he was going on a dangerous mission. The husbandmen had proved time and time again what a rebellious, unscrupulous, and murderous mob of miscreants they were. Yet, grace withheld the coming of judgment one more time. The owner of the vineyard would give them one more chance. Surely, they would have respect to his son! Similarly, the Lord Himself knew perfectly well when He stepped out of eternity into time that the path from the cradle led directly to a cross.

So it was that Jesus came "out of the ivory palaces into a world of woe." He came! It was all of grace! He was God's only begotten and well-beloved Son. He announced Himself to be such (John 5:18–23). The Father proclaimed Him to be such (Matt. 3:17). Peter proclaimed Him to be such (Matt. 16:14–17). The Holy Spirit declared Him to be such (Ps. 2:7–9; John 3:16; Heb. 1:8–14). Now He stood there that day in the temple, confronting His foes, calmly telling them a story in which He, very obviously, once again declared Himself to be the Father's well-beloved Son.

> *But those husbandmen said among themselves, This is the heir;*
> *come, let us kill him, and the inheritance shall be ours. And*
> *they took him, and killed him, and cast him out of the vine-*
> *yard. (12:7–8)*

The Lord took His parable to its inevitable conclusion: the husbandmen would murder the owner's son. What abysmal folly! What pride and arrogance! How descriptive, too, of the Sanhedrin—as represented by its current high priests, Annas and Caiaphas—wicked, unscrupulous, venal, murderous men that they were!

The Lord knew their thoughts and read their hearts. They had already made their intentions perfectly clear and the reason why they hesitated to proceed at once with His murder (11:18). The Lord knew that the bitter hatred now at work in the hearts of His foes could have only one end. They would murder Him. They would cast Him out of the vineyard.

Much good it would do them. The Lord was soon to announce to His disciples a complete change of dispensations. In the Upper Room, He would tell them that the entire scheme of things, centering on the nation of Israel, was about to be changed. *He* was now the *true* Vine, and His *Father* was the Husbandman (John 15:1). He did not tell His enemies that. There was no point in casting such pearls before such swine—to use His own expression (Matt. 7:6). He simply read to these men their doom.

> *What shall therefore the lord of the vineyard do? he will come and destroy the husbandmen, and will give the vineyard unto others.* (12:9)

Their doom was sure. They were about to commit the ultimate crime. All they could henceforth expect was judgment.

As for the vineyard—well, the church has replaced it in God's councils for now. Paul discusses the full significance of this in his Roman epistle (chaps. 9–11).[1]

b. Its natural application (12:10–12)

> *And have ye not read this scripture; The stone which the builders rejected is become the head of the corner: This was the Lord's doing, and it is marvellous in our eyes?* (12:10–11)

The Lord now quotes from Psalm 118:22, the psalm that the chanting multitudes had recited as, a day or so earlier, they had hailed His triumphant entry into Jerusalem (10:9). The Sanhedrin was about to sentence Him to death and have Him crucified and buried. And that would be the end of Him. No indeed! The Scriptures themselves proclaimed His coming exaltation. The grave would not hold Him. He would be back, the headstone of a new building, one of which they could have no conception whatsoever—the church!

Within a few months, Peter would fling this same Scripture in the faces of these same men, pursuing with the same strange blindness, the same terrible policy of rejecting this same Jesus, now ascended on high and continuing His work on earth by means of the apostles, the Holy Spirit, and the church (Acts 5:7–11).

Later still, Peter would write in his first epistle about living stones built by God into "a spiritual house" (1 Peter 2:4–8). The nation of Israel would march on to its predicted doom. God would march on toward a distant future in His church.

---

1. See John Phillips, *Exploring Romans* (Grand Rapids: Kregel, 2002).

Such was the parable of the vineyard. The religious leaders had sought to challenge His authority. He removed theirs altogether.

> *And they sought to lay hold on him, but feared the people: for they knew that he had spoken the parable against them: and they left him, and went their way. (12:12)*

Evidently, at this point, the religious leaders looked around to see if it would be safe to summon the temple police and have the Lord arrested. As before (11:18), the authorities hesitated. The people were still intrigued with Jesus, and the last thing these men wanted was to stir up a riot. They would have to wait for a more favorable occasion.

They went away enraged. They were smart enough to see that the Lord had exposed them and their wickedness publicly. He had given them far more than they had bargained for. They needed allies. They also needed to find some experts who would be able to catch this Galilean peasant by provoking Him to say something incriminating.

2. A deliberate provocation (12:13–34)
   a. In terms of the secular (12:13–17)

Note *how the plot was formed:*

> *And they send unto him certain of the Pharisees and of the Herodians, to catch him in his words. (12:13)*

The word for "catch" here means "to take in hunting," or "to ensnare." A new and unexpected coalition now emerged, a marriage of convenience by two Jewish sects with little or nothing in common. The Herodians accepted the Roman yoke and sought ways to cooperate with the occupying imperial power. The Pharisees bitterly resented the Romans. The two parties squabbled incessantly. The fact that they were acting in concert would not be lost on the Lord, who was a skilled reader of men's thoughts.

Note, also, *how the plot was furthered* (12:14–15a):

> *And when they were come, they say unto him, Master, we know that thou art true, and carest for no man: for thou regardest not*

the person of men, but teachest the way of God in truth: Is it
lawful to give tribute to Caesar, or not? (12:14)

The fulsome flattery of their opening words was certainly wasted on the Lord. He saw through their hypocrisy. Some other person or group might have put the question sincerely because all honest men need to know where to draw the line between church and state. But these men were obviously two-faced.

Behind the buildup to the question is evident sarcasm. He was a fearless teacher. He had not hesitated to take on the Jewish religious leaders, the Sanhedrin. Surely He would be equally bold in taking on the Roman political leaders—Caesar, the senate, the Roman governor, and, if necessary, even the army. After this crafty buildup came the lightning stroke: "Is it lawful to give tribute to Caesar, or not?"

Shall we give, or shall we not give? But he, knowing their hypoc-
risy, said unto them, Why tempt ye me? bring me a penny, that I
may see it. (12:15a)

The trap was obvious. If He said that they should pay tribute to Caesar, He would anger the powerful sect of the Pharisees and compromise His own claim to be the Messiah. In the popular mind, the promised Messiah was to set up His own kingdom, which meant, of course, getting rid of Roman power. If, on the other hand, He said that Roman taxation was unlawful and that they should not pay taxes to Rome, He would be playing into the hands of the Herodians, who would denounce Him to the Roman authorities.

"Bring me a penny!" He said. The "penny" was a denarius, a small coin of little value. He was in the temple at this time, where only Jewish coins were legal tender. Possibly a search was made before the Roman coin could be produced. It says something, incidentally, for the Lord's own personal poverty, that He did not Himself possess the coin He needed for illustration.

Note, moreover, *how the plot was foiled* (12:15b–17):

And they brought it. And he saith unto them, Whose is this image
and superscription? And they said unto him, Caesar's. And Jesus
answering said unto them, Render to Caesar the things that are
Caesar's, and to God the things that are God's. And they mar-
velled at him. (12:16–17)

The Lord took the coin and looked at it, turning it over in His hand to examine both sides. Of course, He knew perfectly well what was engraved on the coin. On one side was the likeness of the Roman caesar. On the other side was an inscription.

He looked up. "Whose image is this?" He demanded. "Whose inscription?"

Reluctantly, they said, "Caesar's." Then came His peerless reply: "Give to Caesar what belongs to Caesar. Give to God what belongs to God." They had never heard anything like it.

They "marvelled." The word in some manuscripts is *ekthaumazō*—"wondered beyond measure." The word *marveled* in the Received Text is *thaumazō* in the imperfect tense, implying continuing wonder—they could not get over it! He had completely avoided the trap that they had set for Him.

b. In terms of the social (12:18–27)

Note *what the Sadducees denied:*

> *Then come unto him the Sadducees, which say there is no resurrection; and they asked him, saying, (12:18)*

The Sadducees were at loggerheads with the Pharisees. The Sadducees denied that the "oral law," so beloved of the rabbis and Pharisees, had any divine authority at all. They did not stop there, however. They also denied the fact of resurrection, the existence of spirits and angels, and the supernatural in general. They did, however, uphold the authority of the written law. It was their turn now to try to cut the Lord down to their puny size.

Note *what the Sadducees declared* (12:19–23):

> *Master, Moses wrote unto us, If a man's brother die, and leave his wife behind him, and leave no children, that his brother should take his wife, and raise up seed unto his brother. (12:19)*

The Sadducees quoted from Deuteronomy 25:5–6. The Mosaic Law provided for the widow by assigning her to her dead husband's brother. He was to marry her and take her into his family to be loved and cared for as one of his wives. A marital relationship was established. The firstborn of this new union was to be named after the deceased brother, thus keeping his name alive in Israel. This arrangement also kept the deceased brother's property within the family—an important consideration under the land laws of Israel.

The system went back much farther than the Mosaic Law, however, having its roots in tribal custom. This rule guaranteed that the Lord was born into the tribe of Judah (Gen. 38:6–30; Matt. 1:3). We see the system operating again, this time under cover of the Mosaic Law, in the case of Ruth. Again, it guaranteed that the Lord would be born of Judah (Ruth 2–4).

The system might have had its flaws. No account was taken of the personal feelings of the parties involved. In the case of Judah, lust prevailed; in the case of Boaz, it was love and mutual respect. But, for all of its limitations, this law was benevolent—how benevolent can be seen when measured alongside the customs of pagan peoples. When an Indian brave died, the people plundered the new widow of her late husband's possessions; and, if she was too despised to be taken into the family of a relative, she was simply abandoned by the wayside to be killed by the wolves or exposure to the weather. Some pagan cultures immolated the widow on her husband's funeral pyre or buried her, alive or dead, with her husband's corpse. The plight of Hindu widows through the centuries has been a damning indictment of that religion.

So, the Sadducees came to Jesus with a hypothetical, cynical, and sneering case with which to challenge the Lord and justify their own rationalistic denial of the resurrection of the dead.

> *Now there were seven brethren: and the first took a wife, and dying left no seed. And the second took her, and died, neither left he any seed: and the third likewise. And the seven had her, and left no seed: last of all the woman died also. In the resurrection therefore, when they shall rise, whose wife shall she be of them? for the seven had her to wife. (12:20–23)*

Picture this poor widow. The possibility certainly existed that this was no hypothetical case, but that it really happened. We see the widow as she comes home from the funeral of her husband. She is still young, perhaps, still reasonably attractive. She might or might not like her brothers-in-law, but that consideration was of no account. She is automatically married to the next brother in line and taken into his home. A hundred stories could be written about that second marriage. What kind of a woman was she? What kind of a man was her brother-in-law? Did he have other wives? Was he loving or lustful? Was he cruel or kind? Did he like her or loathe her? What kind of a business was he in? Was he generous or mean? How long did this marriage last?

Then came the second funeral and the third husband, to be followed by the third funeral and the fourth husband. Story after story of tragedy and torment and triumph and tears could be written.

As husband after husband was buried, the succeeding husbands might well begin to grow apprehensive—we have a recorded case of just such a situation in the story of Judah and Tamar (Gen. 38). What is it about this woman? How come her husbands die with such ominous regularity? Was she suspected of foul play? Probably it took no little courage for husband number seven to step into the vacated shoes of his now dead half-dozen older brothers.

This time, however, the result was just the same and yet totally different. Again, no children resulted from the union, but this time the long-suffering woman herself died.

So much for the story! This could have happened. But then came the sneering punch line: "In the resurrection therefore, when they shall rise, whose wife shall she be of them? for the seven had her to wife."

It was on such a flimsy foundation that these "intellectuals" rejected and ridiculed the great biblical truth of resurrection. Likewise, most of the arguments of agnostics are based on distortion, ignorance, and self-willed conceit. The Lord was not impressed by Sadducean unbelief; it was both shallow and shoddy. If such a case as they cited existed, His heart would have gone out to both the poor woman and her successive husbands. He could see no justification for the levity with which the story might well have been told. As for their conclusion that they had disproved the fact of resurrection by means of this story, He swiftly exposed their error.

Note, moreover, *what the Sadducees discovered* (12:24–27):

> *And Jesus answering said unto them, Do ye not therefore err, because ye know not the scriptures, neither the power of God? (12:24)*

Ignorance of the Word of God is at the bottom of all unbelief. So is ignorance of the power of God. These cynical men were ignorant of the Word of God. The Old Testament Scriptures, their Bible, clearly taught the doctrine of resurrection.

Consider, for instance, Job's magnificent outburst in the midst of all of his woes: "Oh that my words were now written! oh that they were printed in a book!

That they were graven with an iron pen and lead in the rock for ever! For I know that my redeemer liveth, and that he shall stand at the latter day upon the earth: And though after my skin worms destroy this body, yet in my flesh shall I see God: Whom I shall see for myself, and mine eyes shall behold, and not another; though my reins be consumed within me" (Job 19:23–27). Such was Job's magnificent reply to Bildad's sneering prognostication that Job would soon be dead. No greater statement on the bodily resurrection of the believer exists until we come to the fifteenth chapter of Paul's first epistle to the Corinthians.

Consider, too, the notable word of Daniel: "And many of them that sleep in the dust of the earth shall awake, some to everlasting life, and some to shame and everlasting contempt" (Dan. 12:2).

Moreover, three outstanding cases of resurrection are recorded in the Old Testament, one connected with Elijah and two with Elisha (1 Kings 17:10–24; 2 Kings 4:16–37; 13:20–21). So for the Sadducees to deny the fact of resurrection was for them to deny the Word of God—out of sheer willful ignorance.

But they also denied the power of God. What kind of a God did they worship anyway, a God who could not raise the dead? What a poor, puny little God they had invented for themselves, a God no bigger than they were—the God of the so-called "liberals" today! A God who can create galaxies is not a God to be stopped cold by the fact of physical death! A God who can make a body of the dust of the earth (a body so complex that even modern science knows but few of its mysteries); endow that body with life; bestow upon it intellect, emotions, and will; and give it a spirit of its own is not a God to be balked by death. It is no more remarkable that we should live *again* than it is that we should live at all! The Sadducees were small-minded indeed.

> For when they shall rise from the dead, they neither marry, nor
> are given in marriage; but are as the angels which are in heaven.
> (12:25)

The Lord now addresses the basic problem of Sadducean skepticism. He does not say "*if* they shall arise from the dead" but "*when* they shall arise." There is no doubt about it. He Himself was "the resurrection and the life" (John 11:25–26). He had already raised two people from the dead (Mark 5:22–43; Luke 7:11–17). There was no way that the Sadducees could not have known about these events. Moreover, He was on His way to raise a man who, by the time Jesus arrived, would have been dead and buried long enough for his body to begin to decompose (John 11:17–44). So the unbelief of the Sadducees was willful unbelief. All Jerusalem would know of this forthcoming resurrection.

As for the case that they had cited as the grand basis of their denial of resurrection, that, too, was based on ignorance. The fact is that there is no marriage in heaven. The angels do not need to propagate their kind. Nor do the redeemed in heaven. The whole reproductive system is temporal and earthly, necessitated because of death and designed for the propagation of the species. In heaven, all of our relationships will be changed. The Lord spoke with absolute authority and confidence about these things. After all, heaven was His home. He had come from there and was going to return there soon. How petty and poverty-stricken the unbelief of Sadducean and liberal theology seems when placed alongside the confident teaching of Christ!

However, the Lord was not quite through with these sophisticate morons, to borrow a Pauline expression (Rom. 1:22).

> *And as touching the dead, that they rise: have ye not read in the book of Moses, how in the bush God spake unto him, saying, I am the God of Abraham, and the God of Isaac, and the God of Jacob? He is not the God of the dead, but the God of the living: ye therefore do greatly err. (12:26–27)*

With one sharp stab of the sword of the Spirit, the Lord punctured their whole case. When God spoke to Moses at the burning bush, Jacob had been dead for 200 years, Isaac had been dead for 225 years, and Abraham had been dead for 330 years. The point was that *they were not dead at all.* They were very much alive. Indeed, they were still alive when Jesus demolished the Sadducees' argument. The translated beggar, Lazarus, was with Abraham in glory, and the rich fool in hell not only saw Abraham but also pleaded with him and argued with him (Luke 16:19–31). Jesus knew all about it; the deluded Sadducees knew nothing about it.

"Ye therefore do greatly err," Jesus said. The emphasis is on the word *ye.* Willful blindness is inexcusable. Evidence for resurrection was available to these men, as it is available to all, in the Scriptures. In the last analysis, rationalism is not a mental problem but a moral problem. It is not that such people cannot believe; it is that they will not believe. That is the greatest error of all.

    c. In terms of the spiritual (12:28–34)
       (1) What the Scripture said (12:28–31)

And one of the scribes came, and having heard them reasoning
together, and perceiving that he had answered them well, asked
him, Which is the first commandment of all? (12:28)

We do not know if this man was one of the scribes who had, a short while
before, challenged the Lord's authority to minister as He did (11:27). He seems
to be more sincere than the others who challenged the Lord on this day. This
scribe belonged to the sect of the Pharisees, and he was apparently gratified by
the Lord's capable handling of the rival Sadducees.

The scribes, as a group, appear here and there throughout the Scriptures. The early
scribes functioned as secretaries to David and Solomon (2 Sam. 8:17; 20:25; 1 Kings
4:3). By the time of Hezekiah, they transcribed old records and became known for
both their scholarship and their interpretation of the law. They boasted of their wisdom (Jer. 8:8), and they were a dominant force among the repatriates after the
Babylonian captivity. Ezra was a scribe. They gave themselves to the careful study of
the biblical text and developed rules for transcribing it. In time, the words of the
scribes took precedence over the words of Scripture. By the time of Christ, their
casuistry was evident in the clever tricks that they invented for sidestepping the plain-
est duties imposed by the Law of God (Matt. 15:1–6; 23:16–23).

A typical scribe began his training about the age of thirteen. He would go to
Jerusalem and enroll in one of the rabbinical schools. Not until he was thirty,
however, was he inaugurated into his office. Successful scribes rose to high positions in the land. They were doctors of the law and family lawyers. Some of those
who did not rise to such prominence worked at copying the Scriptures. Others
became notaries and were available for writing legal documents, sales contracts,
and so on. The scribes, as a class, had a passion for public recognition and loved
to be given prominent places in formal functions. They enjoyed being hailed in
the marketplace and being called by imposing titles. By the time of Christ, they
were a close, hereditary caste. No priest could compete with them, so many of
the priests joined the scribes.

These scholars debated among themselves which of the commandments carried
the most weight. The Jews recognized 613 commandments of the written Mosaic
Law. In the early days, the ceremonial laws had been deemed the most important.
The prophets who wrote later shifted the weight to the moral laws. In Jesus' day,
the scribes and the Pharisees placed most importance on Sabbath-keeping, tithing,
and the dietary requirements of the law; however, they neglected the more vital
aspects of justice, morality, and truth.

This particular scribe seems to have been dissatisfied with this state of affairs. He was not trying to trap the Lord; he seems to have been genuinely interested in the Lord's opinion.

> *And Jesus answered him, The first of all the commandments is, Hear, O Israel; The Lord our God is one Lord: And thou shalt love the Lord thy God with all thy heart, and with all thy soul, and with all thy mind, and with all thy strength: this is the first commandment. (12:29–30)*

The Lord quoted from Deuteronomy 6:4–5. There is only one God. The Lord restated that simple fact that lies behind the whole Mosaic Law and is basic to the first commandment of the Decalogue. The Lord, however, did not appeal to the Decalogue, as such, in dealing with this scribe. He appealed to the great basic truth that God is God, and He alone is God. The Jewish scribes wrote this truth and carried it with them in a small case, bound either to the forehead or the arm.

There is only one God. His name is "the LORD" (Jehovah). He must be enthroned, Jesus reminded the scribe, in the life of the individual so sovereignly and so supremely that every emotion is a God-centered emotion, every thought is a God-centered thought, every decision is a God-centered decision, and every deed is a God-centered deed. The whole being is thus to be centered in God, who is to be loved and served with all of the strength that we possess.

> *And the second is like, namely this, Thou shalt love thy neighbour as thyself. There is none other commandment greater than these. (12:31)*

This time, the Lord quoted from Leviticus 19:18. Second only to our love for God is to be our love for our fellowmen. The Mosaic Law was summarized in the Decalogue in ten simple commandments. Jesus now reduced it to two. Love is the fulfilling of the law (Rom. 13:8–10).

(2) What the scribe said (12:32–33)

> *And the scribe said unto him, Well, Master, thou hast said the truth: for there is one God; and there is none other but he: And to love him*

> *with all the heart, and with all the understanding, and with all the*
> *soul, and with all the strength, and to love his neighbour as himself,*
> *is more than all whole burnt offerings and sacrifices. (12:32–33)*

It was a remarkable revelation of this particular scribe's heart. He heartily endorsed the Lord's words and added his own comment. The word used for "discreetly" here means that he answered intelligently. Evidently, he had a mind of his own. He was in a better case than the rich young ruler who allowed his money to get in his way, and this scribe was not far from the kingdom, but he was not yet in it. Hence, the veiled warning. The rich young ruler let his money get in his way. This scribe was in danger of letting his mind get in the way. To get into the kingdom, he must pledge allegiance to the King. And the King was passing by right then, on His way to the cross to die for all of those who failed to keep the law as Jesus had just quoted and explained it.

No one dared cross verbal swords with the Lord again. Still, the Lord was aware that questions about the relative importance of the sacrifices and offerings of the law were really only secondary matters. There would be no need for any of the other commandments if a man loved God and his neighbor the way he was supposed to.

He might have gone further. David, in his guilt and despair, recognized in his desperate need that the entire ceremonial law did not help him at all (Ps. 51:16–17). On the contrary, he needed some means of justification quite apart from that provided by the sacrifices of the law (Ps. 32:1–2).

(3) What the Savior said (12:34)

> *And when Jesus saw that he answered discreetly, he said unto*
> *him, Thou art not far from the kingdom of God. And no man*
> *after that durst ask him any question. (12:34)*

The Lord had silenced His critics. The discerning scribe had been answered. Many questions, however, still hovered in the air. The scribe, for instance, was probably wondering what the Lord meant by saying that he was not far from the kingdom.

The scribes agreed that the Messiah was to be the Son of David. They could give Scripture for that fact easily enough (2 Sam. 7:8–16), so they had no dispute about that. Jesus was, Himself, that "son of David" of whom they spoke (Matt.

1:1–16). By inspecting the genealogical records kept in the temple, that fact could be verified. But there was another side to that issue, one to which the scribes had no answer.

> 3. A dramatic punch line (12:35–40)
>   a. A word of wisdom (12:35–37)

And Jesus answered and said, while he taught in the temple, How say the scribes that Christ is the son of David? For David himself said by the Holy Ghost, The Lord said to my Lord, Sit thou on my right hand, till I make thine enemies thy footstool. David therefore himself calleth him Lord; and whence is he then his son? And the common people heard him gladly. (12:35–37)

This time the Lord quoted from Psalm 110:1. David himself must have been astonished at what he had written: "The LORD [Jehovah] said unto my Lord, Sit thou at my right hand. . . ." The Jews acknowledged that this was a messianic psalm. In this psalm, David heard One, whom he knew to be Jehovah, inviting One whom David acknowledged to be his Lord, to come and sit with Him upon His throne, the throne of God. Such a One could only be God. No one else could share God's throne. Yet this One, thus called to sit on high, could be none other than the Messiah—and He was to be David's son!

The Lord now had everyone's attention. He Himself was David's son and Israel's Messiah. His recent triumphant entry had so proclaimed Him. The temple records proved it. Yet David, by divine inspiration, owned this his son to be his *Lord*—a title for Deity. So then—let them answer this question—either David was mistaken, the Scripture was false, and David's "son" was no more than that, a mere human descendant of David, or this Son of David was both David's divine Lord and the Son of God.

That was what the scribe who discussed the law with Jesus must decide. If he wanted to become a member of the kingdom of God, he had to take that step of faith, from giving intellectual assent to truth to personal surrender to Christ. It was not really a question of the *law* but of the *Lord*. What would he do with Jesus? That was the fundamental issue. Would he make the confession that Peter made: "Thou art the Christ, the Son of the living God" (Matt. 16:16), and that Nathanael made: "Rabbi, thou art the Son of God; thou art the King of Israel" (John 1:49), and that Thomas was to make: "My Lord and my God" (John 20:28)?

"And the common people heard him gladly," Mark adds. Doubtless, they were delighted to see the scribes, the Pharisees, the Sadducees, and the chief priests and rulers put in their place.

b. A word of warning (12:38–40)

And he said unto them in his doctrine, Beware of the scribes, which love to go in long clothing, and love salutations in the marketplaces, And the chief seats in the synagogues, and the uppermost rooms at feasts: (12:38–39)

Whether the thoughtful scribe with whom the Lord had just spoken was such a man we are not told. In any case, the Lord was not going to make it easy for him to get into the kingdom of God. He would have to set aside all of his pride in place and race. The scribes, as a class, had a wholly false sense of values, and they were eaten up with pride. Their spirit was completely out of harmony with the Lord's spirit of meekness and lowliness (Matt. 11:29). The Lord warns the people who were listening to all of this about the mistaken notion that such things as the best seats in the synagogue and stylish, expensive robes had anything to do with godliness. On the contrary, all too often, they were a cloak for something else.

Which devour widows' houses, and for a pretence make long prayers: these shall receive greater damnation. (12:40)

One of the duties of the scribes was to make out wills and other deeds. It often happened that, not content with the usual fees for their services, the scribes would play upon the fears, superstitions, and religious susceptibilities of those recently widowed. They would persuade them to deed over their property to the temple as a means of grace. They, themselves, received a substantial proportion of the proceeds. They would cover up this fraudulent activity with hypocritical prayers. Terrible will be the judgment of all such leaders.

4. A deathless principle (12:41–44)

And Jesus sat over against the treasury, and beheld how the people cast money into the treasury: and many that were rich cast in much. (12:41)

Tired of contention the Lord now left the porches and ascended the steps that led from "the terrace" into the temple precincts. The treasury was located in the Court of the Women, which occupied a space of about two hundred square feet and was surrounded by a colonnade. Inside and against the wall were thirteen trumpet-shaped boxes. These "trumpets" bore various inscriptions, designating to what purpose the various gifts were directed. Nine were for legal dues, temple taxes, and the like; four were for voluntary contributions.

The Lord sat down to watch the way people made their contributions. The wealthy were throwing in money by the handfuls. Some people were giving cheerfully, others grudgingly. The Lord observed them all. The word for "beheld" is *theōreō*, suggesting thoughtful observation. The Greek word gives us our English word *theater*. The Lord watched it all with an eager eye. All of the color and drama and, often, the playacting of the ever changing pageant held His interest. Then something of eternal significance caught His eye.

> *And there came a certain poor widow, and she threw in two mites, which make a farthing. (12:42)*

In my boyhood days, we still had farthings in England. It was a small copper coin worth one-quarter of a penny, of no account even in a schoolboy's scale of values. The mite—a small, thin Jewish copper coin—was equally low in the scale of values. But all that the widow had was just two such mites.

It is said that the rabbis forbade the giving of less than two mites. Perhaps that is why she put them both in the box. Or maybe she was torn between giving to support the temple and giving to relieve the poor. She loved God and wanted to give something to Him. On the other hand, she knew what it was like to be desperately poor. In the end, she gave her all, perhaps putting one mite in the box for the Lord and one mite in the box for the poor. In any case, the Lord saw her approach the treasury, the two coins clutched tightly in her hand. He saw the inward struggle, the sudden decision, the swift action, and the woman's hurried departure. He was delighted!

> *And he called unto him his disciples, and saith unto them, Verily I say unto you, That this poor widow hath cast more in, than all they which have cast into the treasury: For all they did cast in of their abundance; but she of her want did cast in all that she had, even all her living. (12:43–44)*

Little did she know whose eyes were watching her that day! Little did she know that the Lord of Glory "sat over against the treasury" that day! Little did she know who had looked into her purse! Little did she know what joy she had brought to the Savior—a ray of sunshine on a dark and gloomy day of controversy, a glow in the gloom that was now gathering all about Him on His way to the cross. Little did she know that her gift that day would find its way into the Gospels, and that for the next two thousand years her generosity would be talked about and preached about to the very ends of the earth!

I have often wondered what she found when she arrived home penniless that day. Did the Lord send Judas with a gift? Just a few days earlier, the Lord had received Zaccheus's pledge: "Half of my goods I give to the poor" (Luke 19:8). Did the Lord touch the heart of that penitent publican and direct his steps to that poor widow's door?

We shall never know. But one thing we can anticipate—great will be her reward in heaven.

Section 2: Predicting the Consequences of Calvary (13:1–37)
A. The temple (13:1–4)
　　1. Their pride (13:1)
　　2. His prediction (13:2–4)
　　　　a. The exact prediction they received (13:2)
　　　　b. The expanded prediction they requested (13:3–4)
　　　　　　(1) Where? (13:3a)
　　　　　　(2) Who? (3:3b)
　　　　　　(3) When? (13:4a)
　　　　　　(4) What? (13:4b)
B. The times (13:5–13)
　　1. False beliefs (13:5–6)
　　　　a. The noting of deceivers (13:5)
　　　　b. The number of deceivers (13:6a)
　　　　c. The nature of deceivers (13:6b)
　　2. Furious battles (13:7–8)
　　　　a. These wars are portrayed (13:7)
　　　　　　(1) Endemic war (13:7)
　　　　　　　　(a) The inevitable (13:7a)
　　　　　　　　(b) The interval (13:7b)
　　　　　　(2) Epidemic war (13:8a–c)
　　　　　　　　(a) Its climax (13:8a)
　　　　　　　　(b) Its coincidence (13:8b)
　　　　　　　　(c) Its consequence (13:8c)
　　　　b. These wars are portentous (13:8d)
　　3. Formal beatings (13:9–11)
　　　　a. Information (13:9)
　　　　　　(1) A word of warning (13:9a)
　　　　　　(2) A word of witness (13:9b)
　　　　b. Intimation (13:10)
　　　　c. Inspiration (13:11)
　　　　　　(1) Their personal incapacity (13:11a)
　　　　　　(2) Their promised invincibility (13:11b)
　　4. Family betrayals (13:12–13)
　　　　a. Their total rejection (13:12–13a)
　　　　　　(1) Their homes will be unsafe (13:12)

        (2) Their hatred will be universal (13:13a)

     b. Their triumphant resolution (13:13b)

C. The Tribulation (13:14–23)

    1. The great profanation (13:14–18)

     a. What they would see (13:14a–b)

        (1) The abomination, described by the famous prophet (13:14a)

        (2) The abomination, dedicated by the future prophet (13:14b)

     b. Where they should be (13:14c–18)

        (1) Go! (13:14c–16)

          (a) The place (13:14c)

          (b) The plea (13:15–16)

            i. Don't go home for anything (13:15)

            ii. Don't get hindered by anything (13:16)

        (2) Woe! (13:17–18)

          (a) Regarding a possible handicap (13:17)

          (b) Regarding a possible hardship (13:18)

    2. The great persecution (13:19)

    3. The great proclamation (13:20–23)

     a. Take heart (13:20)

     b. Take heed (13:21–23)

        (1) Don't believe the lies (13:21–22)

          (a) The lying propaganda (13:21)

          (b) The lying proofs (13:22)

        (2) Do believe the Lord (13:23)

D. The termination (13:24–27)

    1. The signs in the sky (13:24–25)

     a. As to when (13:24a)

     b. As to what (13:24b–25)

        (1) The material sphere (13:24b–25a)

          (a) The solar system affected (13:24b)

          (b) The stellar system affected (13:25a)

        (2) The mystical sphere (13:25b)

    2. The sign of the Savior (13:26–27)

     a. The glory of the sight (13:26)

        (1) His coming will be visible (13:26a)

        (2) His coming will be victorious (13:26b)

     b. The gathering of the saints (13:27)

        (1) The messengers (13:27a)

        (2) The meeting (13:27b–c)

           (a) The remaining earthly saints (13:27b)

           (b) The returning heavenly saints (13:27c)

E. The tree (13:28–33)

  1. The parabolic fig (13:28)

  2. The prophetic focus (13:29–33)

      a. The focus on the time (13:29–30)

        (1) The general theme (13:29)

        (2) The generation theme (13:30)

      b. The focus on the truth (13:31–32)

        (1) A word about the Scripture (13:31)

        (2) A word about the secret (13:32)

      c. The focus on the task (13:33)

F. The test (13:34–37)

  1. The parable (13:34)

      a. The Lord's departure (13:34a)

      b. The Lord's disciples (13:34b–c)

        (1) They must work (13:34b)

        (2) They must watch (13:34c)

  2. The point (13:35–37)

      a. The secrecy of His return (13:35)

      b. The suddenness of His return (13:36–37)

        (1) The silly thing to do (13:36)

        (2) The sensible thing to do (13:37)

—⚅—

Section 2: Predicting the Consequences of Calvary (13:1–37)

A. The temple (13:1–4)

And as he went out of the temple, one of his disciples saith unto him,
Master, see what manner of stones and what building are here! (13:1)

Truly those stones were impressive, a tribute to the skill of Solomon's engineers and Herod's builders. Some of the stones measured twenty to forty feet long and weighed more than one hundred tons. Man's architectural achievements are truly monumental. The ring of obelisks at Stonehenge, the pyramids in Egypt, and the Great Wall of China draw the eye and awe the imagination. How could mere men carve and shape and move and position such massive, heavy, and unwieldy blocks of stone and place them with such mathematical, and often astronomical, precision? It was all a matter of mechanics and manpower.

The disciples were impressed. They thought that Jesus would be too.

> *And Jesus answering said unto him, Seest thou these great buildings? there shall not be left one stone upon another, that shall not be thrown down. (13:2)*

Whichever disciple it was who invited Jesus' comment on the outward magnificence of the temple was impressed by the *construction* of the temple. In fact, this particular temple was not yet completed. Herod the Great had begun work on it in 20 B.C., and it would not be completed until A.D. 64, having taken some eighty-five years to build.

Jesus was more concerned with its *destruction*. Despite the fact that He had already cleansed it twice, the same wicked cartel of unscrupulous men still ran the place. On the cross, He would tear its innermost veil in two and render Judaism obsolete. For the Jewish religion, as authorized in the Old Testament, everything hinged on the temple with its attendant rites and rituals. The veil divided the temple itself in two. It was central to the rituals of the Day of Atonement, the true climax of the annual Jewish religious calendar. The rending of the veil (Matt. 27:51) signified an end to all of this ritualism (Heb. 10:19–22). Some forty years into the immediate future, the Lord would summon the Roman army to come and pull it down altogether.

"There shall not be left one stone upon another." The negative used denotes absolute certainty. Jesus foresaw the day when Roman soldiers would pry the stones apart, heedless of the desire of Titus to preserve the temple, in an eager scramble to get at the gold that so lavishly adorned it. One with greater authority than that of Titus had spoken.

> *And as he sat upon the mount of Olives over against the temple, Peter and James and John and Andrew asked him privately, (13:3)*

This group was the usual inner circle of disciples, but it also included Andrew, Peter's brother. These men, good men though they were, had far less heart than

Jesus had. He had already wept over the city and the temple (Matt. 23:36–38). They were simply curious as to when this unexpected and extraordinary prophecy would be fulfilled.

> *Tell us, when shall these things be? and what shall be the sign*
> *when all these things shall be fulfilled? (13:4)*

When? What? They wanted to know about the time, and they wanted to be given a token. The Lord gave two end-times prophecies, one in the temple and the other on the Mount of Olives (Luke 21 and Matt. 24–25; Mark 13). The prophecy recorded in Luke concentrates on the downfall of Jerusalem that took place in A.D. 70; Matthew and Mark concentrate on the end-times events unveiled at this time by Christ. Some overlap in subject matter occurs, however, between the two prophecies, so it is not always immediately clear whether the Lord is referring to the impending overthrow of the temple (A.D. 70), to the final dissolution of Jewish national life (A.D. 135, at the time of the Bar Chochba rebellion), or to end-times events themselves. Like much Bible prophesy, this end-times prophesy had both a near, impending, and partial fulfillment (the burden of Luke) and a final, end-times, complete fulfillment (the burden of Mark and Matthew).

B. The times (13:5–13)

We begin with *false beliefs* (13:5–6):

> *And Jesus answering them began to say, Take heed lest any man*
> *deceive you: For many shall come in my name, saying, I am Christ;*
> *and shall deceive many. (13:5–6)*

The first ingredient in the recipe of ruin for the last days is to be deception. The Lord emphasizes especially deception that is propagated by false messiahs, particularly the kind of false messiah who actually claims to be Christ Himself. This is a form of deception to which the Jews have been particularly susceptible.

The Jews never had a false messiah until after they rejected the true One; after that, they had a rash of them. There was Moses of Crete, for instance, who promised to smite the sea and lead the Jews on dry land to Canaan; the deluded followers of this false messiah congregated on a cliff and jumped to their deaths. There was Abraham Abulfia, who tried to convert Pope Nicholas III. The pope died the same week! Abulfia was handed over to the Inquisition but actually talked his way out of its clutches! There was even a female messiah, Eva Frank, a seductive temptress who adroitly combined immorality with religion!

As the Christian age draws to a close, we can expect to see a rash of self-proclaimed Christs arise. The Antichrist and his Jewish spokesman, the False Prophet, will eventually deceive both Jews and remaining members of the false church alike (2 Thess. 2; Rev. 13).

Next we have *furious battles* (13:7–8):

> And when ye shall hear of wars and rumours of wars, be ye not troubled: for such things must needs be; but the end shall not be yet. (13:7)

Jesus was God's peace offer to this warring world. The angels sang, and their voices rang out across the Judean hills that cold, clear winter's night: "Unto you is born this day in the city of David a Saviour, which is Christ the Lord. . . . Glory to God in the highest, and on earth peace, good will toward men" (Luke 2:11, 14). Within three and a half decades, the answer was clear: "We will not have this man to reign over us" (Luke 19:14). The Jews handed their Messiah over to the Romans for execution and declared, "We have no king but Caesar" (John 19:15). When Pilate crucified Him, he wrote His title in the three chief languages of the day for everyone to read: "JESUS OF NAZARETH THE KING OF THE JEWS" (John 19:19).

So much for the peace offer connected with the *cradle*. The world has known little but war ever since. There is, of course, another peace offer, one connected with the *cross* (Col. 1:20–21), but that is another matter altogether. So Jesus focused on the wars connected with end-times events. "Such things must needs be," said Jesus. The Prince of Peace (Isa. 9:6) has been rejected. War is all that remains until He comes back.

> For nation shall rise against nation, and kingdom against king-dom: and there shall be earthquakes in divers places, and there shall be famines and troubles: these are the beginnings of sorrows. (13:8)

This is a quotation from Isaiah 19:2, where it had a local application. The Lord broadened the prophecy and gave it a new end-times significance. First, He mentioned the various wars of history that, down to the time of the Napoleonic wars, were essentially wars of armies fighting armies. In the end times, Jesus said, war would take on a vast, new, horrific dimension.

Some ten years after the end of the First World War and ten years before the outbreak of the Second World War, Sir Winston Churchill summarized the dramatic change that had taken place in 1914. War, he said, emerged as the potential destroyer of the human race:

> The organization of mankind into great states and Empires, and the rise of nations to full collective consciousness, enabled enterprises of slaughter to be planned and executed upon a scale and with a perseverance never before imagined. . . .
>
> Instead of fortified towns being starved whole nations were methodically subjected . . . to the process of reduction by famine. The entire population in one capacity or another took part in the war; all were equally the object of attack. . . .[1]

World War II added new dimensions of horror to the waging of war. Weapons became more sophisticated, more nations were involved, casualties skyrocketed—and science gave us the atomic bomb. Two small atomic bombs, dropped on strategic cities, brought Japan to its knees. Now we have sophisticated nuclear warheads, intercontinental ballistic missiles, laser weapons, platforms in space—and even rogue nations willing to arm terrorists with bacteriological weapons and other weapons of mass destruction. These things are merely heralds of the approaching end-times judgments to warn a godless world that the end times have arrived.

The Lord mentioned earthquakes next. We know very much more about earthquakes today than we did, say, twenty years ago. Scientists have mapped the major earthquake zones of the world and have ready explanations about the tectonic forces that cause them. But they are still unable to predict them, much less prevent them. Horrendous earthquakes are becoming increasingly common—Alaska, San Francisco, Mexico, and Japan are just a few of the places that have suffered major earthquakes in recent times—and seismologists are warning us that all indications are that increasingly more catastrophic earthquakes lie ahead.

---

1. From Winston Churchill, *The Aftermath,* quoted by him in *The Gathering Storm,* vol. 1 of his memoirs of World War II (Boston: Houghton Mifflin, 1948), 35–37.

And famines. Our television screens frequently bring the horrifying scenes of mass starvation into our living rooms. We see the helpless little children with their spindly legs and swollen stomachs in the last stages of malnutrition. We see the distraught mothers and the overworked, ill-equipped doctors and nurses struggling to help here and there a handful of the masses of people dying of famine. In country after country and year after year, until even the most tenderhearted philanthropists become discouraged. It seems to be hopeless. So, in the end, millions of people are simply left to starve to death—so many more statistics in the endless horror stories of the twenty-first century.

Mark mentions "troubles." Matthew is more specific; he mentions "pestilences" (Matt. 24:7).

The same twentieth century that brought us global warfare also handed us chemical and bacteriological weapons as a means of adding new dimensions of horror to war. And now we have "the Hot Zone," where a new and deadly virus lurks in the equatorial forests of the world, in remote jungle caves and mountains among the trees.[2] It is called the Ebola virus. It is so deadly that it makes the AIDS virus look like a mild case of the flu. It kills nine out of ten of its victims, and it does so quickly and gruesomely. Even biohazard experts are terrified of it. Those who are infected become human virus bombs. They bleed from all of the orifices of the body. They are deadly to touch or help.

Nor is this virus confined to the jungle. It broke out some time ago among monkeys in the suburbs of a major American city, in a building where the animals were being housed for experimental purposes. The scene that resulted was apocalyptic. A SWAT team of soldiers and scientists wearing biohazard space suits fought the menace for eighteen days, terrified that the virus might break out among the human population and breed an epidemic of unprecedented proportions. The people who were engaged in the battle knew that the virus could kill them quickly and horribly. The emergence of this new and terrible virus coincides with the growing realization that even old-fashioned plagues—such as tuberculosis, leprosy, and the bubonic plague—might soon be immune to modern vaccines and wonder drugs and once again ravage the earth.

"These are the beginnings of sorrows," the Lord added. The word for "sorrows" is ōdin. It is used for both birth pangs and death throes. The Lord pictures

---

2. See Richard Preston, *The HOT ZONE* (New York: Random House, 1994). Stephen King, the author of a number of spine-tingling horror stories, said, "The first chapter of *The HOT ZONE* is one of the most horrifying things I have read in my whole life . . . and then it gets worse. . . ."

the old order in the beginning of its end-times agony and the new order in the travail of its birth. These ingredients in what Jesus called "the beginning of sorrows" are paralleled by the seal judgments of the Apocalypse (Rev. 6).[3]

Then the Lord envisioned *formal beatings* (13:9–11):

> *But take heed to yourselves: for they shall deliver you up to councils; and in the synagogues ye shall be beaten: and ye shall be brought before rulers and kings for my sake, for a testimony against them. (13:9)*

James, the brother of John, became the first martyr of the church, and Peter escaped the same fate only by means of a miracle. It did not take the Sanhedrin long to see the infant church as a threat. Almost immediately after Pentecost, Peter healed a lame man and was arrested for preaching in the temple precincts. He and John, who was with him, boldly charged the Jewish authorities with the murder of Christ (Acts 4:1–21). They were released with warnings not to preach anymore in the name of Jesus and with threats of dire consequences if they did. Peter snapped his fingers at them and defied them.

The rapid expansion of the church infuriated the Jewish leaders who incarcerated the apostles. Again, released miraculously, the apostles returned to the temple and continued preaching. They were arrested again, hauled before the Sanhedrin and beaten. They simply laughed and went on preaching in the temple in open defiance of the Sadducees and the other ringleaders of the official Jewish opposition (Acts 5).

And so it has continued century after century. The church is God's beachhead on this rebel planet. Satan hates it with a malice that defies description. He has persecuted it with tireless persistence down to the present day. He has used Roman caesars, Spanish inquisitors, Holy Roman emperors, Communist commissars, and other dictators as his tools. The roll call of church-age martyrs is beyond count. Persecution of Christians has been endemic throughout the church age. In the twenty-first century it has become epidemic. It is estimated that more Christians, worldwide, have been martyred for the cause of Christ in the last century than in all of the previous nineteen centuries put together. Even worse horrors of persecution lie ahead for the world generally and for the Jews particularly after the church is called home.

---

3. See John Phillips, *Exploring Revelation* (Grand Rapids: Kregel, 2001); and idem, *Exploring the Future* (Grand Rapids: Kregel, 2003).

And the gospel must first be published among all nations. (13:10)

Matthew is more specific. He tells us that the gospel, to which the Lord referred, is the "gospel of the kingdom." True, the church's commission is "to all nations" (Matt. 28:18–20) and "to the uttermost parts of the earth" (Acts 1:8). But with end-times shadows closing in upon us, and despite heroic efforts and modern technology, the task remains far from complete. There remain "untold millions still untold." More than five thousand known language groups are in the world, and some three thousand of them still have no translation of the Scriptures in their language at all.

Once the church is raptured, a fresh outpouring of the Holy Spirit will occur because what happened at Pentecost was only a partial fulfillment of Joel's prophecy (Joel 2:28–32; Acts 2:16–21). Two witnesses (Rev. 11:3) will be raised up (possibly Enoch and Elijah), and they will win 144,000 other witnesses from among the Hebrew people (Rev. 7; 14). These, in turn, will win "a great multitude, which no man could number" (Rev. 7:9). Those people who still are unevangelized will be given a final offer of salvation by angelic proclamation just before the end-times wrath (Rev. 14:6–7). Matthew adds, "Then [once the world has been thus evangelized] shall the end [*telos,* the very end] come" (Matt. 24:14).

> *But when they shall lead you, and deliver you up, take no thought beforehand what ye shall speak, neither do ye premeditate: but whatsoever shall be given you in that hour, that speak ye: for it is not ye that speak, but the Holy Ghost. (13:11)*

Thus it was with Stephen, the first martyr of the church. The Hellinist Jews of the Greco-Roman world (probably including Saul of Tarsus) debated Stephen in their Jerusalem synagogues, but they came off second best. They could not resist the mighty infilling of the Spirit, which gave Stephen an eloquence and a mastery of Scripture that they could not refute. So they plotted against him, had him arrested and falsely accused, and hurried him away to trial.

First, his face arrested them. It looked like the face of an angel (Acts 6:13). Then there was his defense! It was masterly. The words poured out of him like molten lava from a volcano. Their only answer was a monstrous and demonic rage because Stephen testified against them with Holy Spirit fervor, fire, and a flow of facts that they could not deny. The best thing for them to do, they reasoned, was to silence him by killing him.

And so it has been throughout the centuries. We think of Paul before Agrippa, for instance, and Martin Luther before the Diet of Worms.

We are, also, warned of *family betrayals* (13:12–13):

> *Now the brother shall betray the brother to death, and the father the son; and children shall rise up against their parents, and shall cause them to be put to death. (13:12)*

This is a quotation from Micah 7:6. Micah was a younger contemporary of the prophet Isaiah. He preached at a time when the Assyrians were preparing to descend on the kingdom of Israel and make an end of it. In the south, the Judean king, faced with the same threat, vacillated between a pro-Egyptian and a pro-Assyrian foreign policy. In the northern kingdom, all moral and religious restraints were abandoned. The Assyrians arrived; and the terror of siege and sack at the hands of the terrible, ruthless, and bloodthirsty Assyrians must have produced many examples of betrayal by members of one's own family.

In A.D. 70, the terrible siege of Jerusalem by the Romans broke out. The Romans were on the outside; warring Jewish factions fought each other on the inside. The squabbling must have produced chilling stories of betrayal. Down through history, the church, in its hours of torment and terror, has also garnered its own store of horror tales. In the days of the Inquisition, for example, domestic betrayals were common as people sought to save their own skin at the expense of the life of a near kinsman. In modern times, persecutions of the church by the Nazis, the Soviets, and the Chinese Communists have added their quota of sad incidents of betrayal. The Chinese Communists, led by Mao Tse-Tung, sought to brainwash a whole nation, especially the Christians. Many were the treacheries and betrayals that accompanied this terrible time of anguish. The whole system of brainwashing was built on betrayal.

> *And ye shall be hated of all men for my name's sake: but he that shall endure unto the end, the same shall be saved. (13:13)*

Again the scene focuses on the coming horrors that will be the mark of the Great Tribulation. Those who take a stand for God when the Antichrist is here can expect no mercy. He will demand that everyone receive this mark. Those who refuse will be put to death. Martyrdom will be part of the accepted consequence of salvation (Rev. 7:9–17). Great will be the reward in heaven of those who triumph over the Antichrist by defying him to the death or by enduring to the end.

Church history bears testimony to the truth of the Lord's words. Those who bear the name of Christ have been persecuted throughout all ages in all parts of the world. That the Lord particularly had the time of the Great Tribulation in mind, however, is evident from the next verse.

C. The Tribulation (13:14–23)

First, we note *the great profanation* (13:14–18):

> *But when ye shall see the abomination of desolation, spoken of by Daniel the prophet, standing where it ought not, (let him that readeth understand,) then let them that be in Judaea flee to the mountains: (13:14)*

The reference is to Daniel 9:27. When the Antichrist arrives, he will eventually become the world dictator. Satan will have at last achieved the goal for which he has been striving ever since the days of Nimrod—a world empire ruled by his own man. Once the Antichrist is seated on the throne of global power and dominion, he will unveil his secret plans by seizing the rebuilt Jewish temple in Jerusalem. He will put his own image in the Holy of Holies of that temple, endow the image with life, give it the power to kill, and demand that everyone receive his mark (the famous "mark of the beast") as a badge of allegiance and worship his image. Those who refuse will be exterminated.

The believers will have only one hope—flee for refuge to the hills and desolate places the moment the Antichrist seizes the temple. Flight will be particularly urgent for those living in Israel, especially in Jerusalem.

> *And let him that is on the housetop not go down into the house, neither enter therein, to take any thing out of his house: And let him that is in the field not turn back again for to take up his garment. (13:15–16)*

Flee! Run for your lives! The moment the Antichrist's image is in the temple, his police will move to seal off all of the exit routes from the city, and his army will patrol the roads and highways. Once he has secured Jerusalem, posted his guards at the intersections, and sealed off the passes, it will be too late to escape. To go back into the house will be fatal. Just those few minutes devoted to securing life's little treasures, to rounding up supplies of food and clothing, and to gathering up purses and the like will make all of the difference between escape and capture, life and death.

The situation was similar in Sodom in the days of Lot. The angels virtually had to drag Lot and his family out of Sodom! They would have stayed there dithering over taking this or that, even whether to leave a note for this one and that one, until they were overwhelmed in Sodom's doom (Gen. 19).

It was the same situation when Vesuvius exploded. Those who have been to Pompeii tell us of the hundreds of skeletons that have been unearthed in the buried ruins of that ill-fated city. The walls remain fresh, as if they were painted yesterday. The rich mosaic floors retain their colors. In the houses, fragments of the last feast remain. And everywhere are bones and skeletons. A skeleton was found with a key in its bony hand, and nearby was a bag of coins. Beside some silver vases lay another skeleton, presumed to be that of a slave, overwhelmed in the act of plunder. And on and on, evidence of people who perished, thinking that they still had plenty of time to gather their treasures before taking their flight.

"Flee!" That is the Lord's advice to those alive when the Antichrist makes his move.

> *But woe to them that are with child, and to them that give suck*
> *in those days! And pray ye that your flight be not in the winter.*
> *(13:17–18)*

How terrible! What an added burden, anxiety, and woe to be weighed down by an advanced pregnancy or to have the care of little children in that desperate race for life! The *woe* here underlines the added plight and accentuated grief of those people who are so encumbered.

As for the winter, well, it can be severe enough, especially in the highlands around Jerusalem, where snow sometimes falls. So inclement weather would be yet another obstacle to overcome. The Lord urges people living at that time to pray! If they were to watch and pray, they would see the signs and make their escape *before* the hour of crisis. Pray! The Lord can moderate the weather even when winter storms might be expected. Pray!

Then comes *the great persecution:*

> *For in those days shall be affliction, such as was not from the*
> *beginning of the creation which God created unto this time, nei-*
> *ther shall be. (13:19)*

This is a quotation from Daniel 12:1. The Lord believed in Daniel and in the authenticity of both the man and his book. So much for the skepticism of the critics who have tried to tear the book of Daniel apart with their criticism. And so much, too, for those who write off the nation of Israel and spiritualize Old Testament prophecy! Jesus (He who was wisdom incarnate, inerrant, and infallible in all that He said) quoted from the book of Daniel as part of the divinely inspired Word of God. Moreover, He took Daniel's prophecies literally.

Many savage persecutions have been perpetrated in the long, sad march of history, but the Great Tribulation holocaust will dwarf all of them. Satan and the Antichrist will try to make a clean sweep of every last Jew on this planet, of every convert of the 144,000 witnesses, and of every lingering reminder of the Judeo-Christian faith. Scenes of carnage and cruelty will be global in extent and horrific in kind.

We note, also, *the great proclamation* (13:20–23):

> *And except that the Lord had shortened those days, no flesh should*
> *be saved: but for the elect's sake, whom he hath chosen, he hath*
> *shortened the days. (13:20)*

God has more than one elect company that He has chosen throughout the various ages in accordance with His sovereign will and in keeping with His omniscient foreknowledge. The church is one such company, called and predestinated to be like Jesus for all eternity (Rom. 8:29–30). By the time this particular prophecy comes into focus for fulfillment, the elect company of the church will be in heaven.

The 144,000 witnesses (Rev. 7:1–8) are another such elect company. They, too, will be caught up to heaven before the end-times wrath begins (Rev. 14). It is their converts, that "multitude, which no man can number" (Rev. 7:9), who are the elect whom the Lord seems to have in mind here. They, together with the believing Jewish remnant, are the ones for whose sake the period of the Great Tribulation (Matt. 24:15–22) will be "shortened." The period itself will last from the installation of the Antichrist's image in the temple until the Battle of Armageddon. It will be terminated by the personal return of the Lord Jesus "with his saints" (Jude 14; Rev. 19:19–21). This dreadful period will last for three and one-half years—the same time span, indeed, as that covered by the Lord's earthly ministry. The period is stated in various ways: as "a time, and times, and half a time" (Rev. 12:14), as forty-two months (Rev. 13:5), and as 1260 days (Rev. 11:3). Believers, fleeing from the Antichrist and hiding in the hills and dens of the earth, will actually be able to count from day to day how much longer the torment will last.

> *And then if any man shall say to you, Lo, here is Christ; or, lo, he is there; believe him not: For false Christs and false prophets shall rise, and shall shew signs and wonders, to seduce, if it were possible, even the elect. But take ye heed: behold, I have foretold you all things. (13:21–23)*

The False Prophet, the Antichrist's chief minister of propaganda, supported by other false prophets, will perform lying signs and wonders (Rev. 13:13–15). Attempts will be made to lure the hidden and divinely protected end-times believers from their sanctuaries.

The False Prophet, particularly, will be able to perform all kinds of lying miracles. The one miracle actually cited in the New Testament illustrates his satanic power because Satan is able to perform all kinds of spectacular miracles and to endue his emissaries with power to do the same. The False Prophet will actually give life to the Antichrist's image and will empower it to slay those who refuse to worship it (Rev. 13:13–16).

The Lord warns the Tribulation saints not to be duped by the Devil. They have "a more sure word of prophecy" (2 Peter 1:19), they have God's Word, with its divinely given calendar, by which to go. They must remain in hiding until the 1,260 days are over and not be fooled by signs, wonders, and miracles. The warning has a salutary application to us as well. The warning of the Lord about false prophets and their lying miracles is a quotation from Deuteronomy 13.

D. The termination (13:24–27)

Note first, *the signs in the sky* (13:24–25):

> *But in those days, after that tribulation, the sun shall be darkened, and the moon shall not give her light, And the stars of*

heaven shall fall, and the powers that are in heaven shall be shaken.
(13:24–25)

This is a quotation from Isaiah 13:10. It points us to the climax and conclusion of the Great Tribulation because there will be signs, unmistakable signs, signs in the sky, signs from on high. They will make the Devil's signs and wonders look like a bag of magician's tricks. There will be no mistaking it when God finally moves onto the end-times stage.

By this time, the terrible persecutions and purges wrought by the Antichrist will have greatly decimated the believing population on this planet. With all of the wars and famines, earthquakes and disasters, pestilences, and persecutions, millions upon millions of people will be dead.

But now the armies of the Far East are mobilized in rebellion against the Antichrist and the West. Chinese manpower will be married to Japanese technology. The Asiatic hordes beyond the Euphrates will be mobilized. The Antichrist, still preoccupied with wiping out all of those people whom he hates, especially the Jews, will, nevertheless, mobilize the West to meet this new threat from the East. The stage will be set for Armageddon.

Terrifying cosmic disasters will herald the imminent coming of the Lord, affecting the whole course of nature and the very structure and stability of the solar system and outer space.

By this time, war probably will no longer be confined to earth; so-called "Star Wars" will have become a reality. This last battle will bring the threat of nuclear war. Nuclear warheads; state-of-the-art delivery systems; and biological, chemical, and laser weapons—all controlled by advanced computer systems—will threaten the continued existence of this planet once this East-West war begins.

God, however, has no intention of allowing men to incinerate this planet. So what begins as a confrontation between East and West will end up as a confrontation between heaven and earth. The world will indeed eventually be engulfed in a final cataclysmic nuclear holocaust, but God Himself will ignite those consuming fires and, even at that, not until the end of the Millennium (2 Peter 3:10–12; Rev. 20:7–9). The dissolution of the existing structure of things will be a prelude to the creation of a new heaven and a new earth.

Horrendous signs in the sky will be God's answer to man's final, pre-advent insanities. They not only will signal the Lord's immediate return but also will neutralize man's ability to destroy the planet utterly.

Note, also, *the sign of the Savior* (13:26–27):

> *And then shall they see the Son of man coming in the clouds with*
> *great power and glory. (13:26)*

This is a quotation from Daniel 7:13 with a reference to Joel 2:31. It is interesting to observe how much of the Lord's eschatology was based solidly on His knowledge of the Old Testament Scriptures, His unwavering trust in them, and their literal interpretation.

The mobilized millions, massed at Megiddo, will look up. They will see Him. The preceding signs in the sky will have drawn and held their attention and stayed their hands. Those signs, however, are only preliminary. Next, they will see the Lord Himself! What a terrifying, paralyzing sight it will be to those godless men who are mobilized by the Antichrist, inspired by Satan, and deceived by the False Prophet who are massed at Megiddo. They will see the Lord in all of His glory. They will be terrified. The world is being invaded from outer space!

We talk about "the Battle" of Armageddon. One glimpse of Christ, and His foes, from the greatest to the least, will be utterly paralyzed. John tells us of the "sword" that comes out of His mouth (Rev. 19:15). One word from Him, and it all will be over! The Antichrist and the False Prophet will be hurled into the lake of fire. The godless millions will be swept into a lost eternity. Satan will be incarcerated in the Abyss (Rev. 20:1–3). The Lord has come at last!

> *And then shall he send his angels, and shall gather together his*
> *elect from the four winds, from the uttermost part of the earth to*
> *the uttermost part of heaven. (13:27)*

Despite Satan's attempts to kill them all, many saints will still be alive. God has His people, some on earth and, of course, some in heaven. Those on earth will be the believing Jewish remnant and the surviving Gentile converts of the 144,000 witnesses and the converts of the evangelist angel (Rev. 14:6–7). The angels will gather them to meet the long-awaited, now-returned Christ. "What a gathering of the ransomed that will be!"

We learn from the prophet Joel, and from the Lord Jesus Himself (Joel 3:1–2; Matt. 25:31–46), that the Lord will now set up His judgment seat in the Valley of Jehoshaphat. The unregenerate survivors of the various holocausts of the Apocalypse will be summoned there for trial. When it is all over, there will be three companies: the Jewish remnant, now identified with Christ; the Gentile believers; and those who took sides with the Antichrist. This last company will be

banished at once from the earth; the others, Jews and Gentiles, will be the population nucleus of the millennial age.

E.   The tree (13:28–33)

> *Now learn a parable of the fig tree; When her branch is yet ten-*
> *der, and putteth forth leaves, ye know that summer is near: So ye*
> *in like manner, when ye shall see these things come to pass, know*
> *that it is nigh, even at the doors. (13:28–29)*

The day before the Lord gave this Olivet discourse, He cursed a barren fig
tree (Matt. 21:18–20). It was a symbolic act of great significance because it was
the Lord's only judgment miracle. Within a day, that fig tree died. It symbolized the flourishing but Christ-rejecting nation of Israel.

The cursing of the fig tree was accompanied by Christ's actual cursing of the
recalcitrant nation itself (Matt. 13). A series of woes pronounced upon the nation led to the prediction that the nation of Israel would come under the judgment of God within the span of a generation.

In A.D. 70, the Romans destroyed Jerusalem and the temple. In A.D. 135, at
the time of the Bar Chochba rebellion, they terminated what was left of Jewish
national life, built a pagan temple on Mount Moriah, and changed the name of
the country to Palestine—after the Philistines, the Jews' hereditary foes.

So much for the cursing of the fig tree and the nation that it symbolized
(Israel). The Lord then gave the great sign by which we can know that end-times
events are on the verge of fulfillment. "Watch the fig tee!" He said. That is, watch
the nation of Israel, of which the fig tree is a symbol. He intimated that the
people of Israel—suffering under an agelong curse, scattered worldwide, hated,
and persecuted—will come back to the Promised Land in the end times. The
nation of Israel will be revived. But mark this: the revived nation of Israel will
exhibit only "leaves," that is, it will still be a Christ-rejecting nation. But it will be
a nation again! This much has happened in our own lifetime. Israel is back in the
land, back in unbelief, back just in time to experience long-foretold and long-
delayed end-times events. The rebirth of the state of Israel tells us that the Lord's
return is near, even at the doors.

> *Verily I say unto you, that this generation shall not pass, till all*
> *these things be done. (13:30)*

What generation is the "this generation" referred to here? Obviously it is not the generation *to* which the Lord was speaking because that generation has long since passed away. That was the generation that witnessed the cursing of the nation of Israel and the scattering of the Jewish people. Surely, then, it has to be the generation *of* which He was speaking, the generation that actually sees the rebirth of the nation of Israel.

Two factors of uncertainty remain. We do not know the exact date when the fulfillment begins. Some have taken it to be the date when Israel was declared a sovereign state—May 14, 1948. Others have thought that June 7, 1967, the day the Jews recaptured Jerusalem and took the Temple Mount, is more significant. Or it might be some other equally notable event.

Nor do we know the precise length of a generation. It is a very flexible unit of measure. In the Lord's own day, He predicted the doom of the existing nation of Israel (Matt. 23:34–39) just before His Olivet discourse (Matt. 24–25). This prophecy was given in A.D. 33. It was not finally fulfilled until A.D. 135. So, in that case, a generation lasted for a whole century.

One thing is certain: the rebirth of the nation of Israel heralds the beginning of all of those end-times events that will precipitate the rapture of the church, the unveiling of the Antichrist, and all of those other matters that Mark has been describing.

> *Heaven and earth shall pass away: but my words shall not pass away. (13:31)*

Unbelievers may scoff. Professing Christians may embrace schemes of interpretation that allegorize the prophetic Scriptures and explain away what are clearly literal statements. This prophecy, however, read in the light of other relevant prophecies and interpreted literally and grammatically, is quite unambiguous. The Lord said what He meant and meant what He said. We are to take Him at His Word— a word that cannot be broken, a word more sure and steadfast than the starry heavens themselves.

> *But of that day and that hour knoweth no man, no, not the angels which are in heaven, neither the Son, but the Father. (13:32)*

The Lord reminds us that the date of the Rapture is the best-kept secret in the universe. That is the difference between the *Rapture* of the church (the ultimate end-times catalyst) and the subsequent *return* of the Lord to deal with His foes at Meggido and set up His kingdom. The date of the Rapture is concealed; the date of the final return can be calculated by the remnant of God's people still alive on earth.

The *Rapture* is for the church; the *return* is for Israel. The Rapture takes place when the Lord comes to *the air;* the return takes place when His feet split wide the *Mount of Olives* (Zech. 14:1–5). The Rapture is when the Lord comes *for* His church; the return is when he comes *with* His church. The date of the Rapture is *secret;* the date of the return can be *calculated* by those living in the Tribulation age. From the date when the Antichrist seizes the rebuilt Jewish temple to the final coming of Christ in power and glory will be 1,260 days.

It is the height of folly to set dates for the Rapture. One such modern attempt to do that caused national attention in the United States.

A retired National Aeronautics and Space Administration space engineer, Edgar C. Wisenant, published a widely circulated booklet titled *Eighty-eight Reasons the Lord Will Come in Eighty-eight.* The booklet was a strange mixture of truth and error. The author claimed that the Lord would come on Sunday, September 11; Monday, September 12; or Tuesday, September 13, 1988—the preferred date being September 12, the date of the Jewish New Year.

Not content with setting the date for the Rapture, Wisenant listed a whole string of prognostications: the Antichrist would sign his seven-year treaty with Israel on September 21; the 144,000 witnesses would be sealed on September 26; World War III would break out on October 4 and would last for three and one-half weeks. The temple in Jerusalem would be consecrated June 18, 1989; the two witnesses would be killed March 9, 1992; the Battle of Armageddon would take place on October 4, 1995; and the Millennium would begin on December 23, 1995.

When the Lord failed to show up in 1988, Wisenant recalculated. He said that his original book was meant as a warning by God. Wisenant suggested a revised date for the Rapture—September 1, 1989. Another miss! And no wonder—the date of the Rapture is a secret.

> *Take ye heed, watch and pray: for ye know not when the time is.*
> (13:33)

The word *watch* here means "to lie sleepless" or "to lie awake" (through care or anxiety). As the signs begin to multiply, they should drive sleep from our eyes.

We should wake up at night with thoughts of His coming in our minds. We should write across each day the words *Perhaps today!* And sleeplessness should be wedded to prayerfulness, especially when we think of lost loved ones destined, should the Lord indeed come today, to face the horrors of the Apocalypse.

F. The test (13:34–37)

> *For the Son of man is as a man taking a far journey, who left his house, and gave authority to his servants, and to every man his work, and commanded the porter to watch. (13:34)*

That is exactly what the Lord Jesus did. In the Upper Room discourse, He told His disciples that He was soon to leave earth for heaven (John 14:1–6). He was going home to His Father's house. It was to be "a far journey"—not far perhaps in terms of time and travel, not far for One who can annihilate distance. But, from the perspective of His disciples, it was to be a far, far journey indeed. He would be gone! And it would be for a very long time—some two thousand years.

Meanwhile, they must wait and work and watch! As for the "porter," Wuest suggests that he represents the apostolate. Above all others, the apostles were to be on the lookout. They were "to watch." This time, the word used means "to keep awake." Doubtless, Peter would have told Mark about his sad inability to watch in Gethsemane. By the time a few decades had passed, with heresy raising its head and apostasy becoming increasingly daring, the need for watchfulness was all too evident. The spirit of watchfulness is now passed on to us. Paul, for instance, put the Ephesian elders on guard in a farewell speech of great power (Acts 20:17–38). They were to watch out for the wolves.

> *Watch ye therefore: for ye know not when the master of the house cometh, at even, or at midnight, or at the cockcrowing, or in the morning: (13:35)*

Watch! Watch! Watch! The same word is used in verses 34, 35, and 37. It means "to keep awake." Who knows whether the Master's return will be at midnight, at midday, when the sun is setting, or when the rooster advertises the dawn of another day? Again Peter would tell Mark how painful that particular illusion was to him (John 13:37–38; 17:15–27).

Lest coming suddenly he find you sleeping. And what I say unto you I say unto all, Watch. (13:36–37)

The word for "sleeping" implies a voluntary composing of oneself for sleep. Thus, the Lord bombards His people with warnings. As the time approaches for His return, we should keep a weather eye on all that is going on around us. Why? Because He *is* coming! He is coming unannounced! He is coming to take stock of His servants. We cannot afford to let any slackness or slothfulness let His coming catch us unawares.

Section 3: Portraying the Cross of Calvary (14:1–31)

A. The foes (14:1–2)
  1. The period (14:1a)
  2. The proposal (14:1b)
  3. The problem (14:2)
B. The friends (14:3–9)
  1. Adoration (14:3)
    a. The house (14:3a)
    b. The homage (14:3b–c)
      (1) It was precious (14:3b)
      (2) It was personal (14:3c)
  2. Accusation (14:4–5)
    a. An exclamation (14:4)
    b. An evaluation (14:5a)
    c. An explanation (14:5b)
    d. An emotion (14:5c)
  3. Appreciation (14:6–8)
    a. The Lord defended her (14:6)
    b. The Lord deflated them (14:7–8)
      (1) Their social blindness (14:7)
      (2) Their spiritual blindness (14:8)
  4. Admiration (14:9)
C. The follower (14:10–11)
  1. The fact (14:10)
  2. The pact (14:11a–b)
    a. The pleasure of the chief priests (14:11a)
    b. The pledge of the chief priests (14:11b)
  3. The act (14:11c–d)
    a. How deliberate it was (14:11c)
    b. How diabolical it was (14:11d)
D. The feast (14:12–15)
  1. The last Passover of the old dispensation (14:12–21)
    a. The preparation (14:12–16)
      (1) The day (14:12a)
      (2) The disciples (14:12b)
      (3) The directions (14:13–16)

        (a) How simple they were (14:13–14)

            i. A man (14:13)

           ii. A message (14:14)

        (b) How successful they were (14:15–16)

            i. The place was made ready (14:15)

           ii. The Passover was made ready (14:16)

    b. The prediction (14:17–21)

      (1) The word (14:17–18)

        (a) The time (14:17)

        (b) The truth (14:18)

            i. It interrupted a joyous feast (14:18a)

           ii. It injected a jarring fact (14:18b)

      (2) The woe (14:19–20)

        (a) The dismay of the Twelve (14:19)

        (b) The disclosure of the traitor (14:20)

      (3) The warning (14:21)

        (a) What the Scripture declared (14:21a)

        (b) What the Savior declared (14:21b–c)

            i. The doom of the betrayer revealed (14:21b)

           ii. The doom of the betrayer reinforced (14:21c)

  2. The Lord's provision for the new dispensation (14:22–25)

    a. A pictorial view (14:22–24)

      (1) The emblem of His body (14:22)

        (a) The bread blessed (14:22a)

        (b) The bread broken (14:22b)

      (2) The emblem of His blood (14:23–24)

        (a) The cup (14:23)

        (b) The covenant (14:24)

    b. A personal vow (14:25a)

    c. A prophetic vision (14:25b)

E. The forecast (14:26–31)

  1. The conclusion of the Passover (14:26)

  2. The commencement of the Passion (14:27–31)

    a. A quotation (14:27)

      (1) What the Savior said (14:27a)

      (2) What the Scripture said (14:27b)

    b. A qualification (14:28)

      c. A quibble (14:29–31)
          (1) Peter's boast (14:29–31a)
             (a) The boast recorded (14:29)
             (b) The boast refuted (14:30)
             (c) The boast redoubled (14:31a)
          (2) Peter's brethren (14:31b)

—w—

Section 3: Portraying the Cross of Calvary (14:1–31)

A. The foes (14:1–2)

After two days was the feast of the passover, and of unleavened bread: and the chief priests and the scribes sought how they might take him by craft, and put him to death. But they said, Not on the feast day, lest there be an uproar of the people. (14:1–2)

The annual Feast of the Passover, with the accompanying week of eating unleavened bread, was at hand. For some fifteen hundred years, the Jews had thus commemorated their redemption from Egyptian bondage and the commencement of their journey to the Promised Land.

Now the true Passover Lamb was in their midst. The shedding of His blood would open a fountain for uncleanness (Zech. 13:1) that would make redemption available to all mankind. He was without spot or blemish, and well the Jewish authorities knew it. They knew that they could get nothing on Him by testing Him by the law; He had kept it all, in both letter and spirit, every single commandment, every single moment of every single day. So they decided to resort to guile. They would concoct a case against Him.

Part of their problem was to know how to get their hands on Him. They had a healthy respect for the mob. The masses accepted Jesus as a miracle-working prophet, so any move against Him in broad daylight might well provoke a riot. Above all, they must not provoke a riot at Passover time when Jerusalem was teeming with Jews from not only all over the country but also from all over the world. Who could tell what kind of a conflagration might result from a mere spark if they once accidentally ignited the passions of that crowd?

So they sat there in their religious robes and plotted the murder of the Son of God. How blind they were! How blinded they will be on that day when He returns. The stars will explode before Him, disintegrating into fiery sparks like boundless celestial pyrotechnics. The sun will plunge into darkness as it did at Calvary, and the moon will become as black as midnight. And these scheming, plotting, petty little tin-pot dignitaries of a small-time politico-religious court, allowed to hold its sessions only at the whim of an occupying power, will see Him (Rev. 1:7). And they will shake in terror before Him at last.

B. The friends (14:3–9)

> *And being in Bethany in the house of Simon the leper, as he sat at meat, there came a woman having an alabaster box of ointment of spikenard very precious; and she brake the box, and poured it on his head. (14:3)*

We do not know who this woman was. Evidently, this is not the same incident as that recorded by John, which took place six days before the Passover in the house of Lazarus (John 12:1). Neither do we know who Simon the leper was. He was probably one of a number of lepers whose cleansing by the Lord is recorded in the Gospels.

The Lord was his guest. In the same village lived Martha, Mary, and Lazarus. Perhaps the woman of whom Mark writes was inspired by Mary's example. Perhaps, too, Simon, the onetime leper, invited Jesus and His disciples to his home for a meal as a means of expressing his gratitude. With the Sanhedrin spies everywhere, that was a bold thing to do.

Spikenard was a rare and expensive perfume. The alabaster flask in which it was contained was brittle, so it was easily broken. The outpoured perfume anointed the Lord's head and filled the house with its fragrance. It was an act of the warmest and sincerest devotion. With Jesus' enemies multiplying on every hand, these last acts of love and loyalty by these various individuals must have warmed His heart.

> *And there were some that had indignation within themselves, and said, Why was this waste of the ointment made? (1:4)*

At the other anointing, only Judas is mentioned. He was the person who had so crassly put a cash price on Mary's offering. The Lord had rebuked him. But evidently some of the disciples had secretly agreed with Judas and still did at the time of this particular incident. This outpouring of costly ointment rekindled their evil thoughts, although they were at first too prudent to voice their opinion. When they did speak out, they all sounded just like Judas.

> *For it might have been sold for more than three hundred pence,*
> *and have been given to the poor. And they murmured against*
> *her. (14:5)*

In those days, three hundred pence was a considerable sum of money. A man would toil all day in the fields as a hired hand for a penny. The sum that the disciples had in mind represented a good part of a year's wages. To them, that seemed like an enormous amount of money. It must have given Judas a moment's glow of sardonic satisfaction to hear the other disciples saying much the same as he had said. The Lord's true disciples, however, had some real concern for the poor, whereas Judas was a thief and was put out by this loss of an opportunity to plunder the bag (John 12:6).

They "murmured" against the woman. The Greek word implies that they were "deeply moved." They generated some heat over the issue. After all, they knew what it was like to be poor.

> *And Jesus said, Let her alone; why trouble ye her? she hath wrought*
> *a good work on me. For ye have the poor with you always, and*
> *whensoever ye will ye may do them good: but me ye have not*
> *always. (14:6–7)*

The criticism voiced by the disciples struck a sour note. Evidently, the woman herself flinched under their attack. It must have required considerable thought, resolution, and courage in the first place for her to carry out this sacrificial and public act of worship. Perhaps the Lord saw the woman cringe. In any case, He heard the harsh and thoughtless words of the disciples and sprang immediately to her defense.

The ever present poor! The soon departing Lord! They would have endless opportunities to minister to the poor! But now they had only fleeting opportunities to do something personal for Jesus, as this woman had done. "A good work," He called it, a good work in a world where good works are rare.

Ministering to the poor has always been a concern of the church. Widows and orphans, the sick and the suffering, the handicapped and the impaired, the insane, the dropouts of society—one and all have found shelter offered by the ministries of the church in a cold, cruel world. It was Christ who taught His disciples to care for outcasts; it was His church that taught the world to build hospitals and asylums. The annals of the church are filled with its attempts to care for society's failures and misfits.

> *She hath done what she could: she is come aforehand to anoint*
> *my body to the burying. (14:8)*

Thus, Jesus read her act. Her act of worship soared far above the comprehension of the disciples. They constantly blocked out all thoughts of the Lord's impending death, burial, and resurrection. This woman, however, had grasped the fact that the Lord was soon to die and be buried. She could not arrest the onward march of events, the evident intention of the authorities to do away with Jesus. Nor would it be likely that she would be allowed to have a share in His burial. Well, she would do what she could *now.* Thus, she came, and in a magnificently extravagant act of devotion, she anointed Him for burial! Peter might have done that! John might have done that! Thomas might have done that! Any of them might have done that! But none of them did. *She* did! And Jesus was not going to let her be criticized.

> *Verily I say unto you, Wheresoever this gospel shall be preached*
> *throughout the whole world, this also that she hath done shall be*
> *spoken of for a memorial of her. (14:9)*

Instant fame! We shall have to wait until we get to glory, however, before we find out who she was. The gospel story is now published in thousands of languages, and it has been preached for more than two thousand years. In country after country for century after century, this woman's "good work" has been told. It was a fame that she did not seek but one that the Lord instantly bestowed upon her.

No one can do a service to the Lord, one that touches His heart, and not have it one day advertised. It will be told for all to hear at the judgment seat of Christ! It will be heralded across the everlasting hills. It will be remembered for all eternity.

C. The follower (14:10–11)

> *And Judas Iscariot, one of the twelve, went unto the chief priests,*
> *to betray him unto them. (14:10)*

That was the last straw for Judas. The Lord's rebuke of His murmuring disciples and His praise of the woman soured his soul. He had joined the wrong cause. He

could see no political or economic advantage in continuing with such an unrealis-
tic "Messiah." He had thought, a few days ago, at the time of the Triumphal Entry
into Jerusalem, that, at last, the movement was going to get somewhere. But no! It
was more of the same, more upsetting of the establishment, more provoking of the
Sanhedrin. They were serious now about getting rid of this unwanted Messiah. It
would be sheer folly to stay with a sinking ship. The thing to do, of course, was to
cut his losses, get out while he still could, and make a few shekels in the process. So
he slipped away to cut a deal with the priests.

The word for "went" here is arresting. It is "he went off." It implied that he
was smarting under the Lord's latest rebuke of His disciples. Doubtless, he saw
that rebuke as another jab at him.

> *And when they heard it, they were glad, and promised to give him*
> *money. And he sought how he might conveniently betray him. (14:11)*

The religious leaders were delighted at this unexpected solution to their
problem—how to lay hands on Christ at a convenient time, when no crowds would
be there to get in the way. What sheer good fortune to have as their spy one who
was most intimately informed of the Lord's movements and intentions! "They
were glad," Mark says. Imagine that! They rejoiced. What terrible glee! What twisted
souls! There was a hearty handshake all around once the terrible bargain had been
struck and Judas had gone.

As for the traitor, "he sought" how to unobtrusively put Jesus in their wicked
hands. The word used means "kept on seeking" for the desired opportunity. He
"busied himself continually" is the sense conveyed by the imperfect tense of the
verb. He watched Jesus like a hawk. He listened to every word. He was looking
for a clue as to the time and the place when he could cash in and consummate the
dark, devilish deed.

D. The feast (14:12–15)
   1. The last Passover of the old dispensation (14:12–21)

Note first *the preparation* (14:12–16):

> *And the first day of unleavened bread, when they killed the*
> *passover, his disciples said unto him, Where wilt thou that we go*
> *and prepare that thou mayest eat the passover? (14:12)*

Thus, imperceptibly, the Lord's Rubicon was crossed. The public ministry was over. He was the Passover Lamb. He was the One to be killed.

The "first day of unleavened bread" was the fourteenth day of Nisan on the Jewish annual calendar of religious events. The disciples still had not grasped the significance of all of this.

A dozen were in their group, so they would need a large room if they were to keep the Passover together. They would need to buy the usual provisions and kill the lamb. They had much to do.

The disciples must have thought that it was all well and good to be eating in the houses of one's friends, receiving accolades, and handing out implied rebukes. It was time to come back down to earth and get on with the business of living. It was *Passover* time! Vast crowds of people were in the city, and all available space was fast disappearing. They prodded the Lord, as though He had not Himself already made all of the necessary arrangements.

> *And he sendeth forth two of his disciples, and saith unto them,*
> *Go ye into the city, and there shall meet you a man bearing a*
> *pitcher of water: follow him. (14:13)*

The instructions were not nearly as vague as they might seem. It was very rare in those days for men to carry pitchers; women did that. Women took the pitchers to the well, filled them, and carried them home on either their shoulder or their head. If men were to carry any such thing, it would be a wineskin or a water skin. The disciples would have no difficulty spotting a man with a pitcher. Once they had singled him out, they were to follow him. The Lord already knew who the man was and where he lived.

> *And wheresoever he shall go in, say ye to the goodman of the*
> *house, The Master saith, Where is the guestchamber, where I shall*
> *eat the passover with my disciples? And he will show you a large*
> *upper room furnished and prepared: there make ready for us.*
> *(14:14–15)*

Everything had already been arranged. The disciples followed the man with the pitcher who was evidently a servant. They called for the master of the house, and he took them upstairs where all was ready. The couches, the cushions, and all of the basic furniture were there. The Lord had been ahead of His disciples as always. "Omnipotence," as the saying goes, "has its servants everywhere." Despite all of the official enmity, the Lord never lacked a friend who was willing and able to help Him when required. Did He need a boat? Peter had one available. Did He need a donkey, an upper room, or a tomb? Whatever was needed, it was always ready at hand.

Down through the centuries, the Lord's servants have found it so. Did Paul need a home when preaching at Corinth or Philippi? Aquila and Priscilla were there at Corinth—with a job for Paul in the bargain—and Lydia was there at Philippi. Did he need a scribe? Timothy was there. Did he need a doctor? Luke was available. Who, of the Lord's servants, could not produce a sizeable list of people who have been there with what was needed when the time came?

> *And his disciples went forth, and came into the city, and found as*
> *he had said unto them: and they made ready the passover. (14:16)*

Who was this man? Where was this room? What a service he rendered that day! That room sprang to instant fame. There the Lord washed the disciples' feet. There He told them of His imminent departure, told them about the Holy Spirit, taught them of the new vine-branch relationship, and prayed for them with tender eloquence. There Judas received the sop and damned his soul. There the Lord sang His last "Hallelujah Chorus" (Pss. 115–18). There some of the earliest and most memorable resurrection appearances took place. There, it would seem, the Holy Spirit came at Pentecost. There the church was born!

Thank you, Brother Stranger! Great will be your reward in heaven, for the loaning of that room.

Note, also, *the prediction* (14:17–21):

> *And in the evening he cometh with the twelve. And as they sat*
> *and did eat, Jesus said, Verily I say unto you, One of you which*
> *eateth with me shall betray me. (14:17–18)*

It was a bombshell, although not without previous hints during the gathering, that Jesus was expecting to be betrayed that night. He knew perfectly well which one of them it was. Did Judas's heart miss a beat and his blood run cold? Kings and lords in those days made short shrift of traitors.

But that was not the Lord's purpose in making this pronouncement. He was giving Judas every chance to repent, confess, and be restored to the apostolic fellowship. He had gone far down the road to infamy, but he was not yet damned.

> *And they began to be sorrowful, and to say unto him one by one,*
> *Is it I? and another said, Is it I? (14:19)*

They loved the Lord, but evidently they doubted the integrity of their own hearts. But *betray* Him? *Me?* Betray *Him?* "Lord? Is it I?"

Was this a sudden chorus? Or did each speak in turn? "Is it *I,* Lord?" If so, when Judas's turn came, he chanted out the formula boldly enough. He was going to brazen it out. He had too much invested in his betrayal to back out now. Money had changed hands. He had been bought; he was no longer his own. It was as much as his life was worth to let the likes of Caiaphas and Annas down now.

> *And he answered and said unto them, It is one of the twelve, that*
> *dippeth with me in the dish. (14:20)*

The other Evangelists show how the Lord indicated (at least to John) that it would be Judas who would betray Him. He did so by means of the sop. They tell us, too, that as Judas made his way to the door to consummate his nefarious deed, the Lord called after him, "That thou doest, do quickly" (John 13:27). Peter, perhaps, knowing how near he had come to spiritual disaster by his denials of Christ, lets Judas down lightly. And Mark, following Peter's lead, does the same.

> *The Son of man indeed goeth, as it is written of him: but woe to*
> *that man by whom the Son of man is betrayed! good were it for*
> *that man if he had never been born. (14:21)*

Peter might have let Judas down lightly, but the Lord didn't. He spoke very bluntly indeed. He wanted to reach the man's conscience before it was forever too late. Psalm 42:9 had prophesied for a thousand years that one of the Messiah's own intimate friends would betray Him. Psalm 42 referred primarily to Ahithophel, David's onetime friend and gifted counselor. Ahithophel had gone over to Absalom's side at the time of the rebellion and had given Absalom the benefit of his diabolically wicked but exceedingly clever counsel. When Absalom was defeated, Ahithophel (David's Judas) hanged himself. The Lord's warning to Judas needed no interpretation. The treachery and suicide of Ahithophel hung like a menace in the room. Judas beat a hasty retreat.

And how dark was his doom! "That he might go to his own place," Peter said later—in this same Upper Room, after the Lord's ascension, as the disciples were discussing Judas's defection (Acts 1:25). Where that place was, we are not expressly told. Some scholars think that Judas is in the Abyss, being tutored by evil spirits for a possible, yet futile, role in end-times events.

2. The Lord's provision for the new dispensation (14:22–25)

And as they did eat, Jesus took bread, and blessed, and brake it,
and gave to them, and said, Take, eat: this is my body. (14:22)

Thus, the Lord put behind Him the Passover and all that it represented. Within hours, He, the true Passover Lamb, would be slain and the Old Testament type fulfilled. Judaism would be rendered obsolete, and the whole annual ritual of Passover would become no more than an anachronism—full of spiritual lessons, indeed, but now only a type.

A new feast replaced the old one. It consisted of two symbols, the first of which was bread. Now that bread, the Lord said, pictured His body. He broke it. Thus, His body was soon to be broken on the tree. It was a graphic picture that He thus painted, one that the disciples never forgot.

And he took the cup, and when he had given thanks, he gave it to
them: and they all drank of it. And he said unto them, This is my
blood of the new testament, which is shed for many. (14:23–24)

The new covenant! *His* blood! The new covenant is the subject of one of Jeremiah's prophecies (Jer. 31:31). It contains both soteriological clauses (i.e., clauses having to do with salvation) and eschatological clauses (i.e., having to do with the future). The eschatological clauses are *exclusively* for Israel; the soteriological clauses are also for Israel (anticipating a coming day when the Jewish people will accept Christ at the time of His return to earth), but they include the church too.

This new covenant, and the full and free salvation that it offers to Jews and Gentiles alike, is based on the shed blood of Christ. The endless blood sacrifices of the Old

Testament were only temporary expedients. They could save no one. They pointed
forward to Calvary. As Isaac Watts puts it in his hymn "Join All the Glorious Names,"

> Richer blood has flowed
> From nobler veins;
> To give the conscience peace
> And wash away its stains.

So, just as the Lord declared that the broken bread would henceforth depict
His body broken at Calvary, so the wine would henceforth symbolize His blood
outpoured at Calvary. Down through the centuries ever since, the people of God
have celebrated the Lord's Supper in obedience to this command. It has been
distorted by some (as has the other ordinance, baptism), but its significance has
remained. We break the bread and drink of the cup in fond remembrance of His
death for us on the cross.

> *Verily I say unto you, I will drink no more of the fruit of the vine,*
> *until that day that I drink it new in the kingdom of God. (14:25)*

This is another of the great prophetic statements that demands a literal interpretation. Jesus is coming again! He is going to get up off His Father's throne in heaven
and come back to this planet, the scene of His rejection and suffering, and sit down
on the throne of His father David. He will put down all of His foes. He will rule for
a thousand years. Then wine, which is now the token of His blood outpoured, will
be given another meaning: it will symbolize the joy of His return.

E. The forecast (14:26–31)

Note *the conclusion of the Passover* (14:26):

> *And when they had sung an hymn, they went out into the mount*
> *of Olives. (14:26)*

The Jews knew Psalms 113–18 as the Hallel psalms. Psalms 113–14 were
sung before the Passover meal (but after the second of the four cups of wine).
Psalms 115–18 were sung after the Passover meal. These particular psalms comprise "the hymn" that was sung in the Upper Room just before they all left. Very

likely it was sung by the Lord Himself. This group of psalms contains many memorable statements that glow with brighter colors in the light of that Upper Room scene. "The LORD is on my side; I will not fear: what can man do unto me?" (Ps. 118:6). "The stone which the builders refused is become the head stone of the corner" (Ps. 118:22). "This is the day which the LORD hath made; we will rejoice and be glad in it" (Ps. 118:24).

Note, also, *the commencement of the Passion* (14:27–31):

> *And Jesus saith unto them, All ye shall be offended because of me this night: for it is written, I will smite the shepherd, and the sheep shall be scattered. (14:27)*

The Lord was lining up and checking off mentally the many Old Testament prophecies that now demanded fulfillment. This verse was another of them, one recorded in Zechariah 13:7. The word *offended* means "will stumble." The Lord's eye could see Judas already rounding up the men who would accompany him to Gethsemane. Well He knew how quickly the human resolve of His disciples to be loyal to Him come what may would dissolve when the crisis came. He warned them that they would be scattered.

> *But after that I am risen, I will go before you into Galilee. (14:28)*

He was in Jerusalem, but His heart was in Galilee. Jerusalem was sophisticated, cynical, snobbish, and sneering. Jerusalem stoned the prophets and killed those who spoke for God. Galilee was where He had been born. All of His childhood and boyhood memories were there. Galilee was where He had toiled and triumphed. The people of Galilee had received Him gladly; however mistakenly, they would have made Him their king. He would go back to Galilee! He made a date with His disciples: after all of this is over, go to Galilee. "I'll be there!"

> *But Peter said unto him, Although all shall be offended, yet will not I. And Jesus saith unto him, Verily I say unto thee, That this day, even in this night, before the cock crow twice, thou shalt deny me thrice. (14:29–30)*

Peter ignored the Lord's quotation from Zechariah. Instead of looking at the Scripture, he looked at himself. He saw a man, given to bluster, perhaps, but one who loved the Lord with all of his heart. Run away at the first hint of danger? What kind of a man did the Lord think he was anyway? Maybe Matthew or Thomas or all of the others would flee, but not him! He was Peter—as solid as a rock. Others might "stumble," but not him. He said so.

But the Lord knew Peter better than Peter knew himself. "Before the cock crows twice, Peter, you will have denied me three times." Peter was stubborn and angry that the Lord should so confidently dismiss his avowals of loyalty even to the point of death itself.

> *But he spake the more vehemently, If I should die with thee, I will not deny thee in any wise. Likewise also said they all. (14:31)*

He kept on saying it with more and more vehemence. The word used suggests speaking to excess with flowing words and firm gestures. The Lord was not impressed because He knew. He had read Zechariah. The other disciples seem to have caught fire from Peter's eloquence and joined him in protesting loudly their loyalty. The Lord left it at that. Sadly, the crowing cock would prove Him to be right.

Section 4: Paying the Cost of Calvary (14:32–15:47)

A. The will of God (14:32–42)

  1. The place (14:32a)

  2. The pain (14:32b–34)

    a. His command (14:32b)

    b. His companions (14:33a)

    c. His comprehension (14:33b–c)

      (1) His complete amazement (14:33b)

      (2) His crushing anguish (14:33c)

    d. His comment (14:34a)

    e. His command (14:34b)

  3. The prayers (14:35–42)

    a. The first prayer (14:35–38)

      (1) Its torment (14:35–36)

        (a) His prostration (14:35a)

        (b) His plea (14:35b–36)

          i. He had been consulting God's clock (14:35b–c)

            a. The impossible hope (14:35b)

            b. The impending hour (14:35c)

          ii. He had been contemplating our cup (14:36)

            a. His divine relationship (14:36a)

            b. His dread realization (14:36b)

            c. His deliberate resignation (14:36c)

      (2) Its termination (14:37–38)

        (a) What He saw (14:37a)

        (b) What He said (14:37b–38)

          i. A word for Peter (14:37b)

          ii. A word of precaution (14:38)

            a. What He admonished (14:38a)

            b. What He admitted (14:38b)

    b. The further prayer (14:39–40)

      (1) His retirement (14:39)

      (2) His return (14:40)

        (a) The weakness of His disciples (14:40a)

        (b) The weariness of His disciples (14:40b)

    c. The final prayer (14:41–42)

        (1) His resignation (14:41a)
        (2) His realization (14:41b–42)
           (a) The time had come (14:41b)
           (b) The traitor had come (14:41c–42)
B. The wickedness of man (14:43–15:15)
  1. The arrest (14:43–52)
    a. The unthinking mob (14:43–46)
      (1) The rebel (14:43a)
      (2) The rabble (14:43b)
      (3) The rulers (14:43c)
      (4) The ruse (14:44–46)
        (a) Judas approaches (14:44–45)
           i. The traitor's guidance (14:44)
             a. The promised sign (14:44a)
             b. The proposed sin (14:44b)
           ii. The traitor's guilt (14:45)
             a. His sham words (14:45a)
             b. His shameful work (14:45b)
        (b) Jesus apprehended (14:46)
    b. The unflinching master (14:47–50)
      (1) The Lord and His foes (14:47–49)
        (a) The wounded man (14:47)
        (b) The wicked men (14:48–49)
           i. The challenge (14:48)
           ii. The charge (14:49)
      (2) The Lord and His friends (14:50)
    c. The unknown man (14:51–52)
      (1) How he followed (14:51)
      (2) How he fled (14:52)
  2. The arraignment (14:53–15:15)
    a. The Hebrew trial (14:53–72)
      (1) The preface (14:53–54)
        (a) The court (14:53)
        (b) The compromise (14:54)
           i. How Peter followed (14:54a)
           ii. How Peter fared (14:54b)
      (2) The proceedings (14:55–65)

(a) The false witnesses (14:55–61a)
  i. A deliberate search (14:55–56)
    a. What the rulers did (14:55)
    b. What the rulers discovered (14:56)
  ii. A dubious statement (14:57–59)
    a. The testimony of the false witnesses (14:57–58)
    b. The trouble with the false witnesses (14:59)
  iii. A deafening silence (14:60–61a)
    a. What Caiaphas said (14:60)
    b. What Christ said (14:61a)
(b) The faithful witness (14:61b–65)
  i. The solemn question asked (14:61b)
  ii. The solemn question answered (14:62–65)
    a. The reply (14:62)
      1. The Lord's sublime confession (14:62a)
      2. The Lord's Second Coming (14:62b)
    b. The response (14:63–65)
      1. The rent robe (14:63–64)
        (i) The illegal deed (14:63a)
        (ii) The illegal decision (14:63b–64)
      2. The raging rabble (14:65)
(3) The postscript (14:66–72)
(a) Peter's denials (14:66–72a)
  i. Peter in the palace (14:66–68a)
    a. The damsel's remark (14:66–67)
      1. Who she saw (14:66)
      2. What she said (14:67)
    b. The damaging reply (14:68a)
  ii. Peter in the porch (14:68b–72a)
    a. The first crowing of the cock (14:68b–70a)
      1. The setting (14:68b)
      2. The saying (14:69)
      3. The sifting (14:70a)
    b. The further crowing of the cock (14:70b–72a)
      1. A pointed remark (14:70b)
      2. A pitiful response (14:71)

3. A powerful reminder (14:72a)
(b) Peter's despair (14:72b–c)
    i. Peter's memory (14:72b)
    ii. Peter's misery (14:72c)

—⁂—

Section 4: Paying the Cost of Calvary (14:32–15:47)
A. The will of God (14:32–42)

We note, first, *the place* (14:32a):

> *And they came to a place which was named Gethsemane:*

And we note, also, *the pain* (14:32b–34):

> *and he saith to his disciples, Sit ye here, while I shall pray. (14:32)*

An enclosed piece of ground was there at Gethsemane. The Lord seems to have left the main body of the disciples outside. He had a parting word of advice for them, however: "Sit ye here!" He said, "I am going to pray." The implication is that they would be well advised to do the same, especially with Zechariah 13:7 still fresh in their minds. They should stop protesting their resolutions and start praying. Judas and the mob would soon be there.

> *And he taketh with him Peter and James and John, and began to*
> *be sore amazed, and to be very heavy; (14:33)*

The other disciples were getting used to the choice of these three for further revelation. It had happened twice before, once in the house of Jairus, when they had been chosen to witness His *greatness* in the raising of a little girl to life, and once to be with Him and witness His *glory* on the Mount of Transfiguration. Now they were being taken aside to witness His *grief.*

And what grief it was! The word for "sore amazed" occurs in only two other places, both of them in Mark's gospel. We have met the word before. When the Lord came down from the Mount of Transfiguration, we read that "all the people, when they beheld him, were greatly amazed . . ." (9:15). The glory of that other world, revealed in all of its awe-inspiring magnificence on the mount itself, seems to have left its aura about Him. The people were awed by the splendor of another world. It would be the same on the resurrection morning; when the women came to the tomb and saw the angel there, "they were affrighted" and were told to not be "affrighted." Again, it was contact with another world that awed them (16:5–6).

In Gethsemane, the Lord was brought into contact with another world too—the world of our sin, the world of unspeakable horror that lay before Him at Calvary when He would take upon Himself our guilt and be "made sin for us." He was "sore amazed."

The Greek word actually conveys "to be stunned with astonishment." It depicts the pain that results from some great shock. The Lord had lived on this sin-cursed planet ever since He was born at Bethlehem. He had rubbed shoulders with sinning humanity all of His life. But this was different. This was sin in the raw, naked sin, sin in all of its undiluted wickedness. The Lord's first reaction to the full horror and heinousness of human sin seems to have been one of overwhelming shock. The reality exceeded all of His expectations.

He was "sore amazed." Mark adds that He was "very heavy." The word means to be deeply weighed down, to be depressed, to be uncomfortable, to be in a situation in which He no longer felt at home.

> *And saith unto them, My soul is exceeding sorrowful unto death: tarry ye here, and watch. (14:34)*

The words *exceeding sorrowful* mean that He was completely surrounded with grief. "Unto death"—"I almost die!" He adds.

"Tarry ye here, and watch," He said, adding the extra injunction to His chosen three to watch as well as to pray. They had never heard Him speak such words of personal woe before. Surely, they must have made up their minds then and there to do exactly what He requested—to watch and pray.

Next, we note *the prayers* (14:35–42):

> *And he went forward a little, and fell on the ground, and prayed that, if it were possible, the hour might pass from him. (14:35)*

If ever we are shown the true humanity of the Lord Jesus, it is in Gethsemane. The hour was upon Him. The verb for "fell" is in the imperfect tense. He not only fell to the ground but also kept on falling to the ground. He was like some mighty wrestler locked in deadly struggle with some mighty antagonist. The struggle in the darkness was terrible. The word for "prayed" is also in the imperfect tense—He kept on praying. We are told the burden of His prayer:

> *And he said, Abba, Father, all things are possible unto thee; take*
> *away this cup from me: nevertheless not what I will, but what*
> *thou wilt. (14:36)*

The Lord used two words for God here. He called Him "Abba," an Aramaic word that occurs only here, in Romans 8:5, and in Galatians 4:6. The word *Abba* is the word of a child. It answers to our word *Papa,* or *Daddy.* It expresses the deep, emotional devotion and trust that the Lord Jesus had in His beloved Father in heaven.

The word *Father* comes from the Greek word *pater.* It is the word of an adult son. The Lord Jesus fully entered into the mind and will of God. As God, He had been present before time ever began when, in the eternal counsels, the Father, the Son, and the Holy Spirit had planned the redemption of a race as yet unborn. As perfect Man, with perfect understanding of the Scriptures to instruct Him, and with a peerless relationship with the Father to uphold Him, He could thus speak to the Father with every confidence.

The Lord used *both* expressions—not just *Abba* and not just *Father* but both— joined together to express the fullness of the relationship.

It was as Man, however, that He made His request. The horror of that dark and dreadful cup filled His holy soul with loathing. The Lord acknowledged God's omnipotence; all things were possible with God. He asked that some other way be found. And then He capitulated at once to that "good, and acceptable, and perfect, will of God" (Rom. 12:2).

> *And he cometh, and findeth them sleeping, and saith unto Peter,*
> *Simon, sleepest thou? couldest not thou watch one hour? Watch ye*
> *and pray, lest ye enter into temptation. The spirit truly is ready,*
> *but the flesh is weak. (14:37–38)*

On the human level, it must have been a terrible letdown! The Lord, back from a fearful spiritual struggle, came looking for companionship with those three friends of His whom He had invited to have the "fellowship of his sufferings" (Phil. 3:10). He came only to find them asleep. He challenged them, addressing Peter as the one who had boasted the loudest and longest about his loyalty even unto death. To arouse him even more, He called him by his old name—Simon! He warned him. He *must* watch and pray for the good of his own soul. Forces were already afoot that would sift him like wheat to the core of his being. Then, with infinite compassion, He made allowance for their mortal frailty. The flesh was weak, they were only human, they could not possibly enter into His agony, although, in spirit, they were willing enough. More lonely than ever, He returned to His battle.

> *And again he went away, and prayed, and spake the same words. (14:39)*

This is an interesting sidelight on prayer. It does not always have to be original and inventive, always finding new ways to say the same things. Obviously, we must beware against "vain repetition," or allowing our prayers to become mechanical, repetitious, and dead. But no deadness was in His prayer. The onslaught was as fresh and as fierce as before, and the Lord's agony was just as intense. The prospect was as terrible as ever. New words would not have helped. The same words sufficed.

> *And when he returned, he found them asleep again, (for their eyes were heavy,) neither wist they what to answer him. And he cometh the third time, and saith unto them, Sleep on now, and take your rest: it is enough, the hour is come; behold, the Son of man is betrayed into the hands of sinners. Rise up, let us go; lo, he that betrayeth me is at hand. (14:40–42)*

Three times He went away to pray. Three times He came back to find the three disciples asleep. The poor fellows could not keep their eyes open, although He Himself had been in an agony too great for Him even to think of sleep. We learn elsewhere that the agony that He endured was so intense that He not only broke out in sweat but also sweated great drops of blood (Luke 22:44). Indeed, an angel had to come and care for Him—something that Peter could have done, no doubt, had he stayed awake. Satan seems to have tried to kill Him in Gethsemane.

When He returned the third time, He told the disciples that they might just as well finish their sleep. He was wide awake indeed. But He could see what they could not see: Judas consummating his deal with the priests.

Then Jesus said, "It is enough." This was a significant statement. According to one authority, that expression conveys the idea that "he is receiving" (i.e., the money promised in v. 11). The verb as used in the *Papyri* is the technical word for "giving a receipt."[1] So, the omniscient Christ could actually see Judas, at that very moment, receiving the blood money.

Shortly afterward, the sound of the approaching mob could be heard breaking the stillness of the night. Any moment now He, the Son of Man, would be delivered into the hands of these sinful men.

B. The wickedness of man (14:43–15:15)
    1. The arrest (14:43–52)

Note first *the unthinking mob* (14:43–46):

> *And immediately, while he yet spake, cometh Judas, one of the twelve, and with him a great multitude with swords and staves, from the chief priests and the scribes and the elders. (14:43)*

The Sanhedrin was taking no chances. Each of the three groups that made up its membership is mentioned as being involved in this midnight arrest. Swords and clubs were in evidence everywhere. Evidently, the Jewish officials were afraid that the Lord would resist arrest—although what they thought their puny might could do against His almighty power we are not told. In any case, if the disciples did put up a show of resistance, the mob was there in sufficient numbers, hopefully, and well armed enough to overpower them. And there, as bold as brass, was Judas.

> *And he that betrayed him had given them a token, saying, Whomsoever I shall kiss, that same is he; take him, and lead him away safely. (14:44)*

Judas was now totally committed to the enemy. Their cause had become his. He had told them what he would do. He would indicate which of the men was the One they wanted, but then it would be up to them. But they had better act expeditiously, make good their capture, and remove Him to a safe place.

---

1. E. W. Bullinger, "Mark 14:41," in *The Companion Bible* (Grand Rapids: Kregel, 1990), margin.

As for Judas, he was two-faced to the very end. He would betray the Lord with a kiss, the usual Oriental form of greeting. A kiss! The symbol of love and affection employed in deceit and betrayal.

> *And as soon as he was come, he goeth straightway to him, and*
> *saith, Master, master; and kissed him. (14:45)*

Thus, the dreadful betrayal was accomplished. Wuest points out that the verb for "kissed" is *kataphileō*. The simple verb is intensified with a prefixed preposition. In other words, "It was an affectionate, fervent kiss the traitor gave our Lord" even as he addressed Him as "Rabbi! Rabbi!" That kiss will haunt Judas for all eternity.

> *And they laid their hands on him, and took him. (14:46)*

We learn elsewhere that the armed multitude had every right to be apprehensive of Him. They were thrown back as the Lord displayed His deity (John 18:3–9) and made it perfectly clear to these wicked and deluded men that they had no power over Him at all. Then He yielded Himself into their hands.

Note next *the unflinching Master* (14:47–52):

> *And one of them that stood by drew a sword, and smote a servant*
> *of the high priest, and cut off his ear. (14:47)*

We know the name of the swordsman—it was none other than Peter (John 18:10), and we know the name of the servant—it was Malchus, a special body servant (John 18:10) of the high priest himself. Thus, the high priest was present in the person of his personal valet. How like Jesus to perform His last miracle and restore the unfortunate man his ear (Luke 22:51).

> *And Jesus answered and said unto them, Are ye come out, as*
> *against a thief, with swords and with staves to take me? I was*
> *daily with you in the temple teaching, and ye took me not: but*
> *the scriptures must be fulfilled. (14:48–49)*

They could have taken Him just as easily in the temple in broad daylight. He had no intention of resisting arrest or of provoking a riot. Had He wanted to defend

Himself, He had twelve legions of angels attendant on His Word, able and willing to make an end of all of them. In any case, He was not a brigand or a robber chieftain, like Barabbas; He was a teacher. Had they paid any attention to His Sermon on the Mount, they would have known His peaceful and gentle words and ways.

They had been too cowardly and crafty, however, to make a public move against Him in the temple. But the Scriptures had to be fulfilled, and they were helping fulfill them. Isaiah had foretold His arrest and how He would be led as a lamb to the slaughter, acquiescing and unresisting (Isa. 53:7). Zechariah had likewise foretold that, far from mobilizing to the defense of the Lord, His followers would be scattered. The Sanhedrin had nothing to fear from Him, as far as arresting Him was concerned. The truth of Zechariah's prophecy (Zech. 13:7) was instantly demonstrated then and there in the garden.

> *And they all forsook him, and fled. (14:50)*

A sudden panic seized these men. Peter's spurt of carnal heroism spluttered out; in any case, it was quite out of order. Seeing that the leaders of the mob meant business, the disciples took to their heels. Perhaps they caught sight of the Roman soldiers who had come up to reinforce the mob. John tells us that "a captain" was there. The word he uses is *chiliarchos*, "commander of a thousand," that is of ten centurions. Six such tribunes were attached to a legion. Apparently, the Jews had informed the Roman authorities that this was a dangerous case of sedition. The Roman army was there, in the background, to make short work of any outbreak of fighting that might accompany this arrest (John 18:12).

> *And there followed him a certain young man, having a linen
> cloth cast about his naked body; and the young men laid hold on
> him: And he left the linen cloth, and fled from them naked.
> (14:51–52)*

Only Mark records this incident. There has been considerable speculation as to who this young man was. Some scholars think that it was Mark himself and that the recording of this incident is like "the monogram of the painter (Mark) in a dark corner of this picture." Evidently, this young man had arrived at Gethsemane in a hurry, not waiting to dress properly. The linen robe suggests a person of some affluence. Having said all of that, we still do not know who this man was or why this incident is recorded.

Another suggestion is that the young man hovering on the circumference of events was Lazarus. The Lord had made Bethany, and doubtless the home of Lazarus, His final headquarters on earth. The name of Lazarus was high on the list of men whom the Sanhedrin wanted killed (John 12:10). Certainly none of the Lord's immediate disciples could have been this young man.

    2. The arraignment (14:53–15:15)
      a. The Hebrew trial (14:53–72)

First comes *the preface* (14:53–54):

> *And they led Jesus away to the high priest: and with him were assembled all the chief priests and the elders and the scribes. (14:53)*

The *polysyndeton* draws attention to each separate class assembled by order of the high priest for this extraordinary night session of the Sanhedrin. What followed was an official act of the Jewish nation through its recognized rulers. The whole Sanhedrin, in the persons of the high priest and those officials who had responded to his summons, were now ready to make an end of this unwanted, self-proclaimed Galilean Messiah. They were a sorry lot, Caiaphas and his wily old father-in-law, Annas, and the rest of them—priests, scribes, elders, and all.

> *And Peter followed him afar off, even into the palace of the high priest: and he sat with the servants, and warmed himself at the fire. (14:54)*

That fire was to get very hot indeed before long. At last, Peter arrested his headlong flight. He plucked up courage enough to follow Jesus and His captors, but he was careful to keep his distance. Peter did not go right into the palace itself but only into the palace court where the servants were assembled. Even so, he was putting himself in harm's way. What he thought he could accomplish by hanging around with the Lord's enemies is hard to say. But there he stood, warming his hands at the world's fire while, a few yards away, the Lord was being bullied and beaten by Caiaphas and his thugs. And there Peter stood, holding his tongue for once, wondering what to do with himself and seemingly helpless to be of any assistance to the Lord.

Next, we have *the proceedings* (14:55–65):

*And the chief priests and all the council sought for witness against
Jesus to put him to death; and found none. For many bare false
witness against him, but their witness agreed not together.
(14:55–56)*

What a revelation of the abysmal wickedness of men! "Many" false witnesses
came forward. Many! They stood there before priests, elders, and scribes and
spewed out their lies. They took their oath before God and then fabricated testimony against One who had healed their sick, given sight to their blind, cleansed
their lepers, and fed their hungry multitudes. And there He stood—the Lord of
Glory, the Creator of the universe, the sinless Son of God—listening to it all.

Where are you, Peter? Come on, man. Get away from that fire while you still
have your honor. Come on in here. Offer yourself as a witness. Tell them of your
encounter with Christ: "My lords, I know this Man well. He has lived in my
home. He healed my mother-in-law of a fever. I know of three people whom He
has raised from the dead. I was a fisherman when He called me to be His disciple.
To start with, there was my brother and I and our business partners. There were
a dozen of us in all. He went about doing good. That's what He *did*. As for what
He *said*, well never man spoke like this Man. And, as for me, I have seen His
glory. I declare Him to be the Christ, the Son of the living God."

But no! Peter remained outside. It was cold. The world had a fire of coals
there, and Peter warmed his hands.

*And there arose certain, and bare false witness against him, say-
ing, We heard him say, I will destroy this temple that is made
with hands, and within three days I will build another made
without hands. But neither so did their witness agree together.
(14:57–59)*

Of course not! That was neither what He had said nor what He had meant.
True, He had referred to the temple, but He was referring symbolically to His
physical body. He had not said that *He* would destroy it. He had said that if it
were to be destroyed, He would, indeed, rebuild it in three days—a prophecy of
His resurrection. These evil men were planning now to kill Him. They wanted to
destroy His body (the temple of the Holy Spirit) and so get rid of Him. They
would not get rid of Him, even if they managed to kill Him. He was the resurrection and the life. They couldn't kill Him (John 10:18).

The situation was now becoming awkward for the Sanhedrin. They wanted to get rid of Jesus, but, at the same time, they wanted to keep everything "legal." A few consistent liars would have suited their purpose, but the legal farce that they were overseeing was becoming embarrassing. The false witnesses were telling contradictory falsehoods. Caiaphas could not get a conviction on the kind of false testimony being given. At least they could not get a conviction and retain any semblance of a legal trial.

> *And the high priest stood up in the midst, and asked Jesus, saying,*
> *Answerest thou nothing? what is it which these witness against*
> *thee? But he held his peace, and answered nothing. Again the*
> *high priest asked him, and said unto him, Art thou the Christ,*
> *the Son of the Blessed? (14:60–61)*

At one time, the office of high priest had been the highest and holiest position in the country. God planned it and presented it in the Mosaic Law to provide the Jews with a great type of Christ. But it had long since fallen on hard times. A few faithful priests were to be found here and there (men such as Zacharias, the father of John the Baptist, for instance), but the high priests were, for the most part, self-seeking political opportunists, scoundrels of the first degree such as Annas and Caiaphas. Yet, even as they were doing their worst, Jesus was preparing to die for them. Such is the love of God in Christ.

So far, the proceedings had been totally illegal, as Caiaphas knew. The well-established precedent in a capital case among the Jews was first to look for evidence that would acquit the accused. Only later was a search made for incriminating testimony. Moreover, night proceedings were entirely irregular.

Caiaphas, aware that the whole trial was rapidly falling apart, took center stage. He stood and came down to confront Christ face-to-face. So far, the Lord had maintained a fitting but, to His enemies, infuriating silence. He had ignored all of the lies and distortions paraded before the court. This silence only enraged Caiaphas. He wanted something out of the prisoner's mouth that could then be used against Him before Pilate.

"What about all of these things that have been witnessed against You?" He demanded. The Lord maintained His silence. Then the wily priest had a brilliant idea. He would put this Messiah under oath and ask Him an incriminating question, one that He would be bound to answer once the oath was administered. "Are you the Christ, the Son of the Blessed?" He demanded. If Christ answered,

"No!" then He was through as a believable Messiah. If He said, "Yes!" they had Him for sure.

The high priest used the expression *Son of the Blessed* to avoid using the ineffable name of Jehovah, following a superstitious custom going back for centuries. What folly! The ineffable One was there in the midst. The Jesus of the New Testament *was* that very *Jehovah* whose name Caiaphas was too superstitious to use. He did not have to wait long for his reply.

> *And Jesus said, I am: and ye shall see the Son of man sitting on the right hand of power, and coming in the clouds of heaven. (14:62)*

"I AM!" Jesus said. He, the Jesus of the New Testament, was the Jehovah of the Old Testament. Words could not have been plainer. Not only did Jesus audibly pronounce the infallible name, a name that the Jews had not pronounced for centuries, but also He declared that He *was* Jehovah. But there was more. Jesus told Caiaphas that one day he and his crowd would see the overwhelming manifestation of the Lord's glory. They would see Him enthroned on high, sitting on the seat of all power. They would see Him coming back to reign, bursting through the clouds of heaven. It was far more than Caiaphas had hoped for. It was an unequivocal declaration of Deity. Jesus would leave these evil and unscrupulous men in no doubt as to who He was, who He claimed to be, and who it was with whom they were trifling.

> *Then the high priest rent his clothes, and saith, What need we any further witnesses? Ye have heard the blasphemy: what think ye? And they all condemned him to be guilty of death. (14:63–64)*

They had not heard blasphemy at all; they had heard the truth. Moreover, Caiaphas's exaggerated show of horror was quite illegal. Under the Mosaic Law, the high priest was expressly forbidden to rend his clothes (Lev. 10:6; 21:10). The Lord answered this piece of playacting shortly afterward by rending the temple veil (Matt. 27:51), thereby rendering Judaism null and void.

But the high priest's performance won the day. The assembly voted to put Christ to death on the grounds that He had blasphemously declared Himself to be God.

> *And some began to spit on him, and to cover his face, and to buffet him, and to say unto him, Prophesy: and the servants did strike him with the palms of their hands. (14:65)*

These men, the supposed spiritual leaders of the nation, spat upon Him, the Lord of Glory, the Creator of the universe. Then they began to beat Him, the One whom angels worshiped. The horseplay and abuse became worse. They blindfolded Him and cuffed Him. They challenged Him to tell them who had smitten Him. He knew whom it was all right and held back His hand from smiting. He still knows. He is holding that knowledge against the coming judgment day.

When the religious Jewish elite had showed the world their true colors, they handed the Lord over to the servants to have their turn. They "did strike him." The verb form means that they kept on striking Him. "With the palms of their hands," Mark adds. The Greek word means that they struck Him with smart blows. And He, with all power at His disposal, stood there and took their repeated blows and insults with lofty disregard and great sorrow for the men who smote Him thus.

Finally, we have *the postscript* (14:66–72):

> *And as Peter was beneath in the palace, there cometh one of the maids of the high priest: And when she saw Peter warming himself, she looked upon him, and said, And thou also wast with Jesus of Nazareth. But he denied, saying, I know not, neither understand I what thou sayest. And he went out into the porch; and the cock crew. (14:66–68)*

Mark returns in his account to Peter who was still warming himself by the fire. Along came a young woman who took a good look at Peter. The word for "looked" here means to look intently, to look fixedly and to inspect. Something registered in her mind, and out it came: "You are one of His," she said.

Like a flash, in an instant reaction, Peter spoke up. "I don't know what you're talking about," he said. He simply blurted it out, a barefaced lie. The contrast between the Lord inside—boldly telling the crafty Caiaphas the truth, stating just exactly who and what He was, at the cost of His life—and Peter outside—mouthing a cowardly lie to save his own skin—is sad.

Frightened now, Peter moved away from the fire. He went over to "the porch," that is, the vestibule, leading from the outer gate to the court. While he was trying thus to slip away, a cock crowed. Peter does not seem to have heeded it. He was now too busily involved in trying to extricate himself from the dangerous place in which he found himself. He had more important things to think about than the crowing of a rooster.

> And a maid saw him again, and began to say to them that stood by, This is one of them. And he denied it again. And a little after, they that stood by said again to Peter, Surely thou art one of them: for thou art a Galilaean, and thy speech agreeth thereto. (14:69–70)

Back came the maid. This time, she voiced her opinion to the others standing around waiting. Evidently, she was not persuaded by Peter's denial. She drew everyone's attention to Peter. He no longer needed a fire to keep warm; he was sweating enough without it! "He's one of them," the maid said to the loiterers. Again, quickly, Peter denied it.

But his very denial gave him away. They recognized his accent. It took a few minutes for the significance of that fact to sink in. Before long, they put two and two together. "Your speech betrays you," they said. "You are a Galilean. You've got to be one of them." We can read the growing hostility in their accusation.

Peter, now desperate, responded at once.

> But he began to curse and to swear, saying, I know not this man of whom ye speak. (14:71)

He began cursing and swearing, filling the night air with his blistering fisherman's oaths. That put an end to their accusations. *No genuine follower of Jesus would speak like that,* they thought. They were content. Doubtless, he was a Galilean, but a disciple of Jesus? Never! Inside, Jesus had just taken the oath administered by Caiaphas, His implacable foe; outside, Peter poured out the oaths of his former unregenerate days.

> And the second time the cock crew. And Peter called to mind the word that Jesus said unto him, Before the cock crow twice, thou shalt deny me thrice. And when he thought thereon, he wept. (14:72)

This time Peter heard the cock crow, and it put an abrupt end to his profanity. The Lord's warning came back to his mind, and he stood stunned by what he had done. Elsewhere we are told, too, that the Lord caught his eye. Filled with remorse, he went off alone into the dark to weep his heart out. Perhaps he went back to Gethsemane.

The next few days and nights were long and terrible. Jesus was handed over to Pilate. He was crucified and buried in the city. Peter wandered from place to place tormented by his curses, his conscience, and his cowardice. In the end, he found his way back to where some of the other disciples were. It was a sad and miserable group, all of them filled with a sense of guilt for having run away and, perhaps, willing to let a humbled and chastened Peter rejoin their fellowship, a fellowship of grief and remorse.

    b. The heathen trial (15:1–15)
       (1) The challenge (15:1–5)
         (a) The priests (15:1)
            i. The consultation (15:1a)
            ii. The council (15:1b)
            iii. The crime (15:1c)
         (b) The procurator (15:2–5)
            i. The main accusation (15:2)
               a. The question asked (15:2a)
               b. The accused (15:3b–5)
                  1. His silence before the rulers (15:3b)
                  2. His silence before the Roman (15:4–5)
                     (i) Pilate's appeal (15:4)
                     (ii) Pilate's astonishment (15:5)
       (2) The choice (15:6–15)
         (a) The prisoner (15:6–8)
             i. The custom (15:6)
             ii. The criminal (15:7)
             iii. The clamor (15:8)
         (b) The proposal (15:9–11)
            i. How it was offered (15:9–10)
               a. Pilate's obvious sympathy (15:9)
               b. Pilate's obvious sagacity (15:10)
            ii. How it was offset (15:11)
         (c) The problem (15:12–15)
            i. Pilate's struggle (15:2–14)

   a. The first question (15:12–13)
    1. Asked by the magistrate (15:12)
    2. Answered by the mob (15:13)
   b. The further question (15:14)
    1. Asked by the procurator (15:14a)
    2. Answered by the people (15:14b)
  ii. Pilate's surrender (15:15)
   a. His cowardice (15:15a)
   b. His crime (15:15b–c)
    1. The scourging of Jesus (15:15b)
    2. The sentencing of Jesus (15:15c)
C. The way of sacrifice (15:16–47)
 1. The crown (15:16–20)
  a. The Roman military (15:16)
   (1) The courtyard (15:16a)
   (2) The company (15:16b)
  b. The ribald mockery (15:17–20)
   (1) Its completeness (15:17–19)
    (a) Mocking what He was (15:17–18)
     i. The mocking vestments (15:17)
     ii. The mocking voices (15:18)
    (b) Mocking who He was (15:19)
     i. The smiting (15:19a)
     ii. The spitting (15:19b)
     iii. The scoffing (15:19c)
   (2) Its conclusion (15:20)
 2. The cross (15:21–26)
  a. The compulsion (15:21)
   (1) The name of the man (15:21a)
   (2) The fame of the man (15:21b)
  b. The Crucifixion (15:22–26)
   (1) The place (15:22)
   (2) The potion (15:23)
   (3) The penalty (15:24a)
   (4) The play (15:24b)
   (5) The period (15:25)
   (6) The placard (15:26)

3. The criminals (15:27–28)
   a. A fact of history (15:27)
      (1) What they were (15:27a)
      (2) Where they were (15:27b)
   b. A fulfillment of prophesy (15:28)
4. The crowd (15:29–32)
   a. The mockery of the rabble (15:29–30)
      (1) Derisive noddings (15:29a)
      (2) Derisive needlings (15:29b–30)
         (a) The charge they threw in His face (15:29b)
         (b) The challenge they threw in His face (15:30)
   b. The mockery of the rulers (15:30–32a)
      (1) They mocked Him as Savior (15:31)
      (2) They mocked Him as Sovereign (15:32a)
   c. The mockery of the robbers (15:32b)
5. The cry (15:33–37)
   a. The darkness (15:33)
      (1) The time involved (15:33a)
      (2) The territory involved (15:33b)
   b. The despair (15:34)
      (1) When it was (15:34a)
      (2) What it was (15:34b)
   c. The discussion (15:35–36)
      (1) What was thought (15:35)
      (2) What was wrought (15:36)
         (a) What one man did (15:36a)
         (b) What one man declared (15:36b)
   d. The death (15:37)
      (1) The conquering cry (15:37a)
      (2) The confident committal (15:37b)
6. The curtain (15:38)
   a. The reason for the veil (15:38a)
   b. The rending of the veil (15:38b–c)
      (1) The manner of its rending (15:38b)
      (2) The meaning of its rending (15:38c)
7. The confession (15:39)
   a. The centurion's contemplation of the evidence (15:39a)

  b. The centurion's conclusion from the evidence (15:39b)

8. The company (15:40–41)

  a. The outstanding women (15:40–41a)

   (1) Their names disclosed (15:40)

   (2) Their nobility described (15:41a–b)

    (a) Their personal commitment (15:41a)

    (b) Their practical commitment (15:41b)

  b. The other women (15:41c)

9. The counselor (15:42–46)

  a. Who he was (15:42–43)

   (1) The right moment (15:42)

   (2) The right man (15:43)

    (a) His fame (15:43a)

    (b) His faith (15:43b)

  b. What he wanted (15:44–45)

   (1) The substance of his appeal (15:44)

    (a) The boldness he displayed (15:44a)

    (b) The boon he desired (15:44b)

   (2) The success of his appeal (15:45)

  c. Where he went (15:46)

   (1) The body carried to the tomb (15:46a–b)

    (a) How it was enswathed (15:46a)

    (b) How it was entombed (15:46b)

   (2) The body closed in the tomb (15:46c)

10. The comment (15:47)

  a. The two women (15:47a)

  b. The two watched (15:47b)

—ɷ—

  b. The heathen trial (15:1–15)

   (1) The challenge (15:1–5)

And straightway in the morning the chief priests held a consultation with the elders and scribes and the whole council, and bound Jesus, and carried him away, and delivered him to Pilate. (15:1)

The sun had not yet arisen when, by majority or unanimous vote of the quorum of the Sanhedrin, they determined to hand Jesus over to the Roman governor for trial. The Jewish religious leaders had a twofold objective in view. First, the Romans had deprived the Sanhedrin of the right to execute people, and they wanted Jesus to be killed (Gal. 3:13). Second, by delivering Jesus to the Romans, the Jews could shift to them the ill odor of executing Jesus. Moreover, the Romans would crucify Jesus if they passed sentence on Him, and that gave the Jews added satisfaction. It was a much more terrible death than death by stoning. Moreover, it would add the curse of the law to the sentence of death (Gal. 3:13).

We know that it was still dark when the Lord was led before Pilate. It was "about the sixth hour" of the night (John 19:14) when Pilate said, "Behold your King." This fact confirms that the entire Sanhedrin proceedings were illegal because it was against the law not only to try a prisoner at night but also to try one on the eve of a Sabbath. The Lord was tried on the eve of the High Sabbath (Nisan 15). The expression *in the morning* means, "before sunrise."

> *And Pilate asked him, Art thou the King of the Jews? And he*
> *answering said unto him, Thou sayest it. (15:2)*

The Jewish authorities must have kept Pilate informed of what was afoot and that they had a case of high treason that soon would be brought before him. Pilate seems to have been cynical about the entire case. It must have been a novel experience for him to have the Sanhedrin so eager to accuse a Jew of treason against Rome, the nation that they hated. He knew perfectly well what had been going on throughout the country these past few years. Jesus posed no perceptible threat to Rome. The Sanhedrin was jealous of Jesus. Pilate knew that too.

The Jewish authorities adroitly changed the charge against Christ when they brought Him before Pilate. The charge of blasphemy would not carry nearly so much weight with Rome as a charge of treason.

Mark shows Pilate coming to the heart of the matter, as far as he was concerned. He asked Jesus bluntly if He was, indeed, the King of the Jews, a question that Jesus did not avoid. His answer was, "Thou sayest it," or, as we would say today, "You've said it."

> *And the chief priests accused him of many things: but he an-*
> *swered nothing. (15:3)*

The tense of the verb implies that they kept on accusing Him. The Lord simply ignored them. We can hear their strident, angry voices raised. What lies and distortions they dredged up from the dark depths of their evil hearts we are not told. We can almost hear them say, "He claims to be our king. He is a blasphemer. He has stirred up the people from here to Galilee with His claims. We had to arrest Him at night; otherwise, He would have provoked a riot. He resisted arrest!" And on and on. His only answer was silence.

And Pilate asked him again, saying, Answerest thou nothing? behold how many things they witness against thee. (15:4)

At this stage of the trial, Pilate was still trying to get to the root of the matter. He was being fair, giving the accused every opportunity to deny the charges that the vitriolic priests were hurling at Him. Jesus' silence was the silence of absolute self-control. He simply stood there, like a mighty rock in a stormy sea, while the priests, like angry billows, came on and on, hurling their foaming accusations against Him, only to be thrown back by His massive, impenetrable silence. For "as a sheep before her shearers is dumb, so he openeth not his mouth." The prophet had foretold it hundreds of years earlier (Isa. 53:7).

Pilate himself urged the Lord to say something in His own defense, not realizing that His silence said it all. Had He spoken, indeed, legion after legion of angels would have swarmed over the battlements of heaven, turned to blood the waters of the seven seas, stamped flat the high hills of Judah, and made an end of it then and there. But no word passed His lips. The angels put their swords away. The plan of redemption went forward as decided in glory eternities ago.

But Jesus yet answered nothing; so that Pilate marvelled. (15:5)

The Roman governor had never met a man like this Man. He was all too familiar with voluble prisoners, angry prisoners, and frightened prisoners. Never before had he had a silent prisoner, One who steadfastly, under the direst provocation, simply refused to defend Himself. He was astonished.

(1) The choice (15:6–15)

Now at that feast he released unto them one prisoner, whomsoever they desired. (15:6)

Pilate decided to make a gesture of appeasement to a conquered but restless people. Pilate seems to have availed himself of this custom before. It occurred to him that he could avail himself of this custom to give Jesus a chance of life.

> *And there was one named Barabbas, which lay bound with them*
> *that had made insurrection with him, who had committed mur-*
> *der in the insurrection. (15:7)*

Barabbas was all that Jesus was not. He was a rebel against Rome. He had led an armed insurrection and had killed someone in the process. He had been condemned to death and lay in his cell with his fellow insurrectionists awaiting execution. His name is of great interest. It would seem that his full name was Jesus Barabbas. The name *Barabbas* means "son of the father." The word *abbas* suggests that his father was a rabbi. Thus, Barabbas came from a good home. He had turned either to a life of crime or had become a freedom fighter, a Zealot, perhaps, the leader of a group willing to risk life and limb to free his country from the yoke of Rome.

> *And the multitude crying aloud began to desire him to do as he*
> *had ever done unto them. But Pilate answered them, saying, Will*
> *ye that I release unto you the King of the Jews? For he knew that*
> *the chief priests had delivered him for envy. (15:8–10)*

By now, however, the multitude had become a mob. We can visualize the priests' going from one group to another, inciting them to demand their due—the release of a prisoner. The name *Barabbas* passed quickly from mouth to mouth. "Force him to release a prisoner. Make sure that you demand Barabbas. If we must have a messiah, Barabbas is more to our taste. At least Barabbas is a bold man devoted to freedom from Rome!" With such words they prepared the mob to frustrate Pilate's design, which was to have the people demand the release of Jesus.

Eventually, the great question was put to popular vote: "Which one do you want? Jesus which is called Barabbas, or Jesus which is called Christ?"

Pilate was not deceived by the sudden loyalty of the chief priests to Rome. It was not enthusiasm for Caesar that motivated them but envy of Christ. We can be sure that Pilate knew a great deal about the movements and miracles and ministry of Jesus. "This thing was not done in a corner," Paul reminded King

Agrippa some time later (Acts 26:26). The Roman governor was smart enough to see that the root cause of the hatred of the priests toward Jesus was envy. He could perform miracles; they couldn't. The people heard him gladly, but they did so only grudgingly. He spoke with authority; they just mumbled words. So, for now at least, Pilate tried to find an easy way to release the innocent Man who had been handed over to him.

> But the chief priests moved the people, that he should rather re-
> lease Barabbas unto them. (15:11)

Pilate, however, had made a mistake. He had forgotten that Barabbas was some kind of a folk hero to the Jewish nationalists. He had struck a blow for freedom. Pilate had thought that the Jews would have preferred the release of Jesus, who had gone about doing good, and so, perhaps, they might have, had it not been for the chief priests who were here, there, and everywhere, urging the release of Barabbas. A mob is always fickle. The people, who a few days before had been shouting, "Hosanna!" were now ready to cry, "Crucify!"

> And Pilate answered and said again unto them, What will ye
> then that I shall do unto him whom ye call the King of the Jews?
> And they cried out again, Crucify him. (15:12–13)

The chief priests had done their work well. They had mastered the mob, turned its temper into a senseless cry for the crucifixion of their King, and robbed Pilate of his triumph. Probably not a person in that mob—if appealed to soberly, quietly, and individually—would not have demanded the immediate release of the Man who had loved them, cared for them, taught them, and healed them, the Man whom they had hailed as Messiah and Lord and who was, in very fact, the Son of David and the Son of God. Probably when they got home and had time to think dispassionately over the terrible thing that they had done, each of them was ashamed and horrified. They had demanded that Jesus—who had given sight to their blind, cleansed their lepers, raised their dead, and freed their demoniacs— be *crucified*. They would not have wished such a death on any other Jew. How *could* they have been so blinded by senseless rage?

> Then Pilate said unto them, Why, what evil hath he done? And
> they cried out the more exceedingly, Crucify him. (15:14)

Pilate was dumbfounded. He knew that Jesus was a good Man. He was more than a little afraid of Him. He had never received a report about Him from his army of informers and spies that told of any wrong that this good and popular Teacher had done. He had hoped, perhaps, to appeal to Jewish national pride. Surely they would respond if he offered to release their *King*. Rome had nothing to fear from such a King as Jesus.

But no! The cry to crucify rang out again. The cry became a chant. The chant acquired a rhythm, a life of its own. "Crucify! Crucify! Crucify!" So Pilate gave in. Who can argue with a mob?

> *And so Pilate, willing to content the people, released Barabbas unto them, and delivered Jesus, when he had scourged him, to be crucified. (15:15)*

So immortal infamy belongs to Pilate. He knew that Jesus was innocent. He even declared Him to be innocent. He said, in effect, "He is innocent—so I'll have Him scourged." A Roman scourging was a terrible affair. The scourge tore the flesh off the bones and exposed the organs beneath. Many people died under that lash. By his actions, Pilate said, "Jesus is innocent, so I'll not only scourge Him but also crucify Him; I'll give Him over to a slow, agonizing, criminal's death."

All to satisfy the crowd.

So Pilate released Barabbas, and Another died in his place. Doubtless, the mob bore away with cheers their hero of the moment, the activist champion against Rome. Jesus and Pilate remained; Pilate, with his gnawing conscience, and Jesus, a mass of terrible wounds from the savage blows of the scourge.

C. The way of sacrifice (15:16–47)
   1. The crown (15:16–20)

> *And the soldiers led him away into the hall, called Praetorium; and they call together the whole band. (15:16)*

Just as the Sanhedrin's leaders, having blindfolded and buffeted the Son of God to their hearts' content, turned Him over to the servants to give them their turn, so now Pilate, having had Jesus scourged, turned Him over to the soldiers, so that they, too, could have their fun. The Praetorium was the barracks. Once in the barracks, He was in the soldiers' hands. As long as they did not kill Him, they could abuse Him as much as they wished.

News spread fast through the Praetorium: a Jew was to be crucified, and how the Romans hated and despised the Jews! And this Jew was claiming to be the *King* of the Jews! The soldiers came running. This was going to be too good to miss. It was not every day they could practice their buffoonery on a King of the Jews! Soon the whole company had arrived. Jesus stood there, His whole body aflame with the terrible agony of the scourging that He had undergone. Little did these Roman soldiers care about that!

> *And they clothed him with purple, and plaited a crown of thorns,*
> *and put it about his head. And began to salute him, Hail, King*
> *of the Jews! (15:17–18)*

What a joke it all was to these callous men. A king! Well, He must have a robe! Someone flung some purple cloth over His bleeding shoulders. He must have a crown! Someone made a circlet of thorns, with great, sharp spikes, and crushed it on His brow. He must have a court! The soldiers gathered around, saluting Him in mocking tones. But all of this abuse, so far, was mild. Worse was to follow.

> *And they smote him on the head with a reed, and did spit upon*
> *him, and bowing their knees worshipped him. (15:19)*

The tense used implies that they kept on smiting Him. A king needed a scepter. They gave Him a cane. We can picture the scene. As each one of the soldiers took his turn in paying homage to this Jewish "king," he likely would snatch the reed from Christ's hand, give Him a whack over the head with it, and then thrust it back into His hand again ready for the next soldier.

They spat on Him. Again the Greek uses the imperfect tense—they kept on spitting on Him. As each soldier rendered mocking homage, he spat.

Thus, the Lord of Glory, the One whom angels worship, stood there while the whole assembled company of soldiers smote, spat, and sneered: "Hail, King of the Jews!" At length, even that ordeal came to an end.

> *And when they had mocked him, they took off the purple from*
> *him, and put his own clothes on him, and led him out to crucify*
> *him. (15:20)*

To start with, He carried His own cross, a heavy and cumbersome beam of rough-hewn wood. He had to pick it up and hoist it onto His lacerated shoulder and drag it toward Execution Hill. That He was still strong enough to carry it at least part of the way to Calvary says something for the Lord's magnificent physique.

He had been up all night. He had been marched here and there—from Gethsemane to the high priest's palace, fresh from a titanic spiritual struggle that had left Him exhausted—from the high priest's palace to Pilate's judgment hall, from there to Herod's palace, from the palace back to Pilate. He had been manhandled and mauled by the Jews. He had been scourged and then abused by the soldiers. Yet, He could still pick up that heavy cross and start on the way to Calvary! But, at last, He faltered and fell.

2. The cross (15:21–26)

We begin with *the compulsion* (15:21):

> *And they compel one Simon a Cyrenian, who passed by, coming out of the country, the father of Alexander and Rufus, to bear his cross. (15:21)*

We can well imagine the resentment that filled the heart of this man, Simon. He was a native of the Libyan city of Cyrene across from Greece on the Mediterranean. An influential Jewish community was in this city, and it had roots going back to the days of Ptolemy I. This community had its own synagogue in Jerusalem (Acts 6:9), and Jews from Cyrene were present in Jerusalem on the Day of Pentecost. We do not know whether this man was a Jew or a Gentile proselyte.

It is possible that Jesus carried His cross as far as the city gate, where He collapsed. His collapse likely provoked further brutality on the part of the soldiers. However, it soon became evident, even to them, that Jesus had come to the end of His tether. One thing was sure: none of *them* intended to carry that cross. Glancing around, they saw this stranger coming. They seized him and compelled him to carry the cross the rest of the way. We can well believe that, to begin with, he was filled with rage and shame. Everyone would think *he* was on his way to be crucified.

Before it was all over, however, this man's heart might well have been filled with rejoicing. Maybe it was something that Jesus said to him. Maybe he tarried at Calvary and saw and heard the things that, before it was all over, reached the hearts of even the centurion and his men (Matt. 27:54). In any case, he seems to have become a Christian. Mark mentions his sons, Alexander and Rufus, as being well known to his readers. Apparently, one of the sons, Rufus, was a member of the church in Rome because Paul gives both him and his mother honorable mention in his Roman epistle (Rom. 16:13). What a great day it was for this man, Simon, when he met Christ on the road to Calvary. We can well imagine that he never grew tired of talking about it, urging others to take up their cross and follow *Him.*

And what about that other Simon, Simon Peter? If he had not followed so far off and fallen so sadly in the process, *he* might have been the Simon who carried that cross.

Next, we have *the Crucifixion* (15:22–26):

> And they bring him unto the place Golgotha, which is, being interpreted, The place of a skull. (15:22)

Golgotha! The word itself has a gruesome sound, like the word *ghost* or the word *ghoul.* It means "the place of a skull." Visitors to Jerusalem can still see a skull-shaped hill, thought by many to be the true Golgotha. It was a fitting place indeed for men to murder their Maker and for the Jews to murder their Messiah. A skull has a grisly, grinning resemblance to a face. But it is shorn of all that makes a face a face—dancing eyes, mobile lips, changing expressions, warmth and glow. All that remains are teeth and bone and a sardonic grin.

That was where they crucified Him, the Lord of life and glory. The four Evangelists hurry over the dreadful details: the piercing nails, the hammer blows, the searing, stabbing pain, the violent jerk as the cross was hauled aloft and dropped into its waiting hole, the heat and flies and tormenting thirst, and the cramping muscles and screaming tendons. Jesus endured it all.

> And they gave him to drink wine mingled with myrrh: but he received it not. (15:23)

This was one humane concession that the Romans allowed in the dreadful business of crucifying a man. The condemned were offered a cup of wine, drugged with stupefying myrrh, to deaden the first indescribable onslaught of excruciating pain. The Lord refused to drink it. He was there to taste death in all of its undiluted torment. He refused to have His senses muddled and His mind stupefied. He was about His Father's business. He still had things to do while procuring redemption for lost mankind. He wanted a clear mind and full possession of His faculties.

And when they had crucified him, they parted his garments, casting lots upon them, what every man should take. (15:24)

The dreadful deed was done, the most terrible work ever undertaken on this planet—and done with carpenter's tools. The soldiers turned their backs on their finished work and took up the spoils. It was time to share the loot.

All of the material goods that the Lord had in this world were the clothes upon His back. The soldiers distributed them among themselves and then cast lots for His seamless robe. Of what priceless value those garments would be today if they had been preserved. Possibly over time the church of Rome would have acquired them and built a vast cathedral to house them, endowed them with a reputed power to perform miracles, organized pilgrimages for the faithful to come and worship them, offered indulgences for those who prayed at the shrine that housed them, and, at the same time, made a fortune from them. Instead, Roman soldiers of unknown name or fame took their share and made off with His garments and robes. Then, thankfully, they thus passed out of history. God saw to that.

And it was the third hour, and they crucified him. (15:25)

It was nine o'clock in the morning, the time of the morning sacrifice, when they nailed Him to His cross. For the next six hours, the Lord endured an eternity of suffering and woe. The first three hours saw Him suffering at the hands of His foes. These, however, were only the beginnings of sorrow. The last three hours He suffered at the hands of God.

It was nine o'clock in the morning. The world went about its business. People bought and sold in the marketplaces. The priests carried on with their rituals. In the temple, the merchants sold sheep and goats, and the money changers palmed their profits. In the schools, the rabbis taught their pupils. In the procurator's palace, Pilate went on with the business of government or tried to justify to his wife why he had murdered an innocent man. And Jesus endured the first agonies of crucifixion. And, always mindful of others, He found it in His heart to pray for forgiveness for those who were responsible for His pain.

> *And the superscription of his accusation was written over, THE*
> *KING OF THE JEWS. (15:26)*

Such was Pilate's sardonic jibe at the Sanhedrin. He had not wanted to be involved in this case. His wife had warned him against it, and his own judgment had warned him against it, but the Jews had forced his hand. Once the issue of treason was raised, he knew, deep down in his soul, that it would be only a matter of time before he gave in. "This man claims to be our king," they said. "We have no king but Caesar," they added.

"Shall I crucify your King?" he had demanded.

They had won. Pilate was more afraid of Caesar than he was of Christ. Caesar brooked no rivals. Well, there was one thing he could do. He could have the last word. So he wrote up the Lord's accusation and title and nailed it on the cross in three languages for the world to read: THE KING OF THE JEWS. It made the Sanhedrin mad. They demanded that he change it, but, for once, vacillating Pilate stood firm. "What I have written I have written," he said. And what he wrote was the truth.

So there it was, nailed over His head—in Latin, Greek, and Hebrew—a proclamation to the world of what the Jews had done to the last rightful claimant to the throne of David.

3. The criminals (15:27–28)

> *And with him they crucify two thieves; the one on his right*
> *hand, and the other on his left. And the scripture was fulfilled,*
> *which saith, And he was numbered with the transgressors.*
> *(15:27–28)*

The quotation is from Isaiah 53:12. The word for "thieves" here means "robbers." The word for "transgressors" means "lawless ones." Thus, this "friend of publicans and sinners" died in the company of those whom He had come to seek and to save. To one of them He became a Friend indeed. Before it was all over, Jesus opened the gates of paradise for him. The other went on mocking until his mouth was shut by death.

4. The crowd (15:29–32)

And they that passed by railed on him, wagging their heads, and saying, Ah, thou that destroyest the temple, and buildest it in three days. Save thyself, and come down from the cross. (15:29–30)

First, the *rabble!* One does not expect much from a mob. "They that passed by" the cross were much the same as those that pass by in any age. They would be people of all sorts of dispositions, including the type of person who would think it great fun to throw offal and dead cats at unfortunate prisoners in a pillory. At Calvary, they "wagged their heads" in a mocking, "we-told-you-so" gesture. They "railed on him." The phrase means that they were blaspheming. They were repeating words that had leaked out from His Jewish trial. "So! Here He was, the Man who said that He could destroy the temple and build it in three days! Did He not know that they had been working on that temple already for some fifty-three years, and it wasn't finished yet? Who did He think He was? Destroy the temple indeed! Build it in three days, would He? Nonsense!"

Even supposing that He had meant what they mistakenly, for all of their wiseacre head wagging, had taken Him to say, it would not have been hard for Him to build a temple in three days. After all, He had created a universe in six days!

"Save thyself, and come down from the cross!" they added, not knowing that their only hope of escaping hell was for Him to stay where He was. The Lord ignored them. They had already been answered in the noble words of Nehemiah, when Sanballet and Geshem sent unto him to cease what he was doing and come and discuss things with them. "I am doing a great work," he said, "so that I cannot come down: why should the work cease, whilst I leave it, and come down to you?" (Neh. 6:3).

Likewise also the chief priests mocking said among themselves with the scribes, He saved others; himself he cannot save. Let Christ the King of Israel descend now from the cross, that we may see and believe. And they that were crucified with him reviled him. (15:31–32)

First the rabble, now the *rulers.* Some allowance, perhaps, might be made for the thoughtless multitude, but what allowance can be made for these priests and scribes? They were the supposed experts in both the ritual law and the moral law. They were supposed to know the Scriptures. They could not find one single moral law that He had broken. The entire sacrificial system pointed, century after century, to His cross. Priest and scribe alike should have been at His feet in worship. Instead, they stood there and sneered.

They asked for another miracle. Before the day was out, He would put out the sun, shake creation's rocks, rend the temple veil, and burst wide the tombs. And much good those signs were to these evil men who could mock at a dying man and revile the very Christ of God.

Then there were the *robbers*. Even the thieves, writhing on the two crosses alongside His, thought Him fair game for their wicked words. Think of who it really was who hung there on that center tree. Then think that even the criminals thought it appropriate to hurl insults in His face.

The only explanation for such behavior is that it was Satan inspired. Satan with his principalities and powers were there at the cross, gloating over the sufferings of the Savior, goading men out of sheer malice to revile and ridicule the Eternal One. These "principalities and powers" of Satan would sing a different song before long (Col. 2:15).

   5. The cry (15:33–37):

   And when the sixth hour was come, there was darkness over the
   whole land until the ninth hour. (15:33)

At high noon, the sun went out. Darkness reigned from Dan to Beersheba; from the river to the sea; in every city, town, and hamlet; in every vale; and on every hill. People crept about their homes, thinking that the end of the world had come. The work of creation was done in the light (Gen. 1:3); the work of redemption was done in the dark. And how great and awful was that darkness! It was a darkness like that which blanketed Egypt, a darkness that could be felt (Exod. 10:21), a darkness like that which overwhelmed Abraham, "the horror of a great darkness" (Gen. 15:12). The darkness lasted until three o'clock in the afternoon, the time of the evening sacrifice.

   And at the ninth hour Jesus cried with a loud voice, saying, Eloi,
   Eloi, lama sabachthani? which is, being interpreted, My God,
   my God, why hast thou forsaken me? (15:34)

This was a quotation from Psalm 22 in the Aramaic tongue. There is no way that we can comprehend what the Lord suffered during those hours of darkness when He, who knew no sin, was made sin for us (2 Cor. 5:21). During those dread hours, God visited upon our divine substitute the sin of the whole world. This was the climax of all of His woes. It was the prospect of this final ordeal that had overwhelmed Him in Gethsemane. This was the ultimate horror—to be made sin. The Lord was a brave Man. He could have suffered the pain of crucifixion without a word. After all, thousands of people had suffered death by crucifixion. It was commonplace enough in those days in the Roman Empire. But to be made sin! To be abandoned by God! That was what He dreaded. Hymn writer Elizabeth Clephane puts it thus:

> But none of the ransomed ever knew
> How deep were the waters crossed,
> Or how dark was the night that the Lord passed through
> E're He found His sheep that was lost.

And some of them that stood by, when they heard it, said, Behold, he calleth Elias. And one ran and filled a sponge full of vinegar, and put it on a reed, and gave him to drink, saying, Let alone; let us see whether Elias will come to take him down. (15:35–36)

Who was this unknown watcher who so kindly ministered a drink, albeit a bitter one, to the lonely sufferer on the tree? The word for "vinegar" here refers to sour wine mingled with water, such as was commonly drunk by Roman soldiers. Perhaps one day we'll know.

As for Elijah, he had come and gone about a year earlier. On the Mount of Transfiguration, he and Jesus had already discussed the Crucifixion and recognized it as an accomplishment. Jesus did not need Elijah to rescue Him. Elijah had gone on back to heaven, filled with thoughts of the Lord's coming triumph on the tree. The Lord's agonizing cry, "Eloi! Eloi!" consummated the sufferings. From now on, all would be glory! The sin question was settled. Payment had been made. The accomplishment was complete (John 19:28–30). The glory was to follow.

And Jesus cried with a loud voice, and gave up the ghost. (15:37)

He did not die from weakness and exhaustion. The Jews did not kill Him. The Romans did not kill Him. No device of man could kill Him. He knew that all was now accomplished, so He sovereignly dismissed His spirit by a deliberate act of His will. And He did so with a ringing, triumphant shout!

6. The curtain (15:38)

And the veil of the temple was rent in twain from the top to the bottom. (15:38)

Thus, He signified an end to Judaism. The various religious activities on the Hebrew calendar were climaxed on the Day of Atonement (Lev. 16) when, after the most elaborate ritual precautions, the high priest went past the veil into the Holy of Holies. In temple and tabernacle the veil had stood in the Holy Place for some fifteen hundred years to keep all people away from the presence of God. That barrier was passed only by the high priest, on the Day of Atonement, once a year, and, even then, only after the most elaborate ritual precautions (Lev. 16). Now that veil hung, a ruined rag, abolishing Judaism and inviting all men everywhere to come boldly into the presence of God (Heb. 10:19–22). The Jews had killed Him. He put an end to their religion as that religion was depicted in the Old Testament. A new faith would take its place.

7. The confession (15:39)

And when the centurion, which stood over against him, saw that he so cried out, and gave up the ghost, he said, Truly this man was the Son of God. (15:39)

Death by crucifixion was normally a long, slow, lingering death and was usually the last result of exhaustion. People who were nailed to a cross did not die within half a dozen hours and at their own volition. No doubt the centurion, as Matthew implies (27:45–54), was impressed by the darkness, the earthquake, the rent veil, and the opened tombs. But what gripped him most was the absolute lordship of Christ over the moment and the manner of His death. "This," he said, "was the Son of God!"

8. The company (15:40–41)

There were also women looking on afar off: among whom was Mary Magdalene, and Mary the mother of James the less and of

> *Joses, and Salome; (Who also, when he was in Galilee, followed
> him, and ministered unto him;) and many other women which
> came up with him unto Jerusalem. (15:40–41)*

Matthew tells us that many women were looking on, women from Galilee
(27:54). They were braver than the men were; the women loved Him more.
They watched the terrible death of the Lord discreetly from some considerable
distance, where they would be safe from the ribaldry of the crowd and the active
malice of the priests.

Mary Magdalene was there, a woman out of whom Jesus had cast seven evil
spirits and who, thereafter, became one of the Lord's most devoted disciples. The
other Mary seems to have been the wife of Clopas (or Cleophas). Both she and her
husband were followers of the Lord. The other woman Mark names was Salome,
the wife of Zebedee and the mother of two of the Lord's disciples, James and John.

These women loved the Lord. They had hung upon His words, had been thrilled
by His miracles, had been greatly attracted by His character, and had followed His
career eagerly. Salome, however blunderingly, had anticipated the Lord's *coronation*
day (Matt. 20:21). How ravished they all must have been by His *crucifixion* day.
Everything had happened so suddenly. Just a day or so earlier, He had been teaching boldly in the temple. He had shaken city and Sanhedrin alike by raising Lazarus
from the dead. His Triumphal Entry into Jerusalem had raised their hopes.

Not content with admiring Him and giving their sons to His service, these
women had "ministered" unto Him. They supported Him and His disciples fi-
nancially. They rendered Him such service as was open to them, doing things to
help Him; offering Him and His disciples, no doubt, the hospitality of their
homes; and taking care of their laundry, perhaps, or preparing them meals.

And it had all ended like this—a Roman cross on a skull-shaped hill and the
King of Israel brought there by the schemes and machinations of the high priest,
the very man who should have been foremost in bringing Him to the throne.

9. The counselor (15:42–46):

> *And now when the even was come, because it was the prepara-
> tion, that is, the day before the sabbath, (15:42)*

The actual Passover was celebrated on the fifteenth of Nisan. The fourteenth,
the day before Passover, was "the preparation" day, the day on which the Passover

lamb was killed. The daily sacrifice was killed at the sixth hour (noon); the daily sacrifice was offered at the seventh hour. The killing of the Passover lambs began directly afterward—the Lord would then have been on the cross for four hours. Darkness covered all of the land at that time on this particular Sabbath. The Lord died at the ninth hour (3 P.M.). The "high" day (the first day of the feast) began at sunset. They had to hurry to get Christ off that cross and into His tomb. He was likely buried before sunset (about 6 P.M.).

> *Joseph of Arimathaea, an honourable counsellor, which also waited*
> *for the kingdom of God, came, and went in boldly unto Pilate,*
> *and craved the body of Jesus. (15:43)*

The Jews had already taken steps to ensure the removal of the bodies of the three crucified men before the beginning of the high Sabbath. Their deaths were to be hastened to make that removal possible. Doubtless, the authorities, had they dared, would have liked to have thrown the Lord's body into the fires of *Gē Hinnom,* where the offal-consuming fires perpetually burned. In any case, they proposed to dump Him in a common criminal's grave. They were thwarted, however, by Joseph of Arimathea, who was a wealthy man and a member of the Sanhedrin. He, along with Nicodemus (John 3), had dissented from the Sanhedrin's evil doings in arranging for the murder of Jesus.

It was a bold enough move that Joseph made. He now openly broke with his colleagues. He plucked up his courage and went to see Pilate. It was a bold thing to do because, after all, Pilate sentenced Jesus on the grounds that He was a traitor. By now, however, Pilate was doubtless having second thoughts about his own unsavory part in this whole affair. He granted this wealthy and influential Jew immediate access to himself. Joseph came straight to the point: could he please have the body of Jesus to give it a decent burial?

> *And Pilate marvelled if he were already dead: and calling unto*
> *him the centurion, he asked him whether he had been any while*
> *dead. And when he knew it of the centurion, he gave the body to*
> *Joseph. (15:44–45)*

Pilate was just as astonished as the centurion had been at the swift death of Jesus. He had never seen such a magnificent specimen of manhood. In the normal course of events, the Lord should have lingered on that tree for days. As soon as he was satisfied with the centurion's report, Pilate gave the body to Joseph. It was another way to get back at the Sanhedrin. The word for "gave" is one that means that he made a gift of that body to him. The only other place where this word is used in the New Testament is where we are told of what God has *given* to us—"all things that pertain unto life and godliness," and "exceeding great and precious promises" (2 Peter 1:3–4). Pilate made a present of a dead body to Joseph. God makes a present of spiritual and eternal life to us—all because of Calvary.

> *And he bought fine linen, and took him down, and wrapped him*
> *in the linen, and laid him in a sepulchre which was hewn out of*
> *a rock, and rolled a stone unto the door of the sepulchre. (15:46)*

Years earlier, Joseph had bought a piece of ground in Jerusalem suitable for a tomb. Work on it seems to have been still in process at the time of the Crucifixion. The rock-hewn tomb was located in a garden near Golgotha. The tomb was to house the remains of him and members of his family.

As he watched with dismay the wicked tactics of the Sanhedrin and listened to their latest scheme to seize the body of Jesus and give it a dishonorable burial, he came to a swift decision: he would give his tomb to Jesus. And so he did.

Moreover, he provided the expensive linens in which the battered body of Jesus was wrapped when lowered—by loving, caring hands—from the cross. Thus, he helped to fulfill the words of an ancient prophecy, perhaps knowingly and deliberately or perhaps unwittingly: "And he made his grave with the wicked"—or, "they appointed his grave with the wicked," as some render it—"and [he was] with the rich in his death" (Isa. 53:9).

Thus, it came to pass, thanks to this man, Joseph of Arimathea, that the Lord was given honorable burial in a rich man's tomb.

10. The comment (15:47)

> *And Mary Magdalene and Mary the mother of Joses beheld where*
> *he was laid. (15:47)*

The word for "beheld" here suggests that they were looking attentively to see exactly where their Beloved was put to rest. The high Sabbath had put a sudden end to the burying process. The tomb was closed hastily and, then, sealed by Pilate as a sop to the sudden misgivings of the Sanhedrin. Some things still needed to be done. Nicodemus had provided a great quantity of spices, and the body had been hastily embalmed. They must come back as soon as possible to complete the anointing of the body, but that would have to wait. At least, they knew where His body was.

Section 5: Proving the Crime of Calvary (16:1–20)
  A. Conquering the grave (16:1–14)
    1. His resurrection (16:1–8)
      a. The women arriving at the tomb (16:1–4)
        (1) Their desire (16:1)
          (a) Their identity (16:1a)
          (b) Their intention (16:1b)
        (2) Their doubts (16:2–4)
          (a) Their doubts discussed (16:2–3)
            i. The time of the day (16:2)
            ii. The trouble in their way (16:3)
          (b) Their doubts dissolved (16:4)
      b. The women affrighted at the tomb (16:5–8)
        (1) What they dared (16:5a)
        (2) What they discerned (16:5b)
        (3) What they discovered (16:6–7)
          (a) The place (16:6)
          (b) The plan (16:7)
            i. Who they should tell (16:7a)
            ii. What they should tell (16:7b)
        (4) What they did (16:8)
    2. Their reaction (16:9–14)
      a. The unbelief of the disciples recorded (16:9–13)
        (1) The first encounter (16:9–11)
          (a) Mary's encounter with the Master (16:9)
          (b) Mary's encounter with the men (16:10–11)
            i. Their despair described (16:10)
            ii. Their disbelief described (16:11)
        (2) The further encounter (16:12–13)
          (a) The fact of the Resurrection revealed to the two (16:12)
          (b) The fact of the Resurrection relayed by the two (16:13)
            i. Their story recounted (16:13a)
            ii. Their story rejected (16:13b)
      b. The unbelief of the disciples rebuked (16:14)
        (1) The Lord's sudden appearing to them (16:14a)
        (2) The Lord's sad admonishment of them (16:14b)

    B. Conquering the globe (16:15–20)
        1. The Great Commission transmitted (16:15–18)
          a. The simple message (16:15–16)
            (1) Reaching the world (16:15)
            (2) Preaching the Word (16:16)
               (a) The importance of believing (16:16a)
               (b) The importance of baptism (16:16b)
          b. The supporting miracles (16:17–18)
            (1) Divine power released (16:17)
               (a) Supernaturally commanding the foe (16:17a)
               (b) Supernaturally communicating the faith (16:17b)
            (2) Divine protection realized (16:18)
               (a) Unsuspected snares to be harmless (16:18a–b)
                  i. The poisonous creature (16:18a)
                  ii. The poisoned cup (16:18b)
               (b) Unspecified sicknesses to be healed (16:18c)
        2. The glorious Christ translated (16:19–20)
          a. What a thrill (16:19a)
          b. What a throne (16:19b)
          c. What a throng (16:20)
            (1) An obedient people (16:20a)
            (2) An overcoming people (16:20b)
               (a) The wonderful secret (16:20b–d)
                  i. The world evangelized (16:20b)
                  ii. The work energized (16:20c)
                  iii. The Word emphasized (16:20d)
               (b) The wondrous success (16:20e)

—៣—

Section 5: Proving the Crime of Calvary (16:1–20)
    A. Conquering the grave (16:1–14)
        1. His resurrection (16:1–8)

We note, first, *the women arriving at the tomb* (16:1–4):

> *And when the sabbath was past, Mary Magdalene, and Mary*

> *the mother of James, and Salome, had bought sweet spices, that*
> *they might come and anoint him. (16:1)*

The reference now is to the weekly Sabbath, three days and three nights from the day of preparation, when He was buried. The women purchased aromatic spices, not for the embalming of the Lord's body, which had been done by Joseph and Nicodemus, but to further anoint the body. Likely, they purchased these additional spices after the sunset, which closed the regular Sabbath. This act was their way of showing their own love for the Lord. Nicodemus had already given adequate spices for the actual embalming.

> *And very early in the morning the first day of the week, they came*
> *unto the sepulchre at the rising of the sun. (16:2)*

Little did they know that from henceforth the first day of the week would replace the abolished Sabbath!

For three days and three nights the earth had spun on its axis in space cradling the mortal remains of its mighty Maker. Nothing seemed to have changed. People went to bed, arose, and went about their little concerns. And still that august body lay still and cold in death on a rocky ledge in a stone-sealed tomb, immune from the process of decay. And the earth went round and round.

But now the sun was embracing that tomb on a brand-new first day of a brand-new week and a brand-new age. The Sabbath and all that it stood for was past. From now on, men would rest, not in a Sabbath but in a Savior (Matt. 11:28–30; Heb. 4).

> *And they said among themselves, Who shall roll us away the stone*
> *from the door of the sepulchre? And when they looked, they saw*
> *that the stone was rolled away: for it was very great. (16:3–4)*

The door of the sepulchre was a great and heavy stone wheel. It fitted into a sloping groove, so arranged that it ran down an incline. It was, therefore, much easier to close than it was to open. It would have taken several strong men to push that stone back up the groove against the slope. It presented these women with a practically insurmountable obstacle to their plan. They do not seem to have been concerned about either the armed guard or the governor's seal on the tomb. They might not have known about those things.

We can imagine the reaction of these brave women, however, when they saw that someone had been there before them and that the obstacle had already been removed. The grave was open!

Mark says that they "looked up" and *saw*—a word that conveys the ideas of attention, surprise, and joy. Their problem was solved. They had no thought about a resurrection. Very few people took seriously the Lord's words about that. But Mary of Bethany did (John 12), and so did the Lord's enemies. The disciples themselves, however, although the Lord told them repeatedly to expect it, were completely taken by surprise by it and when confronted with mounting evidence, still refused to believe it. They needed a great deal of convincing.

Next we see *the women affrighted at the tomb* (16:5–8):

> *And entering into the sepulchre, they saw a young man sitting on the right side, clothed in a long white garment; and they were affrighted. (16:5)*

The word for "garment" here describes a flowing, stately robe reaching to the feet and sweeping the ground. It depicts a garment of beauty, one associated with opulence and solemnity. It is a fitting word to describe the robe that an angel might have worn. The appearance of this one filled the women with "awe." We have already noted the word in connection with both the Transfiguration (9:15) and the Lord's experience in Gethsemane (14:33). What the women saw was an angel. Some people have thought that the visitor was John Mark and that he had rolled away the stone, but John Mark would not have filled them with wonder and awe. This was a visitor from another world.

> *And he saith unto them, Be not affrighted: Ye seek Jesus of Nazareth, which was crucified: he is risen; he is not here: behold the place where they laid him. (16:6)*

The angelic visitor sought to dispel their fear. He knew why they had come. He announced the glad tidings of the Resurrection just as, more than thirty years earlier, angels had heralded the good news of the Incarnation. What an experience the disciples missed by their unbelief! They had been told how long He intended to remain in the tomb—three days and three nights. They might have themselves come in a body to the tomb, in eager anticipation of His resurrection, a welcoming committee to hail His conquest of the grave. How the angels must have marveled at human unbelief!

The angel invited the women to come into the tomb, where he now mounted guard, and see for themselves that it was empty. In they went. There was the evidence of the grave clothes and the napkin that, shortly afterward, so greatly impressed the apostle John (John 20:3–8). There could be no doubt about it: the Lord was risen indeed, right through the swathing, spice-soaked grave clothes, which now lay as mute testimony to a remarkable resurrection.

> *But go your way, tell his disciples and Peter that he goeth before you into Galilee: there shall ye see him, as he said unto you. And they went out quickly, and fled from the sepulchre; for they trembled and were amazed: neither said they any thing to any man; for they were afraid. (16:7–8)*

The moment that the truth of the empty tomb took hold upon them, the women took to their heels. A little angelic company went a long way! His words, however, still rang in their ears. They were to pass along a reassuring word to poor, grief-stricken, conscience-tormented Peter. They were to tell the disciples to go back to Galilee, away from the dangers of Jerusalem. Jesus would meet them there. For the time being, however, they were too confused and terrified to do much of anything. Even when at least one of them (Mary Magdalene) did tell the disciples about the empty tomb, they would not believe her (v. 11).

Some people reject out of hand the closing dozen verses of Mark. The issues are highly technical and beyond the scope of this commentary. We can note in passing, however, that a considerable number of old versions do contain these verses. The Syriac in its various forms (the "Peshitto" and the "Curetonian Syriac") contains them. Jerome (who had access to Greek MSS older than are generally available today) includes them in the Vulgate, a revision of the Vetus Itala, which goes back to the second century and also contains them. The Egyptian versions (Memphitic and Thebiac) contain them. The Armenian, Ethiopian, and Georgian versions contain them. Many of the church fathers refer to them—Papias, Justin Martyr, Irenaeus, Hoppolytus, Eusebias, Chrysostom, Augustine, Nestorius, and Cyril of Alexandria, for instance.[1]

---

1. E. W. Bullinger, *The Companion Bible* (Grand Rapids: Kregel, 1990), app. 168.

The problem with these verses seems to stem from their mention of the sign gifts (16:17–18), which were discontinued after the fall of Jerusalem. Indications that this would happen are found in 1 Corinthians 13:8–13. For the next hundred years, little or nothing is known of church history. Organized Christianity, as we see it today, did not begin until later. Later scholars, transcribing the Greek manuscripts, saw no trace of these transitional gifts. They concluded that there must be something spurious about these verses, so they left them out!

We have the opposite problem today. Many people are determined to have these gifts regardless of the Holy Spirit's having discontinued them. They go to all extremes and to the most dangerous expedients to get them. Their boasts, claims, and excesses deceive many people. We, however, accept these verses at their face value as part of the God-breathed Word of God.

2. The reaction (16:9–14)

Now when Jesus was risen early the first day of the week, he appeared first to Mary Magdalene, out of whom he had cast seven devils. (16:9)

John tells of this appearing. The evidence of the empty tomb overwhelmed Mary. She jumped to the conclusion, despite the word of the angel, that someone had removed the body. She turned her back on the angel! What did angels mean to her? Jesus was whom she wanted, and now even His body was gone.

Having turned her back on the angel, she saw Jesus! But she did not recognize Him; she thought that He was the gardener. She asked Him if He knew where they had taken the body. He spoke just one word: "Mary!" Instantly, she knew Him, and "heaven came down and glory filled her soul." He at once recommissioned her to go and tell the disciples that He was alive!

And she went and told them that had been with him, as they mourned and wept. And they, when they had heard that he was alive, and had been seen of her, believed not. (16:10–11)

The disciples were still in the throes of shock and grief over the precipitous end of all of their hopes. The hurried trials, the speedy execution, the swift death, the hasty burial—then there was nothing, except broken hearts and shattered hopes.

But when Mary Magdalene, the first person to see Him after His resurrection, brought the news, they wrote it off at once as nonsense.

> *After that he appeared in another form unto two of them, as they walked, and went into the country. And they went and told it unto the residue: neither believed they them. (16:12–13)*

Luke tells the full tale (24:13–33). The two people (probably husband and wife) were on their way to the village of Emmaus. On their seven or eight-mile journey, they were talking sadly about the events of the past few days when Jesus joined them, engaged them in conversation, and then expounded the Scriptures to them. Their hearts were warmed although they failed to recognize Him until, at supper at the end of the journey, some familiar gesture of His opened their eyes. Back they went at once to Jerusalem with eager haste to tell the sorrowing disciples that Jesus was indeed alive! It was a wasted journey, however, because the disciples refused to believe them, so stubborn was their unbelief.

> *Afterward he appeared unto the eleven as they sat at meat, and upbraided them with their unbelief and hardness of heart, because they believed not them which had seen him after he was risen. (16:14)*

Doubtless, this was the occasion when He simply materialized in their midst, ate fish and honeycomb to demonstrate that His body was real, and then, after a while, simply vanished! That put an effective end to their unbelief. Because all eleven of the disciples were present on this occasion, it must have been the second of such appearances to which Mark refers because Thomas was not present the first time that He appeared to them.

The Lord reproached all of them for their persistent unbelief. On this occasion, He specifically admonished Thomas for his resolute agnosticism (John 20:24–29).

B. Conquering the globe (16:15–20)
   1. The Great Commission transmitted (16:15–18)

> *And he said unto them, Go ye into all the world, and preach the gospel to every creature. He that believeth and is baptized shall be saved; but he that believeth not shall be damned. (16:15–16)*

Salvation was purchased at too great a cost to be taken lightly. Those who believe are to be baptized, thereby declaring their union with Christ in His death, burial, and resurrection. They are to spread the gospel tidings far and wide, to earth's remotest bounds. Those who refuse to believe will face condemnation. This condemnation rests on their unbelief, not on their failure to be baptized. We are saved by Christ not by baptism, blood, or water.

> *And these signs shall follow them that believe; In my name shall they cast out devils; they shall speak with new tongues; They shall take up serpents; and if they drink any deadly thing, it shall not hurt them; they shall lay hands on the sick, and they shall recover. (16:17–18)*

These signs belonged to the transitional period. The early chapters of the book of Acts are full of such following signs. Both Peter and Paul healed the sick and raised the dead. Tongues was common in the early church; it was, however, essentially a judgment and a warning sign to the unbelieving Jews. Paul cast out evil spirits. On one occasion, he was bitten by a poisonous snake and came to no harm. Eusebius records instances when both John and Barnabas escaped unharmed after drinking poison.[2]

As the Jewish nation at home and abroad hardened into a settled policy of rejecting the gospel, these sign gifts faded out. They came to an end with the destruction of Jerusalem and the completion of the New Testament canon. They had served their purpose of clear witness to the Jewish people (1 Cor. 1:22). When that witness was rejected, the signs were withdrawn.

2. The glorious Christ translated (16:19–20)

> *So then after the Lord had spoken unto them, he was received up into heaven, and sat on the right hand of God. (16:19)*

From the brow of Olivet, Jesus stepped straight into glory. He found His way through the cheering ranks of the angels to the Great White Throne of God. He took His place on the right hand of God, a Man in a human body, seated on the throne of the universe, with every right to be there because He is God over all, blessed forevermore! There He sits "from henceforth expecting till his enemies be made his footstool" (Heb. 10:13).

---

2. *Eusebius* 3.39.

> *And they went forth, and preached every where, the Lord work-*
> *ing with them, and confirming the word with signs following.*
> *Amen. (16:20)*

As for the disciples of the Lord, they waited in Jerusalem until Pentecost, just as He told them to do. Then, with the outpoured Holy Spirit within them and upon them, they went forth to take on the world—"in Jerusalem, and in all Judea, and in Samaria, and unto the uttermost part of the earth" (Acts 1:8).

From then until now, in country after country, the Good News of the gospel has spread. Countless millions of people have been saved. The Lord, enthroned on high, has watched with the keenest interest as the Holy Spirit has carried on with the task of calling out a people for His name. Workers come and go, but the work itself never stops. Sometimes by the thousands, as on the Day of Pentecost, at other times singly or in pairs—here a child at its mother's knee, there an old man with one foot in the grave—they come. The church is vast. It is "rooted in eternity," as C. S. Lewis puts it, "spread out through all time and space, and terrible as an army with banners."[3]

One of these days, the last person will come to Christ. The roll call will be complete, and the Lord will descend from the sky to summon us all home.

Then will be written the last "amen!"

---

3. C. S. Lewis, *The Screwtape Letters* (New York: Macmillan, 1961), 15.